Other Books by Trailer Life

The RV Handbook, Second Edition
Bill Estes
This encyclopedia of RVing contains a vast array of technical information to help improve RV performance, operate your RV safely, and save money. Included is information on improving engine efficiency and fuel performance, RV handling and proper loading, tire selection, batteries and solar power, and much more. New chapters include practical information on buying an RV and specific details to help RVers understand the systems and details of RV ownership and travel.
7³⁄₈ × 9¹⁄₄, 450 pages
$29.95 ISBN: 0-934798-44-3

Complete Guide to Full-time RVing: Life on the Open Road, Third Edition
Bill and Jan Moeller
This best-selling how-to-do-it book covers a broad range of subjects of interest to fulltimers, those considering a full-time lifestyle, or seasonal RVers. New and expanded chapters include working fulltimers, remodeling your RV for full-time living, and widebody RVs, in addition to chapters on costs, choosing the right RV, safety and security, and more.
7³⁄₈ × 9¹⁄₄, 488 pages
$29.95 ISBN: 0-934798-53-2

The Best of Tech Topics: Volume I
Bob Livingston
Over the years, thousands of RVers have corresponded with Bob Livingston through his monthly "Tech Topics" column in *Highways* magazine. *The Best of Tech Topics* includes their most important questions along with no-nonsense answers, solutions to pressing RV problems, and sources for hard-to-find accessories and replacement parts.
5¹⁄₂ × 8¹⁄₂, 112 pages
$12.95 ISBN: 0-93478-55-9

100 Miles Around Yellowstone
Jim and Madonna Zumbo
This new book is a comprehensive guide that focuses on the sights and activities within a 100-mile radius of Yellowstone National Park. It is a valuable guide for travelers who choose Yellowstone as their destination, but don't want to miss out on the many sights and activities nearby. Particular emphasis is made on RV travel and information in this area.
7³⁄₈ × 9¹⁄₄, 288 pages
$34.95 ISBN: 0-93478-52-4
Available November, 1998

Please Don't Tailgate the Real Estate:
Scouting the Back Roads and Off Ramps to Find True Love and Happiness
William C. Anderson
A hilarious collection of insights, observations, and travel adventures of noted author and Hollywood screenwriter, William "Andy" Anderson, gleaned from more than thirty years of RV travel with his wife and family in their rig, Rocinante. Andy is a rare

combination of gifted humorist and warm-hearted observer whose hilarious accounts of the twists, turns, quirks, and challenges of life on wheels comes from his own personal experience.

$5^1/_2 \times 8^1/_2$, 224 pages
$16.95 ISBN: 0-934798-51-8

These books are available at fine bookstores everywhere. Or, you may order directly from Trailer Life Books. For each book ordered, simply send us the name of the book, the price, plus $3.95 per book for shipping and handling (California residents please add 7.25% sales tax and Indiana residents, 5%).

Mail to:

Trailer Life Books,
64 Inverness Drive East,
Englewood, CO 80112

You may call our customer-service representatives if you wish to charge your order or if you would like additional information. Please phone, toll-free, Monday through Friday, 6:30 A.M. to 6:30 P.M.; Saturday, 7:30 A.M. to 1:30 P.M., Mountain Time; 1(800) 766-1674.

Repair

&

Maintenance Manual

THIRD EDITION

BOB LIVINGSTON

TRAILER LIFE BOOKS

Production Coordinator: Robert S. Tinnon
Technical Illustrations: Randy Miyake
Copy Editor: Rena Copperman
Cover Design: Mirante Almazan
Interior Design: Robert S. Tinnon

This book was set in Giovanni and Futura.

Printed and bound in the United States of America
by Ripon Community Printers.

9 8 7 6 5 4 3 2 1

ISBN:0-934798-45-1

CONTENTS

ILLUSTRATIONS
(A SELECTED LIST)

LIST OF TABLES

TROUBLESHOOTING GUIDES

FOREWORD

In an ideal world, all sorts of vehicles would run virtually forever on miserly amounts of fuel and would never suffer mechanical or electrical breakdowns. Tow trucks would not exist.

Of course, we don't live in an ideal world, and quite a variety of mechanical and electrical problems occur every day, the type and severity dependent on the original quality, age, and condition of the vehicle. That's why we have towing insurance, and why many of us even buy extended service contracts that go well beyond original warranties on items such as the vehicle drivetrain and on motorhome appliances.

Although it may not look like one, the *RV Repair and Maintenance Manual* is an insurance policy—one of a different kind. Given proper attention, this book insures that you will know more about maintenance and repair of your RV, and that you will be better prepared to prevent a broad variety of mechanical and electrical problems through the use of more thorough maintenance. And, this book gives you assurance that you will be better prepared to diagnose problems if they occur. While you may or may not be interested in performing the repairs yourself, you'll be in a better position to deal with professional mechanics.

Many RV owners may regard the technical and mechanical aspects of RV ownership as necessary evils that go along with the enjoyment of motorhome travel, but Bob Livingston, author of the *RV Repair and Maintenance Manual*, enjoys collecting and using knowledge about everything from amperage to Zerk fittings. For Bob, the technical side of RV ownership is a hobby unto itself—something he has enjoyed for more than two decades. It has always been fun for him, which is why he has acquired such a broad range of knowledge.

The result of that knowledge is the very thorough coverage of RV maintenance and repair that you see here. Thus, the book not only can be an insurance policy, it can also be your ticket to the satisfying feeling that comes from knowing how your RV works, how it should be maintained, and how it should be repaired if it breaks. Even RV owners who have no intention of doing any of the work themselves should be armed with the best, most complete, RV repair and maintenance information.

With the *RV Repair and Maintenance Manual*, you're on the way to more enjoyable, less expensive RV travel.

Bill Estes, Publisher
Trailer Life and *MotorHome*

PREFACE

Ten years ago we made the decision to produce a comprehensive technical guide that would provide readers with good reference material to better understand the inner workings of RVs. In 1989, the first *RV Repair & Maintenance Manual* was published, and since then it has helped literally hundreds of thousands of RV owners. The latest edition, the third, has been updated to include detailed information that keeps pace with the changing RV industry. While RVs have always been complex, featuring multiple systems—and multiple service and repair problems—they are now enhanced by sophisticated equipment and electronics. This new edition has been designed to keep up with technology.

You'll probably notice that the inside pages have been three-hole punched. Look closer and you'll find each page micro-perforated. The book is still divided into seventeen chapters designed to give owners more familiarity with individual systems in any trailer, fifthwheel, motorhome, or pickup camper. But these pages can be removed and stored, by chapter, in an optional three-ring notebook. As you peruse this manual, notice that each chapter is individually numbered for quick reference.

Versatility is the key. The notebook is supplied with dividers that have index tabs for each chapter. After being carefully removed, the pages can be placed in plastic sleeves (optional) for added protection. Now you have a very user-friendly notebook, filled with pages that can actually be taken to the job site, one at a time, if need be. The plastic sleeves protect the pages, and there are plenty of opportunities to add notes and receipts from each job. As we update this book, all you have to do is add the specially numbered pages to your personal three-ring binder. It's nice to know that your maintenance manual can be updated without making another book purchase.

Beyond the basic primers, this reference book is designed to instruct the owner on the proper procedures for preventive maintenance, a crucial element for troublefree RV travel. When a rig is delivered by your dealer, it is usually put through an extensive pre-delivery inspection (PDI). Service technicians will thoroughly test each appliance and system for proper operation. But for too many owners, this is the first and last time their rigs get checked out in such detail. Unfortunately, many owners wait for the inevitable breakdown before taking action. And you know what that means: throwing yourself at the mercy of a local repair shop. Knowledge of maintenance procedures and servicing your rig on a regular basis give you the upper hand.

Due to the nature of RV travel, most breakdowns occur far from home, where you're forced to trust the local technician to be honest about necessary repairs and charge you a fair amount. Here is where this manual gives you an advantage. Even if you are not a seasoned mechanic, you'll be far better off if you know something about proper repair procedures. Less-than-honest mechanics are more wary when the owner acts as if he or she knows what's going on.

Troubleshooting guides throughout this manual are designed to lead the owner to the source of the problem, quickly. Checklists give you on-the-spot information, without having to read too much text. In addition, the large number of illustrations, photos, and tables that support the accompanying text can be easily accessed by clearly marked figure numbers.

The information contained in this repair manual will guide you through most procedures. Although your exact appliance or accessory may not be described, the repair and/or service procedure is usually applicable with minor variations.

The information in the *RV Repair & Maintenance Manual* would not be possible without the outstanding cooperation of the industry manufacturers and suppliers. I am forever grateful for their help. Special thanks go to Thetford, Tekonsha, Dometic, Norcold, Onan, Kohler, Generac, Hayes Axle, Atwood Mobile Products, Suburban, Roadmaster, Automatic Equipment, Magic Chef, RV Solar Electric, Winegard, Reese, Eaz-Lift, SeaLand, Microphor, Bargman Products, SHURflo, Sure Power, Thin-Lite, Teton Homes, Fleetwood, Manchester Tank, Intellitec, and a host of other industry suppliers.

Assembling a manual of this magnitude was no easy feat. It took a team of dedicated RV enthusiasts to assist in digesting the material from the various manufacturers and suppliers, integrating their personal experience, knowledge, and talent, and, finally, interpreting and communicating this information to you. Special thanks go to Rich Johnson and Brian Robertson, and to Mike and Pam Steffen, without whose help this book could not have been published in such a timely manner.

Credit Rena Copperman for the editing and Bob Tinnon for the design of this book. Tinnon can now take a deep breath and finally see the sun.

We hope you'll take a moment to fill out the Reader Survey in the back of this book. We always appreciate readers' comments, which, as in the past, will be used during the updating process.

It's nice to know the information contained herein will help get you back on the road. The true reward, of course, is being able to fix the problem yourself.

Happy Trails!

ELECTRICAL SYSTEMS

Recreational vehicles use 12-volt direct current (DC) and/or 120-volt alternating current (AC) power from a number of sources: onboard 12-volt storage batteries, onboard 6-volt storage batteries (wired in series), 120-volt AC campground hookups, 120-volt AC auxiliary generators, power converters, power inverters, or photovoltaic cells (solar). The 120-volt AC in an RV is similar to that in a home and, other than periodic checks for low voltage, usually requires little or no maintenance.

All 120-volt AC wiring for appliances and accessories is protected by a series of circuit breakers located inside the RV. The 120-volt AC system is potentially dangerous and should not be modified unless the user has sufficient understanding of AC electricity.

■ TESTS AND CHECKS ■ FOR ELECTRICAL SYSTEMS

Proper Use of 12-Volt DC Power

Twelve-volt DC power presents little danger of electrical shock. Still, care must be taken when dealing with 12-volt systems because DC power is capable of producing large amounts of current. A short circuit or an overloaded circuit can generate a lot of heat, melting insulation off wiring, damaging appliances, and creating potential for fire. To protect against possible short circuits or fire, all circuits must contain some type of over-current-protection device (OCPD) that is rated no higher-than the conductor's maximum ampere rating. Ideally, the OCPD (fuse or circuit breaker) should be within 18 inches of the power source.

Although troubleshooting RV electrical systems may seem somewhat mysterious, most of these systems can be checked with simple tools. Interruptions in current are the most common problems faced by the RV owner. And these interruptions can be diagnosed by use of an inexpensive 12-volt test light or, preferably, a multimeter. While a test light indicates when voltage exists, a multimeter can help identify breaks or shorts in circuits without the existence of voltage. A multimeter also will show exact voltage. A digital multimeter is the best choice, since it indicates precise voltage.

Using a Test Light

Checking power at a 12-volt DC appliance or a light fixture can be easily accomplished by using a 12-volt test light (Figure 1.1).

CAUTION: Be certain that you have properly differentiated between 12-volt DC and 120-volt AC appliances. Inserting the probe of a 12-volt DC test light into a 120-volt AC wall outlet can cause a dangerous electrical shock.

Most test lights consist of a plastic handle with a small bulb inside. A wire lead with an alligator clip at the end protrudes from the handle. The "business" end of the tester is a sharp probe. A more sophisticated test light has an internal battery, and, rather than using an alligator clip attached to a ground source, the ground is provided by your body. To operate, the user probes the wire or contact with the pointed end and touches a known good ground with his or her hand. While these devices are handy in many instances, they become cumbersome if you need both hands for probing into a wire.

To test for power:

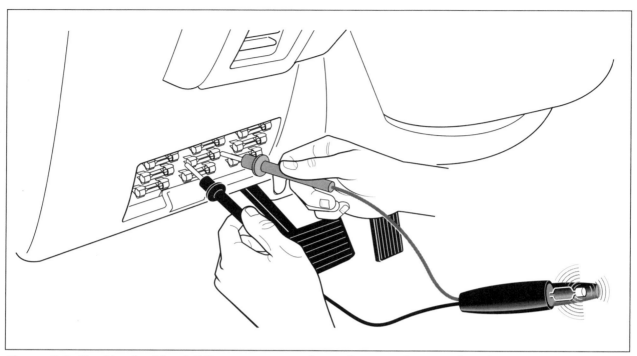

Figure 1.1 Checking for 12-volt DC power at an appliance, fixture, or fuse panel can be accomplished with a simple test light.

1. Touch the probe to the positive post of the battery and the alligator clip to the negative post. The bulb should illuminate, confirming that the tester is functioning. This test should always be done first to determine that the test light is working properly.
2. Connect the alligator clip to a good ground or to the cold (negative) side of the item to be checked, for example, the switch, the light socket, or the wire.
3. With the power on, touch the probe to the hot (positive) terminal or connection that you wish to test. When checking wiring, the probe must break the insulation. If you are using a test light that needs a ground from your body, touch a good ground source with your finger or hand.
4. If the bulb illuminates, power is confirmed.

Using a Multimeter

As its name suggests, a multimeter has many functions, making it one of the most versatile tools available to the do-it-yourselfer (Figure 1.2). A multimeter can be used to check for voltage in either 120-volt AC or 12-volt DC circuits. The ability to read the exact voltage allows the owner to check battery condition, battery-charging effectiveness, and voltage available to appliances and fixtures, regardless of whether the power source is a campground hookup or an on-board AC generator. Before using a multimeter, the battery inside the device should be checked (battery-check position on scale), and the meter should be zeroed according to manufacturer's instructions. This should not be necessary with a digital multimeter.

Checking AC Voltage with a Multimeter

To check AC voltage, follow these steps (Figure 1.3):

1. Connect the probes to the multimeter, as instructed by the manufacturer. Most manufacturers require that the probes be inserted into the multimeter first. Set the range selector to the position that includes 120 volts AC. Most likely, this value will be higher than 120.
2. Hook the RV electrical cord to campground power, start the AC generator, or activate the power inverter, depending on the source you wish to test.

3. Insert the red probe into the larger wall socket slot and the black probe into the other. Read voltage.

4. Voltage range should be between 110 and 127 with no load on the system. Voltage will rarely exceed 120 in campgrounds, but AC generators may produce upward of 130 volts with no load and will drop when a load is switched into the system. If voltage falls below 100 volts AC, motor-driven appliances will be damaged, and 12-volt DC converters may cease to function. Fortunately, most newer AC appliances are protected against low-voltage conditions. Voltage monitored at the wall sockets should be the same as that of the appliances and accessories.

Checking DC Voltage with a Multimeter

To check DC voltage, follow these steps:

1. Connect the probes in the multimeter first. Set the range selector to a position that includes 12 volts DC. Usually the value here will be higher.

2. Touch the red probe to the positive side of the switch, accessory, or wire and the black probe to the negative side or ground location.

3. With the power on, read the voltage. Voltage will vary from near 0 (dead battery) to nearly 15 (output of a GM alternator in cold weather), depending on conditions and the type of equipment used. For example, a fully charged battery that is not connected to a load will produce voltage readings of about 12.6. Appliances will not operate properly when voltage drops to about 10.5. RV converters (battery chargers) will produce 13.8 to 14 volts and alternator output will vary from 13.5 to 15, depending on how much current the alternator is producing and the ambient temperature.

Checking Continuity and Resistance with a Multimeter

The ability to check for resistance to current flow is important in diagnosing electrical problems. If the flow of current is impeded by broken, corroded, shorted, or poorly soldered or connected wires, resistance occurs. To check for resistance:

1. Connect the multimeter probes in the appropriate slots. Set the selector switch to the appropriate position to check continuity.

2. Touch the probes together: the ohms scale or digital screen should read 0. Zero means that there is no resistance while holding the two probe tips together: current is moving freely (Figure 1.4).

3. To check resistance in a wire, touch one probe to one end of the wire and the second probe to the other end. The meter should read 0. If it does not, resistance may be caused by wire damage, corrosion, or poor connections (Figure 1.5).

4. To check for resistance in a solder joint or solderless connection, touch the probes to both sides of the connection and read the scale. Zero means the connection is good; any other position of the needle or other reading of the digital meter means the solder joint is cold or corroded and/or the connector is bad or badly crimped.

5. To check the resistance in a fuse, touch the probes to the metal ends or tabs of the fuse and read the scale. The needle should point to 0. Bulbs can be checked by probing the contact(s) and case and reading the scale (Figure 1.6). The needle should point to 0.

Checking for Proper Polarity

It's important that proper polarity is maintained for both 120-volt AC and 12-volt DC systems. Normally, RV 12-volt DC systems are wired using the black wire as the positive (hot) and the white wire as the negative (ground). In some cases, the rig can be wired using a red wire for the positive and the black as the ground. If the polarity is reversed, many 12-volt DC appliances and accessories can become damaged. If the battery leads are reversed, the converter relays will usually chatter. Do not turn on any appliances if the polarity is reversed. Although the lights will work normally, sensitive electronics can become damaged. If you have replaced or serviced the batteries,

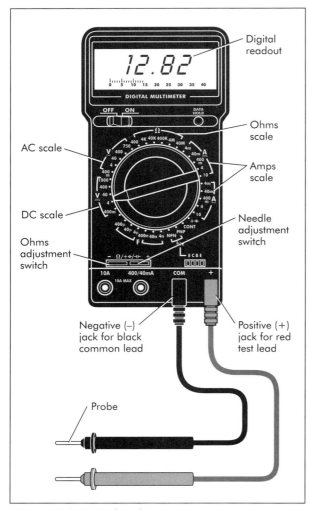

Figure 1.2 Digital multimeter

verify voltage with a multimeter before using any appliances or accessories.

Improper wiring in the campground hookup receptacles—or in the rig—can create electrical problems. It's always prudent to check the polarity at the campground hookup using a polarity and circuit tester (available at RV supply stores) before plugging in the power cord. If the polarity is wrong, inform the campground manager; do not attempt to fix it yourself. Once you initially verify that the receptacles in your RV (new rig, before the first trip) are wired correctly, there should be no future problems here.

The wiring codes for 120-volt AC systems (Figure 1.7) are as follows: white is the common and larger of the slots, black is hot, and green is ground (could also be a bare wire).

Checking Ground-Fault Interrupters

All new RVs must be equipped with a ground-fault circuit interrupter (GFCI). These safety devices are normally used around sinks, tubs, and showers. You'll usually find them installed in the bath area, but some can be found in the kitchen; outdoor receptacles are also tied into GFCI units. They are designed to protect you from electrical shock should you come in contact with an electrical appliance and water. The GFCI reads the variance in current between the hot and ground wires in the outlet. A short circuit draw-

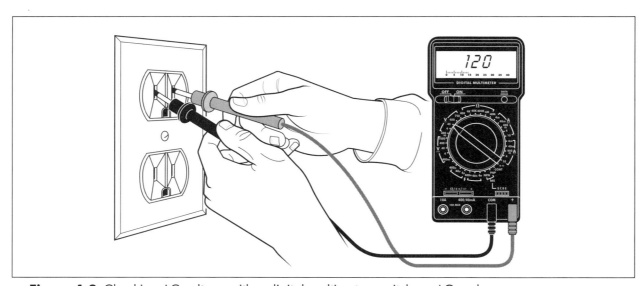

Figure 1.3 Checking AC voltage with a digital multimeter; switch on AC scale

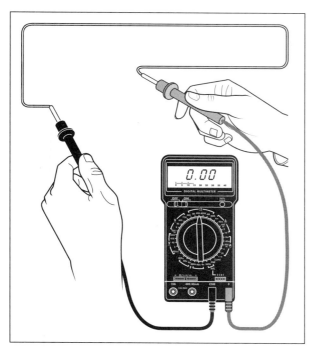

Figure 1.4 The multimeter will show no resistance when the circuit is complete.

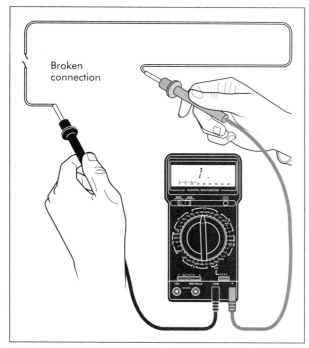

Figure 1.5 The multimeter readout shows a broken connection (resistance).

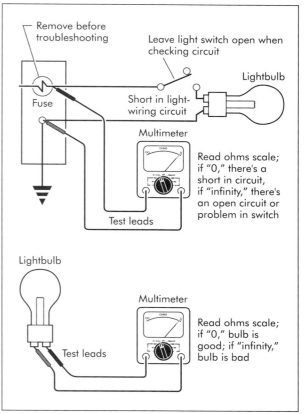

Figure 1.6 Multimeters are versatile tools for checking for shorted circuits or lightbulb conditions.

ing current to ground (through a human body, for instance) will vary the levels of current in the two wires, and the GFCI will shut down the receptacle. Any conductive path from the AC wiring to the ground can trip a GFCI, and it only takes about 5 milliamperes to do the job.

All GFCI units used in RVs are equipped with a test button to verify that the device is working properly. To test, press the "T" or test button; the "R" or reset button should pop out immediately and the receptacle will go dead. Pressing the "R" button should lock in place and restore power. If not, check for faulty wiring or connections. If the wiring checks out, the GFCI is bad and must be replaced.

In some cases, the wiring in the RV can cause the GFCI in the campground hookup to trip. This can be caused by a number of problems, but many times moisture or corrosion on the power cord can cause this problem. Moisture or corrosion in any of the RV's wiring from the rig's GFCI can cause the park's GFCI to trip.

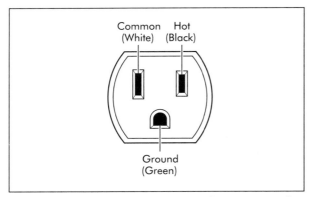

Figure 1.7 Wiring code for 120-volt AC receptacle

Under normal operation, the current supplied by the hot wire returns through the neutral wire. If a different amount of current returns to the neutral wire, the GFCI reads the condition as a ground fault and trips the circuit breaker that's built into the unit. If you suspect that the wiring in your rig is faulty, take the RV to a qualified RV electrical technician and have the system tested. Finding a ground fault can be difficult without precise testing equipment.

Checking the Wiring

In many cases, 12-volt DC appliances and accessories will suffer operational losses when improper wiring size and/or improper wiring techniques are used during installation. The heart of the RV 12-volt DC electrical system is primary wire, which differs from 120-volt wire because it is comprised of many smaller strands of copper wire bundled together to form a specific gauge (size). Although primary wire generally ranges from 10- to 22-gauge (the smaller the number, the larger the wire), most RVs are wired with either 10-, 12-, or 14-gauge wire. Larger wire, such as 6- or 8-gauge, is also used in many cases, especially when connecting the battery or batteries to a fuse box or when wiring a charge line from a tow vehicle to a trailer.

To determine the proper wire size for a specific application, it is necessary to know the current or ampere requirement of the appliance or accessory and the length of wire needed for installation. Wire that is too small for the rated amperage of the appliance will cause a voltage drop (lower voltage at the terminus of the wire than at the power source), which will lead to underperformance and possible damage to the appliance. Most RV appliances and accessories have a label that displays the rated amperage or wattage. Amperage can be determined from known wattage by using the following formula:

$$\frac{\text{watts}}{\text{volts}} = \text{amps}$$

Once amperage (units of electrical flow or volume) is determined, the proper wire can be selected using tables established in the *National Electrical Code Handbook* (Table 1.1).

Caution must be exercised when using the amperage-load chart because under certain circumstances the wire may be capable of handling a specified load for a specified distance but will not

Table 1.1 Amperage load in circuit

Allowable conductor length (in feet) in a circuit before a 1-volt loss occurs																			
Gauge	1	1.5	2	3	4	5	6	7	8	10	12	15	20	24	30	36	50	100	150	200
20	106	70	53	35	26	21	17	15	13	10	8	7	5	4	3	3	2	1	0	0
18	150	100	75	50	37	30	25	21	18	15	12	10	7	6	5	4	3	1	1	0
16	224	144	112	74	56	44	37	32	28	22	18	14	11	9	7	6	4	2	1	1
14	362	241	181	120	90	72	60	51	45	36	30	24	18	15	12	10	7	3	2	1
12	572	381	286	190	143	114	95	81	71	57	47	38	28	23	19	15	11	5	3	2
10	908	605	454	302	227	181	151	129	113	90	75	60	45	37	30	25	18	9	6	4
8	1452	967	726	483	363	290	241	207	181	145	120	96	72	60	48	40	29	14	9	7
6	2342	1560	1171	780	585	468	390	334	292	234	194	155	117	97	78	65	46	23	15	11
4	3702	2467	1851	1232	925	740	616	529	462	370	307	246	185	154	123	102	74	37	24	18
2	6060	4038	3030	2018	1515	1212	1009	866	757	606	503	403	303	252	201	168	121	60	40	30
1	7692	5126	3846	2561	1923	1538	1280	1100	961	769	638	511	384	320	256	213	153	76	51	38
0	9708	6470	4854	3232	2427	1941	1616	1388	1213	970	805	645	485	404	323	269	194	97	64	48

The above table is computed for a 68°F (20°C) ambient temperature.

Table 1.2 National Electrical Code Amperage

Wire Size	Amperage Rating
18	6
16	8
14	15
12	20
10	30
8	40
6	55

Source: *National Electrical Code Handbook*, (Quincy MA:
National Fire Protection Association, 1981), 70–494.

conform to recreational vehicle industry standards. For example, Table 1.1 shows that a 16-gauge wire can be used to operate an appliance that is within 11 feet of the power source and have an amperage rating of 20. However, to meet RV industry standards, a 12-gauge wire must be used—based on Section 551 of the *National Electrical Code Handbook* (Table 1.2).

A typical circuit in an RV consists of a wire running from the positive terminal of the battery to a fuse (or circuit breaker) and then to the appliance or accessory (Figure 1.8). A second wire equal in size to the positive wire must then be used to ground the appliance or accessory to the negative side of the battery. In some cases, the RV chassis may be used as a ground-circuit conductor. When the circuit is completed, electrons flow through wiring to the appliance and return to the battery.

Although wiring is relatively easy to work with and consists of no moving parts, installation inconsistencies can cause failures. When possible, all wiring should be routed inside conduit or wiring looms. Grommets must be used where wires are routed through walls or bulkheads, although silicone sealant, if used properly (Figures 1.9 and 1.10), works well in providing abrasion protection.

Checking Wire Terminals

Modern wire terminals have made soldering virtually unnecessary, but improper use of these connectors can cause a number of problems. The electrical industry has established standards for insulated wire terminals and uses the following color coding: red terminals can be used on 22- to 18-gauge wire, blue represents 16- to 14-gauge, and yellow is for 12- to 10-gauge. There are a number of terminals avail-

able for almost any wiring job. The most common are ring spade, tongue spade, butt splice, and faston terminals (Figure 1.11). The larger terminals repeat the colors; 8-gauge terminals are usually red, and 6-gauge terminals can be blue.

Terminals are made up of three or four parts, depending on the type and quality: *wire barrel, tongue, insulation,* and *strain-relief sleeve*. When crimping a terminal, the wire barrel tends to spread at the seam, so it's best to look for a terminal in which the seam is brazed shut or one that is seamless. This allows the seam to remain closed so that a second crimp can be made for strain relief.

Automotive terminals have either nylon or polyvinyl chloride (PVC) insulation. Nylon is easier to work with and allows a visual inspection of the crimp, but PVC is less susceptible to cuts and moisture. Nylon may be necessary when using the terminals in an environment where certain chemicals are present. Moisture can be sealed out of a terminal by using a small length of shrink tubing over a portion of the wire and terminal. Some terminals have shrink tubing built into the insulation, which is doubly advantageous, although these connectors are more expensive.

How to Crimp a Terminal

Although solderless terminals offer superior connections, they are useless if the crimp is poorly executed. Terminals should not be installed with pliers, vise grips, or a rock. A proper crimping tool is required, preferably one that is made by the terminal manufacturer. If the tool punctures the insulation during the crimping procedure, the terminal should be discarded. Once the proper connector and wire have been matched, the following procedure should be used:

1. Strip off the insulation so that the bare wire will protrude $1/32$ to $1/16$ inch past the wire barrel of the terminal. Some tools have indicators inscribed into the tool (Figure 1.12).
2. Place the terminal into the tool in the correct die according to wire size. Apply gentle pressure to hold the terminal in place.
3. Place the wire into the terminal (Figure 1.13).
4. Close the tool completely (Figure 1.14). Some tools have two points that must be

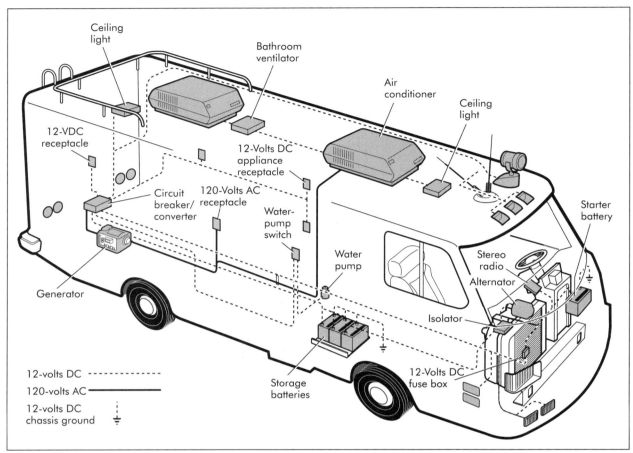

Ceiling light

Bathroom ventilator

Air conditioner

Ceiling light

12-VDC receptacle

12-Volts DC appliance receptacle

120-Volts AC receptacle

Circuit breaker/ converter

Water-pump switch

Water pump

Starter battery

Stereo radio

Alternator

Isolator

Generator

Storage batteries

12-Volts DC fuse box

12-volts DC -----------

120-volts AC ———

12-volts DC chassis ground

Figure 1.8 A typical RV has both 12-volt DC and 120-volt AC wiring circuits. The power converter and batteries supply 12-volt DC power; AC generator and campground hookups supply 120-volt AC power.

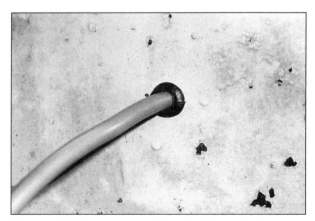

Figure 1.9 A grommet will protect the wire from damage when routed through metal.

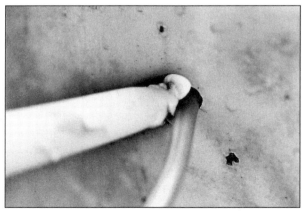

Figure 1.10 Silicone can be used to protect the wire routed through metal if a grommet is not available.

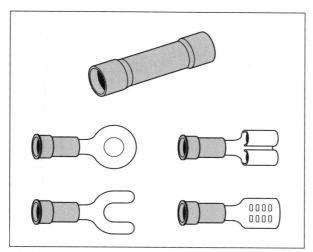

Figure 1.11 Common solderless terminals include butt splice, ring spade, tongue spade, and faston connectors.

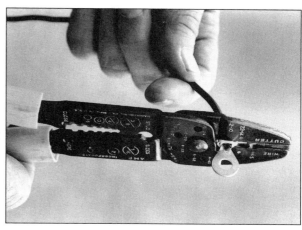

Figure 1.14 Terminals are placed in corresponding slots for crimping.

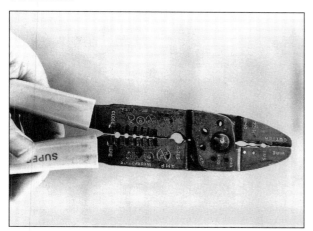

Figure 1.12 Typical crimping tools have inscribed indicators to assist the user.

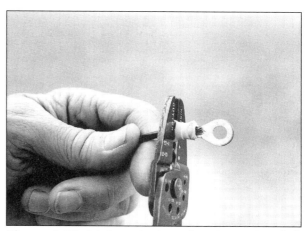

Figure 1.15 It is important to crimp the strain-relief portion of the terminal.

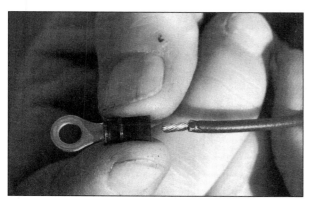

Figure 1.13 Strip off enough insulation so wire fits properly into the terminal.

touched, indicating a proper crimp. The better tools have a ratcheting mechanism that will not release unless the crimp has been executed properly.

5. Move the tool to the strain-relief sleeve (if supplied on terminal) and close the tool completely (Figure 1.15). Many mechanics fail to make this important crimp.

6. If using terminals with heat-shrink tubing (Figure 1.16), apply the flame from a propane torch, match, or use a source of electric heat after crimping. Stop heating when sealant inside the tubing begins to ooze out

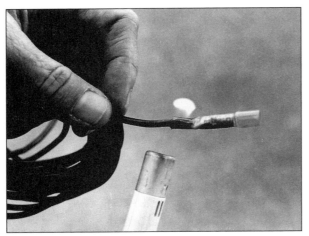

Figure 1.16 Terminals with built-in heat-shrink tubing provide weather protection

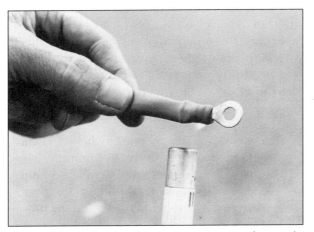

Figure 1.17 Shrink tubing, cut to size, can be used to protect terminals from the elements.

of the terminal insulation. A piece of shrink tubing can be used to seal a connector (Figure 1.17).

Wire Ties

The easiest method of bundling or securing wires and cables is to use wire ties—sometimes referred to as strap ties (Figure 1.18). These are thin nylon straps that can be looped around the wire (and a stationary object, if necessary) and secured using a special closure mechanism. Use only the black wire ties, especially on the exterior; they have superior resistance

Figure 1.18 Use wire ties (or strap ties) to bundle or secure wires and cables.

to the ultraviolet light and the elements. Most wire ties are not reusable and they must be cut off when not needed.

■ BATTERIES ■

Recreational vehicles are usually equipped with two types of batteries: engine starting and deep cycle. The starting battery employed by either the tow vehicle or motorhome engine is designed to provide high amperage discharges for short periods, as required by the starter motor. Deep-cycle batteries are designed for low-amperage discharges to operate accessories such as furnaces, lights, and entertainment systems. Plates in deep-cycle batteries are constructed of higher-density lead, which allows frequent deep discharges without the accelerated shedding of material from the plates that occurs when starting batteries are subjected to this type of use. Starting batteries will fail rapidly if repeatedly discharged heavily.

Engine-starting batteries have thin plates suspended in electrolyte, sulfuric acid combined with water, gel, or glass mat, depending on the design. These batteries are rated in cold-cranking amps (CCA), which is the maximum load a fully charged battery can deliver for thirty seconds at 0°F while maintaining at least 7.2 volts. Some starting batteries can be maintenance free.

Deep-cycle batteries have fewer plates, but they are thicker and coated with antimony or calcium, which increases hardness. This design limits the amount of lead that is sloughed off into the bottom of the case due to repeated charging and discharging cycles. Deep-cycle batteries are available in three styles: conventional flooded-electrolyte, gelled electrolyte, and absorbed glass mat (AGM).

Flooded-cell batteries have been around for decades and use acid and water electrolyte around the positive and negative lead plates. Gel-type batteries utilize a gel to immobilize the electrolyte and calcium on the plates, which reduces the gassing. AGM batteries are similar to gel cells, but the electrolyte is absorbed by a fine glass mat. Like the gel cell, AGM batteries recombine the gases during charging, limiting gassing. Gel and AGM batteries are sealed, virtually eliminating corrosion problems associated with flooded-electolyte batteries.

One plate is positive and the other is negative. As the battery delivers power (discharging), the acid in the electrolyte enters the positive and negative plates. The electrolyte becomes weaker as the acid is depleted until the battery cannot deliver power at a useful voltage. By reversing the current flow (charging), the sulfuric acid is returned to the electrolyte from the plates (Figure 1.19).

Electrolyte management (maintaining proper water levels), combined with proper charging techniques and intervals, can make the difference in performance and battery longevity. Maintenance-free and sealed batteries do not require water replenishment.

Battery Ratings

Reserve capacity is the amount of time the battery can sustain a discharge at a specified level. Different levels are used to rate different batteries. Reserve-capacity ratings are based on how long the battery will sustain a 25-amp load at 80°F before voltage drops to 10.5. In real-world conditions, the 25-amp load does not usually represent the average RV load, which is closer to 10 amps. Battery-reserve capacity lasts longer at lower discharge rates. For example, the common Group 27 RV deep-cycle battery may be rated at 160 minutes. This same battery also may carry the old-style ampere-hour rating—in this case 105 ampere-hours. The amp-hour rating is a measure of reserve capacity and only approximately 60 percent of the capacity that is usable. The amp-hour rating is the amount of current that can be drawn from a battery for twenty hours before voltage drops to 10.5. That's about a 5-amp load for twenty hours.

Table 1.3 Capacities of Typical 12-volt, Deep-cycle, Wet-cell Group 24 and 27 Batteries

Accessory Draw	Power Provided*	
Amps	Group 24	Group 27
5	16.0 hrs	19.0 hrs
15	4.6	5.4
25	2.5	3.0

*Hours of continuous power, based on peak performance.

But it's best to subtract about 20 percent from that figure to compensate for less-than-ideal charging conditions and system losses.

Battery-Depletion Test

Most deep-cycle batteries are rated by their respective manufacturers as to how long they will sustain a specific load. Tables (Table 1.3) are provided by the manufacturers. You can use these tables—minus the 20 percent for real-world conditions—or perform your own depletion test to compare actual performance. This can be especially important when determining your battery needs. To perform a depletion test:

1. Make sure the battery is fully charged. Use a multimeter or hydrometer to confirm.
2. Turn on the interior lights to create a 5-amp load, measuring the load with the ammeter function of the multimeter. Record the time.
3. Monitor time and voltage until voltage drops to 10.5.

Testing the Battery

The three methods for testing a battery are: checking electrolyte with a hydrometer, voltage measurement, and load testing. A hydrometer measures the battery's state of charge by comparing the weight of the electrolyte to the weight of water (specific gravity). Because temperature affects specific gravity, a temperature-correcting hydrometer must be used. An adjustable battery condition/load tester takes all the guesswork out of checking a maintenance-free battery. Load testers are usually only available at repair facilities, but maintenance-free-battery conditions can be determined by reading open-circuit voltage and comparing it to a table (Table 1.4).

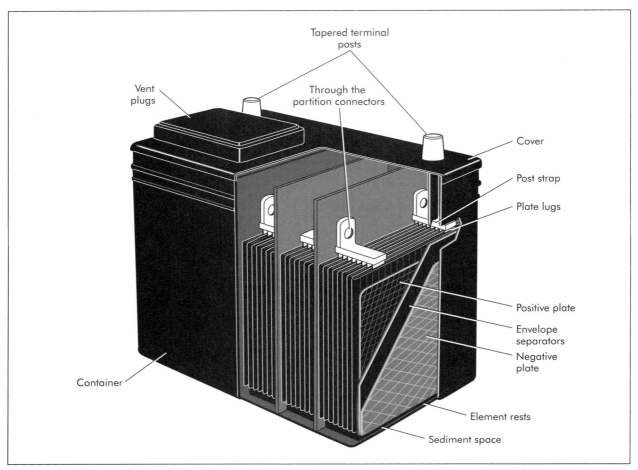

Figure 1.19 Components of a lead-acid, wet-cell battery typically used in RVs.

Table 1.4 Open-Circuit Voltage

Voltage	State of Charge (%)
12.6 or higher	100
12.4	75
12.2	50
12.0	25
11.7	0

CAUTION: Battery acid is corrosive and can damage painted surfaces, metal parts, clothing, skin, or eyes. If spilled, use baking soda and water to neutralize the acid. Flush immediately and seek medical attention if acid is accidentally spilled on skin or squirted in eyes.

Checking Electyrolytye with Hydrometer

To check a battery using a hydrometer, follow these steps (Figure 1.20):

1. Remove battery caps.
2. Insert the syringe into the cell and extract the electrolyte.
3. Hold at eye level and read the specific gravity (Table 1.5).
4. Return the electrolyte to cell.

Open-Circuit Voltage Test

To check a battery's open-circuit voltage, follow these steps:

Table 1.5 Specific Gravity Values

Charge Level (%)	Specific Gravity
100	1.265
75	1.225
50	1.190
25	1.155
Discharged	1.120

CHAPTER 1 Electrical Systems **1.13**

■ TROUBLESHOOTING ■
THE BATTERY

Problem	Possible Cause	Correction
Excessive use of water, corrosion deposits on caps, excessive case heat, warped or broken plates, active material shedding, damaged separators	Overcharging	Check regulator, check converter, replace battery
	Excessive vibration	Repair hold-down
Not holding a charge	Undercharging	Check regulator, check converter
	Loose fan belt	Tighten fan belt
	Sulfation	Perform slow charge
	Bad battery	Replace battery
	Low electrolyte	Replenish
Won't start engine	Low voltage	Recharge battery, load-test.
	Low electrolyte	Replenish
	Loose cable terminal	Tighten terminals
	Bad cable terminal	Replace terminal
	Corroded terminals	Clean corrosion
	Worn or broken cables	Replace (cables)
	Cold/hot weather	Use larger battery
Will not operate appliances and accessories	Low voltage	Recharge battery, load-test.
	Low electrolyte	Replenish
	Loose cable terminal	Tighten terminals
	Bad cable terminal	Replace terminal
	Corroded terminals	Remove corrosion
	Break in wiring	Check wiring
	Bad battery	Replace battery
	No power	Check battery, clean terminals, check wiring. Check fuse box
	Low output from alternator or converter	Check charging sources

1. Perform this test only if the battery has not been charged within the previous twenty-four hours (so surface charge will be depleted). Surface charge can be depleted by turning on a 10-amp load for five minutes.
2. Remove the negative battery cable (to make sure no load is on the battery).
3. Read the voltage with an accurate voltmeter.
4. Reconnect the battery cable.

Battery state of charge can be determined by comparing voltage to the percentage of charge listed in the open-circuit voltage chart (see Table 1.4, page 1.12). For example, if the voltage read at the voltmeter is 12.6 volts or higher, the battery is fully charged. A battery is completely discharged at 11.7 volts.

Charging the Battery

Recreational-vehicle batteries are commonly charged by the vehicle's engine alternator, the power converter, and solar panels. The alternator will do a good job of charging both the starting and house battery(ies),

Figure 1.20 Checking wet cell specific gravity with a hydrometer.

Table 1.6 Battery-charging guide for fixed-rate external chargers

Rated Reserve Capacity* (in minutes)	Slow Charge	Fast Charge
80 or less	10 hrs. at 5 amps 5 hrs. at 10 amps	2.5 hrs. at 20 amps 1.5 hrs. at 30 amps
80 to 125	15 hrs. at 5 amps 7.5 hrs. at 10 amps	3.75 hrs. at 20 amps 1.5 hrs. at 50 amps
125 to 170	20 hrs. at 5 amps 10 hrs. at 10 amps	5 hrs. at 20 amps 2 hrs. at 50 amps
170 to 250	30 hrs. at 5 amps 15 hrs. at 10 amps	7.5 hrs. at 20 amps 3 hrs. at 50 amps
Over 250	24 hrs. at 10 amps	6 hrs. at 40 amps 4 hrs. at 60 amps

NOTE: These charging rates and times are guidelines and should only be used if battery manufacturer's recommendations are not available.
*Indicates the number of minutes the battery will sustain a 25-ampere load before voltage falls to 10.5 (12-volt battery).

provided it is rated high enough to supply the demands of appliances and accessories being operated while driving and still have a surplus for battery charging. All batteries should be returned to a full state of charge before storing the RV. Extended driving with an alternator that is producing voltage levels of 14 to 15 (depending on temperature) will usually bring a battery to a full state of charge.

Most power converters are inefficient when it comes to charging batteries (see page 1.22). Lower line units will only provide 4 to 7 amps for battery charging. A good solar system, on the other hand, can provide efficient charging, providing there's enough sun (see page 1.24).

Batteries that become depleted can be restored to a full state of charge by using a portable charging unit found in many auto-parts and marine-supply stores. Most portable units are designed to taper the charge as battery condition improves, but the use of a nonautomatic charger with a constant, small am-

perage output (about 5 percent of the battery's rated amp-hour capacity) also is effective (Table 1.6).

CAUTION: Careful attention must be paid to prescribed limits of charging time when using a nonautomatic charger. Substantial overcharging can cause case meltdown or serious gassing (release of hydrogen and oxygen), which can cause an explosion.

The latest generation of smart chargers is the most effective. These units provide automatic, multi-stage charging:

Bulk-Charge Stage Provides constant current, up to its maximum rating, for maximum recharging.

Absorption-Charge Stage Current is reduced; voltage is maintained at a specified absorption level to complete the charge without overheating or overcharging the batteries.

Equalization Stage Higher voltage (14.5 to 15 volts) with small current flow is provided to remove sulfate from the plates.

CAUTION: This stage is for flooded-electrolyte batteries only; gel cells do not need this function.

Overcharged Batteries Overcharging is a common reason for premature battery failure. A faulty voltage regulator is usually the culprit. Designed to limit the output voltage of the alternator, it turns the field current on and off so that constant voltage is attained. A voltage regulator can either be an internal part of the alternator or an external piece of equipment.

Electrical converters built into RVs also can cause overcharging over long periods by providing voltage levels that are high enough to cause continual battery gassing. Voltage of the converter should not be higher than 13.8 for long-term use with conventional open-cell batteries. It can be about 14 volts when maintenance free or sealed batteries are being used.

Overcharging can be a significant problem with batteries that have been discharged too deeply. Batteries should not be depleted further than 80 percent (10.5 volts under a 5-amp load). When overdischarging, the acid will not recombine with the electrolyte medium as rapidly as it should. High-current flow creates heat, which can permanently derate the battery. In the case of overdischarging, make sure recharging is limited to the capacity divided by 20 (5.25 amps for a 105-amp battrery) until 20 percent of the battery's capacity has been restored.

Undercharged Batteries Undercharging is a common cause of battery failure. The voltage regulator or a slipping fan belt can be the reason. Fan belts should be tightened to allow for about 1 inch of deflection at the center. Belts should be free from cracks, brittleness, and glazing. It's important to check belts periodically and replace them at the first sign of weakening. During cold weather, batteries will not accept a charge as easily. If the vehicle is used for short trips during winter, the battery may never gain the necessary charge to be effective.

Sulfated Batteries Batteries become sulfated when allowed to remain in a discharged state for too long. Lead sulfate forms on negative plates during the normal process of battery discharge. Problems occur only when the sulfate remains on the plates too long and hardens; this begins within a month if the battery is left in a discharged state. The hard coating acts like varnish, restricting the electrolyte's ability to penetrate the plates. Battery capacity is reduced as sulfation increases. Moderate sulfation may be broken by slow-charging the battery for twenty-four hours at a 6- to 8-ampere rate. This is not effective, though, in severe cases. Once a battery becomes badly sulfated, it should be discarded.

Analysis of voltage output can be helpful in diagnosing problems with insufficient battery-reserve power. Voltage can be checked at the batteries while the engine is running to determine the proper output of the alternator. Using a multimeter, check voltage of each battery; the voltage with the engine

running should be between 14 to 14.8. Voltage checks should not be performed when the battery is in a low state of charge.

Although there may be adequate voltage output from the alternator—or electrical converter—it's important that the available voltage is seen at the battery. Voltage drop can decrease the charging efficiency dramatically. Check the voltage at the alternator or converter and at the batteries. The difference should not be more than 0.2 volts. If a large voltage drop is noticed, install heavier gauge wiring.

Battery-Voltage-Drop Test

The voltage-drop test for vehicles with no isolator but with mechanical relay is as follows:

1. Deplete voltage of auxiliary battery to 10.5 volts by using several interior lights.
2. Set engine idle to 1,500 RPM.
3. Check voltage at the alternator output terminal.
4. Check the voltage at the positive post of the auxiliary battery. If the voltage drop exceeds 0.2 to 0.3 volts, the wire size is inadequate, connections are bad, terminals are bad, or the relay is creating resistance.
5. Recharge the battery when the test is completed.
   NOTE: Check voltage at input and outlet terminals while relay is carrying heavy load. Reading at both terminals should be equal.

The voltage-drop test for vehicles with a solid-state, diode-type isolator is as follows:

1. Deplete the auxiliary battery to 10.5 volts using the preceding procedure.
2. Set the engine speed to 1,500 RPM; check the voltage at the output terminal on the alternator.
3. Check the voltage at the A-post (alternator) on the isolator. The voltage drop should not be more than 0.2 volts.
4. Check the voltage at the auxiliary-battery output terminal of the isolator.
5. Check the voltage at auxiliary battery. The voltage drop should not be more than 0.3 volts.

NOTE: Voltage may not be the same in both preceding tests. Isolator diodes can create a voltage drop of around 1 volt. Fortunately, the isolator causes the alternator output to rise about 1 volt. This compensates for the drop across the diodes.

6. Recharge the battery when the test is completed.

Installing a Battery

To install a battery, follow these steps:

1. Make sure the battery is filled with the proper amount of electrolyte (if not a maintenance-free type). Never add electrolyte after the first filling; add only distilled water.
2. Clean the terminal posts with a wire brush until the metal shines.
3. Turn off all power draw, including lights and accessories. If the negative cable sparks during removal, a draw is still present.
4. Notice the position of the battery in the tray in relation to polarity .
5. Disconnect the cables, negative first, and remove the old battery.
6. Make sure the carrier and the hold-down hardware are free of corrosion.
7. Check terminals and cables.
8. Install terminals, observing polarity.
9. Install hold-down hardware.
   NOTE: Vibration can destroy batteries, so make sure battery is secure.
10. Observe polarity before starting engine or activating the battery switch in motorhomes or trailers. Reverse polarity can damage the battery electrical system, the alternator, and the voltage regulator.

Be sure to properly discard old batteries. Most service stations and auto-parts stores will take the battery in trade or require its return in lieu of a core charge.

Hooking Up Multiple Batteries

Parallel hookup is the common wiring method when more than one 12-volt battery is used to operate appliances and accessories in a motorhome or trailer. This is accomplished when the two positive posts are connected to each other and the two negative posts are also connected. The load can be connected to either battery, but it is preferable to connect the positive load cable to one battery and the negative load cable to the other (Figure 1.21). The number of batteries is usually dependent on electrical needs, recharging capability, and available space. Batteries connected in parallel should be the same brand, type, and age to minimize the interaction that reduces long-term capacity.

Series connection of batteries produces higher voltage. For example, two 6-volt batteries wired in series produce 12-volt output. In a series hookup, the negative cable from one battery is attached to the positive cable of the other. The remaining two posts are connected to the load . A common practice is to connect two 6-volt golf-cart (electric-vehicle) batteries in series. Electric-vehicle batteries usually have high reserve-capacity ratings and can withstand deeper discharges over a longer period of time.

Battery Cables

The selection of battery cables is determined by the size of the battery and the proper routing length (Table 1.7). Battery cables are available as custom or ready-made assemblies. Caution must be exercised when choosing a ready-made cable because a thick insulation may be concealing a much smaller gauge wire. For example, many booster cable sets are only 8-gauge wire, even though the insulation appears as thick as a battery cable used in engine compartments.

Cables can be custom made one of three ways: us-

Table 1.7 Recommended Wire and Cable Sizes for Charging Systems

| Alternator Output Maximum Amperes | | | | | | Wire Size |
To 40	40–60	60–80	80–100	100–130	130–160	(AWG)
Maximum Distance Alternator to Battery (In feet)						
5						14
7	5					12
12	8	6				10
18	12	9	8			8
30	20	15	12	9		6
45	30	23	19	14	12	4
	50	38	30	24	20	2
	50	40	30	25		1
		48	38	30		0

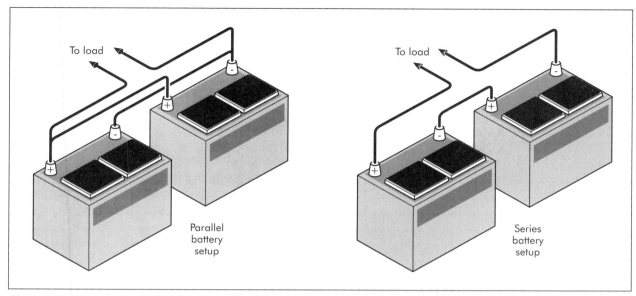

Figure 1.21 Twelve-volt batteries are wired in parallel and 6-volt batterires are wired in series in RVs.

ing bolt-on terminals, soldering, or crimping. Bolt-on terminals should be avoided except for emergency situations because they cannot be properly attached or sealed to prevent corrosion. Corrosion that starts in a terminal can travel, in time, the entire length of the cable. Soldering works well, but the integrity of the connection is only as good as the mechanic's soldering procedures; a cold solder joint can cause resistance, which leads to voltage loss. Crimping usually can only be performed by a qualified mechanic because the tools required to attach solderless terminals to a battery cable cost hundreds of dollars and are not likely to be part of an owner's toolbox (Figure 1.22). Custom cables should be finished with approximately 1½ inches of sealant-filled shrink tubing to protect the cable ends from moisture and corrosion (Figure 1.23).

Care of Cables and Terminals

Cables are the main links to the battery. If a terminal is loose, dirty, or broken, power can be disrupted or become erratic. Periodic inspection should include the following:

- Check cables for breaks, corrosion, or stripped insulation.
- Check terminals for tightness. Make sure terminals are securely fitted to cable.

Figure 1.22 Special crimping tool is used to attach terminals to the battery cable.

Figure 1.23 Heat shrink tubing protects the terminal from the elements.

■ Remove terminals, negative first, and clean with solution of baking soda and water.

■ Clean terminal posts with baking soda and water. Replace all suspect cables and terminals.

■ Apply thin layer of petroleum jelly or commercial protectant to posts; connect terminals, observing polarity. Do not apply too much protectant on the terminals.

Using Jumper Cables

Although the practice of using a booster battery from one vehicle to start the engine of a second vehicle with a dead battery seems elementary, many people are injured by not following safe procedures (Figure 1.24).

The correct procedure is as follows:

1. Make sure terminals on both batteries are tight.
2. Turn off ignition keys and place gear selector in Park or manual shifter in Neutral.
3. Attach the end of one cable to the positive terminal on the discharged battery.
4. Attach the other end of the first cable to the positive post on the booster battery.
5. Attach one end of the second cable to the negative terminal on the booster battery.

6. Attach the other end of the second cable to a good ground source such as the engine block or frame. Do not connect to the negative terminal of the discharged battery.
7. Attempt to start the stalled car's engine. If it does not turn over, start the booster-battery engine and hold at a fast idle for a few minutes or until the stalled engine starts.
8. Once started, disconnect cables in exact reverse order as above.

NOTE: Inferior-grade cables or those made from light-gauge wire are virtually useless in most dead-battery situations. Purchase high-quality cables made from battery cable.

Battery Isolators

Recreational vehicles usually have at least two batteries, one for starting the motorhome or tow-vehicle engine and one (or more) for operating the 12-volt DC house systems. An isolator is used to separate the batteries, allowing the house battery loads to be drained and not allow those loads to drain the main engine battery when the engine is not running. Separating the batteries is called *isolation* and is achieved by using one of two types of equipment: a solid-state isolator or an electrically activated mechanical solenoid switch.

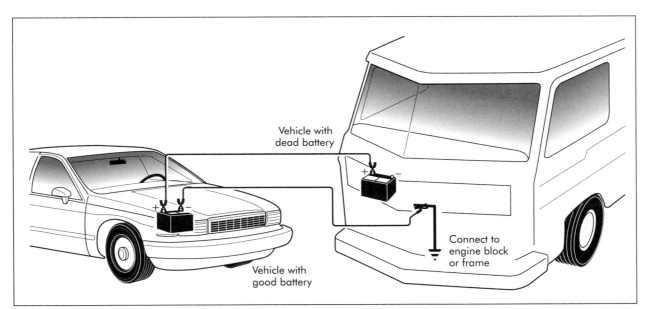

Figure 1.24 Jump-starting a vehicle with a dead battery requires a safe hookup to avoid the possibility of explosion.

How Solenoids Work

The simplest and least durable method of isolating a battery is with a solenoid switch (Figure 1.25). The basic switch—for a two-battery system—has three terminals, one for each battery and one for connection to an ignition-switched 12-volt source. When the power flows to the switch terminal on the solenoid (by turning the ignition switch to the on position), the solenoid connects the batteries in parallel. When the switch terminal is deactivated, the batteries are separated, and only the auxiliary battery can be discharged by the RV appliances. There is an inherent disadvantage with the solenoid switch: If the switch contacts become damaged and are locked together, the owner may assume that the batteries are separated when in fact they are not, causing a dead starting battery. During extended use, the contact points of the switch typically become pitted or coated with black deposits causing voltage drop (loss of potential to transmit current) and reducing the ability of the alternator to charge the house batteries.

These black deposits on the copper contacts are usually caused by the resultant arcing during the switching process. This natural phenomenon is usually more prevalant when the solenoid is switched under minimum load. The arcing created under a higher load will most times wipe the contact area clean. The pitting and black deposits are created when the arc in the atmosphere burns a little bit of oxygen

and mixes with the copper surface of the contacts. This makes cupric oxide. When enough of this material is formed, the contacts become insulated and act as if they are open, when they are actually closed and supposedly completing the circuit. The ingestion of water inside the solenoid casing can accelerate this process. Most RV manufacturers use solenoids with copper-to-copper contacts. If you find that you are experiencing a voltage loss (perform voltage drop tests described on page 1.15), replace the solenoid with one that has silver-to-silver contacts. Many auto-parts stores, such as Napa, sell this type of solenoid.

Solid-State Isolators

Solid-state isolators (Figure 1.26) separate two or more batteries using diodes that are one-way check valves. Each battery receives current from the alternator, but the batteries are never connected in parallel. When the auxiliary battery is being discharged, a diode keeps the starting battery from being discharged with the auxiliary batteries. Current can only flow from the alternator. When the engine is started, the isolator controls current flow to both batteries, charging each as its needs dictate. The solid-state isolator allows effective, independent charging of batteries by the same alternator.

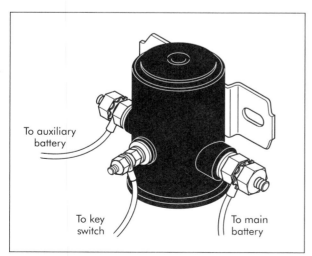

Figure 1.25 Wiring hookup for a dual-battery mechanical solenoid

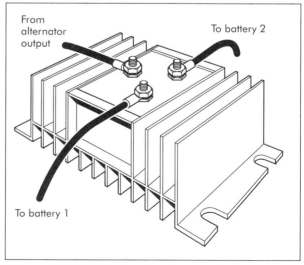

Figure 1.26 Wiring hookup for a multi-battery, solid state isolator

Table 1.8 Electrical Tests to Assure Proper Operation of Battery Isolator*

Test	Operation
"A" terminal (engine off)	May read from 0–12 volts
#1 terminal of isolator (engine off)	Should read vehicle battery voltage
#2 terminal of isolator (engine off)	Should read auxiliary battery voltage
"E" terminal (engine off)	Should read 0 volts
"A" terminal (engine running and alternator charging)	Should be 14.8 to 15.2 volts which is .8 to 1 volt higher than the reading of #1, #2, and "E" terminals
#1 terminal of isolator (engine running)	Should read 13.8 to 14.2 volts
#2 terminal of isolator (engine running)	Should read 13.8 to 14.2 volts
"E" terminal (engine running and alternator charging)	Should read approximately the same voltage as the batteries (13.8 to 14.2 volts)

*For a 12-volt system, the "A" post should read approximately 15 volts. The #1 and #2 posts should read 13.8 to 14.2 volts. If the "A" post reads 13.8 to 14.2 volts the regulator is sensing the alternator output rather than the main battery.

Typically, a diode will cause a voltage drop of about 0.8 volt. If the proper isolator is used and the instructions are followed closely, the alternator's regulator will compensate for the voltage drop (Table 1.8). Thus voltage available to the house batteries is not reduced compared to a direct hookup that does not utilize diodes.

Installing a Multiple-Battery Isolator

To install a multiple-battery isolator, follow these steps (Figures 1.27 and 1.28):

1. Remove negative terminals from all batteries.
2. Mount isolator in a convenient location away from exhaust manifolds or other sources of high heat.
3. Locate the BAT terminal on the alternator (usually the largest wire), remove it, and attach to terminal 1 on the isolator.

4. Crimp terminals on appropriate length of wire to reach from the isolator to the alternator (Table 1.9). Attach one end of wire to terminal A on isolator and the other to the BAT terminal on the alternator. For engines with Delcotron CS Series alternators, follow step 5. For engines manufactured in 1985 and later, follow step 6. For all others, jump to step 7.
5. Delcotron CS Series alternators require an external exciter that is wired from a separate terminal on the isolator, usually marked E. Locate a source of 12-volt DC power con-

Table 1.9 Determining Proper Wire Size

Alternator Rating	Wire Gauge				
	10 ft.	11–15 ft.	15–20 ft.	20–25 ft.	25–30 ft.
Up to 70 amp	10	8	8	6	6
70 to 95	8	8	6	6	4
95 to 120	6	6	4	2	1
120 to 160	4	4	2	2	0

■ TROUBLESHOOTING ■
THE MULTIPLE-BATTERY ISOLATOR SOLENOID

Problem	Possible Cause	Correction
Battery boils or overcharges	Shorted diode	Replace isolator
All batteries go dead	Defective solenoid contacts Open diode	Replace solenoid Replace isolator
One battery not charging	Open diode	Replace isolator
Low battery voltage	Defective diode	Replace isolator

trolled by the ignition switch. Connect a wire from the 12-volt source through a 6–10-amp circuit breaker to the E terminal on the isolator. Be sure not to use the accessory position of the ignition switch as a source of 12-volt power. The use of a kit such as Sure Power's Model 144 is necessary to connect the sense wire to the alternator. Proceed to step 7.

6. Certain late-model Ford alternators do not have a BAT terminal but instead have a plug-in terminal (Figure 1.29). To wire the isolator, first disconnect the battery. Locate the connector on the alternator with one light wire and two heavy black wires. Cut the black/orange wires leaving approximately 2 inches to allow for a butt connector.

   CAUTION: Damage may occur if wire is cut beyond cabling.

   Attach a wire to both cut wires from the alternator (use butt connector) and connect the other end to the A terminal on the isolator. Attach a wire to both cut wires leading from the harness and connect the other end to terminal 1 on the isolator. Proceed to step 7.

7. Attach a length of wire to terminal 2 on the isolator and to one terminal on an appropriately sized circuit breaker (Table 1.10). Attach one end of a length of wire long enough to reach from the isolator to the auxiliary battery to the unattached terminal of the circuit breaker and the other to the positive terminal of the battery.

Table 1.10 Circuit Breakers for Charging Systems

Alternator Rating	Expected Load	Recommended Breaker
Up to 90 amps	40 amps	50 amps
Up to 120 amps	70 amps	80 amps
Up to 150 amps	110 amps	120 amps
Up to 200 amps	140 amps	150 amps

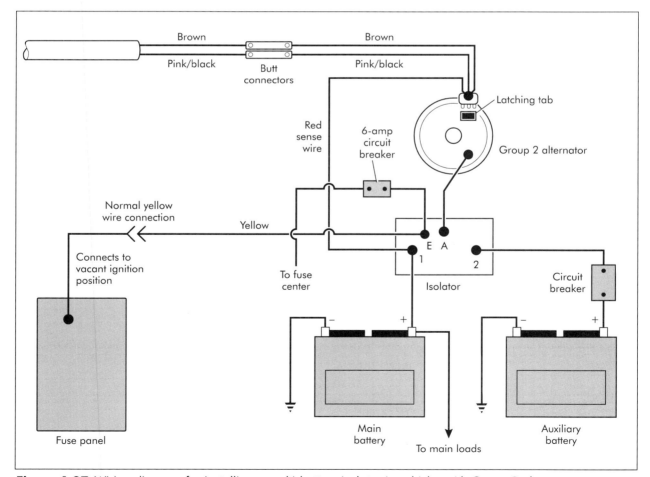

Figure 1.27 Wiring diagram for installing a multi-battery isolator in vehicles with Group 2 alternators.

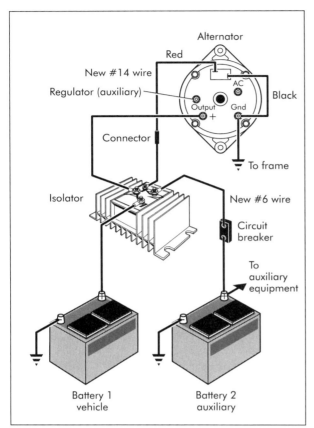

Figure 1.28 Wiring diagram for installing a multi-battery isolator in vehicles with Group 3 alternators.

8. Repeat step 5 for each additional battery when using three- and four-battery isolators.
9. Reconnect negative terminals on all batteries.

■ POWER CONVERTERS ■

Modern recreational-vehicle appliances and accessories operate on two electrical systems: 12-volt DC and 120-volt AC power. In order to avoid duplication of fixtures and some appliances, a power converter is used to transform 120-volt AC power to 12-volt DC power when the RV is plugged into a campground receptacle or when connected to the output of an AC generator. The converter supplies 12-volt DC power to items such as interior lights, fans, and the water pump while the 120-volt AC input to the RV provides household current to the wall outlets, air-conditioner, refrigerator, etc. The converter also charges the batteries, although the am-

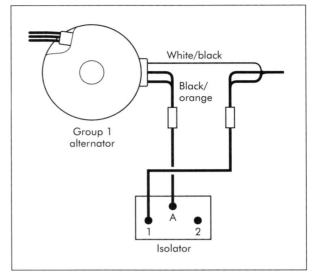

Figure 1.29 Wiring diagram for installing a multi-battery isolator in Ford vehicles using alternators with plug-in connections.

perage output often is too low to be effective for short-term charging. Converters may also incorporate 120-volt AC circuit breakers and a 12-volt DC fuse panel.

CAUTION: Internal converter repairs should be left to a qualified service technician.

There are two types of power converters, dual output (linear) and single output, sometimes called *battery floater*. The dual-output converter (Figure 1.30) is the most common and is usually the least expensive. It has two output circuits, one for operating the RV appliances and one to charge the batteries. With this type of converter, battery charging is usually not very effective. Also, the output for the appliances is often dirty, producing voltage surges that can damage sensitive electronics. Usually there are provisions for hooking up these accessories and appliances.

A single-output converter (Figure 1.31) is more efficient and usually more expensive. The battery is always on line and the voltage is filtered so that ripples and surges are minimal. The older versions used a ferroresonant design (transformers), and the newer units use high-frequency switching (solid-state electronics). Converters do not provide complete charging and cell equalization.

Both types of converters limit voltage to just less than 14 volts, which helps eliminate battery gassing. Since the output of the dual-outlet converter splits the output, battery charging is usually very ineffective. In single-outlet converters, all the output is directed to the battery. The amount of power required by appliances is subtracted from the output available for battery charging. Thus, when demands of appliances are low, the battery-charge capability is higher and vice versa. The charging circuit will automatically taper off as the battery comes closer to a full state of charge.

Low-voltage output can be checked using a multimeter set to the DC-voltage function. When the battery is at full charge, the output of the converter should be 13.8 to 14 volts. If lower voltage is detected, the manufacturer may be able to make necessary adjustments. The converter should be checked for signs of corrosion, and its mounting location should be kept free from stored supplies, especially flammables. Converters create heat and require adequate ventilation.

Some of the higher-line converters feature temperature monitoring or have provisions for the owner to set operating conditions to prevent overcharging. The better converters also have provisions for selecting the type of battery being charged: flooded or gel cell. Completed-charge voltage is slightly lower for gel-cell batteries.

Inverters

Inverters transform 12-volt DC power into 120-volt AC household current (Figure 1.32). Inverters allow use of 120-volt AC convenience items without the need to operate an AC generator or to connect to campground power. The most common use of an inverter is to power color television sets, stereos, food processors, microwave ovens, and computers, with only a specific number of appliances used at one time, depending on the inverter's output rating and the amount of power required by the appliance. Teamed up with good deep-cycle batteries and an adequate charging system, an inverter provides continuous noise-free power. Make sure you use an inverter with a pure or modified sine wave. Inverters pull a great amount of energy from a battery, so judicious use is required.

To determine the size inverter for your particular needs, you first must list the continuous power ratings in watts of all the appliances you intend to operate (Table 1.11). Unless you plan on operating more than one appliance at a time, the inverter's size can be dictated by the appliance with the highest draw. When using multiple appliances, the wattage ratings must be totaled to determine the minimum inverter rating. Wattage can be determined by multiplying the amperage times the voltage. For example, if a 120-volt AC color television is rated at 1 ampere, the continuous wattage rating is 120.

When calculating the proper-size inverter, surge ratings must be considered. Surge power is the additional wattage required to start the appliance; appliances with motors usually need much more power to start than to operate continuously. Surge-power

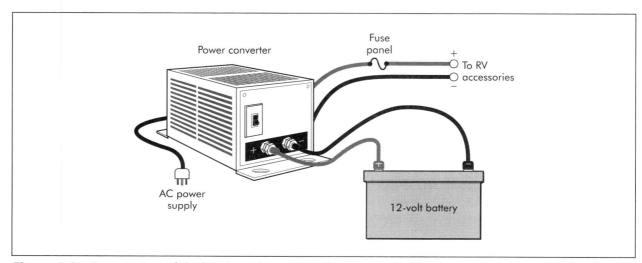

Figure 1.30 Power output of dual outlet or linear converters is split, limiting battery-recharge capability.

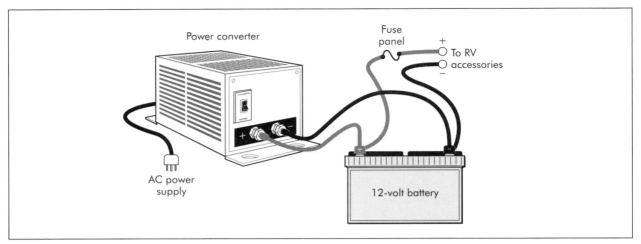

Figure 1.31 Entire output of single outlet is available for battery charging.

Table 1.11 Continuous Power Consumption for Typical 120-volt AC Appliances

Appliance	Wattage
Blender	1,000
Coffeemaker	1,380
Computer	60–100
Drill motor, ⅜-inch	360
Electric blanket	120
Freezer	500
Hair dryers	1,500
Ice maker	600–700
Microwave oven	800–1,500
Popcorn popper, hot-air	1400
Refrigerator	600
Satellite dish	200–250
Soldering iron	40
Stereo	200
Television, 9-inch color	480
Toaster	1800
Trash compactor	800–1,000
VCR	20
Washing machine	600

ratings may be available from the manufacturer of the appliance. A good rule of thumb is to allow two times the rating for televisions, blenders, microwave ovens, entertainment systems, and drill motors, and four times the continuous rating for large appliances such as air compressors, freezers, washing machines, trash compactors, and refrigerators.

Use 00-gauge battery cables when wiring the inverter to the battery bank, and never run these cables longer than 10 feet.

Determining Proper-Size Battery Bank

Although deep-cycle batteries can be discharged 80 percent before experiencing permanent damage, it's best to allow for 50 percent cycling to improve battery longevity. Calculate the amp-hour usage between charging cycles and then use a battery bank twice that capacity. Appliances are rated in AC watts or AC amps. Use the following formula to determine the DC amp-hour draw for a 12-volt DC system (courtesy of Heart Interface):

$$(AC\ amps \times 10) \times 1.1 \times hours\ of\ operation = DC\ amp\text{-}hours$$

$$(AC\ watts \div 12) \times 1.1 \times hours\ of\ operation = DC\ amp\text{-}hours$$

The above formulas should be used to calculate the number of amp-hours used between recharges for each appliance (Table 1.12)

■ SOLAR POWER ■

Solar power is the production of electricity when sunlight strikes a photovoltaic cell, which is made up of a series of solar cells that respond to sunlight by creating electrical current (Figure 1.33). The current can charge batteries used to operate a variety of appliances.

Higher current is produced as the intensity of light increases. Available sunlight and environmental con-

Table 1.12 Average Power Consumption of Typical Appliances

Appliance	Wattage	Run Times/Amp Hours*							
		5 min.	15 min.	30 min.	1 hr.	2 hrs.	3 hrs.	8 hrs.	24 hrs.
Color TV, 13 inch	50	.33	1	2	4	8	12	32	96
Color TV, 19 inch	100	.66	2	4	8	16	24	64	192
VCR	50	.33	1	2	4	8	12	32	96
Lamp	100	.66	2	4	8	16	24	64	192
Blender	300	2	6	12					
Curling iron	50	.33	1	2					
Power drill, 3/8-inch	500	3.3	10	20					
Ice maker**	200			2.6	5.2	10.4	15.6	41.6	83.2
Coffeemaker	1000	6.6	20	40	80	160			
Refrigerator, 3 cu. ft.**	150			2	4	8	12	32	96
Refrigerator, 20 cu. ft.**	750			21	42	84	126	336	672
Microwave, compact	750	5	15	30	60	120	180		
Microwave, full-size	1500	10	30	60	120	240	360		
Vacuum	1100	7.3	22	44	88	176	264		

*The figure in each column represents the total amp hours used (at 12-volt DC) based on various continuous run times.
**Refrigeration is typically calculated using a 1/3-duty cycle.

ditions affect photovoltaic-panel performance. For instance, a panel that generates 11.64 ampere-hours per day in Albuquerque, New Mexico, will only provide 4.76 ampere-hours per day in Pittsburgh, Pennsylvania. Panel-voltage output varies with temperature. The same 33-cell panel subjected to 80°F may charge up to 16 volts, but at 150°F that voltage may be reduced to 14. Therefore, it makes sense to use a panel with at least 32 cells. Most solar experts feel that solar panels with 32 to 36 cells work best for RV use.

Since temperature affects panel performance, make sure that there are at least 2 inches between the bottom of the panel and the roof when mounting. If the panels are installed on the leading edge of the roof,

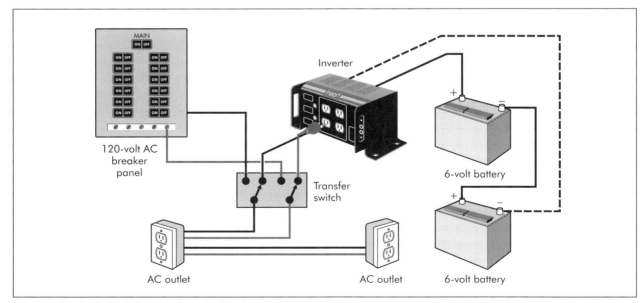

Figure 1.32 Typical inverter installation in an RV

■ **TROUBLESHOOTING** ■
THE POWER INVERTER

Problem	Possible Cause	Correction
No DC power at appliances	Blown fuse	Replace fuse
	Bad battery cable	Replace cable
	Discharged battery	Charge battery
	Tripped load protector	Reset load protector
Load protector continues to trip	Appliance overload	Reduce appliance load

NOTE: Inverters should be repaired internally only by qualified service technicians. If repairs are needed, seek help from an appropriate repair facility.

CAUTION: When connecting the battery to the inverter, it is important to pay close attention to polarity. Some inverters do not have polarity protection, and if the terminals are miswired, the inverter can be damaged.

install some sort of wind deflector on the front edges of the panels to keep the wind from lifting the panels from the roof while on the road.

By including an inverter in the system, a wide variety of appliances and systems can be operated without a 120-volt AC land line or use of an AC generator.

Determining Solar-Power Requirements

The number of solar panels needed depends on individual situations. Power consumption must be calculated by determining the number of hours each appliance will be operated and the total amperage required (Table 1.13). Multiply the consumption rate of the individual appliance by the hours per day it will most likely be operated to arrive at the total ampere-hours per day. Total the ampere-hours per day and divide that figure by the average output of panels in your area (Table 1.14). You can then determine how many panels will be needed to meet your individual demands.

Since photovoltaic panels do not store energy, batteries are integral in any solar system. Good battery-reserve capacity is the key to utilizing a solar system. A large deep-cycle 12-volt battery will suffice in some cases, but several batteries are usually needed.

The number of cells in each photovoltaic module determines its voltage output. Modules that produce higher voltage at no load require the use of a voltage regulator to prevent overcharging; this type is suitable for RV use. Some self-regulating panels can produce enough voltage to overcharge a battery. More sophisticated regulators have provisions for battery-charging equalization and temperature compensation.

Determining Battery-Bank Size When Using Solar Power

While there is no exact formula for determining battery-bank size, you need enough capacity to be able to run the load for the period of time until there is enough sunlight to recharge the batteries. Unless you are using the microwave oven or other high-power-consuming appliance, two 6-volt golf-cart batteries and two 75-watt panels should suffice (and, of course, an external regulator). Add two more golf-cart batteries and two additional panels if you plan on using the microwave oven more often.

Wiring a Photovoltaic System

The panels are wired by routing lengths of wire from the positive and negative terminals of the panel(s) to the regulator and then to the corresponding terminals of the battery(ies), which is connected to the load (Figure 1.34). A fuse or circuit breaker should be installed between the battery and the regulator in the positive lead. The fuse rating should be at least

Table 1.13 Approximate Average Power Consumption of Widely Available 12-Volt DC Appliances

Description	Amps
Lighting	
15-watt fluorescent light	1.0
16-watt slimline fluorescent light	1.2
Dual 8-watt fluorescent tubes	1.2
20-watt standard fluorescent light	1.5
30-watt slimline fluorescent light	2.0
Kitchen	
Coffeemaker	11.5
Toaster	15.0
Slow cooker	20.0
Range hood, fan and light	5.0
Vent fan	2.5
Refrigerator	5.0
Household	
Travel iron	10.0
Electronic bug killer	2.5
Electric razor	1.3
Vacuum cleaner, hand portable	5.0
Electric toothbrush	1.0
Tools	
Winches (for light use)	10.0–100.0
Air compressor	3.5–9.0
Chain saw, 14" blade	100.0
Drill	12.0–15.0
Communications	
TV, B&W, 12"	1.4
TV, color, 9"	4.0
CB radio	0.5
Digital clock	0.1
Tape recorder	0.5
Amplifier (30 watt)	2.0
DC turntable	0.5

Formula to Compute Amp-Hours

Light	1.5 amps × 6 hours = 9.0 amp-hrs
Coffeemaker	11.5 amps × 1 hour = 11.5 amp-hrs
TV	1.4 amps × 3 hours = 4.2 amp-hrs
Total of this example:	24.7 amp-hrs

Table 1.14 Solar Performance Tables

Lat.	Location	Amp-Hrs.	Tilt Angle
32N	AL, Montgomery	7.55	55S
61N	AK, Bethel	6.41	60S
65N	AK, Fairbanks	5.19	90S
62N	AK, Matanuska	5.60	75S
33N	AZ, Phoenix	10.50	45S
35N	AR, Little Rock	7.29	60S
39N	CA, Davis	8.27	60S
37N	CA, Fresno	8.42	60S
34N	CA, Los Angeles	9.57	50S
34N	CA, Riverside	10.28	45S
40N	CO, Boulder	8.40	50S
40N	CO. Granby	10.27	40S
39N	D.C., Washington	6.74	60S
30N	FL, Gainesville	8.72	45S
26N	FL, Miami	9.25	30S
34N	GA, Atlanta	7.80	55S
21N	HI, Honolulu	9.74	35S
44N	ID, Boise	8.17	65S
42N	IL, Chicago	4.57	65S
40N	IN, Indianapolis	6.46	65S
42N	IA, Ames	7.10	65S
38N	KN, Dodge City	10.27	45S
39N	KN, Manhattan	7.35	60S
38N	KY, Lexington	8.09	60S
30N	LA, New Orleans	6.35	55S
32N	LA, Shreveport	7.32	55S
44N	ME, Portland	7.49	65S
42N	MA, Boston	5.92	65S
43N	MI, E. Lansing	6.29	65S
46N	MN St. Cloud	7.50	70S
39N	MO, St. Louis	7.11	60S
47N	MT, Great Falls	7.85	70S
41N	NM, N. Omaha	8.09	60S
36N	NV, Las Vegas	10.89	45S
40N	NJ, Seabrook	6.55	65S
35N	NM, Albuquerque	11.64	40S
41N	NY, New York City	6.26	65S
39N	NC, Ely	10.81	50S
36N	NC, Greensboro	7.43	60S
47N	ND, Bismarck	8.51	65S
41N	OH, Cleveland	6.08	65S
35N	OK, Oklahoma City	9.21	50S
42N	OR, Medford	7.20	65S
40N	PA, Pittsburgh	4.76	65S
41N	RI, Newport	6.68	65S
33N	SC, Charleston	7.95	55S
44N	SD, Rapid City	9.39	55S
36N	TN, Nashville	6.85	60S
32N	TX, Big Spring	9.20	45S
33N	TX, Fort Worth	8.95	50S
41N	UT, Salt Lake City	8.24	65S
38N	VA, Richmond	6.61	60S
47N	WA, Seattle	5.43	70S
48N	WA Spokane	7.37	70S
43N	WI, Madison	6.88	65S
43N	WY, Lander	11.03	45S

5 amps higher than the capacity of the panel(s). Two or more panels can be wired in parallel. Although the charts may show that smaller wire can be used, it is best to use at least an 8-gauge wire throughout any photovoltaic system. The wire length should be kept as short as possible. Route the wires through the refrigerator vent on the roof rather than drilling additional holes in the roof. Make sure the wires are encased in flexible conduit to protect them from ultraviolet light and the elements.

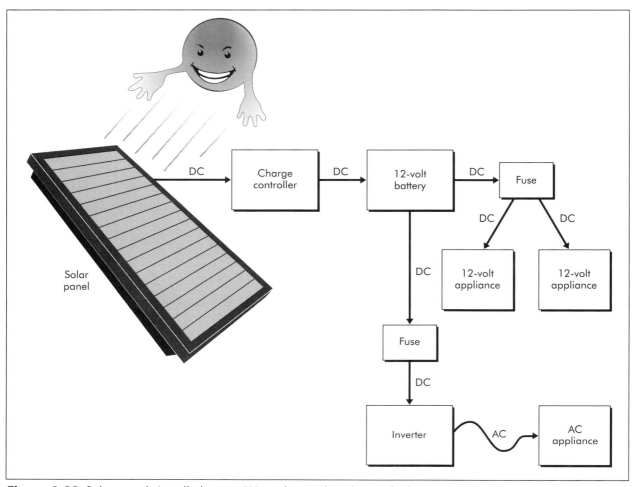

Figure 1.33 Solar panels installed on an RV can be used to charge the batteries.

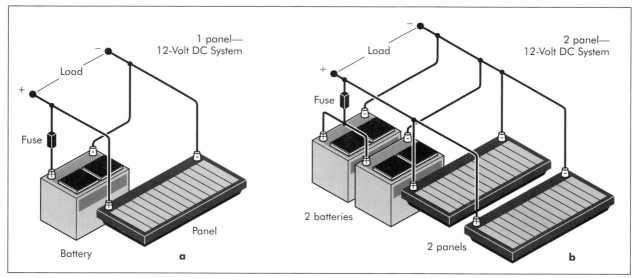

Figure 1.34 Any number of solar panels can be wired into an RV, but most owners use a one-panel system (a) or a two-panel system (b).

Panel Location

Photovoltaic cells work best when faced directly at the sun. It's impractical to use a tracking system in RVs, so the panels usually are mounted flat on the roof. This somewhat restricts their output—which makes proper load management necessary. The use of a good ampere meter will allow you to monitor the electricity production rate and to alter appliance usage, depending upon the solar conditions each day. Most good regulators have this function built in.

The best way to mount the panels is to use Z brackets mounted to the roof. This provides the necessary clearance between the roof and panel. Use nuts and bolts between the Z brackets and panels so that they can be removed easily. Make sure any screws in the roof are sealed with the proper type of lap sealer. Do not use silicone. Make sure the panels are covered when making the installation and wiring. Make sure the panels are installed so that they are not shadowed by other appliances on the roof.

If you are parked for an extended period of time, try to position your RV so that the panels face south, the recommended position for the northern hemisphere.

Photovoltaic-Panel Maintenance

Photovoltaic panels require minimal service. When the panel becomes dirty, clean it with a sponge or soft cloth and water. If necessary, a mild, nonabrasive detergent may be used. Connections, wiring, and mounting hardware should be inspected every six months to assure integrity. Do not walk on or drop items on the panels; broken glass on a panel can become an electrical hazard and cause injury.

Solar panels are not designed to be serviced internally by the user; damage to the cells or diodes can result. Nor should the user wear jewelry when working on photovoltaic panels. It is also important to maintain batteries connected to any photovoltaic system.

12-Volt DC Lighting

Most RVs are equipped with either incandescent or fluorescent fixtures as the primary type of lighting. Some motorhomes and trailers have 120-volt AC lighting, but this type of lighting is usually used to complement 12-volt DC lighting or used for aesthetics in luxury coaches. Other than occasional bulb replacement, interior lighting fixtures are usually trouble free. On the other hand, outside marker lights require constant attention.

Servicing Marker (Clearance) Lights

Check the following on outside marker lights:

- Inspect each marker-light housing for cracks in the red or orange cover. If cracked, replace immediately. Moisture that's allowed to enter the housing will result in corroded sockets and/or shorting.
- Make sure each housing is sealed between the base and side wall. If not, remove the light, clean up the surface and run a bead of silicone before reinstalling.
- If the light socket is corroded, replace the marker light.
- Use marker lights with sealed bulb sockets and two wire leads (Figure 1.35). These are more resistant to water and can be sealed to the side wall more effectively.

    CAUTION: Marker lights that are allowed to leak will create serious dry-rot problems in the future. Frame structures that become damaged due to dry rot can become structurally weak and cause major damage to the RV.

Checking for Low Voltage at a Light Fixture

If the light is dim, the voltage at the fixture must be checked using the following steps:

1. Using a multimeter, read voltage at battery.
2. Remove the lens from the fixture.
3. Unscrew the fixture from the ceiling or the wall.
4. Using a multimeter, touch the positive lead to the black wire and the negative lead to the white wire. If wire nuts are used to connect the wires, remove them; otherwise probe the multimeter leads through the wire insulation.
5. With the bulb/tubes in place and the switch

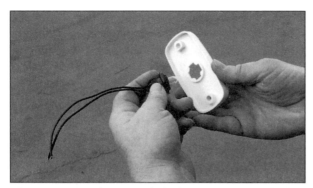

Figure 1.35 Clearance light fixture uses a sealed-bulb socket.

in the on position, read voltage. Voltage should compare to that read at battery.

If voltage is low or incandescent lights are dim or not working, proceed with the following steps:

1. Check and clean the terminals on both the bulb and the socket. Clean with crocus cloth. If outside marker-light sockets are corroded, clean and coat surface with a thin layer of silicone dielectric grease.
2. Check the terminals for proper connections.
3. Rewire to the fixture if necessary, using proper gauge wire.
4. If voltage is okay at connections but lower at the socket, replace the fixture.

   CAUTION: User maintenance on fluorescent fixtures is limited to changing tubes and ballasts. The circuit board and the internal inverter require factory service.

Wiring a Tow Vehicle

In order to operate the marker/taillights, brake lights, electric brakes, and back-up lights, a tow vehicle must be wired so that the trailer plug can be temporarily connected when towing. A charge line must also be routed to the plug receptacle so that the tow-vehicle alternator can charge the trailer batteries. Most lighting and brake actuation failures are attributable to faulty wiring or wiring that has become shorted, corroded, or disconnected (Figure 1.36).

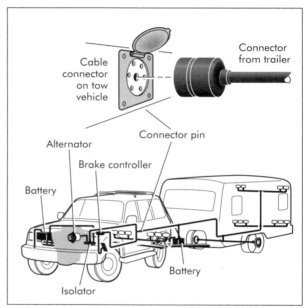

Figure 1.36 The tow vehicle must be wired so the marker lights, turn signals, brake lights, and electric brakes can operate and batteries charge in the trailer.

■ TROUBLESHOOTING ■		
THE INCANDESCENT LIGHTING FIXTURE		
Problem	**Possible Cause**	**Correction**
Fails to light	Burned-out bulb	Replace bulb
	No power	Test voltage and restore power
		Check and charge battery
	Corroded bulb connections	Clean with crocus cloth and reinstall
Low light	Improper voltage	Check and charge battery
	Fogged lens	Replace fixture lens
	Bad fixture socket	Replace fixture

Installing a Charge Line

To prevent voltage drop (restriction of current flow), an 8-gauge charge-line wire should be used. Proper connections will insure that the trailer battery or batteries will receive a good charge.

To install the charge line, follow these steps:

1. Route a number 8 automotive, stranded copper wire from the tow vehicle's engine compartment to the rear bumper. Route the wire so that it cannot be chafed by the chassis or other sharp edges found under a vehicle. Encase in flexible conduit for maximum protection. Secure with black (ultraviolet-protected) tie wraps so the wire does not sag at any point. Make sure the wire is away from sources of extreme heat such as the exhaust system.
2. Connect the wire lead in the engine compartment to one side of a 50-ampere circuit breaker that has been mounted either on the fender well or engine fire wall. Use a good-quality ring terminal.
3. Connect another length of number 8 wire to the other side of the 50-ampere circuit breaker and connect the other end to the battery terminal on the alternator. The charge-line wire may also be attached to the positive terminal of the starting battery.

Wiring Brake Lights, Marker/Taillights, and Back-up Lights

For brake lights, marker lights, taillights, and back-up lights, follow these steps:

1. Locate the wiring harness in the vicinity of the tow vehicle's taillights.
2. Using a 12-volt test light or a multimeter, turn on taillights and left and right turn signals, one at a time, and probe the wires in the harness until the light indicates the presence of current. The back-up-light wire must also be located if trailer is so equipped. Probing can be avoided if you have a service manual that identifies the wiring code.
3. Connect a length of number 16 automotive wire to each of the wires of the taillight, right and left turn signals, and back-up light using quick connectors.

    NOTE: Quick connectors will cause erratic operation if not used properly. A good way to prevent a quick connector from collecting moisture and corrosion is to coat the connector with RTV silicone sealant after it has been locked into place on the wire. If possible make your wiring additions the same color as the original wiring in the vehicle.

There are specially designed wiring kits on the market (Figure 1.37) that allow connection of the taillight, right, and left turn signals and back-up light without using quick connectors or cutting the orig-

---

■ TROUBLESHOOTING ■
THE FLUORESCENT LIGHTING FIXTURE

Problem	Possible Cause	Correction
Fails to light	Reversed polarity	Rewire with black wire to positive, white to negative
	Bad tubes	Replace tubes
Tube ends turning black	Frequent on/offs	Limit on/offs
	Low voltage	Check and recharge battery Check connections
	Bad tubes	Replace tube
Frequent ballast failure	Failure to replace bad tubes	Replace ballast and tubes
	Low voltage	Check and recharge battery Check connections
	High transient voltages (spikes)	Check power converter

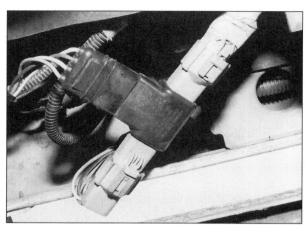

Figure 1.37 Quick connect kits provide a convenient method for wiring a tow vehicle.

inal wires. To use, simply disconnect the specified multipin terminal and insert the adaptor with the wire leads.

Grounding Wires

To provide a good ground, attach one end of a length of 8-gauge automotive wire to a clean portion of the chassis in the proximity of the receptacle. This should be accomplished using at least a ¼-inch bolt and corresponding ring terminal. Sheet-metal screws or smaller bolts attached to the receptacle bracket are not adequate sources of a good ground.

NOTE Never use the hitch ball as the only ground. This will cause erratic operation of the lights.

The Trailer-Plug Receptacle

Most trailers use a 7-way Bargman or Pollak flat pin plug and receptacle (Figure 1.38). Trailers equipped with Dometic 3-Way Automatic Energy Selector refrigerators require a 9-way version of' the same type of receptacle (Figure 1.39). Receptacles should be mounted below the rear bumper, on the left side of the hitch receiver. Mounting the receptacles in such locations is standard in the RV industry, but makes them highly susceptible to moisture, dirt, and corrosion. If the wire attachments are connected prop-

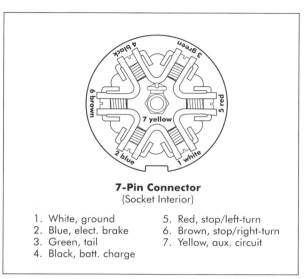

7-Pin Connector
(Socket Interior)

1. White, ground
2. Blue, elect. brake
3. Green, tail
4. Black, batt. charge
5. Red, stop/left-turn
6. Brown, stop/right-turn
7. Yellow, aux. circuit

Figure 1.38 Seven-way wiring

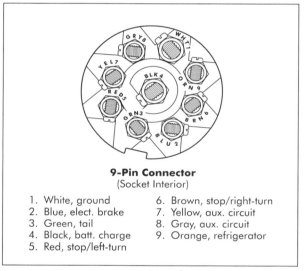

9-Pin Connector
(Socket Interior)

1. White, ground
2. Blue, elect. brake
3. Green, tail
4. Black, batt. charge
5. Red, stop/left-turn
6. Brown, stop/right-turn
7. Yellow, aux. circuit
8. Gray, aux. circuit
9. Orange, refrigerator

Figure 1.39 Nine-way wiring

erly, they should not work loose or break off. A coating of RTV silicone to the very back portion of the receptacle housing helps prevent moisture and dirt from entering the connections, greatly improving durability of the receptacle. Sealed receptacles with pigtails are also available at RV supply stores.

CAUTION: Do not apply the silicone too deeply into the receptacle. If the silicone coats the wire connections inside the plug, shorting may occur under certain conditions.

■ CHAPTER 2 ■
LP-GAS SYSTEMS

Propane is derived from the distillation of crude oil into lighter products such as gasoline. Each gas exhibits distinctly different properties. Although the flame each gas produces is nearly the same, the physical qualities of the raw gas are quite different.

Liquid petroleum gas is made up of a number of hydrocarbon gases that turn into liquid when under pressure. Propane (chemical formula C_3H_8) is used almost exclusively for RVs since it performs well in all climates. The gas used in RVs is called commercial propane, and it consists of 95 percent propane and/or propylene and 5 percent other gases, mainly from the butane family. Butane (chemical formula C_3H_{10}) is not used as often in RVs; it has the disadvantage of freezing at 31°F, making its use in climates where the temperature drops below freezing impractical. Propane is usable down to minus 44°F.

Both gases are easily liquefied under moderate pressure (150 psi), which makes their storage easy. Because they are stored in liquid form and are petroleum products, they are both referred to as *liquid petroleum gas* or *LP-gas*. Containers are constructed to hold pressure, and, because the gas is concentrated in liquid form, there is an abundance of heat potential in a relatively small package. Approximately 91,500 Btus of heat are contained in one gallon of liquid propane. This can be compared to natural gas, which has 36,600 Btus. Even a small 5-gallon cylinder of propane offers approximately 436,000 Btus of heat; this is enough to operate a 25,000-Btu/hour furnace continuously for more than seventeen hours.

Propane looks somewhat like water, but it boils at minus 50°F rather than at 212°F. Since the vapor from propane burns, flammable gas is produced when the temperature is above minus 50°F. Pressure varies with temperature and volume. Propane inside a closed vessel (cylinder or tank) will have zero pressure at minus 50°F; at 0°F it has about 24 psi. At 100°F pressure will exceed 200 psi.

The specific gravity of these gases makes them heavier than air. Propane is about 1½ times heavier than air. This creates a safety hazard if there is a leak. Propane tends to pool much like water, seeking the lowest point. Because it does not dissipate easily, and the gas expands as the temperature rises, a spark in the immediate vicinity can cause an explosion. Leak detectors are mounted near the floor, which provides good protection, but air currents caused by convection will move the gas around. Therefore, it's critical that during a leak, you refrain from causing any source of ignition, even if it's well above floor level.

Both gases are colorless and odorless, which, combined with their tendency to settle in low places, make them difficult to detect. To make detection easier they are odorized at the time of manufacture. The smell, sometimes described as a "rotten-egg" odor, is a sign of a possible leak. At the first sign (smell) of a leak, open doors and windows. Do not turn a light switch on or off, extinguish all flames, and turn off the cylinder/tank supply valve. Keep in mind that even slamming the entry door can cause a spark, depending on the latch and frame adjustment. Many RV leak detectors automatically shut off the storage vessel via an electronic solenoid when a gas concentration at the sensor reaches the danger level.

These gases are heavier than air, but they are lighter than water. Propane is only one-half the weight of water, with a liquid specific gravity of .51 (water equals 1.0).

NOTE: The weight of propane, 4.24 pounds per gallon, should be taken into account when you are weighing an RV to determine usable load capacity.

■ **TROUBLESHOOTING** ■
THE LP-GAS TANK

Problem	Possible Cause	Correction
Propane (rotten-egg) odor	Leaking gas	Leak-test all connections and fittings with soapy water; check connection tightness with a wrench; if tightening the connection does not solve the problem, turn off gas until repairs are made
Tank will not fill	Defective stop-fill valve	Have replaced by qualified technician
	Incorrect valve installation	Install per stop-valve manufacturer's instructions.
Low tank capacity	Misadjusted stop-fill	Have valve adjustment done by qualified technician.
	Surging of fuel	Allow fuel to stabilize and resume filling
Tank overfills	Defective stop-fill valve	Have replaced by qualified technician
	Improper filling procedure	Follow correct fill routine

As a motor fuel, propane has less Btus, or heat value, than gasoline (about 12 percent less); therefore it reduces the power output of any given engine by that amount. The big advantage of propane lies in its high octane rating (near 120), which reduces ping (detonation). Many vehicles were converted to propane or gasoline/propane (dual fuel) in the early 1970s to circumvent the skyrocketing cost of gasoline and long lines at service stations. Since then, propane cost has reached prices that are closer to gasoline, and, with the reduction of power and poorer availability of propane, it lost its advantage.

■ **STORAGE VESSELS** ■

There are two methods of storing LP-gas on RVs: Department of Transportation (DOT) cylinders and American Society of Mechanical Engineers (ASME) tanks (Figure 2.1). Both vessels are constructed to rigid standards and are designed to provide many years of service with very little maintenance.

DOT cylinders are typically mounted on the front of trailers, in fifth-wheel exterior compartments, and inside a dedicated compartment in a pickup camper (Figure 2.2). They come in various sizes; the most common for RVs are 5-, 7-, and 10-gallon cylinders.

These cylinders are usually about 12 inches in diameter and are at least .078 inch thick; aluminum cylinders must be at least .140 inch thick. DOT cylinders also utilize the same port for filling as for withdrawing gas.

ASME tanks are in a horizonal configuration and are used almost exclusively for motorhomes (Figure 2.3). They have a separate port for filling and are designed to be bolted permanently to the RV's frame; they must be filled in place. The metal used in construction is half again as thick as DOT cylinders in the diameter. They do not have to be recertified every twelve years. Inspection, though, is still very important.

The latest generation of DOT cylinders is fitted with Quick Closing Coupling (QCC) valves (Figure 2.4). The QCC valve has three safety attributes: If you open the service valve without having a fitting and hose attached properly, there's no flow of gas. It also has a "fuse" that will shut the flow of gas should the valve get hot (while in use) in case of a fire. And, if the pigtail should break, the flow will be restricted automatically.

The threads are on the outside of the valve and use a 1½-inch ACME fitting with right-hand threads that require only hand tightening. The POL fitting can also be used; gas will not flow unless both types of fittings are installed (seated) properly.

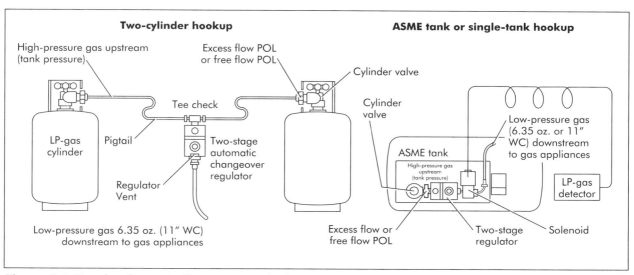

Figure 2.1 Travel trailers typically use a two-cylinder LP-gas system with a two-stage automatic changeover regulator. Motorhomes use an ASME tank and a two-stage regulator.

Figure 2.2 DOT cylinders typically come in 5-, 7-, and 10-gallon sizes.

Figure 2.3 ASME tanks are used on motorhomes

Figure 2.4 Cylinders with QCC valves are fitted with a 1½-inch ACME fitting.

■ **CHECKLIST** ■

LP-GAS TANKS AND CYLINDERS

- Inspect the cylinders for rust, pits, gouges, scrapes, and dents frequently. These defects can compromise the integrity of the cylinder.
- Keep the cylinder painted with a light-color paint. Many RV stores sell spray paint specifically designed for propane cylinders. Dark colors can create additional heat.
- Inspect the bottom of the cylinder for rust and other problems associated with condensation. Moisture usually collects here. Make sure this area is well painted.
- Cylinders are available in vertical and horizontal configurations. Always store, transport, and fill these cylinders in the position they are designed for in use.
- Check for leaks around the valve stem (using soapy water, see page 2.10) frequently. Leaks here are common. The O-ring seal can become defective from the cold, dirt and/or age, causing a leak around the stem threads. If a leak occurs, you may be able to curtail the leak by opening and closing the valve all the way. Try gently backseating the valve stem when opening—this may get you by until repairs can be made by a qualified technician. Opening and closing of the valve a few times may help remove any dirt that may have accumulated around the O-ring.
- Never close the valve more than hand tight. Overtightening, even by hand, can damage the valve.
- Cylinders are only certified for twelve years and must be recertifed by a qualified service center after that period before refilling.
- Never cut or modify a valve guard.
- POL plugs (Figure 2.5) must be used when transporting cylinders that have 45 pounds capacity or less (must be plugged also when not hooked up). These caps prevent air and moisture from entering the cylinder when empty, which helps prevent internal rust and odorant oxidation.
- Inspect the racks on the trailer A-frame (or inside a fifth-wheel storage compartment). These racks are designed to hold eight times the filled cylinder's weight. Hold-down bars should be checked before each trip.
- Make sure the cylinders are mounted with relief-valve openings facing the trailer.
- Check mounting brackets and bolts for corrosion and looseness. Loose bolts can lead to potential accidents and stress cracks in the welds.
- Never weld anything to a tank, or attempt to repair the tank by welding.

NOTE: All frame ASME tanks and DOT cylinders that are enclosed in compartments must be clearly marked on the outside of the RV with one-inch-high letters "LPG" indicating the location of the tank.

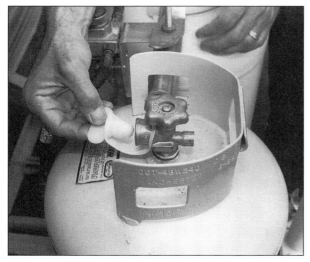

Figure 2.5 POL plugs must be used when transporting cylinders with 45-pound or smaller capacity.

LP-gas tanks/cylinders are equipped with an outlet valve that dispenses gas in vapor form to the RV's appliances through a regulator (Figure 2.6). This regulator is attached to the valve via a left-hand-threaded connection known as a POL connector. The hex portion of the fitting has a small groove machined around its circumference indicating that it has left-hand threads.

Pressure in a full cylinder is about 150 pounds per square inch (psi). This pressure is necessary to keep the gas in liquid form within the tank and will vary with temperature changes as described above. As pressure is reduced during withdrawal, the gas vaporizes and exits the tank through the regulator. Improper positioning of a tank may allow liquid fuel to flow into the regulator. Since the regulator is designed for gas, not liquid, damage to the regulator

Figure 2.6 Outlet valve dispenses gas in vapor form through a regulator.

could occur. Excessive gas quantities could enter the appliance, causing dangerous flareups. The appliances in an RV are designed to operate at a much lower pressure level; the regulator is designed to reduce the high cylinder/tank pressure to a steady 11 inches water-column pressure (about .4 psi).

■ REGULATORS ■

Regulators are durable instruments, but once in a while they may get out of adjustment. In order to verify/adjust the pressure, a gauge called a *manometer* is used (Figure 2.7). This gauge accurately measures very low pressure readings in inches of water column. A water-column gauge consists of a glass or plastic tube bent in a U-shape filled midway with water. Pressure is applied to one end of the tube, which displaces the water. The total displacement is measured in inches of water column. Most RV appliances work best when the regulator is set to 11 inches of pressure. The water in the gauge is pushed down 5½ inches in one tube, which pushes the water up the other tube 5½ inches. The total displacement is 11 inches. Most commercial gauges do not use a glass tube with water, but a special low-pressure dial gauge (Figure 2.8) that is calibrated to water-column pressure. Never attempt to adjust pressure with a conventional gauge calibrated in pounds per square inch. As stated earlier, 11 inches of water-column pressure is only .4 psi—a number

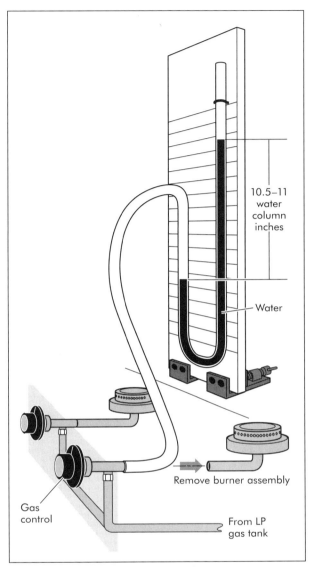

Figure 2.7 LP-gas is checked with a manometer or water-column gauge.

that would hardly register, even on a low-psi type of gauge. Commercial gauges are available through most RV supply stores for around $70. These gauges are also useful in performing leak-down tests to determine the integrity of the system.

Pressure is checked by slipping a connector over an appliance gas outlet (usually the galley-stove burner) that leads to the pressure gauge. The appliance is turned on, and a direct pressure reading is taken. If an adjustment is necessary, the protective cover on the regulator cap is removed to reveal the pressure-adjusting screw. Turning the screw clock-

■ TROUBLESHOOTING ■
THE REGULATOR

Problem	Possible Cause	Correction
Regulator freeze-up	Overfilled tank	Seek qualified help to bleed excessive pressure from tank
	Clogged regulator vent	Clean vent opening
	Water in tank	LP-gas facilities can inject alcohol to absorb moisture
Pilot lights fail	Low regulator pressure	Check regulator output pressure, set to 11 inches water-column pressure
	Low LP-gas level	Replenish supply
	Clogged regulator vent	Clean vent opening
	Defective thermocouple	Install new thermocouple
Regulator vent clogs	Road dirt and debris	Install shield to protect regulator from debris

Figure 2.8 The commmercial manometer is a special low-pressure dial gauge calibrated to water-column pressure.

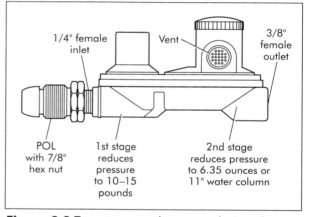

Figure 2.9 Two-stage regulators are designed to reduce LP-gas pressure to 11 inches water column.

wise increases the pressure; counterclockwise reduces the regulator's pressure output.

CAUTION: Do not attempt to adjust the regulator unless you know what you are doing. Take the RV to a certified LP-gas technician.

The building code was changed in 1977 to require the use of two-stage regulators. Older, single-stage regulators could not maintain constant pressure in cold weather due to low inlet pressures. Two-stage regulators are actually two regulators in one (Figure 2.9). The first stage reduces the pressure to about 10 to 15 pounds, and the second stage is needed to further reduce pressure to the necessary 11 inches of water column. You should get about fifteen years of service from a regulator, but dirt, vibration, road salts, and other elements can decrease usable service life. Faulty regulators can be dangerous; they are not repairable. Opening the valve quickly can be hard on the regulator diaphragm and create leaks; open this valve slowly.

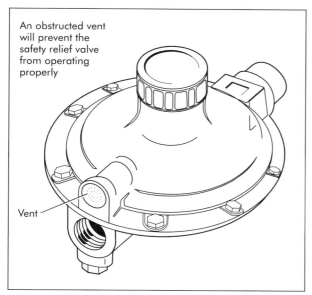

Figure 2.10 Regulator vent location

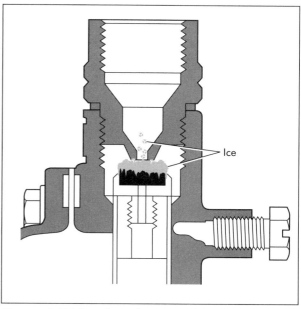

Figure 2.11 Regulator freeze-up during extremely cold temperatures can prevent LP-gas from flowing.

Regulator Service and Repair

The diaphragm vent is located in the top cover of the regulator and is designed to allow air to enter and exit from the spring side of the diaphragm. If this vent becomes blocked by dirt, insects, or road debris, the regulator can be rendered useless and/or dangerous. A small blockage may cause enough pressure drop to allow pilot lights to blow out, or the condition could lead to excessive gas pressure being forced to the appliances, causing a safety hazard. The vent is covered with a fine-mesh screen that should be checked and cleaned periodically (Figure 2.10).

Driving in icy or freezing rain conditions may cause water to enter the vent and freeze the opening shut (Figure 2.11). If these weather conditions bring about odd behavior of propane appliances, a clogged vent may be the culprit. Regulators that lie horizontally are most apt to have the vent fill with water and ice. A shield or hood can be purchased at RV supply stores (or constructed) that will protect vents. Install the regulator so that the vent is pointing down, or at least at a 45-degree angle toward the ground.

Another problem can arise when water enters the tank/cylinder and causes the regulator to freeze from the inside. The pressure-control valve inside the regulator will freeze if water is present in the propane tank/cylinder. As propane is vaporized from liquid to gas, it becomes very cold. If there is water present, it is possible for the temperature inside the regulator to drop below 32°F. This results in regulator freeze-up. Water can enter the tank through a contaminated supply or through a tank valve that is left open by the consumer when the tank/cylinder is empty. If it is determined that moisture has entered the tank/cylinder, methyl alcohol can be injected along with propane by the supplier on the next fill-up. The alcohol absorbs the moisture and allows it to be carried out of the tank/cylinder without causing freeze-ups. It only takes about a pint of methyl alcohol for every 100 gallons of propane, so this procedure should be done by a qualified technician.

Automatic Regulators

Automatic regulators are designed for use when two cylinders are connected by high-pressure pigtails (Figure 2.12). Typical use for such a setup includes installations in travel trailers, fifth-wheels, and pickup campers. Both cylinders are left on at the same time, and the regulator uses the cylinder (service cylinder) indicated by a mark or arrow on a knob or lever. When the service cylinder is empty, the regulator au-

Figure 2.12 Automatic regulator used when two cylinders are connected by high-pressure pigtails.

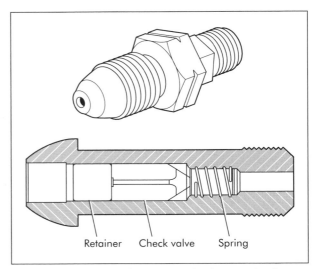

Retainer   Check valve   Spring

Figure 2.13 Excess-flow device built into POL fitting automatically reduces gas flow in event of a line break.

tomatically switches to the other cylinder, and an indicator (usually red) pops up to inform the user that one cylinder is empty.

When the indicator is showing that one cylinder is empty, you can close the valve, rotate the knob/lever to the service cylinder, and remove the empty cylinder for refilling. If you experience a leak when disconnecting the pigtail from the empty cylinder, you probably forgot to turn the arrow or close the empty tank valve.

To use the automatic regulator as a leak detector, you should:

1. Turn off the valve on the cylinder(s).
2. Make sure all burners and pilots are off.
3. Turn on the cylinder valve slowly.
4. Listen to the regulator for the sound of gas flow.
5. If no flow is heard, turn off the cylinder(s).
6. Wait for thirty minutes and visually check the full–empty indicator.
7. If the indicator turns red, there is most likely a leak somewhere in the system.
8. Test with soapy water to find the leak before using the system.

■ POL FITTINGS ■

Special fittings (Figure 2.13) are used to hook pigtails up to the tank/cylinder. These POLs are high-pressure fittings with left-hand threads. (The name

POL comes from the initials of the Prest-O-Lite Company.) Use a 7/8-inch open-end wrench to install/ remove these fittings. Do not apply too much pressure or you will damage the fitting.

Inspect the POL fitting for nicks or deep scratches; any defect can create a poor seal, resulting in a leak. Do not use POL fittings with the O-ring built into the end; current code requires the use of a brass-against-brass seal. Check for leaks using soapy water.

■ FILLING AND OVERFILLING CYLINDERS ■

Many mistakes are made when filling cylinders as uninformed attendants try to sell that "last drop" of propane. All cylinders are fitted with fixed liquid-level gauges in the service valve (Figure 2.14). These valves can be called *outage, 20 percent,* or even *release,* but they all do the same thing. Older models used a finger-operated knurled fitting; the very cold propane could easily damage your skin. Later model liquid-level gauges are operated by a screwdriver.

This valve opens a small passageway to the internal tube extended into the cylinder to its 80-percent level— or the level where it's safe to fill. This hole is very small; it's actually the size of a number 54 drill bit. The filling process must stop when a steady stream of white liquid appears.

The stamping on the cylinder guard shows water

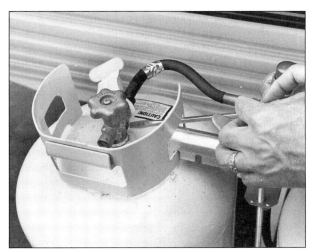

Figure 2.14 Liquid level indicator (bleeder) is a screw on the side of the valve.

capacity in pounds and can be used as a guide for filling (Figure 2.15). For example, the stamping on a 5-gallon cylinder reads "WC 47.7." If you move the decimal point one place to the left, you get the propane capacity in gallons for this particular cylinder. There are about 4.7 gallons in a 20-pound cylinder, about 7.2 gallons in a 30-pound cylinder, and approximately 9.2 gallons in a 40-pound cylinder.

Using the weight method of filling, weigh the cylinder and subtract the tare weight (stamped on the guard); divide that number by 4.24 (weight in pounds per gallon of propane).

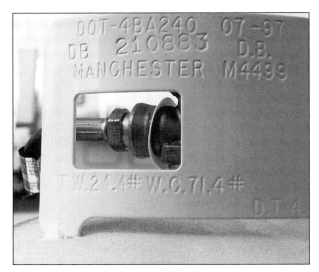

Figure 2.15 Cylinder guard stamping

If the cylinder is overfilled, take it to an open area where there are no flames or sources of ignition. Open the liquid-level gauge (outage valve) very slowly—one-half to one turn is all that is needed. Continue bleeding until the white vapor turns clear. Make sure you are at least ten feet from a flame or source of ignition. Although the propane should not be capable of being lit as long as the flame or source is at least ten feet away, it's a good idea to allow more distance, just for added insurance. Propane is only flammable when there's a 2.2- to 9.6-percent mixture of gas in the air.

■ STOP-FILL VALVES ■

For more than thirteen years, the RV industry has been using automatic stop-fill devices in ASME tanks (Figures 2.16 and 2.17). These devices automatically

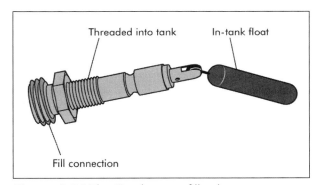

Figure 2.16 The Ceodux stop-fill valve uses an in-tank float to prevent LP-gas overfilling.

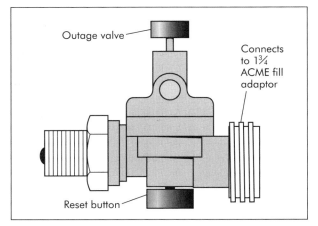

Figure 2.17 The Auto-Stop stop-fill valve automatically stops the flow of LP-gas when the tank becomes 80 percent filled.

■ **CHECKLIST** ■

FILLING, REMOVING, OR INSTALLING AN LP-GAS CYLINDER

- Close valves on appliances and pilot burners.
- Make sure POL fitting is tight between the regulator and the cylinder/tank valve. This nut has a left-hand thread. Be sure to use a properly fitting wrench to prevent deforming the brass fitting (Figure 2.18). Slowly open the cylinder valve.
- Check for leaks with a soapy-water solution at fittings and connections(Figure 2.19). Never use soap with harsh chemicals or ammonia; these chemicals can corrode the lines and brass fittings.
- Replace the regulator immediately if bubbles indicate leaks at the diaphragm seal or vents.
- Retest for leaks.
- Relight the pilots and check them for proper flame (light blue—no yellow).
- Light the main burners to check for proper flame color.
- Check to see that the regulator vent is clear and free of debris.
- Close the cylinder/tank valve when the appliances will not be used.
- Never store cylinders indoors in an unvented enclosed area or near an open flame or source of sparks.

NOTE: Regulators that are not in enclosed compartments must have covers.

Figure 2.18 The regulator coupling nut has a left-hand thread and can be deformed easily if forced in the opposite direction.

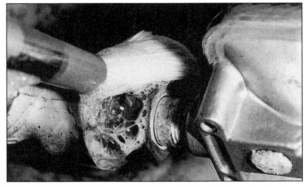

Figure 2.19 LP-gas leaks should only be checked with soap and water.

stop the filling process when the tank reaches the safe capacity (80 percent).

Stop-fill devices eliminate the guesswork or the ignorance of station attendants by automatically stopping the propane flow when the level reaches the 80-percent mark. The most common stop-fill valves operate like the float mechanisms in residential toilet bowls. The float is simply pushed up by the rising liquid entering the tank. At the 80-percent level, the float exerts enough pressure on the valve to stop the flow of gas from the fill-station pump.

Early-model stop-fill valves were more troublesome, but the later models work well. Early-model devices or other float-type stop-fills are not repairable

and must be replaced by a qualified technician. The Auto-Stop device is serviceable, even without emptying the tank, but again, this must be done by a qualified technician. Since all stop-fills are sensitive to dirt, you must keep the dust caps on when the tank is not being filled.

■ **LEAK DETECTORS** ■

LP-gas leaks are serious business. Many RVs come equipped with electronic leak detectors. These units have sensors mounted low to the floor (propane gas is heavier than air and will seek the lowest level) that "sniff" constantly to detect the presence of gas. When gas is detected, they sound an alarm and, in many cases, send a signal to a tank-mounted electric solenoid shutoff valve that will immediately shut the gas off at the cylinder.

NOTE: If your appliances mysteriously fail to operate, check the solenoid valve first. You can bypass it temporarily to determine if it is the cause of the problem.

■ SAFETY ■

Safety around LP-gas should be your number one priority. Leaks are serious. Never use an open flame to check for leaks; always use a solution of soapy water. In the preceding checklist are a few common-sense rules when filling, removing, or installing an LP-gas cylinder in an RV.

■ CHAPTER 3 ■
WATER SYSTEMS

The freshwater system probably does more to make an RV like a home than any other feature. You'd think a system that provides so much convenience would be difficult to maintain and repair, but it's not. Many people have a mental block when it comes to plumbing, but the RV's water system can be maintained and repaired easily with a little pre-planning and a few basic tools.

An RV's water system consists of a metal or plastic water-storage tank, a connection for city water, copper tubing or plastic water lines, a 12-volt DC-powered demand water pump or 12-volt DC air compressor, an accumulator tank, a strainer system, check valves, a water-filter system, and faucets to control water flow (Figure 3.1). A particular system may contain all or just a few of these components.

Basically there are two types of water systems. The most common is the demand system, where water is available "on demand" by either a hand vacuum pump pulling the liquid from a storage tank or by opening a faucet and allowing an electric pump to push water to the fixture. The other type of system, no longer popular with manufacturers, operates by air pressure. In this type of system, an air compressor pressurizes a tank filled with water, forcing water through the system to each valve or faucet.

A hand-pump system uses a handle that is physically pumped back and forth until water is drawn to the fixture. This type of system is common in tent trailers and small campers. An electric demand pump has a telltale whirring-sound pump motor that comes on almost instantly when a faucet is opened. The air-compressor system, on the other hand, will delay several seconds, or if a small amount of water is drawn, several minutes, before the compressor can be heard.

■ WATER TANKS ■

Most RVs utilize polyethylene water tanks. They are lightweight, durable, impact resistant, sanitary, and easily manufactured in a variety of shapes and sizes.

RVs with air-pressure systems will have a metal tank of stainless steel or aluminum. Some of the high-line motorhomes feature stainless-steel tanks in concert with a demand system. The average RV water-tank capacity is about 40 gallons. This translates to about 340 pounds of liquid weight that the tank must contain. When 340 pounds of water are sloshed around due to road movement, the forces that the tank must contend with are considerable. Even so, water tanks seldom require repair.

Maintenance consists of keeping the tank fresh by sanitizing with chlorine and making sure nothing is stored near the water tank that could puncture it. It's also important to drain the water system during cold-weather storage or make sure the tank area is insulated from the cold when using the rig in winter.

Tank Removal

The most difficult service procedure involving water tanks is the removal of the tank itself. Although many repairs can be made to tanks while they are in the RV, it is best to remove the tank for leak repair.

Repairing the Freshwater Tank

Cracks or holes may appear in the freshwater tank if severe impact or abrasion is encountered. Overfilling the tank may also create stresses that may lead

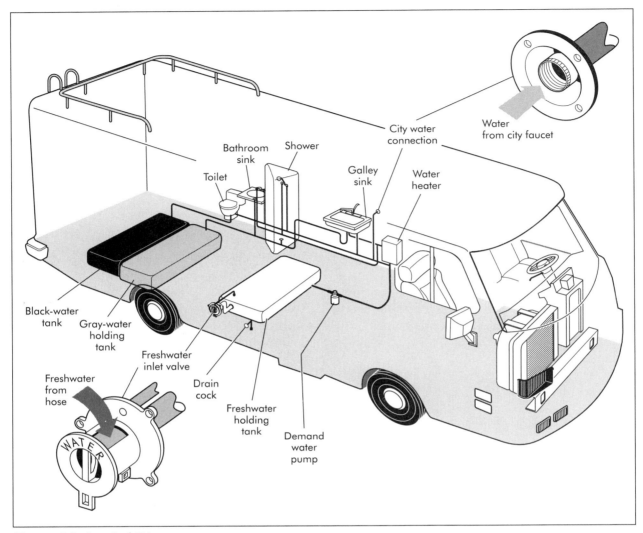

Figure 3.1 A typical RV water system

to a rupture (and damage to the surrounding compartment). After many miles of travel, the constant vibration may cause a crack to appear. Plastic tanks can be repaired with a special epoxy resin and fiberglass patch (Figure 3.2) following these steps:

1. Drain the tanks so the area around the crack is dry. If the crack is in an inaccessible area, the tanks must be removed.
2. A small hole (⅛-inch diameter) should be drilled at each end of the crack. This prevents the crack from propagating from under the patch you will apply.
3. Sand the area around the crack until the tank

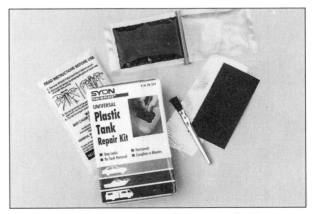

Figure 3.2 Plastic tanks can be repaired using special kits.

| ■ **TROUBLESHOOTING** ■ |||
| THE WATER TANK |||
Problem	**Possible Cause**	**Correction**
Tank will not fill	Vent hose clogged	Clear vent hose
Tank leaks	Loose hose or tubing	Check and tighten
	Crack in tank	Repair or replace tank
	Freeze damage	Repair or replace tank
Odor or bad taste	Bacteria	Sanitize water system

surface is roughed up to allow a good adhesive bond.

4. Cut a fiberglass patch about 1 to 2 inches larger than the crack in all directions.

5. Mix the epoxy resin with its catalyst. After the catalyst is added, there are only about fifteen minutes of working time before the resin "sets up" and starts to harden.

6. With a small brush, dab a layer of resin over the area that was rough-sanded. Then lay the fiberglass-cloth patch over the resin. Pat the patch with the brush until all the fiberglass is soaked with resin.

7. Add more resin to the patch area until it takes on a glossy appearance and the cloth fibers are covered.

8. The resin will become tacky in about fifteen to twenty minutes and will fully harden in a few hours. It's best to wait twenty-four hours before filling the tank with water and inspecting for leaks.
   NOTE: These kits work best when on cracks up to 5 inches and holes 1 inch in diameter.

Some plastics—especially larger repairs—can be welded using a hot-gas procedure and special plastic welding rod. This is a specialized method that is used most often in plastic-tank manufacture. Many RV repair shops are equipped to perform this type of repair (Figure 3.3).

Metal tanks, stainless steel, or aluminum should not be repaired with the fiberglass/epoxy method. The best way is by welding. Since stainless steel and aluminum are difficult to weld, they are best repaired by a professional with gas-tungsten-arc (sometimes known as Heliarc or TIG) welding. The tank should

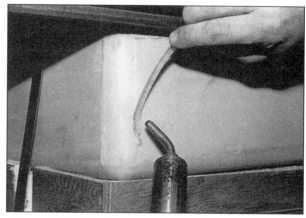

Figure 3.3 Polyethylene tanks can be repaired with a special plastic welding rod and heat gun.

be removed from the RV before welding. Tanks that have been damaged by freezing can be repaired if the damage is not too severe. Permanent bulges, long cracks, or split tank seams warrant tank replacement. Although temporary repairs may be made, this type of damage often will cause the tank to fail in a relatively short period of time. If you need to replace a metal tank, consider making the conversion to a demand system using a polyethylene tank.

Vent Hose Inspection and Repair

A water tank will fill slowly (or not at all) if the vent hose is clogged. The vent hose is usually made of a vinyl plastic section that leads from a fitting on the top of the tank to a fitting that terminates at the outside water-fill door (Figure 3.4). The usual problem is that the hose becomes bent and kinked, making

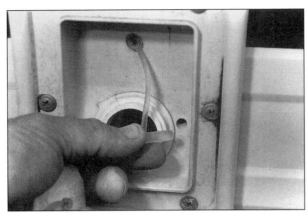

Figure 3.4 Opening the water-fill vent plug facilitates the job of adding water.

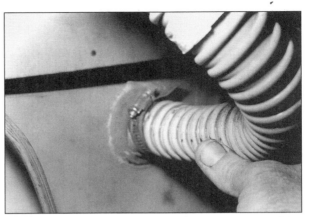

Figure 3.5 The hose connection from the water fill to the tank should be checked for leaks or kinking.

it impossible for air to pass. The problem can be remedied by either shortening the hose to remove the kink or by replacing the hose if it is too short. In both cases, the hose should make a smooth transition from the top of the tank to the outside fill port. It is also important not to store objects on the water tank that could restrict the vent hose's ability to allow air to flow.

Leaking Hose Connections and Fittings

Since the water in the tank and the associated plumbing on the suction side of the pump cannot be pressure tested (except for air-pressure systems), leaks can be deceptive. Small leaks may go unnoticed until water damage has been done to the RV. A simple method for checking for small leaks in a demand system is to pressurize the lines (allowing the pump to cycle off) and allowing the rig to stand without using the water. If the pump blips, there's most likely a small leak in the system.

Hose connections to the water tank can be the cause of a leak (Figure 3.5). Depending on the situation and type of fitting, repairs can usually be performed while the tank is in the RV. If fittings are damaged by freezing, the tank may have to be removed for fitting replacement. If there is inadequate room near the tank to position a wrench to rotate a fitting, the entire tank has to be removed.

Check hoses and fitting connections for excessive side pressure. If a hose is routed around a sharp bend or abrupt turn, the pressure may be enough to de-

flect the hose fitting and cause a leak. Hoses should be rerouted so that pressure is not applied to the fittings or hose.

The most popular type of water supply pipe used in RVs is polybutylene (PB), but in some older RVs you may also find copper. Flexible, braided, vinyl tubing may be used for the first 12 inches on the inlet and outlet sides of the pump. Most rigs during the past twenty years are equipped with the gray-colored tubing, usually under the Qest nameplate.

Copper tubing uses compression-type connectors that can be tightened if a leak appears (Figure 3.6), or in the case of older installations, the fittings may have been soldered (sweat connections). The leak may also be caused by damage to the compression ring. The seating surface on the fitting must be clean and free from nicks and scratches. If the sealing surface is damaged, the fittings should be replaced.

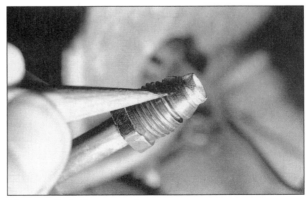

Figure 3.6 Compression-type connectors on copper tubing must be tightened if a leak occurs.

The use of flexible vinyl hose with braided reinforcement may be recommended by your pump manufacturer. This type of hose should only be used on the first 12 inches from the inlet and outlet sides of the pump. Barbed fittings are used at the pump, and the hose is secured with a worm-gear-type hose clamp; do not overtighten or allow the clamp to cut into the hose material. The other ends of the hoses are fitted with barbed fittings that terminate with the proper configuration for hookup to the PB tubing or other accessories like an accumulator tank. If a leak is detected here, the best solution is to cut the hose, reinstall over the barb fitting, and tighten the clamp.

Polybutylene (PB) is the most common water pipe found in RVs as it can transport both hot and cold water and is soft enough to turn some corners without the need for additional fittings. Being a soft hose, it can also expand to a small degree and therefore can resist some freezing before bursting; copper, on the other hand, is not very resistant to freezing. Burst tubing is usually the reason for having to replace the lines.

The newer type of plastic tubing is clear, gray, red, or white in color and is much more flexible. In a typical water system, this plastic tubing will be interconnected with two types of fittings: barb and crimp rings or flared cone-and-nut types.

Installing barbed fittings with crimp rings requires a special tool. Manufacturers use high-quality crimp tools that can cost more than $150. Do-it-yourselfers who find the need to install crimp rings once in a while can purchase less expensive—although much slower to use—tools. When installing a crimp ring, make sure the tool is fully seated before releasing. Crimp rings must be cut off and are not reusable.

Installing Qest Flared Cone-and-Nut Type Fittings

Follow these steps in installing Qest fittings:

1. Make sure the tubing is cut to the proper length. Cut the end square.
2. Install the nut over the tubing with the threads toward the end of the tubing.
3. Slip the ring over the tubing with the flare (or extrusion) facing away from the nut.
4. Slide the cone over the tubing with the taper toward the end of the tubing. Make sure

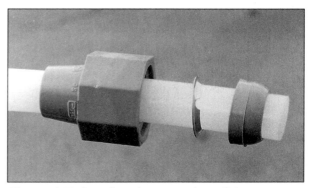

Figure 3.7 Qest flared cone-and-nut fittings are used to connect water tubing.

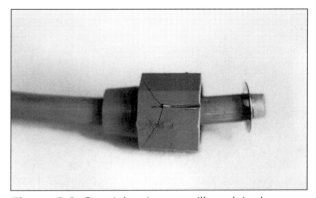

Figure 3.8 Overtightening nut will result in damage.

¼ inch of the tubing shows past the cone (Figure 3.7).
5. Push the end of the tubing into the fitting; slide over the nut, the ring, and the cone until secure, and hand tighten the nut. Do not overtighten (Figure 3.8).

If you need to remove and reinstall the fitting, it's best to use a new ring and cone. It may be necessary to cut back the tubing since the cone will usually be difficult to remove.

Installing Flair-It Cone-and-Nut Fittings

To install Flair-It fittings follow these steps:

1. Make sure the tubing is cut to the proper length.
2. Slide the nut over the tubing.
3. Firmly press the tubing onto the flare of the

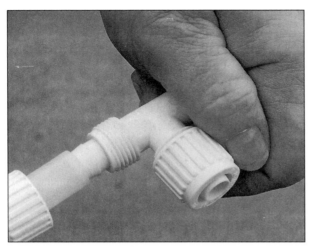

Figure 3.9 Flair-It cone-and-nut fittings are easy to install

fitting—go to the end of the flare portion (Figure 3.9).
4. Slide the nut to the threads and hand tighten. Do not overtighten or use a wrench.

These fitting are the easiest to use and are reusable. Keep a few unions handy; they can simplify on-the-road repairs of broken tubing.

■ WATER SYSTEM SANITATION ■

It is not uncommon for RV owners to complain of bad water. The first sign of a contaminated water system is usually a bad taste, followed by strange odors emanating from the water supply. Bacteria may have built up in the water tank, especially if the water tank's supply has not been used frequently and has not been replenished with fresh, clean water on a regular basis. When a rig comes out of storage or is being used extensively on a city-water connection, the tank and entire water system should be sanitized before use. Some of the bacterial buildup can cause serious illness; don't take chances!

Here are the steps to sanitize the water tank:

1. Drain the water tank completely, then refill halfway with clean, fresh water.
2. Mix ¼ cup of household bleach for every 15 gallons of tank capacity in a container with a gallon or two of clean water.
3. Pour this mixture into the water tank.
4. Top off the water tank with fresh water. Drive the rig around the block to mix the solution.
5. Pump water through each faucet so that all the lines are filled with the water/bleach mixture from the tank. Usually, running a quart of water out each faucet is adequate.
6. The hot-water tank holds at least 6 gallons of water. Run the hot-water faucets until this much solution has passed to insure that the old water has been purged from the hot-water tank, and it is now filled with the water/bleach solution from the water tank.
7. Let the water stand for several hours.
8. Drain the entire water system, hot-water tank included.
9. To remove the bleach odor, mix ½ cup of baking soda with a gallon of water and pour into the freshwater tank.
10. Fill the tank completely and pump this solution through the water heater and the rest of the water lines. This solution can sit in the system for a few days. Driving the rig around the block will slosh water around and thoroughly clean the tank.
11. Drain the entire system and refill with fresh, clean water.

Water Filters

Water filters perform the primary function of removing sediment and particles from the water, and secondly, the task of removing odors and improving the taste of the water. Filter systems can use throwaway canisters (Figure 3.10) or one or two replaceable cartridges (Figure 3.11). Filters work by screening out impurities in the water, and over a period of time they become clogged with sediments and mineral particles. When the filter becomes full of these impurities, you will notice a reduced flow of water and decreased water pressure; this is a clear signal to replace the canister or cartridge(s). Due to the wide range of water conditions, it is impossible to establish a definitive schedule for water-filter replacement; however, a rough interval for filter replacement would be every three months of use.

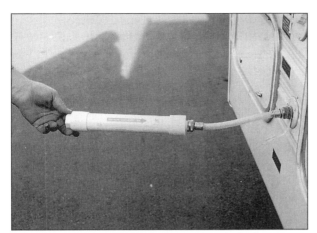

Figure 3.10 The water filter is discarded after its useful life is expired.

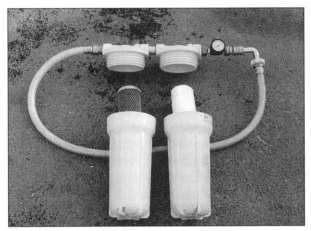

Figure 3.11 Some water filters use replaceable cartridges.

◼ WATER PUMPS ◼

Water pumps seem to be the biggest cause of RV water-system difficulties. The pump is a heavily-used component in the water system, relying on a number of moving parts and electrical components.

There are a variety of electric pumps on the market; make it a point to be familiar with the one installed in your RV. Most RV pumps use some type of rubber diaphragm and a 12-volt DC electric motor. Some pump manufacturers use a rotary-impeller system. The main advantage of a diaphragm pump is that it operates more quietly than the rotary-impeller design and will not be damaged if accidentally run dry.

Service and Repair

Servicing a water pump is easy with a few basic tools: A couple of screwdrivers (Phillips and flat), a set of small wrenches and sockets (¼ inch through ½ inch), an adjustable-end wrench that will open to 1 inch, pliers, a pair of water-pump pliers, and a multimeter for checking electrical components.

If the water pump runs but fails to deliver water, the cause is most often a restriction in the suction or inlet side of the pump.

Testing the Suction-Water Line

To evaluate the condition of the suction-water line, follow these steps:

1. Carefully follow the water line from the pump inlet to the water tank. Look for any signs of pinching or kinks in the line. If necessary, reroute the line to avoid this condition.
2. Check the tightness of all connections from the water tank to the pump (Figure 3.12). A leak here will allow air to be drawn in with the water flow, causing the pump to lose its prime.

If an anti-backflow valve (check valve) is installed in the line, it may be stuck closed, shutting off water flow to the inlet side of the pump. Remove the check valve from the line. An arrow should indicate

Figure 3.12 If the pump connections are not tight, air may be drawn in, allowing the pump to lose its prime.

Figure 3.13 Arrow shows direction of water flow from tank to faucets.

Figure 3.14 Checking the water-pump backflow valve with air will determine its integrity.

the direction of water flow (Figure 3.13). Blow through the valve in the direction of the arrow (Figure 3.14). Air should pass this way but not in the opposite direction. If air fails to pass through the valve, it should be replaced.

If it is determined that water is reaching the pump through the suction line from the water tank, the lack of water flow is usually caused by a broken drive belt on the Jabsco pump (Figure 3.15), a diaphragm problem, or a leak in the inlet tubing (vacuum leak). It's also possible that the inlet tubing is kinked or restricted. If the RV is equipped with a Jabsco belt-drive pump, make sure the belt has not broken or slipped off the pulleys. This belt is a toothed, positive drive belt that is easily replaced. Simply slip a new belt

into position, making sure that the teeth of the belt mesh with the cogs of the pulleys. If you have a SHURflo pump (Figure 3.16), check for debris in the inlet/outlet valves or for swollen and/or dry valves. Also, check the pump housing for cracks or for loose drive-assembly screws. For both types of pumps, make sure the diaphragm is not pinched or ruptured. A defective diaphragm can cause failure to the pump, low water volume, and intermittent cycling when all faucets are turned off.

If water still fails to flow, check the pump's wiring (Figure 3.17) for polarity and check voltage. If the 12-volt DC leads are reversed, the pump will run backward, failing to pump water. Reverse the pump-motor wires and operate the pump. If water now pumps, permanently connect the wiring leads in this position. If the water still fails to flow, check for low voltage. Using a multimeter, check that the voltage is at least 12 volts (plus/minus 10 percent), while the pump is running (Figure 3.18).

Overhauling the Water Pump

To inspect the pump diaphragm, the pump assembly should be disconnected and removed from the RV. All pump manufacturers supply a service kit that contains a new diaphragm, a pump-check valve, a drive belt (if needed), and gaskets. Purchase this service kit before you start to overhaul the pump. To overhaul the water pump:

1. Remove electrical connections from the pump, marking the wires for their correct location.
2. Drain both the freshwater tank and the hot-water tank to keep water from flowing out of the inlet line when it is removed.
3. Remove the inlet and outlet lines from the pump housing. Use the proper-size wrench so that the fittings are not damaged. This procedure should be easy if the original installation included swivel barb fittings.
4. Remove the pump-housing mounting bolts and rubber vibration pads from the mounting location on the RV.
5. When the pump is free from the RV, take it to a clean work area for disassembly.
6. All pumps have retaining screws that hold the

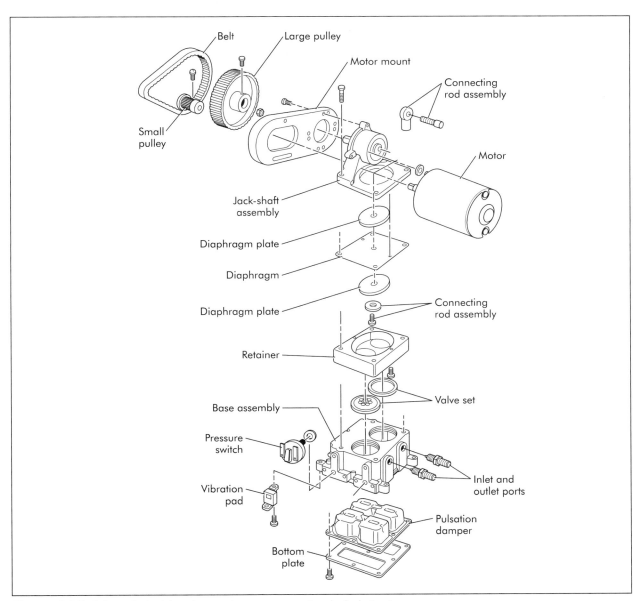

Figure 3.15 Jabsco belt-drive demand water pump (exploded view)

diaphragm cover in place. By removing these screws, the diaphragm can be removed (Figure 3.19). Jabsco pumps require that the motor and jack-shaft assembly be removed before the diaphragm screws can be reached. SHURflo pumps have the pressure-sensing switch located in the diaphragm cover. The switch and the pressure spring will pop out when the cover is removed.

7. With the diaphragm removed, inspect the rubber for cracks and defects (Figure 3.20). Check the small flapper-check valves for signs of sticking or foreign objects that may prevent them from seating fully (Figure 3.21). If the pump has an internal filter screen on the inlet side, replace the screen or clean it before reassembly.

8. Replace the diaphragm. Reassemble the pump and mount it back in the RV. Connect the inlet- and outlet-water lines and the

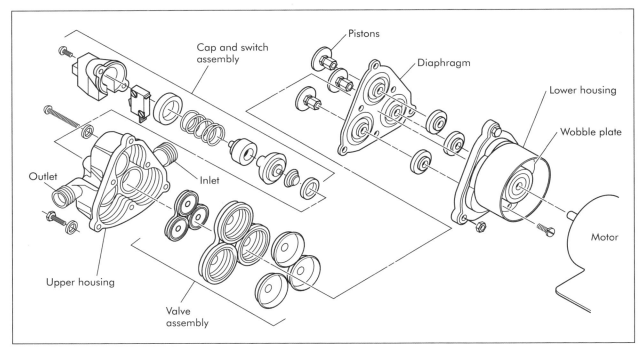

Figure 3.16 SHURflo demand water pump (exploded view)

Figure 3.17 Water pump will run backward if 12-volt DC wiring polarity is reversed.

Figure 3.18 Multimeter showing low voltage at water pump.

12-volt DC wiring. If you are using swivel barb fittings, make sure they are only hand tightened. Overtightening can damage the taper seal, causing leaks. Never use Teflon tape or other sealing compounds on the threads. Sealer can cause pump failure, which will not usually be covered by the warranty.

9. To test the pump, fill the water tank, inspect the connections for leaks, turn on the water-pump switch, and open a faucet. The pump should start, prime, and pump water. Run water from each fixture until the air is bled from the system. The pressure switch should automatically turn off the pump when pressure builds.

Figure 3.19 SHURflo demand water pump diaphragm is accessed after removing cover screws.

Figure 3.20 The water-pump diaphragm should be inspected for cracks or defects after removal.

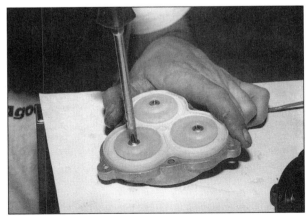

Figure 3.21 Debris can prevent the flapper-check valves in the water pump from seating.

Testing Other Water-Pump Components

A pump that fails to operate may have a defective master control switch or simply low-battery voltage. Make sure the control switch is rated at 15 amps or better. To check these components, a multimeter is needed. Follow these steps:

1. Battery condition can be determined by taking a voltage reading across the positive and negative terminals or by trying other 12-volt DC appliances. Low voltage will prevent the pump from operating. Voltage at the battery should be not less than 11 volts.
2. If voltage is normal, locate the 12-volt DC fuse that protects the water pump. See if the fuse is intact. Using the multimeter on the DC volts setting, check for voltage on both sides of the fuse. If not, replace the fuse and recheck.
3. With the pump's master control switch in the on position, voltage should be present to one side of the pressure-sensitive control switch. If not, the master switch is defective or there is a break in the wiring from the switch to the pump.
4. If there is voltage to the switch and the pump still will not function, the pressure switch should be removed and tested. On Jabsco belt-drive pumps, the pressure switch is located on the outside of the pump housing and can be removed without removing the pump housing. On SHURflo pumps, the pressure switch is located under the pump-housing diaphragm cover, which must be removed.
5. With the switch removed from the pump, the test can be done with a multimeter (Figure 3.22). These pressure switches are normally closed; the circuit is complete without pressure. After calibrating the multimeter, touch the leads to each side of the switch; there should be a zero-resistance reading on the multimeter (ohms). If not, replace the switch, reassemble the pump, and turn on the master switch to test the pump. The motor should run until pressure is established, and then the pump should shut off.

■ TROUBLESHOOTING ■
THE WATER PUMP

Problem	Possible Cause	Correction
Pump runs but no water flows at outlets	Low water level in tank	Replenish supply
	Clogged water lines	Locate, remove obstruction
	Kink in suction line	Straighten line
	Air leak in suction line	Repair air leak
	Loose hose clamps on suction side of pump	Tighten clamps
	Stuck pump-check valve	Repair or clean valve
	Punctured diaphragm	Replace diaphragm
	Cracked pump housing	Replace pump housing
	Stuck backflow valve	Replace backflow valve
	Broken pump-drive belt	Replace belt
	Worn pump impeller	Replace impeller
	Pump running backward	Reverse pump wiring
	Plugged in-line filter	Replace element or screen
Pump cycles off and on with faucets closed	Water leak in plumbing	Locate and repair
	Leaking faucet sets	Repair faucet sets
	Defective toilet valve	Repair valve
	Internal leak in pump	Install pump-repair kit
	Failed pressure switch	Replace pressure switch
Pump motor fails to run	Blown fuse	Locate and replace
	Master switch off	Turn on master switch
	Low battery charge	Charge battery
	Loose wiring connection	Check all connections
	Poor ground	Check ground connection
	Defective pump motor	Replace motor
Pump fails to shut off when faucet is closed	Empty water tank	Replenish water supply
	Low voltage condition	Charge batteries
	Leaking faucets	Repair faucets
	Failed pressure switch	Replace pressure switch
Excessive pump noise or vibration	Restricted intake line	Clear suction hose
	Inadequate pump mounting	Mount per manufacturer's specs
	Loose mounting bolts	Tighten bolts
	Worn mount bushings	Replace with new bushings
	Failed pulsation damper	Replace with new damper
	Loose drive pulleys	Tighten pulleys
	Worn pump bearings	Replace bearings

■ **TROUBLESHOOTING** ■
THE WATER PUMP, continued

Problem	Possible Cause	Correction
Inadequate water flow	Air leak at pump suction	Check suction line
	Undersized suction line	Replace with larger line
	Kinked outlet line	Straighten line
	Clogged intake strainer	Clean strainer
	Leaking pump diaphragm	Replace diaphragm
	Inadequate pump wiring	Rewire with larger wire
Sputtering water flow	Air leak in suction line	Repair leaks
	Air not bled from lines	Bleed air from lines
	Air in water heater	Bleed hot-water lines
Pump will not prime	Empty water tank	Fill water tank
	Air leak in suction line	Repair suction line
	Restricted suction line	Clear obstruction
	Defective pump diaphragm	Replace diaphragm
	Defective pump impeller	Replace impeller
	Broken pump-drive belt	Replace drive belt
	Clogged intake strainer	Clean strainer

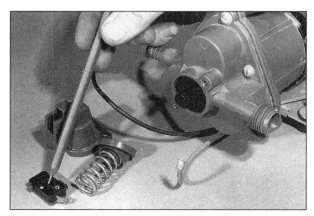

Figure 3.22 The pressure switch can be checked for condition after its removal from the water pump.

This same test procedure should be done if the pump fails to shut off. The pressure switch may fail to open as pressure builds. The switch will test with a 0-ohm reading even when pressure is applied. Replace the switch if it will not open with pressure applied.

Another common cause of pump run-on is low battery voltage. When the battery is low, the pump motor cannot produce sufficient pressure to open the pressure-sensing switch. This can lead to motor overheating and potentially permanent damage to the motor and pump. Wiring that is too small a gauge may also cause this condition. If the voltage is not correct, check that the wiring is at least 14 gauge; wiring should be 12 gauge if the length from the power source exceeds 20 feet (up to 50 feet).

Accumulator Tanks

An accumulator tank (Figure 3.23) has an internal bladder that prevents air from being dissolved into the water. It is usually installed close to the outlet side of the pump and can be mounted in virtually any position. The air bladder is compressed when the pump charges the water system and returns pressure to the water system when a valve or faucet is opened. This provides a smoother flow of water and reduces the number of times that the water pump must cycle to deliver the same volume of water.

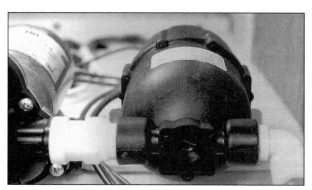

Figure 3.23 Accumulator tank in water line reduces pump cycling.

Reducing Pump Noise

Excessive pump-motor noise is a common complaint among RV owners. See the checklist below for some tips to reduce pump noise.

Although it's not common, an older pump may have defective motor- or drive-mechanism bearings. If the pump becomes progressively noisy with age, it is likely the pump needs to be replaced.

■ WATER-PRESSURE REGULATORS ■

The water lines in the normal RV are designed to withstand 45 pounds per square inch (psi) water pressure. Most demand water-pump systems produce approximately 35 to 45 psi. The water connections from city water can easily exceed 100 psi, which can damage the RV water system by rupturing a line or fitting and cause leaking. To control this excess pressure, a pressure regulator is placed in the faucet end of the hose going to the RV's city-water connection.

These regulators are normally factory set to allow 45 psi to enter the RV. Because an RV water hose is used to contain water pressure, it is important to place the regulator at the supply faucet and then connect the hose to it. This limits the water pressure inside the hose, preventing it from ballooning or bursting from excess pressure.

Regulators can be purchased with an integral gauge to show the line pressure going to the RV. You can also use adjustable regulators with a line-pressure gauge to suit local conditions. If you use an adjustable regulator, be sure not to exceed the pressure rating of the water-supply hose and your RV plumbing system.

If your RV is fitted with an internal water-pressure regulator, there is no need for the inline regulator. If this is the case, it's best to use a rigid hose when hooking up to water systems with high pressure, especially in extremely hot weather.

Figure 3.24 Rubber mounts on the base reduce noise when the water pump is operating.

■ CHECKLIST ■
FOR PUMP NOISE

- Make sure the pump is mounted on a solid surface that is not flimsy or prone to vibration; the RV floor is usually the best surface since it is likely to be the most rigid.
- Mount the pump on the manufacturer's rubber mounts; they are designed to minimize noise (Figure 3.24).
- Make sure all mounting connections, pulleys, and the associated drive mechanisms are tight.
- The compartment where the pump is located can be insulated with fiberglass, Styrofoam, or Reflextix to provide a sound barrier.

■ REPAIRING FAUCETS ■

Leaks can occur in the water inlet and the drain portions of sinks, showers, and bathtubs. The most common problem results from the inlet fittings loosening due to road vibrations; these fittings only have to be tightened to correct the problem. On occasion the seals and gaskets inside the faucets may become worn and need to be replaced (Figure 3.25). Some faucet leaks are created when the plastic gasket seats become worn to the point that a gasket will no longer hold a good seal. These seats are not repairable and it may be faster and cheaper to replace the entire unit rather than attempt to seal the unit with new gaskets (Figure 3.26).

Replacing a Faucet

Follow these steps when replacing a faucet:

1. Turn off the water supply to the faucet. This is generally located beneath the sink or lavatory.
2. Open both the hot and cold handles on the existing faucet.
3. Disconnect water supply lines from the existing faucet. These are normally secured by hand-tightened nuts under the faucet. You may need to use a basin wrench to reach these nuts (Figure 3.27).
4. Remove the existing faucet by unscrewing the winged plastic hold-down nuts.

Figure 3.26 Repair kits are available for most water faucets.

5. Clean the top surface of the sink or lavatory where the new faucet assembly will rest.
6. Most RV-type faucets come with a mounting plate. With the mounting plate in place, insert the two shank ends of the faucet into the sink (or countertop) and set the faucet in place.
7. Install the winged plastic locknuts onto the two shank ends of the faucet and hand tighten firmly against the underside of the sink. Make sure these nuts are only hand tight; do not use a wrench or other tools on plastic threads.
8. Replace the plastic water-line-supply nuts and thread them onto the faucet shanks. Again, hand tighten only.
9. Turn the water supply on again and test for leaks.

Figure 3.25 Seals and gaskets in faucets can become worn and cause leaks.

Figure 3.27 A basin wrench can help reach nuts in tight, hard-to-reach locations.

■ SEALING SINKS AND BATHTUBS ■

Bathtubs and sinks have a collar-type drain that is sealed to the bottom using a locknut. In almost all cases a leak can be attributed to the locking collar working loose because of road vibrations. The leak can usually be stopped by simply reaching under the sink and hand tightening the collar. Do not use any tools; the fitting is usually plastic and very easy to damage. If tightening doesn't stop the leak, the rubber or closed-cell foam gasket located in the bottom of the drain fitting may be defective. Replacement requires loosening the locking collar and removing the old gasket, installing a new one, and hand tightening the locking collar back onto the drain fitting.

A good substitute for the gasket—if it cannot be located—is to use plumber's putty or butyl tape (the same material used to seal RV windows).

■ HOT-WATER TANKS ■

RV water heaters come in two main types. The most common consists of an insulated water tank (usually 6, 8, 10, or 12 gallons in capacity); a flue assembly for routing hot gases through a passage in the tank, so that heat transfers to the water; a gas burner; a gas-control valve; and an electronic direct-spark ignition, an electric pilot-light ignition, or a manual gas-pilot ignition system. The two major suppliers are Atwood (Figure 3.28) and Suburban (Figure 3.29). Another type is an instantaneous or continuous-flow appliance (Figure 3.30), where the water is heated in a central core by applying a flame directly to the copper tubes that contain the water. With this type, water is heated on demand, eliminating the need for a storage tank. The hot-water supply is almost endless, although technically there is actually a limit—beyond the usual freshwater capacity of most RVs.

The water in most hot-water tanks is heated via a propane-fired burner, although some may use 120-volt AC power to take advantage of campground hookups. Electric (120-volt AC) is used when hooked up in campsites, while gas is used when hookups are not available. Both fuel sources can be used simultaneously for faster recovery rates.

Water heaters are rated for Btu input and the rate of 100-degree rise (the number of gallons of water per hour that the heater can raise 100 degrees). Wa-ter heaters require little maintenance but should be subject to periodic tank flushing, winterizing, and minor burner adjustments.

Water Heaters with Pilot Assemblies

Consistent pilot-light outage (for models so equipped) may be caused by a number of things, most often a weak pilot caused by a dirty orifice and/or low gas pressure. Check gas pressure (see LP-gas section, page 2.5), to confirm that there are 11 inches of water-column pressure. When the control knob is held in the pilot position, gas is supplied to the pilot orifice, which is manually lit with a match or appliance lighter. The pilot flame engulfs the thermocouple, which generates millivolts to the gas control's magnet assembly. When the magnet receives the specified millivolts (depending on brand), it allows the gas to flow to the pilot without holding the control knob in the pilot position. If the water temperature exceeds 180°F, the ECO (energy cutoff) limit switch in the gas valve trips open permanently. If this happens, you'll have to replace the gas valve.

CAUTION: Never light the water heater without first filling it with water.

Cleaning the Pilot

Cleaning the orifice is a delicate job since the hole the gas passes through is only slightly larger than the diameter of a human hair. Do not attempt to clean the orifice with any metal object; the hole will be enlarged and the pilot flame will be too large. Cleaning can be done with rubbing alcohol and a wooden toothpick.

To clean the pilot, follow these steps:

1. Remove the pilot tube and orifice from the main burner assembly (Figure 3.31).
2. Soak the orifice end in alcohol.
3. Use a toothpick to clean the orifice hole (Figure 3.32). Be careful not to break any wood off in the hole.
4. Reinstall the pilot tube and burner assembly and try to relight. If there still is an inadequate flame and the orifice is clogged, replace the tube and pilot burner assembly.

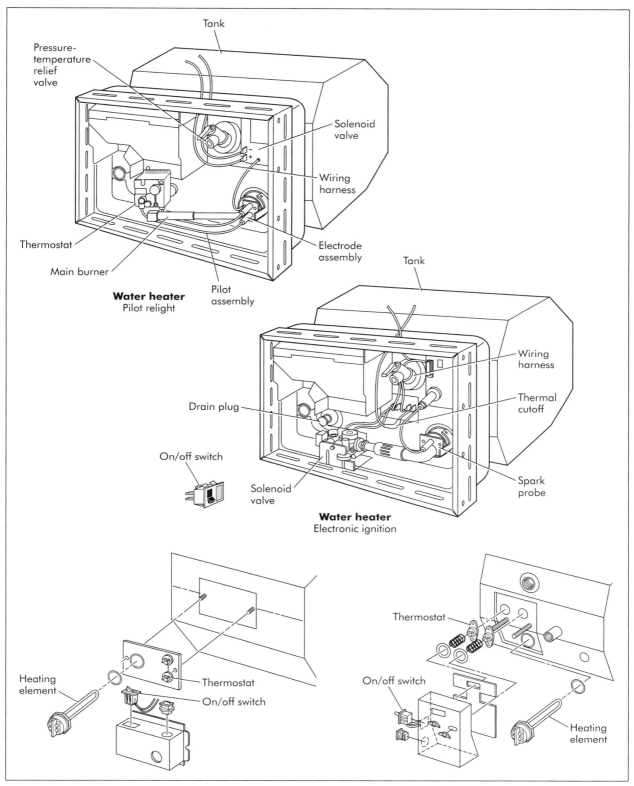

Figure 3.28 The Atwood water heater (exploded view)

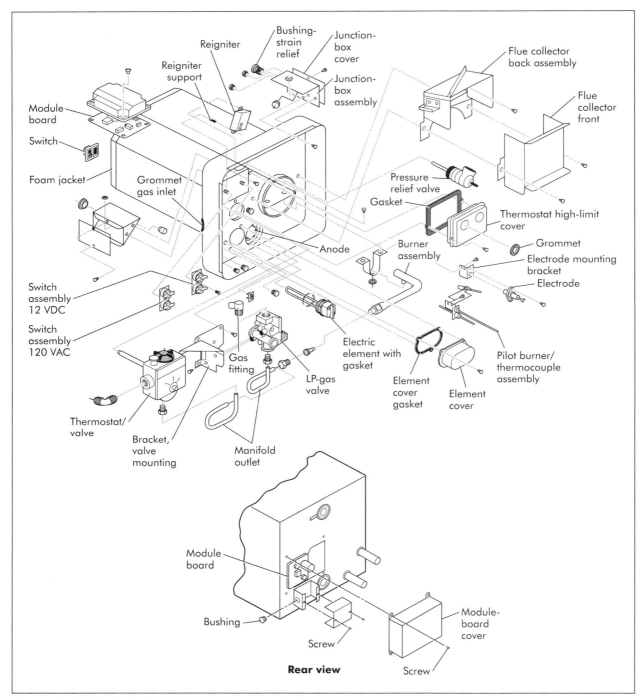

Figure 3.29 The Suburban water heater (exploded view)

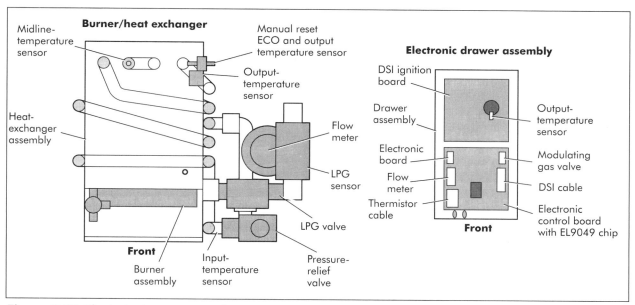

Figure 3.30 The instantaneous water heater

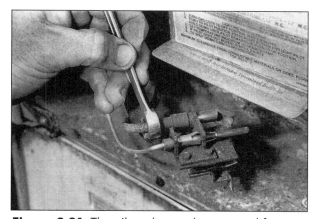

Figure 3.31 The pilot tube can be removed from the hot-water tank burner assembly with a line wrench.

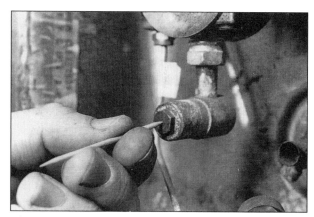

Figure 3.32 A toothpick should be used to clean the pilot orifice.

5. Dirt and debris lodged in the pilot burner can also create a frequent pilot-outage situation. Make sure the air passage around the pilot burner is clean—free of dirt, insects, and corrosion.

Atwood Pilot Assembly

There are two pilot assemblies used in Atwood hot-water tanks. The earlier model is made by Robertshaw (Figure 3.33), and it has a ¼-inch pilot gas line mounting on the left side of the main burner. The current pilot is made by Jade (Figure 3.34), and it has a ⅛-inch gas line and pilot mounting on the right side of the main burner. The Robertshaw is no longer available, and the Jade must be substituted. If there is no location on the right side of the main burner to mount the Jade pilot, a new burner with the proper holes will have to be replaced as well.

Atwood Pilot Adjustment

The flame height for the pilot is regulated by the gas valve and pilot orifice. Early-model gas controls have

■ TROUBLESHOOTING ■
THE HOT-WATER TANK

Problem	Possible Cause	Correction
Pilot outage	Poor pilot flame	Replace pilot orifice
	Fluttering pilot flame	Clean or replace orifice
	Weak thermocouple	Replace thermocouple
	Insufficient gas pressure	Adjust to 11 inches water-column pressure
	Weak gas-control magnet	Replace control unit
	Obstructed air intake	Clean intake tube
	Improper air adjustment	Adjust air shutter
Pilot extinguishes itself when attempting to light flame	Thermocouple needs more time to heat	Wait 30 seconds
	Loose thermocouple	Tighten connection
	Weak thermocouple	Replace thermocouple
	Weak gas-control magnet	Replace gas control
No spark (direct ignition heaters)	Spark gap incorrect	Adjust gap
	Corroded terminals	Clean terminals
	Cracked insulators	Replace electrodes
	Cracked wires	Replace lead wire
	Overly long high-voltage wire	Shorten lead
	Dirt and dust on wires	Clean system
Flame will not establish (direct ignition)	Wrong spark-gap adjustment	Adjust spark gap
	Malfunctioning valve	Replace valve
Early lockout	Reversed polarity	Reverse wires to power and ground
	Poor ground	Establish good ground
	High gas pressure	Lower to 11 inches water-column pressure
	Sensor probe	Adjust position in flame
Erratic burner flame	Blocked burner orifice	Clean orifice
	Misaligned main burner	Align burner tube
	Obstruction in burner	Remove obstruction
	Improper air adjustment	Adjust air shutter
	Insufficient gas pressure	Adjust gas pressure
	Poor gas supply	Replace gas in tank
Yellow-colored flame	Improper air mixture	Adjust air shutter
	Plugged burner orifice	Clean orifice
	Obstruction in tube	Clear burner tube
	Wrong gas pressure	Adjust to 11 inches water-column pressure
	Obstructed heater grill	Clear grill
	Misaligned burner jet	Align burner jet

■ TROUBLESHOOTING ■
THE HOT WATER TANK, continued

Problem	Possible Cause	Correction
Smoking and/or sooting	Improper air mixture	Adjust air shutter
	Misaligned main burner	Align burner jet
	Obstruction in main jet	Clear main burner jet
	Poor gas supply	Replace gas supply
Main burner will not light	Blocked burner jet	Clear burner jet
	Improper air adjustment	Adjust burner jet
	Defective gas control valve	Clear burner jet
	Improper air setting	Adjust air shutter
	Obstruction in tube	Clear obstruction
	Incorrect thermostat setting	Set higher or lower
	Defective gas control	Replace valve
Relief valve leaks	Foreign material in seat	Flip valve handle to clear
	Air in system	Purge all air in system
	Defective valve	Replace valve

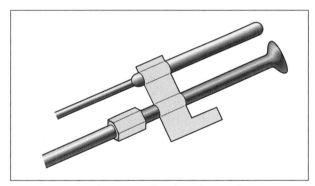

Figure 3.33 The Atwood-Robertshaw pilot

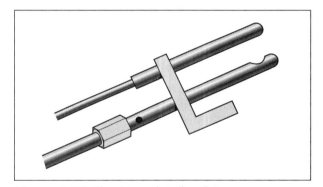

Figure 3.34 The Atwood-Jade pilot

a pilot-adjustment screw, which actually has very little effect on the pilot. There is no pilot adjustment in the current White Rodger controls. The flame should be high enough to engulf the thermocouple. If the pilot is larger, the ECO in the gas valve could blow, stopping the gas flow.

Replacing the Thermocouple

Many times a pilot light will go out almost immediately after lighting. Here are some simple checks and remedies for this problem:

1. Make sure the thermocouple is given adequate time to heat, at least thirty seconds. If more than thirty seconds are required, replace the thermocouple.
2. The thermocouple is removed with a ⅜-inch open-end wrench at the gas-control valve. The other end is held in a spring-clip arrangement that allows the thermocouple to be pulled straight out of the holder (Figure 3.35).
3. Slip the new unit into the holder until one-third of the end will be exposed directly to the pilot flame. The other end is tightened finger tight in the gas-control valve. Then

Figure 3.35 The thermocouple can be removed from the gas control valve with a ⅜-inch wrench.

Figure 3.36 Magnet assembly thermocouple tester

tighten one-quarter turn with the wrench. Do not overtighten or undertighten, or the unit will not function.

4. Open the gas valve to the pilot position, depress the pilot-light button, and hold while lighting the flame. Release the button after thirty seconds; the pilot should remain lit.

Testing the Thermocouple

If you have access to a magnet-assembly thermocouple tester (Figure 3.36), you can check the thermocouple function. Screw the thermocouple into the tester and heat for fifteen seconds. Press the plunger down; if the plunger pops up in less than fifteen seconds, replace the thermocouple.

Suburban Pilot Adjustment

Two types of gas valves (Figure 3.37) are used for manual-light Suburban water heaters: Robertshaw (Unitrol) and SIT. The current models (as of mid-1995) use the SIT valves. A pilot-flame-adjustment screw is provided for both model's gas valves. The adjustment is on the front and to the right in the Robertshaw valve and on the right side in the SIT. This is the only way to adjust the pilot flame. The pilot flame should engulf the tip of the thermocouple and be blue or orange-blue in color.

Main-Burner Adjustment

The main-burner flame can also affect the pilot flame and determine the overall performance of the water heater. The proper steps for adjustment are as follows:

1. Slide the air-shutter valve so that it is about one-quarter of the way open (Figure 3.38).
2. The flame should burn predominantly blue with a short tip of yellow.
3. If the flame is too yellow, open the shutter slightly until only a tip of yellow is visible. This may be necessary for optimum heater performance at high elevations.
4. The flame should not roar excessively. If it does, it is likely that the air shutter is open too far and the gas mixture is too lean. Close the shutter slightly until you see a slight tip of yellow on a blue flame. Tighten the shutter-locking screw or nut.
5. If the flame will not adjust, it is possible that the main-burner jet is clogged, incorrectly centered in the burner tube, or the burner tube itself contains dirt and obstructions.
6. Turn off the flame, loosen the burner-tube hold-down screws, and remove the tube from the end of the gas-control valve (Figure 3.39).
7. The burner jet is located in the end of the gas-control valve and is removable with a small wrench. Check to see that the jet is

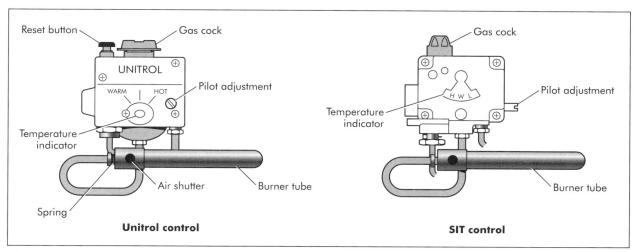

Figure 3.37 Suburban hot-water tanks use Unitrol (left) or SIT (right) gas valve.

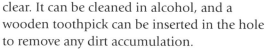

Figure 3.38 Adjust air-shutter valve for proper air/gas mixture.

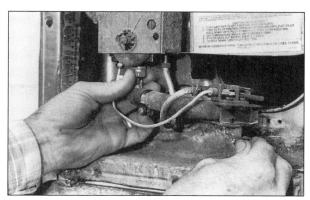

Figure 3.39 The burner jet in the hot-water tank is located in the end of the gas-control valve.

clear. It can be cleaned in alcohol, and a wooden toothpick can be inserted in the hole to remove any dirt accumulation.

8. Clean the inside of the burner tube (Figure 3.40).
9. Install the jet and burner tube and attempt to light; adjust the air shutter to attain a proper flame.

Suburban Late-Model Main-Burner Adjustment

The burner flame cannot be adjusted on later-model Suburban water heaters; the older ones with an air-shutter control can be adjusted as previously described. The burner assembly is preset from the factory. Generally, the water heater is certified to work

as designed in altitudes up to 4,500 feet. Operation above this elevation should be derated (orifice change) by 4 percent for every 1,000-foot gain in elevation (Figure 3.41). If you live in a high-altitude area, have your qualified service technician (certified by Suburban) make the orifice change. This should not be necessary when traveling briefly in high-altitude areas.

Main-Burner Alignment

The manifold and main burner must align with the center of the burner tube for the gas to mix properly with the incoming air (Figure 3.42). Check to see that the center of the jet is parallel with the center of the burner tube, so that the orifice disperses the gas

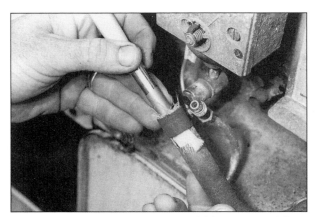

Figure 3.40 The burner jet should be inspected for any accumulation of dirt.

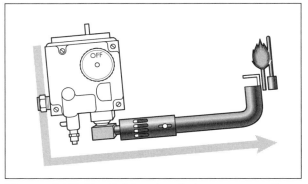

Figure 3.42 Manifold and main burner must align with the center of the burner tube.

straight down the center of the burner tube. If it is not, the tube can be loosened and rotated slightly up or down until the jet is parallel, or the control can be moved. If the control is backed off to make the alignment, make sure there are no water leaks at the coupling. Tighten the tube hold-down screws.

Atwood Electric Element

Some Atwood hot-water tanks are equipped with a 120-volt AC heating element. If it fails to heat the water, the following steps should be taken:

CAUTION: Always use care when diagnosing 120-volt AC appliances. If you are not experienced with 120-volt AC voltage, have a professional technician make the diagnosis and repairs.

1. Make sure the power to the water heater is off.
2. Remove junction-box cover in the rear of the water heater.
3. Make sure the control switch is in the on position and that there is power to the water heater. Use a multimeter to measure voltage.
4. Locate and manually reset the ECO high-limit switch.
5. Make sure there is continuity (use a multimeter) between the wire leads connected to the electric thermostat (Figure 3.43).
6. Move temperature dial to high if water is not sufficiently hot.
7. Make sure the connection between the heating element and electric thermostat is good.
8. Confirm that there is continuity between

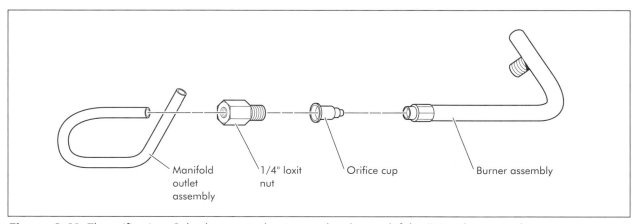

Manifold outlet assembly   1/4" loxit nut   Orifice cup   Burner assembly

Figure 3.41 The orifice in a Suburban water heater can be changed if the RV is always used in high-altitude areas.

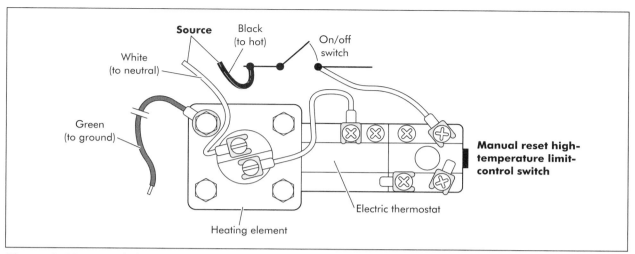

Figure 3.43 Atwood electric heating element and thermostat used in later model water heaters.

center screws in the heating element (the ones with wire connections).

9. If there is continuity between the flange of the heating element and the screw in the heating element (the one with a wire lead that goes to the electric thermostat), the heating element has shorted and must be replaced.

10. Make sure there is a good ground to the heating element.

CAUTION: The heating element will self-destruct if allowed to operate for an extended time with the tank empty. If the heating element is allowed to run in a dry tank, allow the tank to cool for two to three hours before adding water. This will prevent the tank from possibly collapsing.

Atwood Bolt-on Heating Element

Early model Atwood water heaters used a bolt-on 120-volt AC heating element (Figure 3.44) and a one-piece thermostat/ECO limit switch. The adjustable rectangular thermostat is surface mounted to the inner tank using a steel clip. If this thermostat is making unobstructed contact with the aluminum tank, and the temperature is set to the high position, the water should heat to 130°F. Keep in mind that the heating process is slower on electric than on gas. Heating elements in 1996 were changed to have a 1,400-watt rating (from 1,500 watts) to provide a better cushion for the 15-amp breaker (it now draws 12.7 amps). This increases heating time slightly.

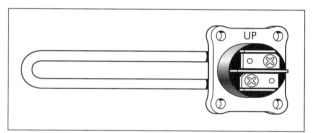

Figure 3.44 Atwood bolt-on heating element

Atwood Screw-in Heating Element

Current Atwood water heaters use a screw-in 120-volt AC heating element (Figure 3.45) and a separate preset thermostat and ECO limit switch. It is rated at 1,400 watts. The thermostat is set at 140°F and is the same type of unit that's used on the gas side of the electronic-ignition water heaters. The ECO is a backup thermostat and will trip if the thermostat fails and the water temperature exceeds 180°F.

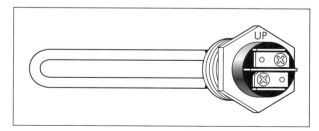

Figure 3.45 Atwood screw-in heating element

Suburban Electric Element

The most common problem is energizing the water heater before filling with water. This may trip the RV circuit breaker or the high-limit switch in the water heater. If the unit fails to heat, follow these steps:

1. Check the circuit breaker in the RV panel. Reset if tripped.
2. Check for 120 volts AC to the on/off switch in the lower left-hand corner of the control panel. If voltage is present on one side of the switch, and the heater still doesn't work, replace the switch.
3. Press the reset button in the control panel.
4. Check all wire connections if the unit fails to heat after resetting the button.
5. Check the heating element for continuity using a multimeter.
6. If the water heater becomes too hot and activates the reset control, push the reset switch pad.
7. Make sure the thermostat is being held tightly against the tank.

Atwood Electronic Ignition (DSI) Water Heater

Water heaters with a direct-spark ignition (DSI) system rely on a circuit board that provides a spark to light the flame when the switch is placed in the on position. Electrodes sense the flame within six to eight seconds; if a signal is not sensed, the circuit board will shut down the gas valve, and the system goes into safety lockout. The thermostat uses a normally closed, nonadjustable temperature switch that sends current to the circuit board; it opens when the water temperature reaches 140°F. A one-shot heat-

sensing fuse (thermal shutoff) will trip when water temperature exceeds 190°F. This fuse is located on the incoming power wire and connected to the thermostat. Obstructions in the main-burner tube or flue tube due to spiders or mud wasps are the usual cause for the thermal cutoff to trip. These obstructions cause the main-burner flame to burn outside the main-burner tube, a very dangerous situation. If this happens, consult your dealer for repairs. An ECO limit switch sends voltage to the solenoid valve and will open if water temperature exceeds 180°F. The dual-solenoid valve will only open and send gas to the electrodes when there's a minimum of 10.5 volts DC.

Suburban Electronic Ignition (DSI) Water Heater

The Suburban DSI water heater is designed to work when DC voltage is between 10.5 and 13.5. Excessive voltage can damage the circuit board. Voltage should be supplied from the filtered side of the converter. When there is a call for heat, a high-voltage spark is generated from the spark electrode to ground. The spark gap (between the electrode and ground) should

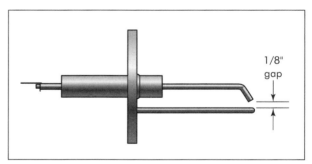

Figure 3.46 Spark gap in an Atwood DSI water heater

■ CHECKLIST ■
ATWOOD DSI SYSTEM

- Make sure battery voltage is more than 10.5 volts.
- Tank must be filled to operate. If water heater is lit before filling, ECO will almost immediately shut down operation.
- Make sure main-burner tube is clear of spider webs and corrosion.
- Check that the spark gap (the space between electrode and ground) is ⅛ inch (Figure 3.46).

CAUTION: A gap that is too wide and arching to ground can damage the circuit board.

be ⅛ inch. The unit is designed to allow for a fifteen-second purge at the start of the heating cycle followed by a 6 to 8-second trial for ignition. Sparking ceases when the flame is present. The water heater is protected by a high-temperature-limit ECO switch that trips when water temperature exceeds 180°F. Thermostats are preset for 130°F water. The burner cannot activate unless water temperature falls below 100°F. The water heater uses a thermostat/ECO switch (Figure 3.47) in a bracket that must keep both switches tight against the tank. The ECO can be reset manually by pushing a button.

Suburban Electrode Assembly

The igniter will go into lockout if the signal from the electrode is too small. It locks when the DC current falls to 1.5 microamps. Using a microamp meter, the flame current should be 3 microamps. To measure flame current, use the following procedure:

Shut off power to the system and remove the flame-sensing wire from the electrode terminal and insert the microamp meter in series with the sensor electrode and ground. The positive terminal of the meter goes to the component board and the negative terminal to the sensing electrode.

Energize the igniter. The reading should be 3 microamps.

If the microamps are too low, continue with the following:

1. Check input polarity. Terminal 1 should be hot (12 volts DC) with respect to ground. Terminal 6 is neutral (0 voltage) with respect to ground.
2. Check for proper grounding. If a flame is present during the trial for ignition period, but the system shuts down, make sure the burner is properly grounded.
3. Check the electrode ceramic for cracks or carbon.
4. Make sure electrode leads are not corroded. Clean if necessary.
5. Check the sensor-wire continuity with a multimeter.
6. Check the spark gap; it must be ⅛ inch.

If no spark is present, check the following:

1. Terminal 1 at the circuit board should have voltage. If not, clean the connections at the circuit board with a pencil eraser first.
2. Check the voltage through ECO and the thermostat. If voltage is on one side and not the other, replace thermostat or ECO. Inspect the connections.
3. If voltage is present through ECO and the thermostat to the module board, and there is still no sparking, replace the circuit board.
4. If replacing the circuit board fails to correct the problem, check the high-voltage wire for cracks or breaks, and replace if necessary.

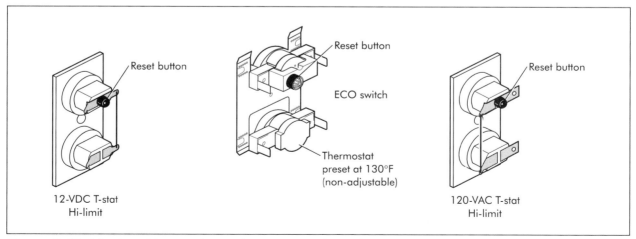

Figure 3.47 Suburban DSI water heater thermostats and reset buttons: Models SW6D, SW6DE, and SW6DM (left); V-series (center); Models SW6PE, SW6PER, SW6DE (right).

Sparking should occur and the gas valve should open simultaneously if power is supplied to the igniter. If sparking occurs and the valve fails to open, check the following:

1. Place a voltmeter (multimeter) between terminal 4 on the input connector and ground (or across the valve). Recycle the ignitor by turning the on/off switch to off for five seconds and then back on. Voltage should be present at valve.
2. If voltage is present and the valve fails to open, remove the wires from the valve terminals and retest the valve on a known voltage source. If the valve fails to function, replace it.
3. Make sure circuit board connections are good.
4. If voltage is not present at terminals 4 and 6 or at the valve, replace the circuit board.

Tank Cleaning

If the hot-water tank is used a great deal during the year, you may want to flush it out a number of times to remove accumulation of dirt and scale that can shorten tank life. To clean the tank:

1. Turn off the main water supply, either the city supply or the 12-volt DC pump.
2. Drain the tank by removing the plug, the anode rod, or opening the wing-shaped drain petcock on the outside of the tank, depending on the style of water heater (Figure 3.48).

Figure 3.48 Some water heater models use a petcock for draining the water.

Figure 3.49 Pressure relief valve will open when the temperature exceeds 150°F.

3. Open the relief valve to admit air to speed draining (Figure 3.49).
4. If the drain valve becomes clogged while draining, a small wire, such as a coat hanger, pushed through the drain opening will dislodge any scale blocking the water's path.
5. With the city water connected and turned on, flush the heater for about five minutes through the drain valve. This will dislodge and flush corrosive scale particles from the tank.
6. Close the drain or replace the plug/anode rod; open a hot-water faucet inside the RV to bleed air from the tank. Close the faucet; the tank is now clean and flushed.

Replacing the Suburban Anode Rod

Certain Suburban water heaters are protected by an anode rod (Figure 3.50) that also serves as the drain plug. Replacement of this rod is recommended when the consumption of the material or weight loss is greater than 75 percent (Figure 3.51). The anode is a sacrificial rod that provides cathodic protection for the tank. It is very important; failure to replace the anode rod in a timely manner may lead to premature tank wear and void the manufacturer's warranty.

Leaking Pressure-Temperature Relief Valve

All hot-water tanks are protected by pressure-relief valves designed to "pop" when water temperature ex-

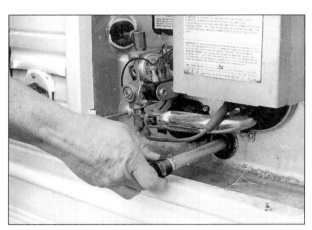

Figure 3.50 An anode rod is used to protect the tank in certain Suburban water heaters.

ceeds 150°F. In most cases, weeping or dripping of this valve does not mean it's defective. Most likely the air space needs to be returned to the top of the tank. To replace the air, follow these steps:

1. Drain the hot-water tank while the faucets remain open.
2. Close the faucets and turn the water pump on. Make sure there's water in the freshwater tank.
3. Allow the hot-water tank to fill—until the water pump cycles off.
4. Light the water heater (or turn on the switch for DSI models).
5. When the water heater cycles off (water is up to temperature), slowly open each hot-water faucet until the water flows smoothly.

6. Air is now returned to the top of the hot-water tank and normal use can continue.

PrecisionTemp Instantaneous Water Heater

The RV 500 instantaneous water heater supplies continuous hot water upon demand. It uses a microprocessor to control the heating of the water. The tank holds less than a pint of water, making winterization very simple. All you have to do is open a valve and drain the water from the tank or fill the tank with nontoxic antifreeze. There's no need for a bypass kit (see Winterizing the Water System, page 3.31).

When LP-gas and 12-volt DC power are supplied to the RV 500 water heater, and there's no water flow, the unit will remain dormant except for a green LED (Figure 3.52) flashing once each second. The microprocessor is actively monitoring the three temperature sensors, the set temperature request, and the water flow each half second in anticipation of a request for hot water. When the hot-water faucet is opened and flow is at least 0.4 gallons per minute (GPM), the microprocessor sends ignition voltage to the modulating valve and powers the ignition relay on the board. The voltage must be at least 10.8 volts DC for the water heater to function.

If there is no green LED flashing or it stays on but does not flash, take the following steps:

1. Check that the power is on and the panel breaker is not tripped. With the power off, detach the ¼-inch spade terminal leads of the

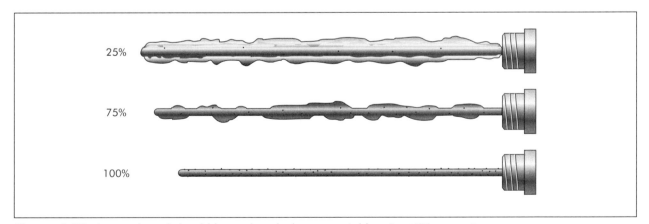

25%

75%

100%

Figure 3.51 An anode rod should be replaced when material loss is at 75 percent.

Figure 3.52 PrecisionTemp instantaneous water heater uses LEDs for diagnosing problems. Microprocesser is in a pull-out drawer.

power supply. Turn the power on and check for voltage with a multimeter.
2. Be sure all electrical connectors are secure and that polarity has not be reversed
   CAUTION: Reverse polarity will damage the circuit boards.
3. If you have connected the power supply (12-volt DC) lead from the converter, make sure it is hooked to a filtered terminal. If you cannot find a filtered connection, hook the power lead directly to the battery. The RV 500 must have clean DC voltage to operate properly. It can only tolerate less than plus or minus 0.3 volts AC (dirty voltage).

If the green LED flashes, but no ignition (igniter sparks, no gas), take the following steps:

1. Check that the pop-out button in the ECO limit switch is pushed in. This switch opens when the water temperature exceeds 165°F and requires manual reset.
2. Make sure the propane supply is on and that there is propane in the storage tank/cylinder. Gas pressure may be too low to operate the unit. The supply line should be at least ³⁄₁₆ inch in diameter and shorter than 25 feet in length.
3. Check for a faulty on/off solenoid at the tank/cylinder that works with the propane-leak detector. Also, if the unit is equipped with an on/off solenoid, make sure the orifice is at least ³⁄₁₆ inch in diameter.

If your RV 500 water heater has a large fluctuation in temperature, take the following steps:

1. If operating a demand water pump, you probably need to install an accumulator tank with a rubber bladder. The pulsing of the water pump confuses the flowmeter.
2. Check the aerators and strainers used on the faucets and showerhead. If they become clogged, water flow is restricted below the minimum required to activate the system.
3. Make sure the water connections in back are not reversed. The RV 500 is opposite the standard-type RV hot-water tanks on the market.
4. Check the flowmeter for direction. It should turn counterclockwise.
5. The flame may be cycling between minimum burn and off. If so, check the water flow as described below.

Determining Cold-Water Bypass for RV 500

A cold-water crossover may occur when the cold water is connected to the hot-water line, and is allowed to enter the hot-water line between the water heater and the point of use. Examples include showers, hot-water-tank bypass kits, showers with a shutoff in the showerhead, washing machines, dishwashers, and in plumbing to water-use appliances (usually in parallel instead of in series). There can also be a planned crossover in the shower. The federal government has mandated that shower-mixing valves have anti-scald provisions built into them. If so equipped, you cannot get 100 percent hot water from the showerhead when the cold-water valve is off—designed to allow bleeding of cold water. Thus the lavatory sink may have hotter water than the showerhead.

Flowmeter Checkout

To check the flowmeter, follow these steps:

1. Find the 3-pin connector in the circuit board. Using a multimeter, hook the positive probe to the red wire in the back of the connector and the negative probe to the black wire.

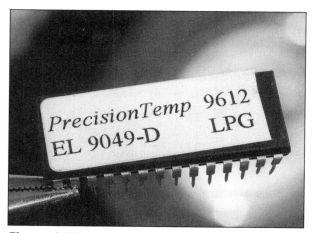

Figure 3.53 Latest microcontroller provides additional diagnostics for RV 500 instantaneous water heater.

With the power on, voltage should read 4 volts DC. If not, the flowmeter must be replaced.

2. Move the positive probe to the middle or white wire of the flowmeter. Turn water on so that flow is greater than 0.5 gpm. The meter should jump to values between 0 and 5 volts DC. If not, replace the flowmeter.

3. If your unit has an EL 9049-D or later version microcontroller (Figure 3.53), conduct the following test: With the power on and the water running, watch the green LED. The LED will flash approximately once each second. Watch the LED to find one delay between flashes (1.5 seconds versus 1 second). Begin counting green LED flashes until the next longer delay. The flashes correspond to water flow. Each flash is ⅛ of a gallon. Use the formula: *Water flow, GPM=number of green flashes ÷ 8*. You can confirm this by running water into a gallon bucket and using a stopwatch.

Service Codes

As long as your RV 500 has the EL 9049-D or later microcontroller, you can use a series of red LED flashes to diagnose problems.

- *Red double flash per second*: T_mid thermister has failed.
- *Single red flash*: T_out thermister has failed.

- *Two red flashes*: T_in thermister has failed.
- *Three red flashes*: T_mid thermister is not in the 30° to 160°F operational range.
- *Four red flashes*: T_out thermister is not in the 30° to 180°F operational range.
- *Five red flashes*: T_in thermister is not in the 30° to 110°F operational range.
- *Six red flashes*: Water is flowing through the unit backward. Water inlet and outlet connections must be reversed.
- *Seven red flashes*: Direct spark ignition (DSI) has timed out after two 3 to 5-second ignition attempts and the DSI board has locked out. Sequence will be repeated after 45 seconds. You can also reset the DSI by turning off the water for a few seconds, and then on. The red LED will continue to flash even though the unit is now operating. To reset the LED, turn the power off, then on.

■ WINTERIZING THE WATER SYSTEM ■

Winterizing the RV's water system is necessary to protect all components from freezing. There are two ways to accomplish the job:

1. Drain all water from the system and use compressed air to blow out remaining water that may lie in low spots within the system.
2. Fill the system with a potable nontoxic antifreeze until all water is removed from the system.

In each case, the hot-water tank must be drained. When a nontoxic winterizing fluid is used, it is best to install a winterizing (bypass) kit that allows the water system to bypass the hot-water tank so that expensive antifreeze is not needed to fill the heater.

Winterizing Using Compressed Air

To winterize using compressed air, follow these steps:

CAUTION: Use only nontoxic antifreeze designed for RV use.

1. Open all drains in the system, including the hot-water tank.

2. If you are going to use the compressed-air method, purchase an air-fitting adapter for the city-water connection so that you can blow the air from that location (Figure 3.54).

3. Operate the 12-volt DC pump with a faucet open until it runs dry. You can also drain the system from the water-heater drain plug while running the water pump.

4. Connect the air fitting to the city-water hookup and close all the drains except the one for the hot-water tank.

5. Blow air through the city-water hookup until all the water is removed from the hot-water tank.

6. Close the bypass valves to the water heater. Open the faucet farthest from the water pump. Blow air through the city-hookup line until only air comes out of the faucet.

7. Open another faucet (farthest ones first) and then close the first one; blow out the line until all the water is gone. Continue this procedure until all faucets, including the shower, are drained.

8. Open the toilet valve; allow the air to force out any water there.

9. Close all faucets; the system is winterized.

Winterizing Using Nontoxic Antifreeze

CAUTION: Use only nontoxic antifreeze designed for RV use.

If you choose to fill the system with nontoxic antifreeze there are a couple of methods you can use (Figure 3.55). Installation of a hot-water-tank bypass kit will avoid having to fill the entire water heater with antifreeze.

Pour a couple gallons of potable nontoxic antifreeze directly into the freshwater tank of the RV. Operate the water pump so that the solution will flow through all the lines, starting with the faucet farthest from the pump. Leave the faucet open until the antifreeze is visible (pink in color). Operate each faucet in the same fashion until all lines are filled with the fluid.

Another method requires less fluid since you do not pour it into the water tank. A connection is made at the inlet side of the water pump, and the antifreeze is drawn from the container through the pump, filling all the lines and accessories in the water system. You must make sure that the freshwater tank and the hot-water tank are drained completely.

Shut off all faucets and turn off the water pump; the system is winterized. After the winter storage period, the hot-water bypass valves must be turned on after the antifreeze has been flushed out of the system. The fluid is tasteless, odorless, and nontoxic, but it's a good idea to sanitize the system (see page 3.6) after a winter-long storage stint.

Figure 3.54 Commercial air-fitting for city-water hookup is used to blow out the water lines.

Figure 3.55 Use only non-toxic antifreeze to winterize the RV water system.

CHAPTER 4

SANITATION SYSTEMS

Manufacturers of RVs have several approaches to handling sanitation but they almost exclusively use a black-water holding tank to capture sewage from the toilet, a gray-water holding tank to capture drain water from the shower, lavatory, and kitchen sink, and myriad lines leading to the dump valves. Depending on floor plans, some large fifth-wheels and motorhomes may have a separate gray-water holding tank to service the galley area.

■ TOILETS ■

Three types of toilets are used in RV applications: freshwater, recirculating, and portable. The most common type of toilet, the freshwater, is mounted permanently, flushing with clean water from the RV's onboard freshwater storage tank. The flushing mechanism, whether a foot-operated pedal or a hand-operated lever, allows a valve in the bottom of the bowl to open, permitting the contents to be flushed into the holding tank. A stream of water under pressure from the RV's water system swirls around the bowl, cleaning it and flushing the contents into the holding tank. Many models have two levers, each working independently of the other so the bowl can be filled with water prior to use. Other types of toilets have a dual-position foot-operated lever.

Freshwater toilet bowls are made of either durable plastic or porcelain, depending on the brand and model. These toilets flush using simple, dependable components. A vacuum breaker (back-flow restrictor) mounted at the rear of the toilet prevents water from the toilet from backing into the RV's freshwater system. The vacuum breaker works by cre-

ating a vacuum in the toilet water supply line so that water flowing to other faucets in the RV will not suck water from the toilet.

Maintaining the Freshwater Toilet

While freshwater toilets require little maintenance, certain precautions must be taken to prolong the life of the mechanisms, especially the slide ball, or flapper valve. The first rule of thumb is to make sure all the contents are removed (flow into the holding tank) from the bowl before closing the valve. If toilet paper gets caught between the valve and seal, the toilet may emit odors from the holding tank. If paper or contents become lodged in the seal, the cleaning process is not pleasant. Do not use a sharp object (Figure 4.1) to clean the seal area since damage may occur.

To clean the toilet, use a nonabrasive cleaner and a soft rag or paper towel. Do not use a highly concentrated or high-acid-content household cleaner. Scouring powder or other abrasives can damage the seal and other plastic parts in the toilet mechanism.

Thetford Freshwater Toilets

If the toilet must be removed to replace a leaky flange seal, proceed with the following steps for the various models of Thetford freshwater toilets.

Replacing the Aqua-Magic Aurora To replace the Aqua-Magic Aurora model toilet (Figure 4.2):

1. Turn off the water supply to the toilet.

Figure 4.1 A Q-tip can be used to clean the valve seal in the toilet

2. Insert a 2½-inch object to prop open the slide valve in the flush hole. Attach a cord or wire to keep it from falling into the holding tank.
3. Remove the side-access covers. These snap out from the top of the cover.
4. Remove the water line from the water-valve elbow while supporting the elbow with a wrench.
5. Use a 12-point, ½-inch ratcheting box-end wrench to remove the hold-down nuts.
6. Lift the toilet from the mounting flange.
7. Reverse the procedure when replacing the toilet. Use a new toilet seal. The Aurora toilet has a universal flange designed to fit the bolt patterns of all current-model RV toilets.

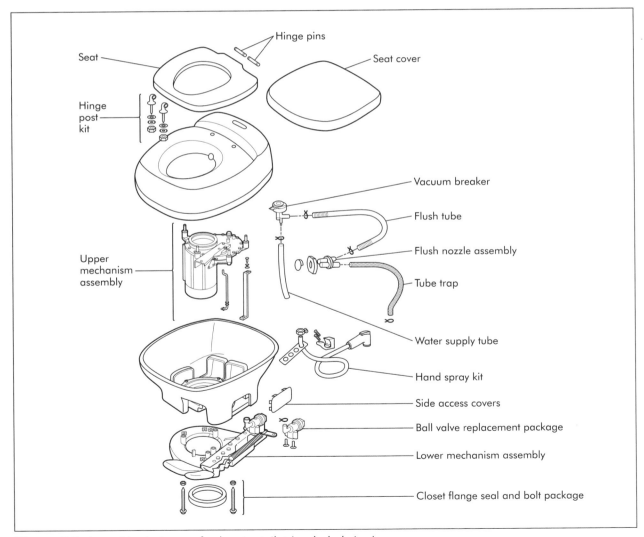

Figure 4.2 Aqua-Magic Aurora freshwater toilet (exploded view)

■ TROUBLESHOOTING ■
THE THETFORD AQUA-MAGIC IV TOILET

Problem	Possible Cause	Correction
Water keeps running into bowl	Sticking levers	Make sure levers return all the way to left
	Sticking slide valve	Remove foreign material from blade or seat; replace if cleaning does not work.
Toilet leaks on floor	Leaking water-supply line	Tighten as necessary
	Loose closet-flange nuts	Tighten as necessary
	Wrong closet-flange height	Make sure flange height is between ¼ and ⁷⁄₁₆ inch
	Defective closet flange	Replace seal
Poor flush	Flush duration too short	Hold levers open for at least two to three seconds
	Bad water flow	Adjust flow rate to 10 quarts per minute

CAUTION: Do not overtighten the water-line fitting or damage will result.

Replacing the Aqua-Magic IV Model Toilet To replace the Aqua-Magic IV model toilet (Figure 4.3):

1. Turn off the water supply to the toilet. If you do not have a valve behind the toilet, make sure the water pump is off or the water-hookup faucet is shut. Purge any pressure from the line by releasing the toilet valve.
2. Disconnect the water-supply line from the water valve located at the rear of the toilet. Hold the water-valve hex nut with an $^{11}/_{16}$-inch wrench while loosening the water-line fitting. Be careful not to exert too much force or the fitting can become damaged.
3. Remove the mounting flange bolts.
4. Lift the toilet from the mounting flange.
5. Reverse this procedure when replacing the toilet. Use a new toilet seal.

CAUTION: Do not overtighten the water-line fitting or damage will result.

Replacing Aqua-Magic Galaxy or Starlite Models To replace either the Aqua-Magic Galaxy or Starlite model toilets (Figure 4.4):

1. Turn off the water supply to the toilet.
2. Insert a 2½-inch object to prop open the slide valve in the flush hole. Attach a cord or wire to keep it from falling into the holding tank. Use a 12-point, ½-inch ratcheting box-end wrench to reach the front bolt through the opening above the foot pedal.
3. Remove the rear bolt—positioned at about 11 o'clock—using the ratcheting box-end wrench if there is room between the toilet and the wall. If there is not adequate room, the bolt can be reached via the access hole in the top of the toilet. Pry the plug open with a coin and insert a deep ½-inch socket and universal swivel attached to a 12-inch extension to remove the nut.
4. Lift the toilet from the mounting flange.
5. Reverse this procedure when replacing the toilet. Use a new toilet seal.

CAUTION: Do not overtighten the water-line fitting or damage will result.

Winterizing Thetford Freshwater Toilets The water-supply line can be drained by propping open the slide valve in the flush hole. This can be accomplished by using a soft-drink bottle or like object to hold the valve open. Attach a cord or wire to keep object from falling into the holding tank. Blow out the lines using compressed air or fill the lines with nontoxic antifreeze. If you are using antifreeze, open the toilet valve until the antifreeze flows constantly. (See Winterizing the Water System, page 3.31).

CAUTION: If compressed air is used to purge the water from the RV system, the toilet valve must be held in the open position. Do not attempt

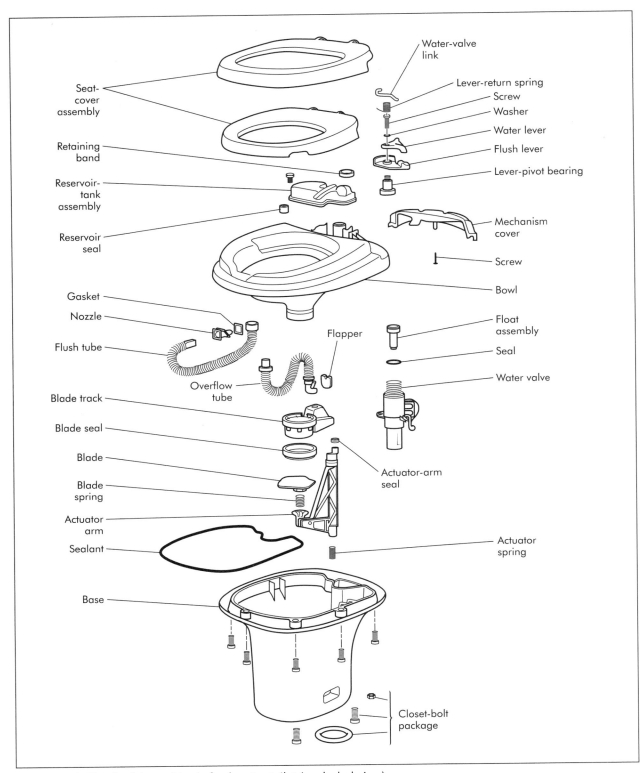

Figure 4.3 Thetford Aqua-Magic freshwater toilet (exploded view)

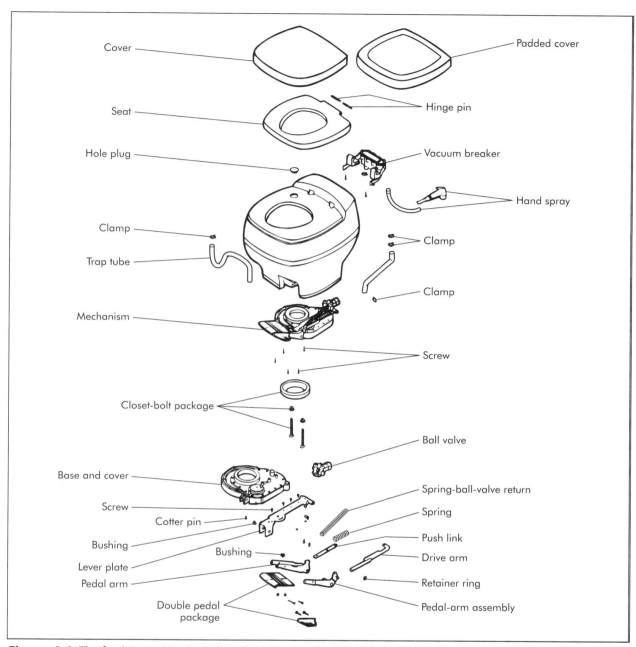

Figure 4.4 Thetford Aqua-Magic Galaxy freshwater toilet (exploded view)

■ **TROUBLESHOOTING** ■

THE THETFORD AURORA, GALAXY, AND STARLITE TOILETS

Problem	Possible Cause	Correction
Water keeps running into bowl	Slide valve is not seated	Clean all foreign material in groove where valve blade seats when closed
Leaks	Leaking water-supply line	Tighten as necessary
	Leaking vacuum breaker	Replace vacuum breaker; replace ball valve if vacuum breaker leaks without flushing
	Defective bowl-to-mechanism seal	Replace seal
	Defective closet-flange-to-floor seal	Tighten flange nuts; remove toilet and check flange height; adjust to ¼ to ⁷⁄₁₆ inch above floor; replace flange seal.
Harder than normal foot pedal or	Mounting bolts too tight	Check for oversight condition and adjust sticking blade
	Restricted valve blade	Apply light film of silicone spray on blade **CAUTION**: Do not use hydrocarbon-based lubricants; damage to seals and other surfaces can occur.

to flush the toilet if it contains ice. Doing so will damage the toilet's internal valves.

SeaLand Traveler Freshwater Toilets

The SeaLand Traveler freshwater toilet is available in several models (Figures 4.5, 4.6, 4.7, and 4.8). If the Traveler toilet needs to be removed to replace a defective flange seal or to remodel the bathroom, proceed with the following steps:

Replacing the SeaLand Traveler Freshwater Toilet

To remove and/or replace the SeaLand Traveler toilet, follow these steps:

1. Remove the shroud near the floor by reaching behind the edges and pulling outward while the shroud is pulled forward. Do not force; the shroud should be removed with light pressure.

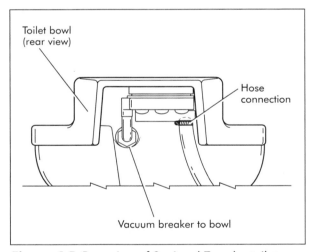

Figure 4.5 Rear view of SeaLand Traveler toilet showing vacuum breaker and water connection

2. Disconnect the water-supply line by loosening the ½-inch fittings.
3. Remove the four flange nuts.
4. Lift and remove the toilet.
5. Reverse this order to reinstall. Use a new flange seal.

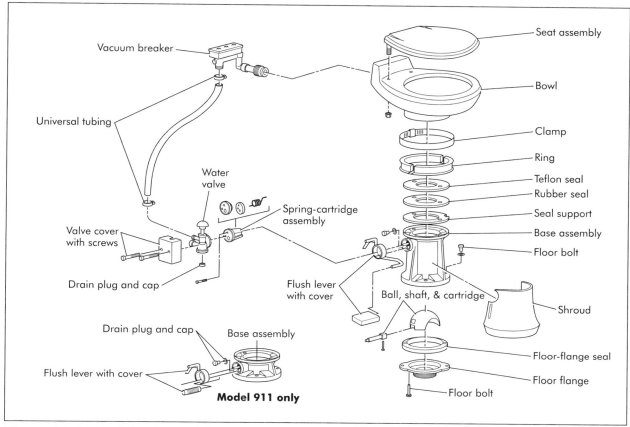

Figure 4.6 SeaLand Traveler models 910 and 911 freshwater toilets (exploded view)

CAUTION: Do not overtighten the water-line fitting or damage will result.

Winterizing the SeaLand Traveler Toilet

To winterize the SeaLand Traveler toilet, follow these steps:

1. Clean and flush the toilet.
2. Turn off the water supply in the RV.
3. Remove the drain plug.
4. Remove the drain cap from the bottom of the water valve in Models 910 and 510 (Figure 4.9).
5. Depress the flush lever until all water is drained from the system. Blow out the lines using compressed air or fill the lines with nontoxic antifreeze. If you are using antifreeze, open the toilet valve until the antifreeze flows constantly. (See Winterizing the Water System, page 3.31).

CAUTION: If compressed air is used to purge the water from the RV system, the toilet valve must be held in the open position. Do not attempt to flush the toilet if it contains ice. Doing so will damage the toilet's internal valves.

Microphor Microflush Toilets

The Microphor Microflush freshwater toilet is usually found only in high-line coaches and trailers. The toilet is similar in size and style to a home model, but uses both water pressure and compressed air to operate. Air pressure is used to expel wastewater over the trapway to the holding tank. The compressed air reduces water consumption by almost 90 percent. Microphor toilets, when installed and adjusted properly, are rated to flush using only a half-gallon of water.

The Microflush uses the following sequence to

■ **TROUBLESHOOTING** ■
THE THETFORD ELECTRA MAGIC RECIRCULATING TOILET

Problem	Possible Cause	Correction
Toilet wobbles	Closet flange too high; mounting surface too high	Check by laying straightedge across flange and measuring gap to floor at four leg locations; height should be ¼ to ⁷⁄₁₆ inch.
Flush action too weak or noisy	Pump running backward	Check wire polarity: black is positive, white is negative
	Cycling without sufficient water	Charge with 3 gallons of water or to charge-level-indicator lens

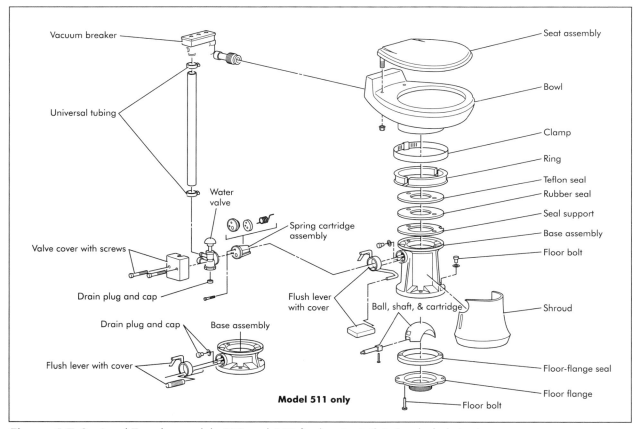

Figure 4.7 SeaLand Traveler models 510 and 511 freshwater toilets (exploded view)

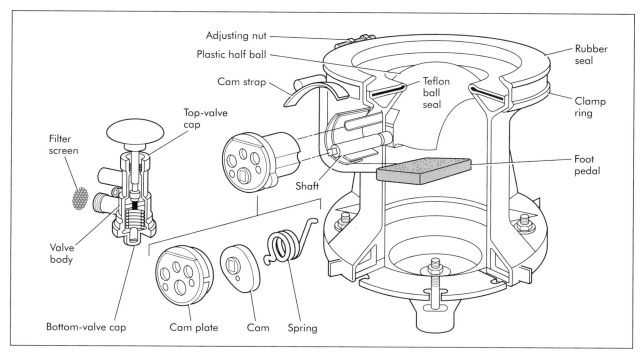

Figure 4.8 SeaLand Traveler freshwater toilet base (exploded view)

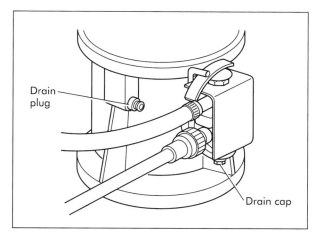

Figure 4.9 Location of the water valve drain cap in the SeaLand Traveler freshwater toilet.

flush (Figure 4.10): The handle is pressed, opening a flapper valve and allowing the water in the bowl to flow into the lower chamber. Clean water enters from around the rim, washing the bowl. After a few seconds, the flapper valve closes, and clean water continues to flow into the bowl, ready for the next use. After the flapper valve is closed, compressed air is released into the lower chamber, forcing the contents out the discharge line (Figure 4.11).

Adjusting the Microflush Toilet   To adjust the Microflush toilet, follow these steps (Figure 4.12):

1. Turn on water to the toilet.
2. Adjust the flapper cycle to five to seven seconds by turning the flush-cycle timing adjustment: to lengthen the cycle, turn the timing adjustment clockwise: to shorten, turn counterclockwise.
3. Adjust the water level in the bowl to the top edge of the flapper opening by turning the water-shutoff valve (angle stop) next to the toilet.

Cleaning the Microflush Toilet   To properly clean the Microflush toilet, follow these steps:

1. Depress the flush activator, turn off water, and allow bowl cleaner to flow to the lower chamber while the activator continues to be depressed. Any liquid toilet-bowl cleaner is acceptable, but do not use caustic drain openers.
2. Insert a bowl brush into the lower chamber and agitate.

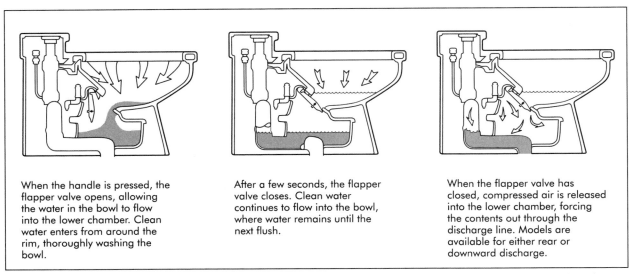

When the handle is pressed, the flapper valve opens, allowing the water in the bowl to flow into the lower chamber. Clean water enters from around the rim, thoroughly washing the bowl.

After a few seconds, the flapper valve closes. Clean water continues to flow into the bowl, where water remains until the next flush.

When the flapper valve has closed, compressed air is released into the lower chamber, forcing the contents out through the discharge line. Models are available for either rear or downward discharge.

Figure 4.10 Microphor Microflush freshwater toilets use compressed air and water pressure to complete the flushing cycle.

3. Remove the brush and release the flush activator.
4. Turn on water and flush twice to rinse thoroughly.

Routine Maintenance of Microflush Toilet   Water pressure should be maintained at levels below 50 psi. Air pressure should be regulated at 60 psi. The air-operated flush valve requires lubrication every five years. The Microflush toilet becomes more complicated when installed in RVs. Internal repairs and adjustments other than those detailed here should be performed by an authorized service center.

■ THE RECIRCULATING TOILET ■

Thetford Electra Magic Toilet

A recirculating toilet (Figure 4.13) requires no pressure-water connection or holding tank. This type of toilet uses a 12-volt DC pump and a system of filters to recirculate the contents. The liquid portion is separated from the solid contents and is used to complete the flushing cycle. When the contents fill the internal holding tank, the toilet must be dumped by use of a 3-inch termination valve, similar to those used to dump holding tanks. A holding tank can be installed to increase toilet capacity.

Replacing the Electra Magic Toilet Fuse   To replace a fuse in the Thetford Electra Magic toilet, follow these steps:

1. Remove the two cover-mounting screws and motor cover.
2. Check the fuse with a multimeter.
3. Replace if detective.

Replacing the Electra Magic Toilet Switch   To replace the Electra Magic toilet switch, follow these steps:

1. Disconnect the lead wires from the power source.
2. Remove the two cover-mounting screws and the motor cover.
3. Remove the switch-retaining nut and remove the wires from switch terminals.
4. Check with a multimeter.
5. Replace if defective.

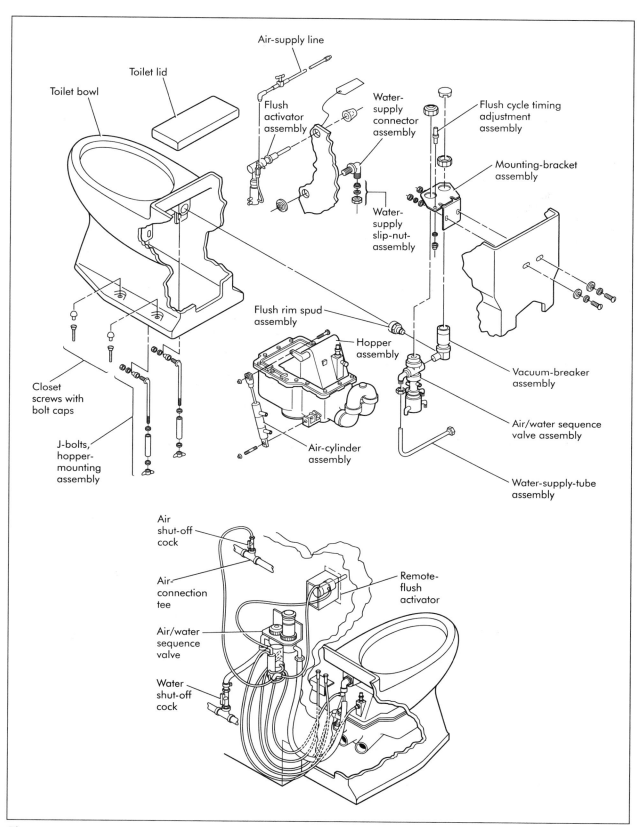

Figure 4.11 Microphor Microflush freshwater toilet (exploded view)

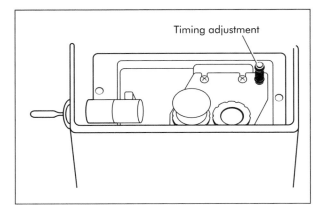

Figure 4.12 The flush cycle in the Microphor Microflush is controlled by the timing adjustment under the toilet lid.

Replacing the Electra Magic Toilet Pump   To replace the Electra Magic toilet pump, follow these steps:

1. Disconnect the lead wires from the power source.
2. Remove the two cover-mounting screws and the motor cover.
3. Remove the cover and bowl-assembly screws in the rear from the top side and the two screws from the bottom side; remove the cover and bowl assembly.
4. Remove the four pump-mounting screws.
5. Disconnect the flush tube from the pump outlet.
6. Remove the pump assembly.
7. Replace if defective.

Replacing the Electra Magic Slide-EZ Valve   To replace the Electra Magic Slide-EZ Valve, follow these steps (Figure 4.14):

1. Disconnect the lead wires from the power source.
2. Empty the toilet completely.
3. Remove the cotter pin and the extension handle, if so equipped.
4. Remove the two molding-mounting screws and remove the two base moldings.
5. Remove the slides by catching tabs with a hooked instrument and pulling forward.
6. Lift the toilet from the closet flange and invert unit.

7. Remove the four screws and remove the valve.
8. Replace if defective.

Cleaning the Electra Magic Toilet   The bowl and outside of the Electra Magic toilet can be cleaned using the same type of nonabrasive cleaners specified for freshwater toilets. For cleaning the tank, use Thetford's Aqua Bowl or diluted household laundry detergent (2 to 4 ounces to 1 gallon of water).

Winterizing and Storing the Electra Magic Toilet   To winterize the Electra Magic Toilet, follow these steps:

1. Completely empty the unit via the termination valve.
2. Refill the unit to the bottom of the bowl with fresh water.
3. Add 8 ounces (1 cup) of Aqua Bowl or a diluted solution of laundry detergent.
4. Cycle three times by depressing the flush button for ten seconds each cycle.
5. Let stand for a few minutes.
6. Completely empty unit via the termination valve.
7. Add one-half charge with nontoxic RV antifreeze.

Maintaining the Portable Toilet

Portable Toilets

Portable toilets are used in smaller RVs that are not equipped with holding tanks and the appropriate plumbing. This type of toilet is commonly found in folding trailers or in truck campers that are not self-contained. Portable toilets are very simple to use and can be dumped into a conventional toilet, pit toilet, or at a dump station. Most portables are comprised of two pieces: a top half consisting of a bowl, a seat, and a freshwater reservoir, and a bottom half containing the slider valve and handle, the waste-holding tank, and an evacuation tube. Various models offer larger holding tanks (Figure 4.15). Cassette-

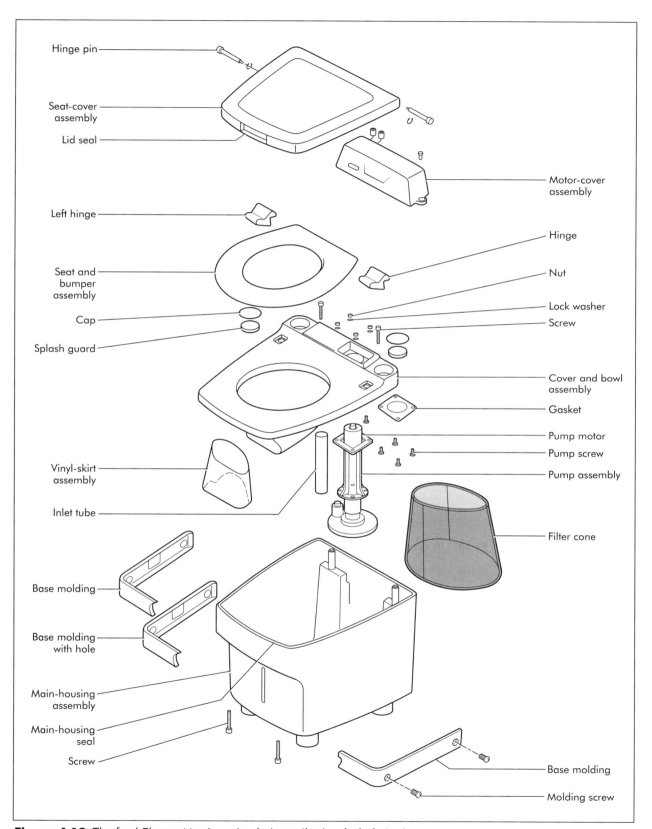

Hinge pin

Seat-cover assembly

Lid seal

Motor-cover assembly

Left hinge

Hinge

Nut

Seat and bumper assembly

Cap

Lock washer

Screw

Splash guard

Cover and bowl assembly

Gasket

Pump motor

Pump screw

Pump assembly

Vinyl-skirt assembly

Inlet tube

Filter cone

Base molding

Base molding with hole

Main-housing assembly

Main-housing seal

Screw

Base molding

Molding screw

Figure 4.13 Thetford Electra Magic recirculating toilet (exploded view)

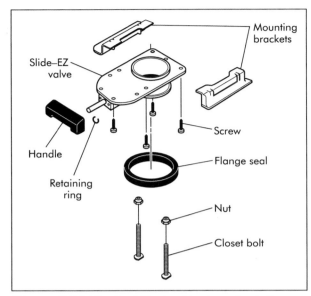

Figure 4.14 Thetford Electra Magic recirculating toilet Slide-EZ Valve

style portable toilets offer built-in convenience with portable versatility (Figure 4.16).

Other than periodic cleaning, the only maintenance needed is to keep the slider valve and seal clean of debris. The holding tank should be thoroughly rinsed before storing the toilet. To winterize, simply add propylene glycol-type antifreeze to the freshwater holding tank.

■ HOLDING TANKS, DRAINPIPES, ■ AND VENT PIPES

Self-contained RVs have a system of plastic pipes that allow the sinks, the shower, and the toilet to drain into holding tanks. In most RVs, the shower and sinks drain into one holding tank, and the toilet waste is routed into a separate holding tank. The drain water goes into a gray-water holding tank, and toilet wastes end up in the black-water holding tank. Toilet-waste holding tanks can also be referred to as sewer or waste tanks (Figure 4.17).

Both holding tanks terminate at a 3-inch dump valve usually located under the motorhome or trailer or in compartments on the left side, within 16 feet of the rear bumper (Figure 4.18). Although only one dump valve is the norm, some coaches use two dump valves. The contents from each tank are separated by

individual slide valves. A typical RV system will have a section of 3-inch pipe from the black-water holding tank connected to a 3-inch slider valve and the main dump connection. A 1½-inch pipe with a separate slide valve will be routed from the gray-water holding tank to the main slider valve. The plumbing is set up so that the valves can be used independently.

Dumping the Holding Tank

The main dump valve is fitted with extruded pins that allow the attachment of a flexible sewer hose. The hose is then routed to a 4-inch pipe in a dump station or campsite hookup. To properly dump the holding tanks, the black water should be evacuated first. After the black-water tank finishes draining, the gray-water tank should be emptied. This allows the gray water to rinse the hose. Make sure the smaller slide valve is *closed* when draining the black-water holding tank so that waste material cannot be forced into the gray-water plumbing.

When hooked up to a campsite sewer, the black-water valve should remain closed until the tank is at least three-quarters full. The tank cannot be flushed properly unless there is a sufficient amount of liquid material to gravity-flow from the tank. Clogging of the termination valve can result if an insufficient amount of liquid waste is flushed.

To make sure that the black tank has been completely emptied, you may want to use one of the several tank-cleaning tools on the market. Some of these tools are spray wands that you attach to a non-drinking water hose. You place the spray wand through the opening in the bottom of the toilet, and the spray head insures that the water reaches all areas of the tank to completely rinse it free of sewage. Another method is to have fresh water spray heads installed into the black-water tank. You connect a nondrinking water hose to the sprayer connection, and the water pressure from the sprayers insure the tank is rinsed free of sewage.

IMPORTANT: Never use a drinking-water hose to flush your black- or gray-water tanks. Dedicate a green or black garden hose to this task. Always use an anti-backflush valve on the hose to insure that water does not go back up into the water-supply hose attached to your sprayers.

Normally only a couple of holding-tank rinses are needed before storing the RV, however, after pro-

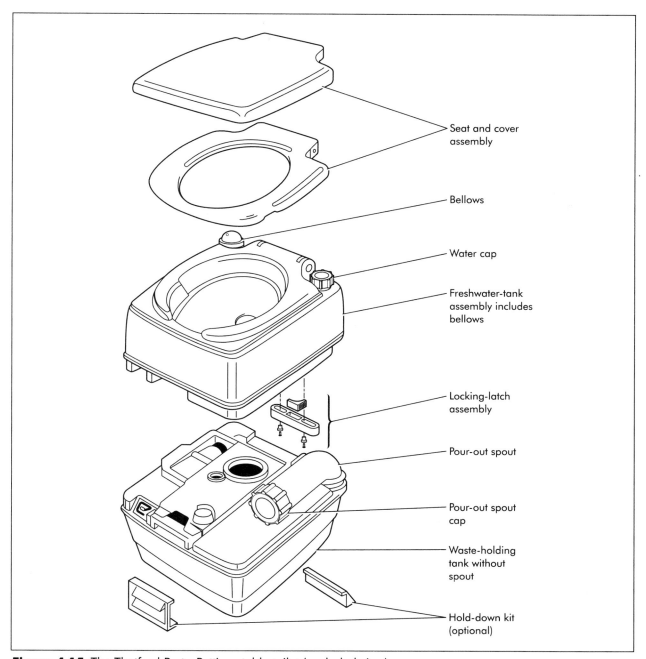

Seat and cover assembly

Bellows

Water cap

Freshwater-tank assembly includes bellows

Locking-latch assembly

Pour-out spout

Pour-out spout cap

Waste-holding tank without spout

Hold-down kit (optional)

Figure 4.15 The Thetford Porta-Potti portable toilet (exploded view)

longed use it may be necessary to clean the tank with a holding-tank cleaner and fresh water. This procedure requires a warm day with the temperature at least 75°F. Fill the black-water tank to the appropriate level of fresh water, depending on the tank-cleaner directions, and then add the chemicals. Drive or tow the RV for about one hour and then park it for a twenty-four-hour period. After the twenty-four

hours, drive the RV for about one hour to loosen deposits, and then go to a dump site and empty the tank. Holding-tank cleaners are available in most RV supply stores.

CAUTION: Do not use household detergents or cleaning compounds when cleaning holding tanks. These may contain chemicals that could damage the drain system or termination valves; cleaners that contain petroleum distillates can damage toilet seals and termination valves.

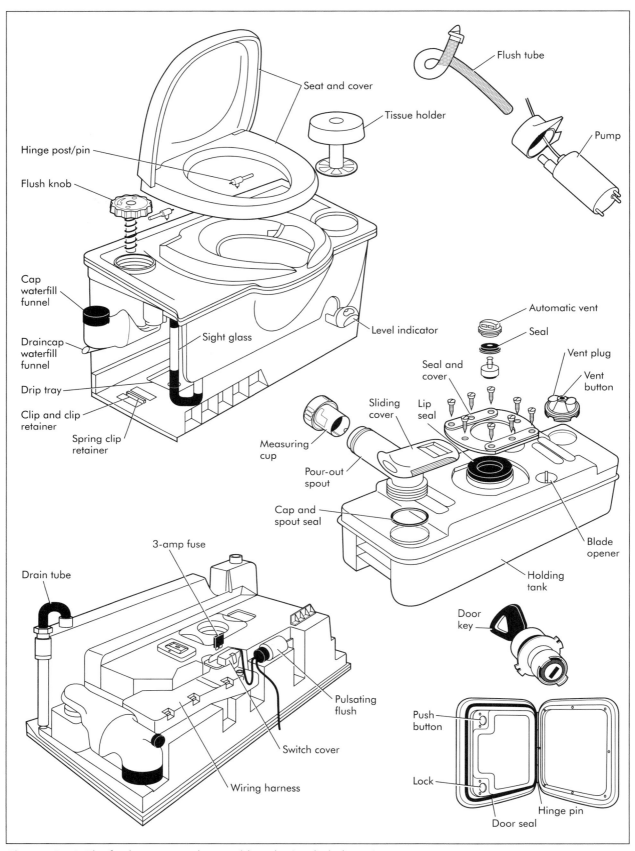

Figure 4.16 Thetford cassette-style portable toilet (exploded view)

Macerator Pumps

There are times when your holding tanks will be full and you may not have access to a standard dump site. Quite often you will be able to find a sewer-cleanout port in gas stations or other public service areas. After getting permission from the owner or manager of the site, you can use a macerator pump and hose to empty your full tanks. Macerator pumps are designed to aid in emptying a holding tank by grinding waste down to a particle size no larger than 1/8 inch and pushing it out a l-inch discharge hose. This pump can handle body wastes, toilet tissue, and facial tissue, but not hard, solid objects, sanitary napkins, or rags. The Jabsco Par macerator pump, for example, will empty a typical 30-gallon waste-holding tank in three minutes (Figure 4.19).

A macerator pump will perform properly if the following recommendations are followed:

- Flush the holding tank with several gallons of water after each pumpout.
- Do not run the motor dry.
- Operate the pump only when the battery is fully charged or outside hookups are available.

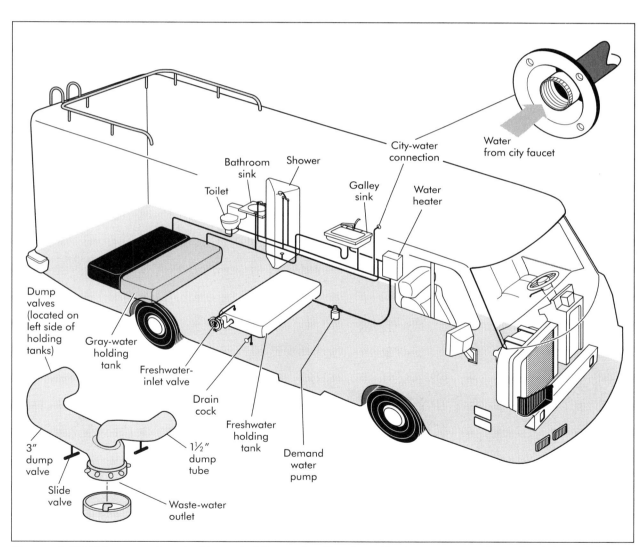

Figure 4.17 RVs are equipped with two holding tanks: One for collecting gray water from the sinks and shower and the other for storing waste from the toilet. Dump valves are used to control removal of contents from the individual tanks.

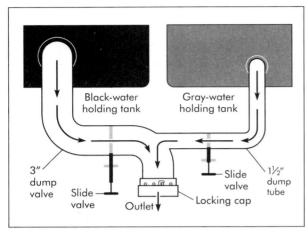

Figure 4.18 Holding tanks terminate at a 3-inch exit pipe that is fitted with a 3-inch slide valve for the black-water tank and a 1½-inch slide valve for the gray-water tank.

- Do not run the motor for more than fifteen minutes in continuous duty.
- Be sure the pump is wired with 10-gauge wire for distances up to 20 feet and 12-gauge wire for distances under 10 feet. Use a 20-amp fuse.

     NOTE: After long periods of nonuse, the pump may not turn freely. Pour a cup of water down the pump discharge line to help free the impeller.

Replacing the Seal, Impeller, and Gasket in the Par Macerator Pump

To replace the seal, impeller, and gasket in the Par Macerator pump, follow these steps:

1. Remove the acorn nuts and the inlet housing.
2. Unscrew the cutter plate from the shaft by turning the facing cutter blades counterclockwise. Hold the motor shaft behind the plate to prevent turning.
3. Remove the gaskets, the wearplate, and the slide-pump assembly from the mounting studs.
4. Remove the seal by pushing out evenly with a screwdriver from the impeller-bore side of the body.
5. Remove the gasket and the impeller.
6. Replace with the new gasket and the impeller.
7. Reassemble the seal by coating the outside of the metal case lightly with sealant and pressing into the body with the lip facing the impeller.
8. Press the star retaining washer (with con-

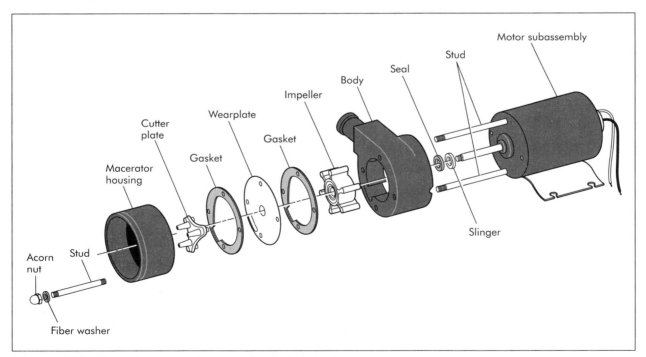

Figure 4.19 Jabsco Par macerator pump (exploded view)

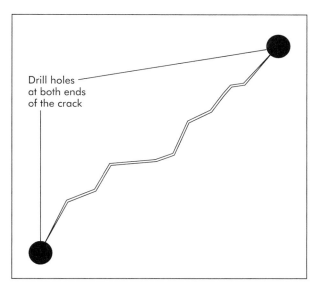

Figure 4.20 A crack in the holding tank can be stopped by drilling holes at each end of the damaged area.

cave side up) into the seal bore and against the seal case.

9. Apply light coating of grease to the impeller bore and wearplate to aid in initial startup.
10. Reassemble the body, the impeller, the gaskets, the wearplate, the housing, and the acorn nuts.

Repairing the Holding Tank

Holding-tank leaks are a messy proposition. Most holding tanks are made from black ABS, which is very durable. But holes and breaks can be caused by flying rocks or by dragging on steep driveways and rough terrain. If a crack develops, the ends of the crack should be drilled to keep the crack from getting any longer before repairing (Figure 4.20).

Obviously, holes or cracks that are too large cannot be repaired, and the holding tank must be replaced. Smaller holes and cracks can be repaired using a commercially available patch kit, such as the Syon Seal-N-Place kit. (See the step-by-step instructions that follow, "Repairing Polyethylene Tanks.") Another good method is to use fiberglass cloth and a gap-filling cyanoacrylate adhesive, found in most hobby shops. This glue is similar to Super Glue but is much thicker and takes longer to set—sometimes as long as two minutes. The thicker adhesive allows adequate

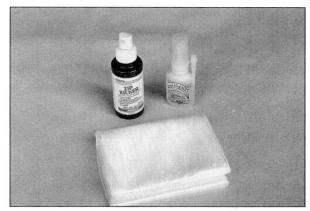

Figure 4.21 Cyanoacrylate adhesive, found in most hobby stores, can be used to fix holding tanks.

time to cover the crack or break. The key to using gap-filling cyanoacrylate adhesive is the accelerator compound that will instantly set the glue (Figure 4.21). The owner has enough time to saturate the fiberglass cloth, position it over the break, and then zap it with accelerator to instantly set the glue. Use the following steps to fix a holding-tank break.

1. Empty the holding tank and, when dry, clean the area around the damage.
2. Cut a piece of fiberglass cloth a couple of inches larger than the damaged area.
3. Saturate the fiberglass cloth with the cyanoacrylate adhesive.
4. Place the saturated fiberglass cloth over the damaged area. Smooth out with your hands (use disposable gloves for this job).
5. When the fiberglass is in position and smooth, zap the area with the accelerator. The fiberglass cloth and adhesive will bond instantly to the damaged area.

The preceding procedure can be used to make emergency repairs to ABS pipes, tanks, or exterior fiberglass.

Repairing Polyethylene Tanks

Polyethylene tanks (translucent) can be repaired with a commercially available kit, Syon Seal-N-Place, or by "welding" (heat). The welding process is more complicated and requires specialized equipment and the expertise available at larger RV repair shops.

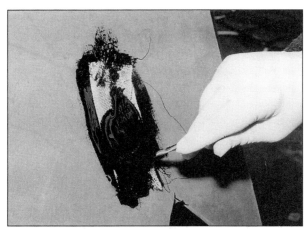

Figure 4.22 Repairing a crack with the Seal-N-Place kit.

The Seal-N-Place kit (Figure 4.22) is designed for permanent repairs but must be used quickly because the resin mixture begins to harden in six to eight minutes. The resin is cured in twenty minutes. The resin can be used in temperatures down to 30°F. Allow yourself five minutes to make the repair after mixing the material so that you will have a slight time cushion before the resin hardens. Repairs can be made using the Seal-N-Place kit and following these procedures:

1. Remove grease, road dirt, tar, and any oil from the repair surface.
2. Rough up the surface with the sandpaper.
3. Cut enough of the fiberglass cloth to overlap the damaged area.
4. Break off the tip on the metal tube within the plastic bag holding the resin.
5. Using the key over the metal tube, empty the hardener from the tube into the plastic bag.
6. Knead the plastic bag until the resin and hardener are thoroughly mixed (approximately twenty seconds).
7. Brush a layer of resin over the area to be covered by the fiberglass.
8. Lay the cut fiberglass over the resin-coated area.
9. Brush on a heavy coat of resin over the fiberglass until it is completely saturated. Flare out the edges of the resin.
   NOTE: Seal-N-Place kits can also be used for repairing ABS, polypropylene, and other plastic surfaces.

Toilet Chemicals

Unlike home sewage that drains into a large underground septic system or a city sewer, the waste in RV holding tanks remains in close proximity to the living quarters. To eliminate offensive odors, chemicals must be used in the black-water holding tank. Normally the tank is charged with a dose of toilet chemicals after dumping. But during hot summer days, additional chemicals may be necessary. Products are also available to freshen gray-water holding tanks.

Many municipalities require that biodegradable chemicals, devoid of formaldehyde, be used. Therefore, a wide variety of environmentally safe chemicals is available. There are many home remedies that have surfaced during evening campfire conversations, but some of these household products may damage the toilet seals, plumbing, or termination valves. Home-brew chemicals can also cause an explosion inside the tank under certain conditions. It is always safer to use a commercially available toilet chemical.

Although it is not absolutely necessary, it is advisable to use single-ply, white toilet paper in all RV toilets. Not only is the bulk limited because the paper is thin, but it also tends to break down faster, which is easier on the plumbing system, especially the termination valves.

Drainpipes

An RV's plumbing system, which drains the water from the sinks and shower, is comprised of a series of black ABS pipes, configured much the same as a home system. Pipes fitted to the sinks and shower are routed to nearby P-traps and then on to the holding tanks. P-traps are U-shaped curves in the pipe that allow columns of water to remain temporarily trapped until the next amount of water is drained. This column of water prevents the gases in the holding tank from backing up into the sinks and shower, preventing nasty smells from entering the living quarters. Traps can become clogged with accumulated hair, grease, and other small food particles. To break a clog, hot water can be flushed down the drain. If this does not work, the P-trap can be dismantled by unscrewing the fittings on each end. Do not use sharp objects to free a clog, or damage to the pipe may result.

Pipes made of ABS are usually hardy enough to last the life of the RV. Occasionally, a leak will develop or a break will be caused by a heavy item that has fallen on the pipe. Repairing or rerouting is fairly easy, requiring only a hacksaw, new ABS pipe sections, connectors, and ABS cement to dissolve the surfaces of the pipes to be connected, allowing two sections to be welded together. The cementing process is fast and requires forethought and organization before proceeding.

Slide valves usually must be replaced if a jam or break develops. This is also an easy process since termination valves are universal and often are only attached to the pipe with large hose clamps. If that is the case, the hose clamp can be removed, the valve twisted off, and a new one attached. If the valve is ABS-cemented to the pipe, it must be cut and a new valve installed, using appropriate couplers.

Vent Pipes

In order for the waste water and sewage to flow properly, the holding tanks must be vented, usually to the outside, terminating on the roof. The vent covers should be inspected once a year, or after making contact with low tree branches or other low obstacles. Usually, the vent pipes are covered with plastic caps that snap onto the roof fixture (Figure 4.23). If the base is in good shape, all you have to do is replace the cap. If the entire fixture must be replaced, consider using a metal counterpart (Figure 4.24). These metal fixtures cost only a few dollars more, but will last much longer.

Figure 4.23 Vent pipes are covered with plastic caps that snap onto the fixture.

Figure 4.24 Metal vent-pipe cups will last longer.

Make sure the roof vents are kept free of debris. If necessary, use a long stick or broom handle to clear the passageway. Failure to keep the vent pipes clear may create foul odors throughout the RV.

Toilets that Spit Back

If the toilet spits back when flushed, the vent pipe may be too long. Using a flashlight, inspect the inside of the holding tank. Look for a pipe that protrudes into the holding tank. If the pipe is too long and becomes covered by the tank contents, it will fail to vent properly. You may have to remove the toilet for access, or peer through the dump valve (Figures 4.25 and 4.26).

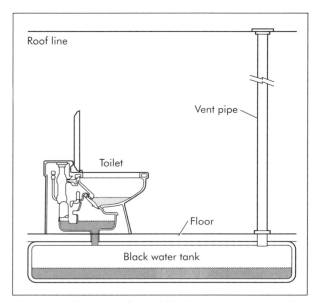

Figure 4.25 Properly installed vent pipe in typical black-water tank set-up

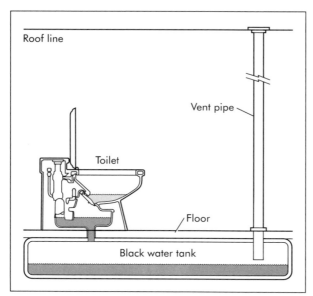

Figure 4.26 Improperly installed vent pipe in holding tank. Note how far the pipe intrudes into the tank.

Repairing a Long Vent Pipe

To repair a vent pipe that is too long:

1. Establish access after either removing the toilet or opening the dump valve. If you are using the dump valve for access, make sure the holding tank is empty and cleaned thoroughly.
2. Affix a hacksaw blade to any object that allows the protruding pipe to be reached.
3. Cut off the excess pipe to a point just below the top of the holding tank.
4. Replace the toilet, using a new flange gasket or close the dump valve.
5. Flush the tank with water to remove any plastic shavings.

■ CHAPTER 5 ■
AC GENERATORS

AC generators, the types found on RVs, are compact power plants designed to provide 120-volt, 60-cycle-per-second alternating current to household-type appliances when outside hookups are not available. AC generators are either single- or multi-cylinder, 4-cycle engines powered by gasoline, propane, or diesel fuel.

AC generators are sized and classified by the amount of power they are able to produce, expressed in kilowatts (thousands of watts). Those for RVs range from a 2.5-kw propane-powered unit (2.8 kw in the gasoline version) to large diesel-powered sets that can produce up to 20 kw. Determining the type and power rating of your AC generator is easy. A nameplate affixed to the side of the unit contains the following information: model and serial number (both are necessary to order parts), AC voltage output, phase, kilowatts (sometimes expressed as KVA), ampere rating, hertz (cycles per second), engine-governed RPM, and type of fuel required.

Table 5.1 AC-Generator Maintenance Schedule

	Startup	50 Hours	100 Hours	500 Hours
Check RV battery	X			
Check oil level	X			
Check fuel supply	X			
Check air inlet and outlet	X			
Check compartment for debris	X			
Check air cleaner	X			
Lubricate governor linkage		X		
Change oil			X	
Replace oil filter			X	
Clean fuel filter			X	
Replace spark plug			X	
Check breaker points			X	
Check electrical connections			X	
Check mounting bolts			X	
Adjust carburetor			X	
Check brushes				X
Service cylinder heads				X

■ MAINTENANCE OF AC GENERATORS ■

It's important to keep the AC generator well maintained for optimum performance. Maintenance procedures and time intervals vary from manufacturer to manufacturer. Make sure you refer to the owner's manual for your particular generator and follow the recommended procedures carefully. Refer to Table 5.1 as a generic maintenance schedule.

Service and Repair

Battery

Without a fully charged battery and clean, tight electrical connections, starting the generator will be difficult or impossible. The battery electrolyte level should be checked regularly and the cable terminals and battery posts cleaned at least on a yearly basis.

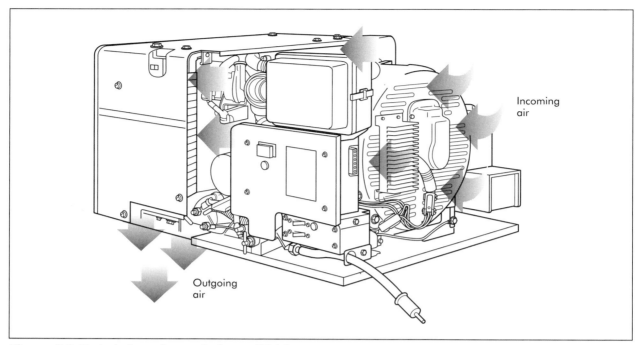

Figure 5.1 Typical air-cooling paths for an RV AC generator

Removing Battery Corrosion Follow these steps to remove battery corrosion:

1. Remove the terminals from the battery posts using a battery-terminal puller if necessary.
2. Soak the terminals in a mixture of 1 quart of water and ½ cup of baking soda.
3. Mix another quart of water and ½ cup baking soda and pour over the battery top. (Allow this mixture about five minutes to work). Make sure that none of the battery-cell caps—if so equipped—are open. If the baking-soda mixture enters the cells, it will reduce the acid strength, possibly damaging the cell.
4. Rinse the terminals and battery top with clean water, then dry.
5. A battery post/terminal brush should be used to thoroughly clean the inside of the terminal fittings and the outside of the posts.
6. Use a light grease or commercially available terminal protectant on the terminals and posts; install terminals to posts and tighten firmly.

Cooling-System Intake/Outlet

Check and clean the air-inlet screen. Cooling air is drawn over the AC generator, then exits by passing over the engine (Figure 5.1). Make sure there is no debris such as leaves or paper that may block the flow of air.

For liquid-cooled generator units, check the radiator for any signs of debris buildup. Airflow that is blocked across the radiator will lead to overheating. Liquid-cooled engines have a few more maintenance requirements. The water pump and cooling fan are driven by a fan belt. It should be inspected at regular intervals. Look for signs of fraying, cracks, or any other abnormalities. The belt's tension should also be checked and set to the AC-generator manufacturer's recommendations. Experts usually recommend belt replacement every three or four years, regardless of the number of hours of operation.

The engine's ethylene glycol coolant should be checked with a coolant hydrometer each year to make sure it offers enough freezing/boiling protection. At a minimum, a 50-percent mix of coolant to water

Figure 5.2 High-water temperature shut-off switch protects the engine in the event of a broken fan belt or clogged radiator.

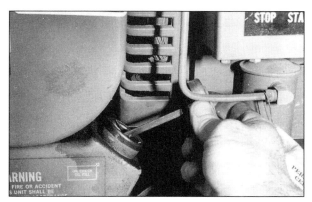

Figure 5.3 The AC-generator oil level should be checked at the outset of each trip.

should be present in the system. This will offer freeze protection to −34°F. If colder temperatures are expected, the concentration can be increased to 70 percent. The coolant should be drained and replaced every other year.

CAUTION: Hot coolant and steam can cause severe burns. Before removing the pressure cap, stop the engine and allow it to cool. Loosen the cap slowly to relieve pressure.

Most liquid-cooled generators are fitted with a high-water-temperature shutdown switch (Figure 5.2). This switch will shut down engine operation if the coolant temperature exceeds 220°F to 230°F. This is to protect the engine in the event of a clogged radiator, broken fan belt, etc. Be aware that this switch is *not* a low-coolant-level switch and coolant levels should be checked regularly; proper level must be maintained for these safety devices to function. If the engine is shut down due to overheating, the cause of the heating problem must be rectified before the engine is restarted.

Crankcase-Oil Level

When checking the oil level (Figure 5.3), make sure you follow the AC-generator manufacturer's recommendations. Kohler generators require that the level

be checked with the oil cap resting on the oil-shaft collar; do not thread the cap on. Onan requires the opposite method: the cap should be screwed into its fully seated position before reading the dipstick. Generac requires that the oil be checked by removing the dipstick and wiping it dry with a clean cloth, reinstalling the dipstick, and tightening it into the fill tube, then removing it again to read the oil level. If additional oil is needed, make sure you add the correct viscosity and API (American Petroleum Institute)- rated oil as recommended by the AC-generator manufacturer.

Most AC generators today are equipped with a low-oil-pressure shutdown switch (Figure 5.4). This device will stop engine operation due to an oil pump failure or other mechanical malfunction which affects the oil pressure—such as a blown oil-filter gasket. Be aware that this switch is not a low-oil-level detection switch. You must regularly check the engine-oil level visually on the dipstick.

Changing the Oil and Filter Most manufacturers recommend that oil changes should be performed every 100 hours or once every twelve months. Drain the oil while engine is warm, after running the generator at half load for thirty minutes.

To drain the oil and change the filter:

1. Stop the AC generator.
2. With the drain pan under the AC generator, remove the drain plug if so equipped, or open the drain valve (Figure 5.5). Drain the oil completely and dispose of properly.
3. Remove the old oil filter (Figure 5.6).

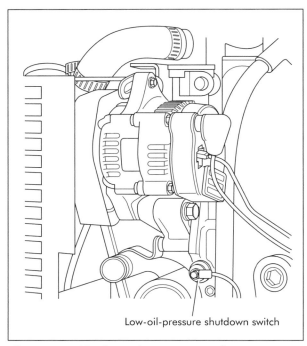

Low-oil-pressure shutdown switch

Figure 5.4 The low-oil-pressure switch prevents engine damage by shuting off the engine if there is a lack of oil pressure.

Figure 5.5 A drain plug or petcock is used to remove oil from the AC-generator.

4. Clean the filter base on the engine.
5. Wipe a film of clean oil onto the new filter's gasket.
6. Screw a new filter to the base until the gasket contacts, then tighten an additional half-turn.
7. Replace the drain plug or close the drain valve.

Figure 5.6 Removing the oil filter should be part of the oil-change maintenance program.

8. Refill the crankcase to the proper level with the recommended grade and weight of oil for the operational service temperature expected.
9. Start the engine and run for a few minutes, checking for leaks at filter base and drain plug or valve.
10. Record the hour-meter time of the oil change in a log to keep for future reference.

Setting Ignition Points and Timing

NOTE: Newer model gasoline or propane-powered AC generators equipped with electronic ignitions require no periodic maintenance. Most older AC generators can be fitted with an electronic conversion kit to eliminate the conventional point-ignition system.

If your AC generator is equipped with a points-type ignition, follow these steps:

1. The battery cables, negative cable first, should be removed to prevent accidental engine startup during point-adjustment procedure.
2. The points are found under a sheetmetal cover on the engine block or governor (Figure 5.7).
3. Point contact surfaces should be clean and smooth. If points are rough and pitted, they will require replacement.
4. Gap settings vary greatly, depending on the make and model of the AC generator, but generally are between .016 and .025 inch (Figures 5.8 and 5.9).

Figure 5.7 Points for this Onan AC-generator are located under a box that is easily accessible.

5. Point gap must be set with the points in their fully open position. Using a wrench or socket, rotate the engine by turning the AC generator shaft until the points are fully opened.

6. A clean, flat feeler gauge (Figure 5.10) of the recommended thickness should be used to check the gap.

7. If the gap is incorrect, loosen the hold-down screws and move the stationary member of the points until the proper gap is attained.

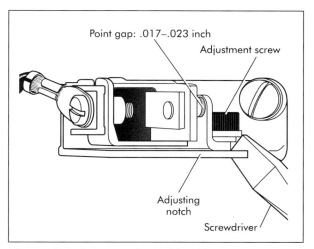

Figure 5.8 Point gap for Kohler AC generators should be set between .017 and .023 inch.

8. Tighten the hold-down screws, replace cover, and reconnect the negative battery terminal.

Air Cleaners

Virtually all AC generators use a pleated-paper air-filter element (Figure 5.11) that requires service approximately every fifty hours; some may be backed

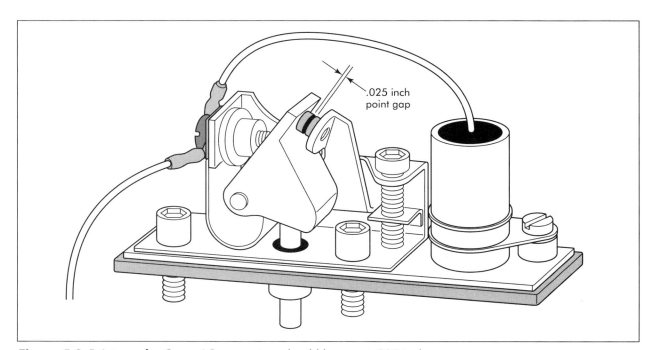

Figure 5.9 Point gap for Onan AC generators should be set at .025 inch.

■ TROUBLESHOOTING ■
THE AC GENERATOR

Problem	Possible Cause	Correction
Will not start	Low battery	Charge or replace
	Out of fuel	Replenish
	Bad battery connection	Clean terminals
	Clogged fuel filter	Replace filter
	Dirty air cleaner	Clean or replace
	Faulty ignition points	Clean, adjust, replace
	Worn or dirty spark plug	Clean or replace
	Faulty ignition coil	Replace
	Oil too heavy	Replace with lighter grade
	Stuck carburetor choke	Clean and adjust
	Blown starting-circuit fuse	Check and replace
	Fuel-shutdown solenoid	Replace or remove
Hard to start	Stale fuel	Replace
	Wrong carburetor adjustment	Adjust
	Incorrect point setting	Adjust gap
	Dirty air cleaner	Replace
	Worn spark plug	Replace
	Engine running too hot	Check cooling system
	Faulty fuel pump	Replace
Engine runs, then stops	Low fuel level	Replenish supply
	Low oil pressure	Check/add oil
	Oil level too high	Check/remove oil
	Wrong fuel mixture	Adjust
	Faulty spark plug	Clean or replace
	Clogged fuel filter	Clean or replace
	Fuel-shutdown solenoid	Replace or remove
Emits black smoke	Rich fuel mixture	Adjust carburetor
	Clogged air cleaner	Replace element
	Choke stuck closed	Clean and adjust
Engine lacks power	Clogged air cleaner	Replace element
	Rich fuel mixture	Adjust carburetor
	Overloaded engine	Reduce electrical load
	Bad or stale fuel	Replenish with fresh fuel
	Dirty or faulty spark plug	Clean or replace plug
	Engine carbon buildup	Service/remove carbon
	Ignition points	Adjust or replace points
	Overheated engine	Check cooling system

■ TROUBLESHOOTING ■
THE AC GENERATOR, continued

Problem	Possible Cause	Correction
Engine surges	Clogged air cleaner	Clean or replace
	Worn ignition points	Replace
	Worn spark plug	Replace
	Fuel starvation	Check filter and pump
	Incorrect carburetor adjustment	Adjust
	Stale fuel	Replace with fresh fuel
	Sticking linkage	Clean and lubricate
Engine overheats	Clogged airflow ducts	Clean inlet and outlet
	Carburetor mixture too lean	Enrich mixture
	Incorrect point adjustment	Adjust
No AC current output	Tripped circuit breaker	Reset breaker
	Breaker continues to trip	Reduce load
	Breaker still trips	Short in wiring
	Internal generator defect	Seek professional service
Low AC output	Engine speed too low	Adjust carburetor or governor
	Power overload	Reduce load

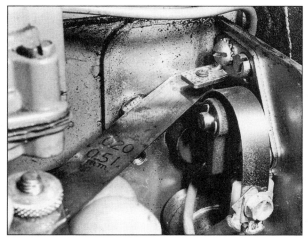

Figure 5.10 An automotive feeler gauge is used to set the point gap.

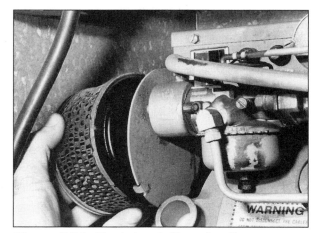

Figure 5.11 Check the air filter often if you are operating in dusty areas; it needs to be checked on a weekly basis or as specified by the AC generator manufacturer.

with a foam filter (Figure 5.12). The element can be cleaned after the first fifty hours by lightly tapping it against a flat surface to dislodge any loose dirt and debris. Paper elements should not be washed in any type of solvent solution since damage to the element will occur. Replace the element every 100 hours, but if the AC generator is operated in extremely dusty or dirty environments, replace the element more often (Figure 5.13).

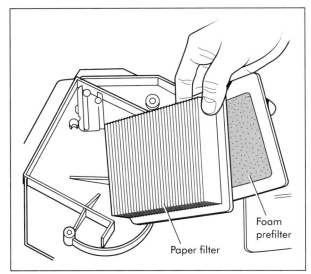

Figure 5.12 Combined paper filter and foam prefilter

Spark Plugs

Spark plugs should be replaced after approximately 100 hours of running time, or, if upon inspection, they show signs of burning or deposits of carbon. Spark plugs that show heavy, black-colored deposits could indicate excessive oil consumption or a carburetor that is adjusted so the mixture is too rich.

Replacing Spark Plugs   To replace spark plugs, follow these steps:

1. Remove the spark plug with a spark-plug socket, either a ⅝ inch or ¹³⁄₁₆ inch, depending on the spark-plug type.
2. Make sure that the gasket-seating surface of the cylinder head is clean.
3. Set the plug gap to .025 inch or as specified by the manufacturer.

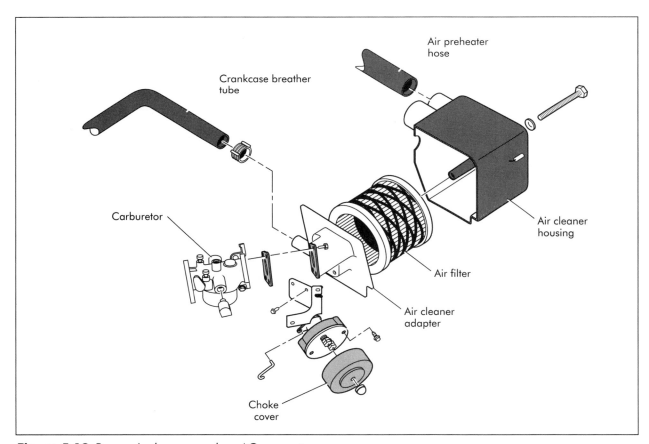

Figure 5.13 Paper air cleaner used on AC generator

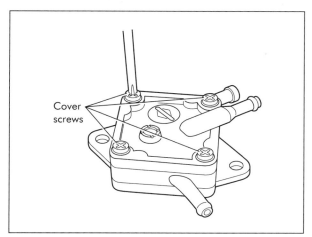

Figure 5.14 AC-generator fuel pump

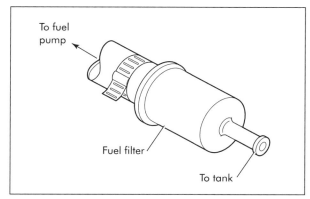

Figure 5.15 An inline fuel filter is designed to trap water, dirt, and metal particles.

4. Tighten the spark plug carefully. *AC generators use an aluminum cylinder head and the threads are prone to stripping if overtightened.* If you are using a torque wrench, tighten the plug to 10 to 15 foot-pounds.

Fuel Filters and Pumps

Gasoline-powered, AC-generator fuel pumps are either solid-state, electrically operated by 12-volt DC power (Figure 5.14), or are mechanically actuated by an eccentric lobe on the engine's camshaft. Most AC generators since the mid-1980s use the electric system. These electric pumps cannot be serviced; only the filter assembly may be replaced. The diaphragm may be replaceable in mechanical pumps.

The fuel system in a diesel-powered AC generator uses an injector pump to send fuel to the engine. Often, a small electric pump is also used to assist the injector pump. Service of these pumps should only be done by qualified technicians.

Diesel-fuel filters should be changed at approximately 250 hours. Most diesel AC generators have two fuel filters. The first, or primary filter, may be either a spin-on type or in-line plastic filter (Figure 5.15) designed to trap water, dirt, and metal particles before they get to the secondary or final filter.

Changing the spin-on diesel-fuel filter is easy, just like changing a spin-on oil filter found in vehicle engines.

Changing a Spin-on Filter To change a spin-on filter:

1. Loosen the filter by turning in a counterclockwise direction. Some fuel will spill out; use rags to catch the excess. Discard the old filter. Do not reuse.
2. Wipe the new filter's gasket surface clean.
3. Lightly lubricate the rubber gasket on the filter with some clean fuel or light motor oil.
4. Thread the filter on until the gasket contacts the base; hand tighten an additional half-turn.
5. One additional step is required when opening a diesel-fuel system: bleeding. If a diesel engine runs out of fuel, has an air leak on the suction side of the pump, or if you change the filter, the system must be bled of all air. Erratic operation and hard starting will result if air remains in the fuel lines.

Bleeding the Diesel-Fuel System To bleed the diesel-fuel system:

1. Make sure the fuel tank is filled.
2. Loosen the small bleeder valve on top of the fuel-filter housing a couple of turns.
3. Using the start switch on the AC generator controller, crank the engine over until air stops flowing from the vent.
4. Tighten the fitting.
5. Loosen the fuel-line-inlet connection at the fuel-injection pump. Operate the start switch

as above until bubbles disappear. Tighten the connection.

The fuel system should now be purged of air and operate normally.

Replacing the Fuel Filter (Gas Engines)   To replace the fuel filter:

1. The fuel filter is located in the suction line between the tank and fuel pump.
2. Using a screwdriver, loosen the clamps. Remove and discard the old filter.
3. Install the new filter in-line and tighten clamp connections.
4. Start the engine and check for leaks and normal operation.

Testing the Electric Pump   To test the electric pump:

1. Remove the fuel-outlet line to the carburetor and install a fuel-pressure gauge.
2. Press the start switch and hold until a pressure reading is constant.
3. Check the specifications in the owner's manual for the proper pressure output; usually the pressure should read between 4 and 5 psi. Pressure should stay constant or drop off slowly.
4. These pumps cannot be serviced; if the pump fails to perform properly, the entire assembly must be replaced.

Fuel-Shutdown Solenoid

Some manufacturers equip their carburetors with a fuel-shutdown solenoid that prevents runon (dieseling) after the engine is shut down. The solenoid is mounted on top of the carburetor and is energized by battery current when starting the engine. When the engine is shut down, the solenoid is de-energized, dropping a plunger to stop fuel flow. If the solenoid fails, fuel cannot reach the engine.

Bypassing the Solenoid   To bypass the solenoid temporarily, it can be removed, the plunger removed

from the body, and the solenoid reinstalled. Follow these steps:

1. Turn the main fuel adjustment in until it bottoms.
2. Record the number of turns in.
3. Turn the main screw out far enough to shift the solenoid retaining bracket.
4. Lift out the solenoid and remove the plunger.
5. Reinstall the solenoid and its retaining bracket.
6. Turn the main fuel adjustment screw in until it bottoms.
7. Back the screw out the recorded number of turns.
8. Minor adjustments may have to be made in the fuel mixture.

Carburetor Adjustments

There are three main carburetor adjustments: main fuel mixture, idle fuel mixture, and the choke setting. Improper carburetor adjustment can lead to serious engine trouble. A mixture that is too rich can wash away lubricating oil from the cylinder walls, causing accelerated piston-ring wear. A mixture that is too lean can cause overheating and burned valves and pistons.

Main-Fuel Mixture (Kohler)   The main fuel-mixture adjustment screw (Figure 5.16) is centered on top of the carburetor, except for the 2.5-kw model, where the screw is centered on the bottom.

For 2.5-kw Kohler AC Generators   To adjust the 2.5-kw Kohler AC generator:

1. Turn main mixture screw clockwise until it lightly bottoms.
2. Back screw out 1¼ turns.
3. Minor adjustments may have to be made with the engine running at full load to achieve maximum power.

For all other Kohlers   To adjust all other Kohlers:

1. Turn main fuel-mixture screw until it lightly bottoms.

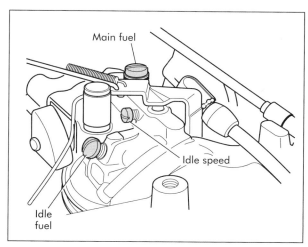

Figure 5.16 Typical carburetor adjustment points for the Kohler AC generator

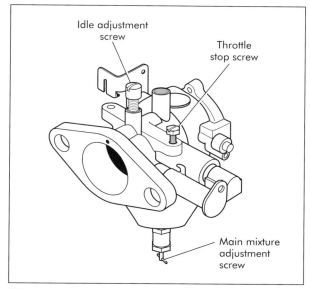

Figure 5.17 Typical carburetor adjustment points for an Onan AC generator

2. Back the screw out 2¼ turns.
3. With the engine thoroughly warmed up and running under full-rated load, turn the screw until the engine slows down (lean setting).
4. Turn screw out (rich setting) until the engine regains speed and then starts to slow down.
5. Turn screw back in until the position is halfway between rich and lean.
6. Engine should operate with a steady, smooth governor action.

Main-Fuel Mixture (Onan) Onan AC generators have the main mixture adjustment screw centered on the bottom of the carburetor (Figure 5.17). To adjust an Onan follow these steps:

1. Start the AC generator and apply full-rated load; run for ten minutes.
2. Connect a multimeter (voltage) to the AC output.
3. Turn the adjustment screw inward until the voltage drops.
4. Turn the screw outward until the voltage drops again.
5. Locate the point where voltage is the highest. From this setting turn the screw out an additional ¼ turn.

The idle circuit of the carburetor only functions as the engine comes up to speed through the idle range and if there is no load on the AC generator.

1. Locate the idle screw on the upper side of the carburetor.
2. Turn the screw in until it lightly bottoms.
3. Back the screw out ¾ turn.
4. No further adjustment is necessary.

Idle Fuel-Mixture Adjustment (All other Kohler Models) For Kohler's other models, the screw is on the top of the carburetor, offset from the center, and is slightly smaller than the main adjustment screw.

1. Turn the screw in until it lightly bottoms.
2. Back out 1½ turns.
3. No further adjustment is necessary.

Idle Fuel-Mixture Adjustment (Onan) To make the mixture adjustment:

1. Run the AC generator until it is warmed up, about ten minutes.
2. Remove all loads.
3. Connect a multimeter (voltage) to the AC output.
4. Turn the screw inward until the voltage drops

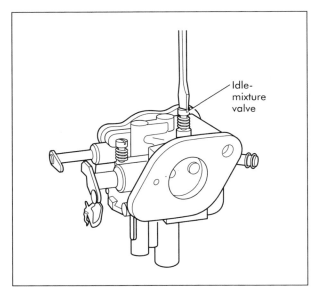

Figure 5.18 Typical carburetor adjustment points for an AC generator

and the engine begins to run roughly.

5. Back out the screw until the engine runs smoothly without any surging.
6. Add and remove a full load several times to make sure engine does not bog or surge.

Idle Fuel-Mixture Adjustment (Generac) For all vertical and horizontal-engine models (excluding automatic-idle-control models):

1. Turn the idle-mixture valve (Figure 5.18) clockwise until it just seats. *Do not force it.*
2. Turn the idle-mixture valve counterclockwise 1¼ turns. This setting will permit the engine to be started and operated.

   NOTE: The Generac Automatic Idle Control System requires several special tools and equipment and is best left to an authorized Generac repair facility.

Carburetor Overhaul

Many carburetor problems can be corrected by adjusting the mixture or float, but to effectively clean gummed-up fuel passages and/or worn internal parts, a complete overhaul is necessary. The instructions that follow for overhauling a carburetor pertain to Onan's BGE model, but represent the same type of service necessary for rebuilding carburetors found in

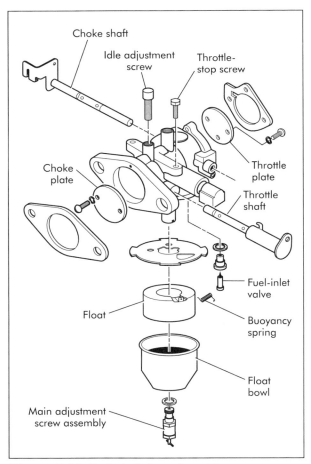

Figure 5.19 Exploded view of an AC-generator carburetor.

most AC generators. Carburetors have very small parts associated with their operation. These parts are easily lost or misplaced. If you are not completely familiar with working on such precision components, it is best left to experienced technicians.

Carburetor Removal and Disassembly

To remove and disassemble the carburetor, follow these steps (Figure 5.19):

1. Remove the crankcase breather hose and the air preheater hose from the air-cleaner housing.
2. Remove the air-cleaner-housing center cap screw and lift off the housing and air filter.
3. Remove the choke-cover retaining nut and lift off the choke cover.

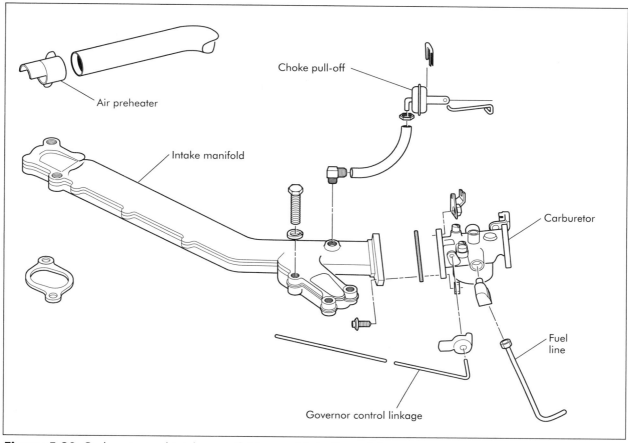

Figure 5.20 Carburetor and intake manifold assembly in Onan AC generators

4. Disconnect the choke lead wires at the choke terminals.

5. Remove the three cap screws that secure the air-cleaner adapter to the carburetor and lift off the adapter. The choke linkage must be disengaged from the choke assembly.

6. Disconnect the fuel line and governor control linkage from the carburetor.

7. Remove the intake-manifold cap screws and lift off the carburetor preheater. Lift off the carburetor and manifold as one assembly.

8. Remove the two intake-manifold gaskets and plug the intake ports with a rag to prevent loose parts from entering ports.

9. Remove the two cap screws that secure the carburetor and choke pulloff assembly to the intake manifold. Disengage the choke-pulloff linkage from the carburetor and carefully separate the carburetor from the intake manifold (Figure 5.20).

10. Remove the air-cleaner adapter and the automatic-choke assembly.

11. Remove the throttle and choke-plate retaining screws and plates. Carefully pull out the throttle and choke shafts, making sure not to damage the Teflon coating.

12. Remove the main and idle-mixture screw assemblies.

13. Separate the fuel bowl (lower section of the carburetor) from the fuel-bowl cover (lower section).

14. After noting the position of the float assembly, slide out the retaining pin and remove the float assembly, springs, clips, and the needle valve.

15. Unscrew and remove the needle and the valve seat.

16. Soak all metal parts in the carburetor cleaner that are not replaced by the repair kit. Most automotive-parts stores carry carburetor

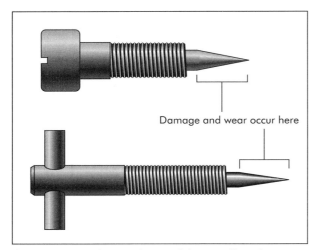

Figure 5.21 The condition of the needle valve should be checked when performing a carburetor overhaul.

cleaner in a can that has a wire basket. Make sure not to soak nonmetal parts such as the float itself. Soak for the time prescribed by the manufacturer of the cleaner.

CAUTION: Carburetor cleaner is flammable and should not be used around flames or while smoking.

17. Clean the carbon deposits from the carburetor bore, especially where the throttle and choke plates seat. Make sure the idle or main fuel ports do not become plugged.

18. Blow out all the passages with compressed air. Do not clean with a wire or other metallic object that may increase the size of the orifices.

19. Check the condition of the needle valve and float (Figure 5.21). Replace the needle valve if damaged and the float if saturated with fuel or damaged. Needle valves and floats may not be part of the repair kit and may have to be purchased separately.

20. Check the condition of the choke and the throttle shafts for excessive play in their bore and replace if necessary.

21. Replace the old components with new parts from the repair kit.

Reassembly of Carburetor Reassemble the carburetor when parts are clean and dry, following these steps:

1. Slide in the throttle shaft and install the

throttle plate using new screws (if supplied in repair kit). The plate must be centered in the bore before tightening. To center, back off the throttle lever. Seat the plate by gently tapping with a small screwdriver, then tighten screws.

2. Install the choke shaft and plate using the same procedure as in step 1.

3. Install the idle-mixture screw assembly. Turn the screw in until it becomes lightly seated and then out one turn, plus or minus ¼ turn for Onan, or the number of turns specified by the AC-generator manufacturer. Do not force the mixture-adjustment screw; overtightening can damage the needle and seat.

4. Install the needle and seat, the fuel-bowl gasket, and the float assembly (Figure 5.22). Make sure the clips and springs are properly placed and the float can move freely.

5. Invert the float-and-needle valve assembly and check the float level between the float and gasket (Figure 5.23). The full weight of the float should be resting on the needle valve and spring. The distance between the float and the bowl-flange gasket should be

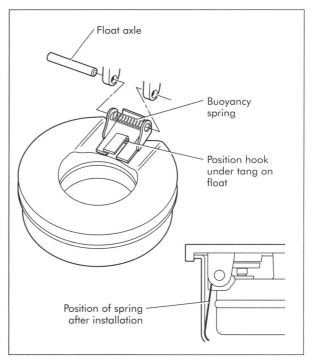

Figure 5.22 Procedure for installing a float and a needle and seat assembly in Onan AC-generator carburetors

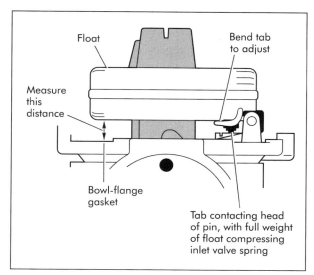

Figure 5.23 Adjusting the carburetor float level in Onan AC generators

$\frac{1}{16}$ inch, plus or minus $\frac{1}{32}$ inch. This figure is for the Onan; other measurements will vary depending on the AC-generator manufacturer. To achieve the proper distance, remove the float and bend the tab, but only at the point specified by the float manufacturer (marked on the float). The needle and seat can become damaged if the float is adjusted while in the carburetor.

6. Install the float bowl and main-mixture screw assembly. Turn the screw in until lightly seated, then out two turns, plus or minus $\frac{1}{4}$ turn for Onan or the specified figure for other manufacturers.

7. Reverse steps 1 through 9 under Carburetor Removal and Disassembly on page 5.12 to reassemble the carburetor, the manifold, and the air cleaner.

8. Readjust mixture screws as described on page 5.11.

Propane Conversions

A number of RV manufacturers are using LP-gas-powered AC generators in rigs where it is not practical to use a separate gasoline tank (for example, diesel-powered motorhomes and fifth-wheels). One drawback of a propane-powered AC generator is that it uses the same propane supply needed to operate the stove, the refrigerator, the water heater, and the furnace in the RV, and that consumption must be monitored carefully. The other major drawback is that propane does not produce as many Btus of energy as gasoline, so an LP-gas-powered AC generator will usually be downrated from its gasoline-powered counterpart.

A gaseous fuel system consists of four primary systems: the supply tank, the electric propane-fuel-lock-off solenoid, the regulator, and the carburetor (Figures 5.24 and 5.25).

The supply tank used in RVs is a "vapor-withdrawal" type, that is, the vapors that form above the liquid fuel in the tank are used for the appliances. The normal method of linking to the standard RV-propane system is to install a tee fitting into the gas line. Care must be taken to insure that all fittings are sealed with approved thread sealants and not tape-type sealants, which can break off and get into the valve seats in the lockout solenoid, the regulator, or the carburetor and cause a gas leak. Also make sure that only gas-type "black pipe" and LP-gas-approved flexible pipe is used when connecting the system to the propane source.

The fuel-lockoff solenoid is operated by the start/run circuit in the AC generator. It opens when the AC generator is first started and remains open while it's running. When the AC generator is shut down, the solenoid closes to prevent fuel from escaping.

The regulator supplies the proper amount of fuel pressure to the carburetor. Normally, the regulator

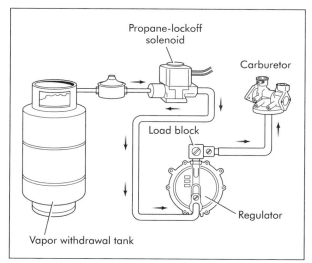

Figure 5.24 LP-gas fuel system for AC generators

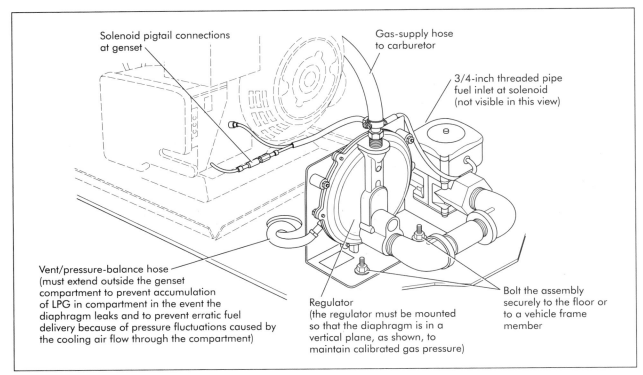

Solenoid pigtail connections at genset

Gas-supply hose to carburetor

3/4-inch threaded pipe fuel inlet at solenoid (not visible in this view)

Vent/pressure-balance hose (must extend outside the genset compartment to prevent accumulation of LPG in compartment in the event the diaphragm leaks and to prevent erratic fuel delivery because of pressure fluctuations caused by the cooling air flow through the compartment)

Regulator (the regulator must be mounted so that the diaphragm is in a vertical plane, as shown, to maintain calibrated gas pressure)

Bolt the assembly securely to the floor or to a vehicle frame member

Figure 5.25 The gaseous fuel system consists of four primary systems.

is set to provide 9 to 13 inches water-column pressure (3½ to 5 psi) under all conditions. Care must be taken to make sure the pressure does not exceed that recommended by the AC-generator manufacturer. In some systems, a secondary regulator called a *load block* is used and should be adjusted only by persons familiar with its operation.

Propane-gas carburetors (Figure 5.26) are quite different from the gasoline type and no attempt to interchange them should be made. The carburetor is normally provided by the AC-generator manufacturer to fit the specific model.

The AC-generator manufacturer will provide the specifications, installation, and test data for the installation but safety has to be one of the primary concerns of the end user.

Choke Adjustment (Kohler)

AC generators utilize a 12-volt DC electric-choke system (Kohler's 2.5-kw unit has a manual, hand-operated choke) to enrich the fuel mixture when the engine is cold. To adjust the choke:

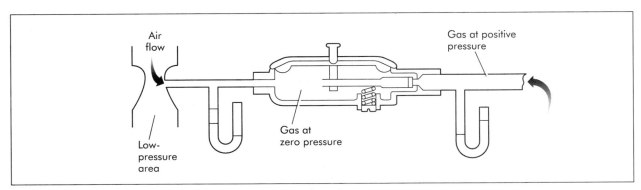

Air flow

Gas at positive pressure

Low-pressure area

Gas at zero pressure

Figure 5.26 LP-gas carburetor operating systems in the AC generator

1. Loosen the two screws securing the choke assembly to its bracket.
2. When properly set, the choke plate will be within 5 to 10 degrees of full open at 70°F.
3. Rotate choke housing to attain this setting.
4. Tighten the retaining screws.

Choke Adjustment (Onan)

To adjust Onan models:

1. Allow the engine to completely cool.
2. Remove the plastic choke cover and mounting nut.
3. Loosen the heating-element screws.
4. Rotate the element housing until the choke plate is halfway open.
5. Slowly rotate the cover counterclockwise while tapping the carburetor choke lever and making the choke lever bounce slightly. Continue the rotation until tapping the lever no longer makes it bounce. This is the fully closed position and becomes the reference position.
6. Refer to Table 5.2 to determine the number of degrees the cover must be rotated from the reference position. Marks on the housing are in 5-degree increments.
7. Rotate the cover as specified in the chart, depending on the air temperature.
8. Tighten the screws and move the lever back and forth to check for binding.
9. Install the choke cover and tighten the mounting nut.

Generac Choke Adjustment

To make the adjustment:

1. When the choke solenoid is not actuated, the carburetor choke plate should be about ⅛ inch from its full-open position. If necessary, use needlenose pliers to bend the tip of the bimetal piece on the automatic choke assembly to obtain the desired setting (Figure 5.27).
2. Loosen the screws that retain the choke solenoid to its bracket. Slide the choke solenoid

Table 5.2 Choke Adjustments

Ambient air temperature	Rotation from reference mark*
40°F (4°C)	0°
45°F (7°C)	4°CW
50°F (10°C)	8°CW
55°F (13°C)	12°CW
60°F (16°C)	16°CW
65°F (18°C)	20°CW
70°F (21°C)	24°CW
75°F (24°C)	27°CW
80°F (27°C)	32°CW
85°F (29°C)	35°CW
90°F (32°C)	39°CW
95°F (35°C)	43°CW
100°F (38°C)	47°CW

*Each mark on the choke housing equals 5° of angular rotation.

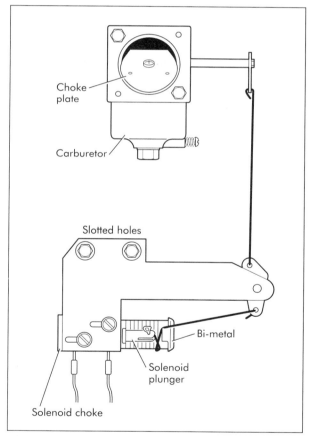

Figure 5.27 Generac automatic choke assembly

in the slotted holes of the bracket to adjust the axial movement of the solenoid plunger. Adjust the axial-plunger movement so that with the carburetor choke plate closed, the choke-adjustment-solenoid plunger is bottomed in the solenoid coil (full-bottomed position). With the choke plate closed and plunger bottomed in the coil, tighten the two screws.

Governor Adjustment

Voltage output and frequency of the AC generator are affected by engine speed, which is controlled by the governor. In most late-model AC generators, this is done with an electronic sensor working in conjunction with the ignition system to control engine RPM. These governors are not adjustable; if they are suspected of failure, the unit must be replaced.

Increasing engine speed increases voltage and frequency, and vice versa. The governor maintains constant engine speed as the load conditions vary so that voltage and frequency remain within factory parameters. The most popular generators operate at 1,800 RPM at a voltage range between 120 and 132 volts and a frequency range between 59 and 63 hertz. The owner should limit adjustment of the governor to checking voltage by changing the linkage position.

Adjusting the frequency requires instrumentation not normally available to the average mechanic. If voltage is too high or too low after checking with a multimeter, the governor linkage can be adjusted to temporarily improve voltage. A factory-certified service center should fine-tune voltage and frequency as soon as possible.

If you are the owner of an older AC generator that uses a mechanical speed regulator, read the following section.

Adjusting the Kohler Governor

To adjust the Kohler governor, follow these steps (see Table 5.3):

1. Probe the closest 120-volt AC plug receptacle to the AC generator using a multimeter.
2. Make sure all appliances and the circuit breaker to the power converter are off.
3. Start the AC generator and read the voltage.
4. If an adjustment is necessary, shut down the AC generator and loosen the outside locking nut on the speed-adjusting arm.
5. Restart the AC generator.
6. To increase speed and voltage, turn the adjusting nut (next to the locking nut) so that it tightens or draws back the speed-adjusting arm (Figure 5.28).
7. To decrease speed and voltage, loosen the adjusting nut.
8. Tighten the locking nut after proper voltage is achieved.

Table 5.3 Kohler Voltage and Frequency Specifications

No load	62–63 Hz	1,800 RPM	120 volts, ± 5 volts
Full load	59–60 Hz	1,800 RPM	120 volts, ± 5 volts

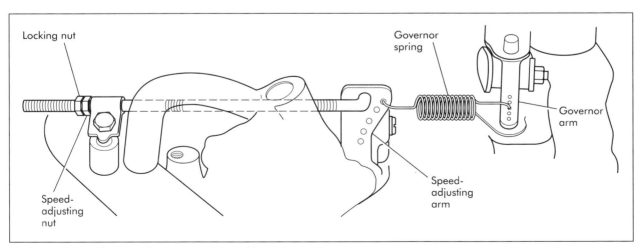

Figure 5.28 Adjusting the governor in Kohler AC generators

9. Open circuit breaker(s) for the power converter and appliances.

If the governor is too sensitive, engine speed will surge as the load changes. If a big drop is noticed when a normal load is applied, the governor must be set for greater sensitivity. This is accomplished by changing the position of the governor spring in the governor arm holes. Move the spring in to make the governor control more sensitive or out to make it less sensitive. Recheck the engine speed after changing sensitivity.

Adjusting the Onan Governor

To adjust the Onan governor, follow these steps (see Table 5.4):

1. Run the AC generator for ten minutes under a light load to allow engine to reach its normal operating temperature .
2. Make sure all the appliances and the circuit breaker to the power converter are off.
3. Probe the closest 120-volt AC plug receptacle to the AC generator using a multimeter.
4. Make sure the carburetor is properly adjusted.
5. Adjust the length of the governor linkage (Figure 5.29) and check for binding or looseness.
6. Adjust the length so that the stop on the throttle-shaft assembly almost touches the stop on the side of the carburetor. This should be done with the engine stopped and with tension on the governor spring. The adjustment is correct if one more turn on the ball joint will allow the throttle-shaft stop to touch the carburetor. Tighten the locknut.
7. With the AC generator running at no load, turn the speed-adjusting nut in to increase speed and voltage, or out to decrease speed and voltage. Then check the voltage under load (close

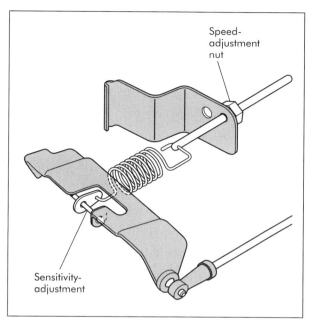

Figure 5.29 Adjusting the governor in Onan AC generators

the circuit breakers and turn on 120-volt AC appliances) using the same technique.
8. The sensitivity-adjustment screw must be set to insure minimum (or no) speed and voltage difference between no load and full load, without causing the engine to hunt. To increase sensitivity or allow closer regulation, turn the screw counterclockwise; to decrease sensitivity, turn the screw clockwise.
9. Recheck speed and voltage after readjusting sensitivity.

Generac Governor Adjustment

This static governor adjustment must be made prior to starting the engine or attempting to perform governor adjustments while the engine is running (Figure 5.30).

1. Loosen the governor-lever bolt and nut.
2. Push on the governor lever until the throttle is wide open. *Do not bend the governor linkage.*
3. Hold the governor lever in the "wide-open-throttle" position and rotate the governor shaft counterclockwise as far as it will go.

Table 5.4 Onan Voltage and Frequency Specifications

Maximum no load	63 Hz	1,890 RPM	132.0 volts
Minimum full load	57 Hz	1,710 RPM	108.0 volts
Normal no load	62 Hz	1,800 RPM	127.5 volts, (± 4.5 volts)

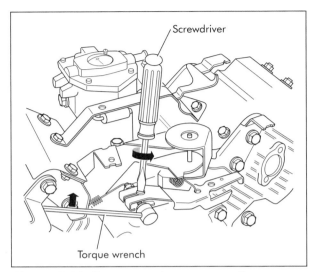

Figure 5.30 Generac static governor adjustment

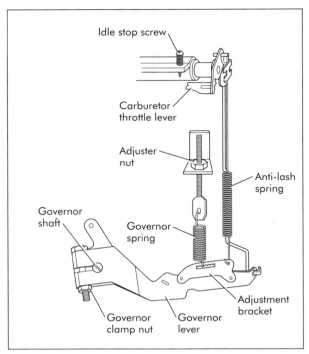

Figure 5.31 Governor adjustment for vertical-shaft units

4. Hold the shaft in the fully counterclockwise position and tighten the governor-lever bolt and nut. Torque the governor-lever bolt and nut to 8 N-m (70 inch-pounds).

The dynamic-governor adjustment is performed with the engine running. With the static-governor adjustment and choke adjustments completed:

1. Inspect the anti-lash spring (Figure 5.31) to make sure it is not broken or disengaged.
2. Connect an accurate AC frequency meter to the AC generator's output leads.
3. Start the engine: let it stabilize and warm up without any load attached to it.
4. Turn the adjuster nut to attain a frequency reading as close as possible to 62 hertz.
5. Apply electrical loads and test AC generator operation with loads applied. Apply electrical loads as close as possible to the AC generator's full-rated wattage capacity. Note the amount of frequency drop when loads are applied. Also note whether excessive hunting occurs when loads are disconnected.
6. If frequency drops below about 59 hertz with a load applied, disconnect the load and move the governor spring in the adjustment bracket closer to the anti-lash spring, then readjust with the adjuster nut to obtain a no-load frequency as close as possible to 62 hertz.

Again apply a load and check drop.

7. Continue the above procedures until the no-load speed is as close as possible to 62 hertz and excessive drop does not occur under load and until excess hunting does not occur when the load is removed.

Exhaust System

The exhaust system routes exhaust gas from the engine away from the vehicle (Figure 5.32). A properly designed system will require little maintenance, just regular inspection.

1. Inspect the exhaust-system installation. It should be routed so that harmful gases may not be drawn into the vehicle through windows, doors, air conditioning system, etc. Make sure the system is fitted with steel tubing, not the flexible tailpiping material that can crack and leak, possibly causing exhaust poisoning of the occupants.
2. Check the tailpipe outlet to make sure it has not been crushed closed, which will cause

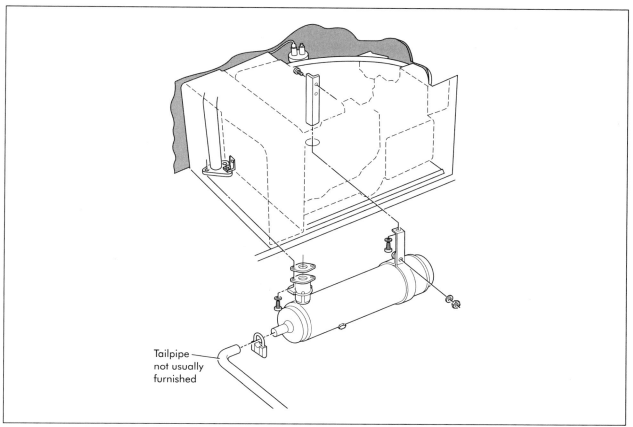

Figure 5.32 Typical exhaust system for an AC-generator set

Tailpipe not usually furnished

excessive back pressure, poor AC generator performance, and possible overheating.

3. Make sure all components of the exhaust system are at least 3 inches away from any combustible material in the AC generator compartment, floor, or exterior panel of the vehicle.

4. Make sure the muffler and tailpipe are in good condition, with no heavy corrosion or holes in the piping or muffler.

5. Most AC generators are fitted with a spark-arrestor-type muffler. Check your owner's manual for any cleaning/replacement requirements.

■ CHAPTER 6 ■
HEATING SYSTEMS

Propane-fired furnaces are used for comfort heating in all RVs, with the exception of a few luxury motorcoaches. The forced-air ducted furnace is the most prevalent technology in use throughout the industry. This type of furnace operates in much the same manner as a household furnace, heating air in a heat exchanger, then employing a blower to force the heated air through a system of ducts routed to various points in the RV.

A second style of propane-fired RV furnace is the undercounter unit. In this type of furnace, air is heated by a heat exchanger and is blown into the RV directly from the furnace, without the use of ducts. Undercounter furnaces are most often installed in smaller RVs, such as tent trailers and pickup campers, where heat distribution over a wide area is not required.

Another source of heat is the catalytic heater. These units are normally used as auxiliary heat sources. Catalytic heaters mix propane and air in a silica wool pad impregnated with platinum. Platinum is the catalyst that allows combustion to take place without a flame. Catalytic heaters produce warmth that heats objects and people, but not the air. Even though catalytic heaters are nearly 100 percent efficient, they still consume oxygen and therefore require attention to ventilation in the living space. As a comparison, forced-air units operate at about an 80-percent efficiency level.

A fourth type is the perimeter heating system, found only in a few large, luxury motorhomes. Installation of a perimeter heating system requires the living area be specifically designed for use of the system. These systems heat water, which is then circulated by means of a small electric pump through pipes around the perimeter of the RV's floor. It is a radiant-heat system that produces a very even and comfortable level of warmth throughout the coach.

■ FORCED-AIR FURNACES ■

All forced-air furnaces share similar basic operating principles (Figure 6.1). The term *forced air* is derived from the fact that outside air is force-fed to a sealed combustion-chamber assembly while interior air is moved through a heat exchanger.

The typical sequence of operation for a modern RV forced-air furnace is as follows:

■ The thermostat is first in line of the controls for the furnace operating circuit. By reacting to room temperature, the thermostat opens or closes a set of contact points that permit electric current to flow to the on/off switch and then to the delay relay.

■ The delay relay incorporates a heater coil that activates a bi-metal disc closing the relay circuit.

■ The current then flows to the motor and activates the blower. The motor shaft powers one wheel for circulation air and another that provides combustion air to the burner.

■ The circulating air blows against the sail switch, and as the switch is activated it completes the circuit. The sail switch is in the system as a safety device to insure that there is adequate air for combustion.

■ The limit switch is a safety device that protects the furnace against overheating. At a given temperature, the switch opens, thereby shutting off power to the ignition system that controls the gas valve.

■ Furnaces with electronic-ignition systems incorporate a timing circuit to allow the blower to purge the chamber of combustion products

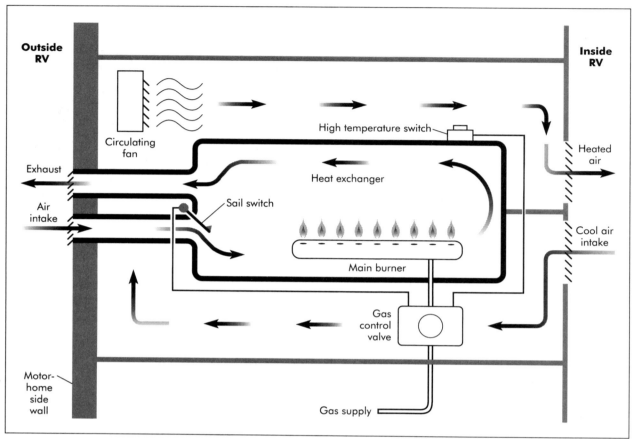

Figure 6.1 The operation and flow of a typical RV heating furnace

or gases. Then the system will apply current to the gas valve and simultaneously produce a high-voltage-current supply to the electrode to generate a spark at the burner. A sensor confirms the presence of a flame. If a flame is not sensed after a few seconds, the system will try again to ignite the furnace. If there is repeated failure to ignite, the furnace will go into lockout mode.

■ As the room temperature rises, the thermostat will sense this and the contacts will open, thus removing power from the controls. The blower will remain active until the relay opens and stops the motor.

There are three types of ignition systems. The most basic ignition system is a manual match-lit pilot (called a *standing pilot*) that remains on until it is manually turned off. More technologically advanced is the piezo-electric spark ignition used to light the standing pilot

(this eliminates the need for a match). Most advanced is an electronic-ignition system in which a transformer generates a spark to light the main burner upon demand from the thermostat, resulting in a fully automatic, pilotless lighting system.

Furnace operation is controlled by a wall-mounted thermostat. The thermostat monitors the RV's interior temperature and signals the furnace when to turn on and off. It does this through a set of electrical contact points that open and close, depending upon the relationship between the thermostat setting and the ambient temperature. When the room temperature falls below the adjusted setting on the thermostat dial, the contacts close. This energizes the furnace circuitry that starts the heating cycle.

What happens next depends upon the type of ignition system being used. In standing pilot furnaces, the gas-control valve opens, sending propane to the pilot flame, and the burner ignites. In electronic-ignition furnaces (direct spark ignition or DSI), the gas-control valve opens and a spark is simultaneously generated to ignite the main burner.

Gas-burning furnaces consume oxygen and must be vented to the outside to prevent the oxygen inside the RV from being consumed. The way the furnace heats room air without consuming the oxygen in the room is ingenious. The flame burning in the combustion chamber heats the air in a sealed heat exchanger. A fan pulls cold air from inside the RV through the heat exchanger where it is heated and forced back into the living compartment. It is the separation of air used for combustion and air used for heating the interior of the RV that makes the furnace safe.

Safe Use of Forced-Air Furnaces

Safe use of a propane-fired forced-air furnace is further enhanced by several other features. Chief among these is the thermocouple (Figure 6.2), a heat-sensing device that detects a level of heat and responds by generating a small electric current. This current is sent to the gas-control device that will shut off the gas supply if current is not available. An example of how this works is as follows: If the pilot flame were to blow out, the thermocouple would sense the lack of heat and fail to produce an electric current—which would, in turn, signal the control valve to shut off the gas supply.

Another important safety feature is a special switch called a *sail* or an *air-prover* (Figure 6.3). It is so-named because it is sensitive to airflow. The purpose of the sail switch is to detect airflow to the burner assembly and take certain safety steps if the airflow is not

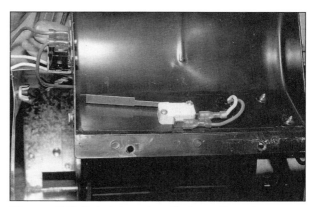

Figure 6.3 Switch here is called a *sail* or *air-prover*.

proper. If, for example, airflow is inadequate to the combustion chamber, the sail switch will not permit the gas-control valve to open, and the main burner cannot be ignited. If, for any reason, the air supply to the burner is blocked, restricted, or hampered by slow fan speed due to low system voltage, the sail switch will prevent the furnace from operating.

Critical to the safe operation of a forced-air furnace is the temperature-limit switch (Figure 6.4). This safety switch is normally closed and will open only if the furnace assembly becomes overheated. When the switch opens, it causes the gas-control valve to close, discontinuing gas flow to the main burner. An example of a situation in which the temperature-limit switch would come into operation, shutting the system down, would be if the furnace outlet were blocked, resulting in an an overheated furnace.

At the end of the heating cycle, the heat exchanger needs to be cooled down and the combustion cham-

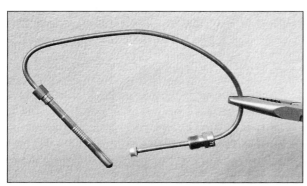

Figure 6.2 Thermocouple for propane forced-air furnace

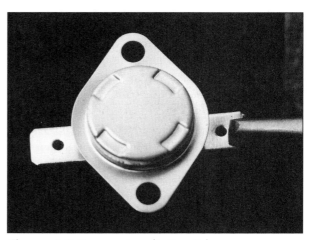

Figure 6.4 Temperature-limit switch

Figure 6.5 Furnace fan switch

ber purged. This task is accomplished by a furnace fan switch (Figure 6.5). When the interior living space is warm enough, the thermostat contacts open, shutting the gas-control valve, and the flame dies. Even though the burner is no longer operating, the combustion chamber and heat exchanger remain hot and must be cooled and purged. The furnace-fan switch permits the fan to operate until the assembly is cool, before shutting off. At that point, the furnace can be reignited by simply turning the thermostat dial to a higher temperature.

A malfunction in any of the integrated safety systems discussed can cause a problem with furnace operation. Following a logical course of troubleshooting can reveal the defective component.

Preventive Maintenance Inspections of Forced-Air Furnaces

The forced-air furnace should be inspected on an annual basis. This is essential if an RV owner is to have reliable and safe operation of the furnace. Here are the major check areas:

1. *Inspect the furnace monthly during the heating season*: Look for soot buildup on the vent. This is an indication of incomplete combustion and is a warning that the furnace is operating in an unsafe condition. If soot is observed on the vent, shut down the furnace immediately and contact a qualified service technician.

2. *Air Wheel*: This should be clean and clear of obstructions. Starting the furnace with something in the blower air chamber will damage the wheel.

3. *Burner*: The burner requires no adjustments but should have a clear blue flame. If the burner has a yellow or wavering flame, the burner should be cleaned and inspected. Burners should be cleaned with a wire brush to remove debris, rust, and corrosion buildup. If this fails to rectify the situation, the burner should be replaced.

4. *Combustion Chamber:* Check the air intake and the flue areas of the furnace for internal obstructions such as wasp or bird nests. The life span of the chamber is in direct proportion to the amount of usage; therefore, it is essential to inspect the chamber for cracks or holes. The unit is not field repairable and should be replaced if it is damaged.

5. *Control Compartment*: This is the area around the furnace. It should be free of dirt and lint.

6. *Direct Spark Ignition Module*: If the DSI or control-module board is found to be defective, it must be replaced; there is no field repair for this part. Make sure that the replacement part is the exact board called for by the manufacturer.

7. *Ducting*: All heat ducts should be clear of sawdust, lint, and obstructions. Make sure all the ducts are firmly connected to the furnace and that there is a minimum of ¼ inch clearance where they pass through combustible construction or cabinetry. There must be a minimum number of ducts as required by the individual furnace manufacturer (for the specific model furnace). Failure to use the minimum number of ducts can create overheating problems.

8. *Gas Pressure*: The normal pressure is 11 inches water column and can be checked by a manometer (see page 2.5). If you do not have a manometer or don't know how to use one, have the pressure checked by a qualified RV technician.

9. *Gaskets*: Inspect all gaskets for tight seals. *Do not reuse gaskets.*

10. *Motor*: The motor is a sealed unit and is

permanently lubricated. If the motor makes unusual noises or drags when it warms up, replace it with an exact replacement part.

11. *Physical Support*: Inspect the flooring, supports, and frame around the furnace.

12. *Return Air*: The return-air passage should be clear of obstructions and free of lint, spider webs, or other combustibles. Do not use "wasp filters" over the return air or exhaust. These screens can eventually restrict airflow, leading to a dangerous situation. Also, use of these screens will void the warranty provided by the furnace manufacturer.

13. *Voltage*: There should be between 10.5 and 13.5 volts DC at the furnace during operation. The gas valve will not open if voltage is below 10.5. If the battery is okay, check for faulty or light-gauge wiring and/or defective terminals.

Cautions and Warnings

Before you attempt to perform any repair work on your furnace, you need to be aware of these precautions:

1. RV furnaces and propane systems involve potential hazards. These systems should only be serviced or repaired by those who are familiar and comfortable with the proper procedures. Major repairs should be performed only by professional service technicians.

2. If any of the gas lines are to be disconnected, make sure the source is turned off and the gas in the lines has time to dissipate before beginning work. All spark sources must be turned off or disconnected.

3. Never operate the furnace with the electrode wire disconnected or with the electrode assembly removed from the furnace.

4. Never use a battery charger to provide power to check the furnace operation. Use only a 12-volt battery.

5. Never use a screwdriver on any part of the electrode assembly while the furnace is operating.

6. Be sure the spark from the electrode never reaches the flame-sensor portion of the electrode assembly.

Figure 6.6 RV furnaces fail to perform properly when electrtic power to the system is lower than 10.5 volts.

7. Be sure the electrode assembly screws are snug at all times.

Service and Repair of Forced-Air Furnaces

RV furnaces fail to perform properly when electric power to the system is lower than 10.5 volts (Figure 6.6). When operating on power from the house batteries, it is not uncommon for furnace-function problems to be caused by low battery voltage. Many circuit boards are replaced when the actual problem is only a weak or dead battery. See page 1.11 to determine the battery's state of charge.

Furnaces that use electronic ignition systems generate high voltages to create a spark to light the main burner. This voltage can cause severe shock. Keep your hands and tools away from the igniter area when you are testing.

Correcting Pilot-Light Failure

One of the most common furnace problems is pilot-light failure. Check the following to correct this difficulty:

■ Check the propane tank to make sure there is an adequate amount of fuel.

■ Check that the gas-cylinder valve is open and the manual valve to the furnace is rotated so it is parallel with the gas-supply tubing (open position).

■ Make sure the gas-control valve in the furnace is turned to the on position and that the pilot-light button is fully depressed.

■ Check that the gas-pressure regulator is set to 11 inches of water-column pressure with the propane tank filled (see page 2.5).

■ If the furnace in question utilizes a piezoelectric spark lighter for the flame, there must be a spark present when the lighter is energized. If not, check the gap from the spark electrode to ground. It should be about ⅛ inch.

■ If the gas supply has been shut off during prolonged storage, the lines may be full of air (Figure 6.7). Try lighting the stove to purge air from the system. It may take several minutes and many attempts before the air in the lines is purged and gas reaches the pilot orifice.

■ The pilot gas orifice is very small and is prone to clogging. To check for a clogged orifice, place a small amount of soapy-water solution over the end of the orifice and push the pilot-light button on the gas-control valve. If no bubbles appear, the orifice is clogged.

■ Pilot orifices are so small that it is best to replace them rather than attempt to clean them. Do not try to insert any metal object through the orifice in an attempt to clean it; the precision-size hole in soft brass may become deformed.

■ Manual pilots usually have an adjustment screw located behind a cover screw in the gas controller. This screw is to adjust the height of the pilot flame. If it is closed too far, the flame will not ignite. Remove the cover screw (there will be a small O-ring located under this screw). The O-ring must be in place when the cover screw is returned, or gas will leak into the interior of the RV. Once the pilot flame is established, it should be adjusted to envelop the end of the thermocouple. Check for leaks, using soapy water when done.

Correcting Pilot-Light Outage (Manual-Control Models Only)

Sometimes the pilot is easy to ignite, but continually extinguishes. If constant pilot outage is a problem, there are several areas that can be checked and serviced.

■ The flame can be adjusted in two ways: With the flame-adjustment screw in the gas-control valve (Figure 6.8), or by slightly bending the pilot flame mounting bracket with needlenose pliers to direct the flame at the thermocouple (Figure 6.9). The pilot flame should be directed so that the entire end of the thermocouple is engulfed in flame.

■ If the pilot still goes out, it is possible that the

Figure 6.7 Gas supply to furnace is controlled by an in-line valve.

Figure 6.8 Flame-adjustment screw in the gas-control valve

Figure 6.9 Bend the pilot-flame-mounting bracket slightly with needlenose pliers to direct the flame at the thermocouple.

thermocouple is defective (Figure 6.10). The thermocouple unit is inexpensive and easy to replace. Turn off the gas supply at the valve on the propane tank. Using a tubing wrench, remove the connector nut where the thermocouple's tube connects with the gas-control valve. Remove the connection between the thermocouple tip and the furnace's combustion chamber.

■ To replace the unit, reverse the above procedure, making sure the tip of the thermocouple

Figure 6.10 If the pilot still goes out, it is possible that the thermocouple is defective.

is set at the correct distance from the pilot-flame orifice. Tighten the tubing nut into the gas-control valve finger tight, plus one-quarter turn. Do not overtighten, because it will damage the end of the tube and destroy the thermocouple.

■ Relight the pilot. The flame should continue to burn.

Checking for a Leaking Control Valve (Manual-Control Models Only)

Other reasons for pilot outage may be lack of venting, incorrect gas pressure, a leaking control valve, or improper pilot-flame adjustment. A leaking control valve allows a very small amount of raw gas to enter the chamber, where over a period of time it consumes the oxygen in the chamber, eventually causing the pilot to go out. To check for a leaking control valve:

■ Observe the main burner assembly when it is shut off. The presence of even a small flame will cause the pilot to fail.

■ If there is a flame present, other than the pilot flame, the gas controller should be replaced.

Replacing the Gas Controller (Manual-Control Models Only)

To replace the gas controller (Figure 6.11):

1. Make sure you have obtained an exact replacement, as stated in the furnace owner's manual. Use a controller designed for your specific application.
2. Shut off the propane supply at the main tank.
3. Carefully remove and mark all control wires so they are installed in the correct location on the new valve assembly.
4. With a tubing wrench, remove the propane inlet, the outlet to the main burner, the thermocouple, and the pilot tube from the control valve.
5. The control valve is now free from the furnace and can be removed.

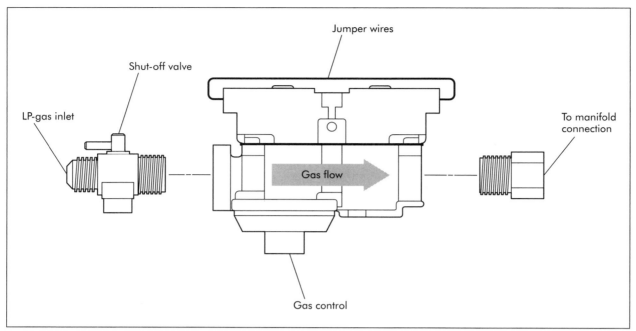

Jumper wires

Shut-off valve

LP-gas inlet

To manifold connection

Gas flow

Gas control

Figure 6.11 The gas-control valve in the furnace must be replaced with the identical part specified by the manufacturer.

6. Some furnaces may have the burner-manifold assembly connected directly to the gas valve. If this is the case, the burner assembly should be removed with the valve assembly so the valve can be placed in a bench vise to remove the burner.

7. Replace the new valve in the reverse order, connect the wires, turn on the gas, and check all connections with soapy water for leaks.

8. If there are no leaks, turn on the control valve, ignite, and adjust the pilot. Adjust the thermostat so the main burner will light. Check the condition of the pilot flame and main burner flame. When the main burner cycles off, the pilot should continue to burn.

Erratic furnace performance will result from gas-pressure fluctuation. Outside temperature and level of fuel in the propane tank play roles in determining gas pressure. Here's what Duo-Therm has to say about the importance of proper gas pressure:

Low gas pressure can lead to unsatisfactory furnace operation (nuisance lockouts, high-pitched noise during operation, reduced heat output and pilot outages, etc.). Be sure that the gas-line pres-sure at the furnace is 11 inches (water-column) pressure during furnace operation. This line pressure will result in a 9.5 to 10.5 manifold pressure at the gas-valve manifold outlet tap. Low gas-line pressure can be corrected by adjusting the propane-tank regulator. This adjustment should be made by a qualified service person.

At low temperatures, partially filled propane tanks may not be able to deliver sufficient gas to maintain adequate line pressure. For example, a 50-percent-full, 30-pound (7½-gallon) propane cylinder at 0°F can only supply 22,600 Btus of gas each hour, a 30-percent-full tank will further reduce this supply to 17,600 Btus per hour, and a 50-percent full tank at −10°F will deliver only 11,300 Btus per hour. When the demand on the system is greater than it can supply, line pressure will be reduced, which will adversely affect the operation of the appliance.

Checking for Other Burner-Light Failures

Even though the pilot is operating properly, the main burner may still fail to light. If that happens, here are some areas that should be checked:

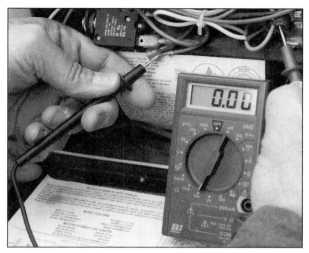

Figure 6.12 Checking the thermostat with a multimeter (ohms)

- Make sure the thermostat is turned on and set to a temperature high enough to activate the gas-control valve.
- To check the thermostat, disconnect the thermostat wires from the furnace. Then connect the leads from a multimeter (ohms) across these two wires. When the thermostat contacts close (thermostat set to high temperature), there should be a zero-ohm reading; when the contacts open (thermostat set to low temperature) there should be an infinity-ohm reading (Figure 6.12). If this does not occur, replace the thermostat with an exact duplicate. There are many different types of thermostats used in the RV industry. An incompatible replacement may render the furnace inoperable.
- Low-battery voltage will not allow the furnace fan to operate fast enough to close the sail switch. Make sure voltage is at least 10.5.
- A stuck sail switch that does not respond to airflow will not allow the gas-control valve to open. The furnace must be removed from its compartment to gain access to the switch and associated linkage. The sail switch can be checked with a multimeter (ohms). It should be in the open position (infinity on the ohm meter) normally, and closed (zero ohms) only when there is sufficient airflow.
- Reversed battery polarity will cause the fan motor to operate in reverse. This will not allow the sail switch to close and activate the

burner. If the furnace is ducted, make sure the ducting and register grates are not blocked or kinked. If airflow cannot escape the furnace at an adequate rate, the limit switch will overheat, causing the gas-control valve to shut down the burner. The burner intake and outlet on the exterior of the RV must be clear. Any blockage here will reduce airflow to the combustion chamber, making the flame nearly impossible to light. Check for animal nests or other obstructions in the vent inlet and outlet.

- If the furnace has electronic ignition, the spark may not be adequate to start the gas burning. Check to see that the electrode gap is correct. For all models of furnaces the gap should be ⅛ inch, plus or minus 1/32 inch. If there still is no spark, check the electrode lead for cracks and broken insulation. If there are high voltage leaks, the spark will fail to appear.
- The spark is controlled by a modular printed circuit board. It is important that the board's wiring connections and terminals be clean. Corrosion and dirt at these terminals can cause the spark ignition to fail. Remove the connections and check for dirt and corrosion. Use a cotton swab and alcohol to clean the terminal connections.
- If the main burner still fails to light, the problem could be a clogged main burner jet. To clean the jet, the burner assembly must be removed from the gas-control valve (Figure 6.13). Do not attempt to clean the jet with a metal object, as the jet can become damaged, producing an incorrect amount of gas flow. Clean the jet with a wooden or plastic toothpick (Figure 6.14). If the clog cannot be removed by this method, a new jet should be purchased and installed.

Checking for Burner Lockout (Electronic-Ignition Furnaces Only)

Burner lockout occurs only in electronic-ignition furnaces (Figures 6.15 and 6.16). It is noticeable when the main burner momentarily ignites, then goes out. The furnace must be shut off for several minutes while it resets, then the attempt can be made to

■ **TROUBLESHOOTING** ■
THE FORCED-AIR FURNACE

Problem	Possible Cause	Correction
Pilot will not light	Empty LP-gas supply	Replenish
	Wrong LP-gas pressure	Adjust to 11 inches water-column pressure
	Defective piezo lighter	Replace lighter assembly
	Incorrect spark gap	Set spark gap
	Clogged pilot orifice	Clean or replace
	Air in gas line	Purge gas line
	Adjustment screw wrong	Adjust pilot screw
Pilot will not stay lit	Defective thermocouple	Replace thermocouple
	Air leakage	Check for leakage
	Lack of air	Check for venting
	Leaking control valve	Check control valve
	Incorrect gas pressure	Set to 11 inches water-column pressure
	Clogged pilot orifice	Clean or replace orifice
	Pilot-adjustment screw	Adjust pilot-flame level
Noisy operation	Low input voltage	Charge or replace battery
	Unbalanced blower wheel	Replace blower wheel
	Loose blower wheel	Tighten wheel
	Loud burner	Adjust air shutter
	Rubbing blower wheel	Check clearance with housing
Main burner will not light	Thermostat off	Turn on thermostat
	Thermostat contacts open	Reset thermostat
	Gas off	Turn on gas supply
	Empty propane tank	Replenish supply
	Low gas level in tank	Refill tank
	Low gas pressure	Adjust to 11 inches water-column pressure
	Low battery voltage	Charge battery
	Stuck sail switch	Clean switch
	Defective sail switch	Replace switch
	Defective limit switch	Replace limit switch
	Reversed battery polarity	Check wiring
	Blocked ducting	Check duct hoses
	Blocked air intake	Check air intake
	Blocked burner exhaust	Clear burner exhaust
	No igniter spark	Check electrode lead
	Incorrect spark gap	Reset spark gap
	Dirty module connections	Clean connections
	Clogged main burner jet	Replace or clean jet

■ TROUBLESHOOTING ■
THE FORCED-AIR FURNACE, continued

Problem	Possible Cause	Correction
Burner lights but shuts off (lockout)	Misaligned flame sensor	Adjust flame sensor
	Loose sensor wire	Tighten connections
	Dirty sensor probe	Clean probe
	Defective sensor	Test sensor
	Defective module board	Replace board
	Low gas pressure	Set to 11 inches water-column pressure
	Low gas level in tank	Refill tank
Main burner will not shut off	High thermostat setting	Reduce temperature setting
	Stuck thermostat points	Replace relay
	Defective gas valve	Replace gas valve
Blower will not run	No or low voltage	Check voltage at furnace
	Blown 12-volt DC fuse	Check fuse and replace if necessary
	Reversed battery polarity	Check wire connections
	Open thermostat points	Check points for closing
	Locked motor	Rotate by hand to check
	Defective motor relay	Replace relay
	Defective motor	Replace motor
No igniter spark	Improper input polarity	Check 12-volt wiring
	No voltage present	Check voltage at furnace
	Poor electrode ground	Check ground connection
	Corroded connections	Clean connections
	Loose connections	Tighten connections
	Wrong spark gap	Set spark gap
	Broken electrode lead	Replace electrode lead
	Cracked insulators	Replace insulators
	Faulty module board	Replace module board

reignite the furnace. Chronic lockout may be attributable to one or more of the following causes:

■ Instead of a thermocouple, the electronic furnace utilizes a flame sensor. The flame sensor is mounted next to the spark-ignition system and is exposed to the main burner when it lights. If the sensor is not exposed directly to the flame, it will cause lockout. The sensor can be bent slightly to aim it into the flame area.
■ If the sensor tip is dirty and corroded, it should be cleaned with steel wool or crocus cloth for better heat contact.
■ The electronic sensor and control board re-

quire special testing equipment that can measure microamps of current. Seek help at a qualified service center.
■ Low gas pressure can reduce the flame output to a level that is too low to activate the heat sensor. Have gas pressure set to 11 inches of water-column pressure.

Checking for Burner-Shutoff Failure

The opposite problem of lockout is failure for the main burner to shut off. If this situation occurs, check the following:

Figure 6.13 To clean the jet, the burner assembly must be removed from the gas-control valve.

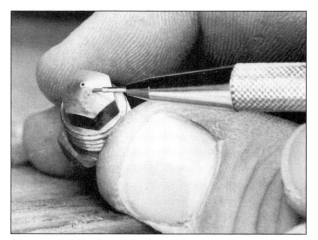

Figure 6.14 Clean the jet with a wooden or plastic toothpick.

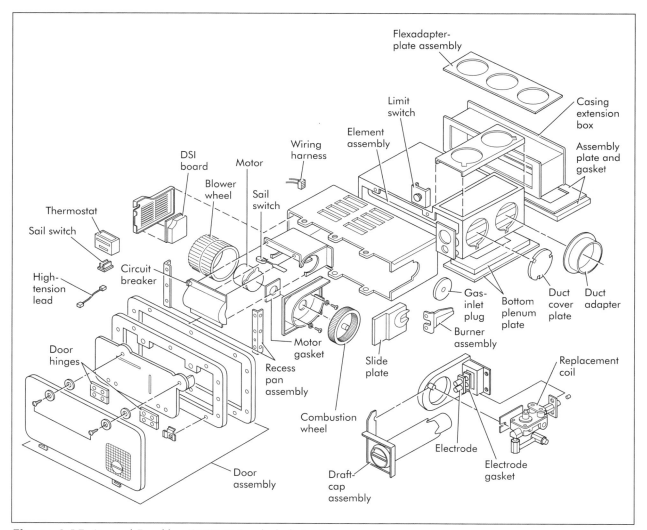

Figure 6.15 Atwood Excalibur 8500-III (exploded view)

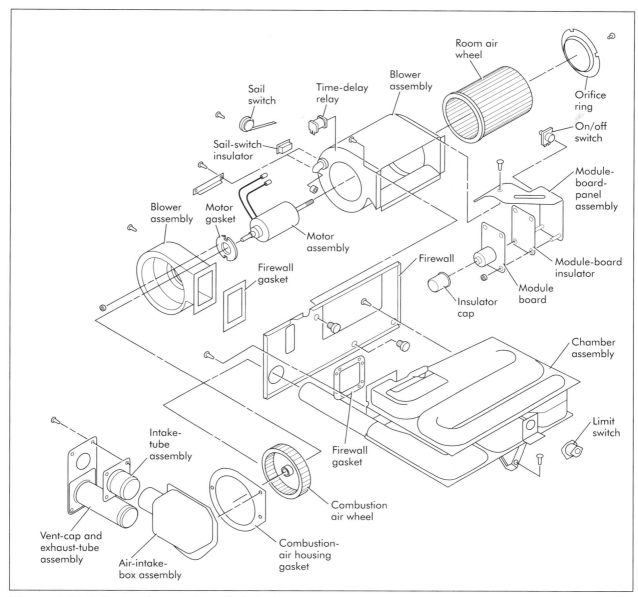

Figure 6.16 Suburban furnace (exploded view)

- The thermostat must be set to a lower setting. If this does not correct the problem, the points in the thermostat may be stuck closed; they can be examined by removing the thermostat cover.
- The points can also be checked with a multimeter (ohms). If the multimeter reads zero when the thermostat is turned to its lowest temperature, the points are stuck closed. They probably are pitted and will stick again, even if they are manually pushed apart. Replace-

ment of the thermostat is recommended.

- If the thermostat responds to temperature, the problem may be in the gas-control valve. Remove the wires from the control valve while the main burner is activated. This should allow the valve to shut immediately. If it does not, the valve is defective and should be replaced.
- The thermostat also contains a small internal adjustment called a *heat anticipator*, which can delay furnace shutdown if it is set too high

Figure 6.17 Furnace heating cycles can be controlled by adjusting the heat anticipator in the wall thermostat (arrow).

Figure 6.18 The points in the wall thermostat should be checked with a multimeter to insure that proper contact is being made.

(Figure 6.17). By moving a small lever, you can change this setting. A move toward a smaller number will cause the furnace to shut off sooner (a shorter heating cycle), and a move to a larger number will cause the heater to run longer (a longer heating cycle). Most furnaces will cycle five to six times an hour. Expect short cycling in warmer weather when the inside temperature comes up to the thermostat setting faster. Experiment to see which settings give the best results. For example, the anticipator on all hydro-flame furnaces should be set at 1.0.

Checking for Blower-Motor Failure

Failure of the blower motor to start is another furnace problem that may occur. If the blower fails to operate, the sail switch cannot close and the main burner cannot light. Following are some problem areas to look for if the blower motor fails to start:

- Check the 12-volt DC fuse or circuit breaker that protects the furnace. If the fuse is blown, replace it with a new fuse of the proper amperage. If the fuse continues to fail, this is an indication of a problem that may require expert assistance.

- Low battery voltage can cause the furnace to become inoperable. Make sure that a minimum of 10. 5 volts are present at the furnace.
- Crossed wires may cause the blower to fail to operate. Make sure correct polarity is observed.
- Check the thermostat points (Figure 6.18). If they fail to close, the motor cannot start (Figure 6.19). The points can be manually closed with a small screwdriver, and they can be checked with a multimeter (ohms) to insure

Figure 6.19 The furnace motor cannot operate if the thermostat points fail to close (arrow).

that when they make contact, a good connection occurs. With the wires to the thermostat removed from the furnace, there should be a zero-ohm reading on the meter when the points are closed.

■ Some furnaces have a motor relay that can fail. Check with an authorized service center for your brand of furnace.

■ If all else is determined to be good, the motor should be removed from the furnace and tested. If it will not function with a direct 12-volt DC hookup, it is defective and should be replaced.

Checking for Noise

If noise is the primary complaint, it usually comes from the blower-fan assembly but can also be caused by an improperly burning flame or low battery voltage. Check the following:

■ Low voltage can cause the fan motor to run at a less than optimal speed. The noise generated is generally a low-frequency groan. The low blower speed can also affect combustion in the burner chamber, allowing the flame to make a roaring noise. The problem is easily solved by charging the battery, replacing it if necessary, or using campground electrical hookups.

■ In rare cases, the blower wheel may be out of balance or loose on the motor shaft. If this is

the case, the entire furnace must be removed and disassembled to gain access to the fan. A metallic scraping sound may indicate that the blower is rubbing against the surrounding housing. The furnace must be removed and disassembled to correct this problem.

Checking for Spark Failure

Electronic-ignition furnaces employ a high-voltage spark that jumps a gap, much like a spark plug, to ignite the propane-air mixture in the combustion chamber. If the spark fails to fire, there are several things you can do to solve the problem. For additional information, see the Spark Failure Checklist below.

■ CATALYTIC HEATERS ■

Catalytic heaters (Figure 6.22) operate very efficiently. Because there is no combustion chamber, heat exchanger, or exhaust to the outside, nearly all the heat generated by a catalytic heater is released to the living quarters. Catalytic heaters radiate infrared rays that warm objects and people, but do not heat the air in the enclosed area. The radiated heat is absorbed by objects and people and is then radiated back to heat the surrounding area.

In spite of their impressive efficiency, catalytic

■ CHECKLIST ■
FOR SPARK FAILURE

■ Check input polarity and voltage. Corrosion of the electrode-terminal connections can create a poor ground. The sparker assembly has a side electrode that must have a good ground in order for the spark to jump across. Check the electrode-assembly mounting screws for tightness. Make sure they are clean to insure a good ground.

■ Connection terminals to the modular printed circuit board must be clean. Contamination by dirt can cause spark failure. Remove the terminal connections and make sure that both the male and female parts of the plug are clean.

■ Using a flashlight, check to see that the spark gap between the sparking and ground electrodes is ⅛ inch, ± ¹⁄₃₂ inch (Figures 6.20 and 6.21). Bend only the ground electrode with needlenose pliers to establish the correct gap.

■ Cables that carry high voltages are subject to breakdown. Make sure the lead to the electrode is free of cracks. There are also ceramic insulators where the cable joins the furnace combustion chamber; make sure the ceramic is not cracked. If cracks are found in either the cable or insulators, replace the cable and electrode assembly.

■ If everything seems in order but still no spark appears, the failure may be in the modular control board itself. There are no on-the-road diagnostics; the board is simply unplugged from its mounting and replaced with a new one.

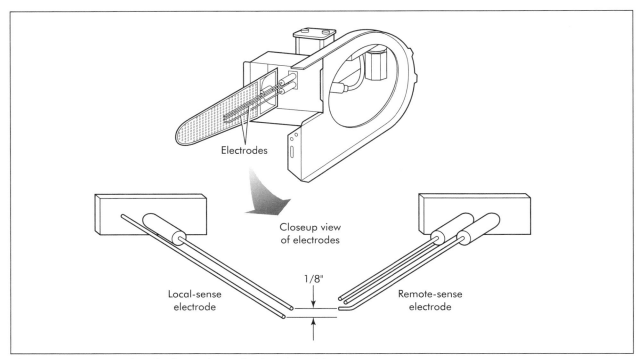

Figure 6.20 Burner head, electrode, and valve assembly

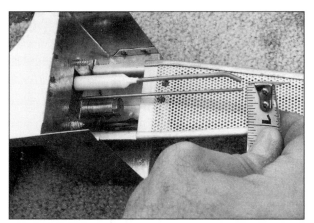

Figure 6.21 The electrode spark gap must be ⅛ inch, ± ¹⁄₃₂ inch, in furnaces with electronic ignition.

heaters require provisions for fresh-air ventilation because these heaters consume oxygen. At the very minimum, not less than one square inch of open window area per 1,000 Btus of heater output should be provided. For example, if the catalytic heater is rated at 8,000 Btus, the absolute minimum safe ventilation requirement would be eight square inches of open window area to prevent depletion of the oxygen inside the RV. Folding camping trailers are sometimes

Figure 6.22 Catalytic heater mounted on legs

thought of as not being air-tight because of the fabric walls. However, manufacturers of catalytic heaters are quick to point out that the fabric, when wet, can become almost impervious to the passage of air. So it is important to provide adequate free-air circulation when using a catalytic heater in a tent trailer.

Some catalytic heaters are equipped with oxygen

depletion sensors (ODS), which are designed to shut off the heater when the oxygen content of air surrounding the heater falls below 17.9 percent. Normal air at sea level contains 20.9 percent oxygen. A heater equipped with an ODS system will not function at altitudes much higher than 5,000 feet, because the oxygen content of the atmosphere at that elevation is not sufficient to satisfy the sensor.

Because there are no moving parts to wear out, other than the control-valve assembly, manufacturers of catalytic heaters do not recommend that owners attempt repairs. If a problem exists with the heater, call the manufacturer to obtain the name of an authorized repair station or return it to the manufacturer for necessary work.

Maintaining Catalytic Heaters

Care and maintenance of a catalytic heater is relatively simple. Following are a few maintenance tips, but you will note that most of them stress that excessive cleaning is neither necessary nor desirable.

- Do not clean the heater while it is hot.
- Keep the heater and the area around the heater clean and dust-free.
- Use a damp cloth to wipe away dust or accumulated grime from the grill and surrounding housing.

- Attempting to clean the catalyst pad will cause damage.
- Do not use a vacuum to clean the heater. The silica wool element can be easily damaged by vacuum suction.
- Do not use compressed air to clean the heater. Doing so will damage the pad.
- Some manufacturers recommend that, in order to maintain high-efficiency operation, the catalyst pad be replaced every three years or sooner if abnormal operation is noticed.

Troubleshooting

Even though catalytic heaters are relatively simple, there are still some areas where trouble can show up.

- On piezo-ignited units, if there is no spark when the igniter button is pressed several times, the igniter may need replacement.
- If the thermocouple will not stay lit when the control knob is released, the thermocouple is either not tightly connected to the control valve, or it is improperly positioned on the catalyst pad, or it is faulty and needs to be replaced. When replacing the thermocouple, care must be taken to position the new one in exactly the right place.

■ CHAPTER 7 ■
AIR-CONDITIONING SYSTEMS

Because the majority of RV travel takes place during warm seasons or to regions of the country where it is relatively warm even during winter months, personal comfort depends a great deal upon the use of an air conditioner. It has not been too many years ago that RV air conditioning was reserved for large luxury motorcoaches, but nowadays almost every RV—including small travel trailers and campers—is equipped with air conditioning. Roof-mounted air conditioners are most common, although some luxury RVs are equipped with central air systems. RV air conditioners are compressor-type units and work on the same operating principle as residential air conditioners.

■ COMPRESSOR AIR CONDITIONERS ■

Compressor-type air conditioners (Figures 7.1 and 7.2) are capable of transferring heat from one place to another, because the laws of physics dictate that heat tends to move toward cold. In order to remove heat from the interior of an RV, a refrigerant (Figure 7.3) is circulated through a closed system that includes an evaporator, where the refrigerant absorbs heat from the interior of the RV and then vaporizes. The refrigerant is then routed through the condenser, where the heat is removed and dissipated outside the RV.

A secondary benefit of an air-conditioning system is that, as it cools the interior air, it also acts as a dehumidifier, and dry air is more comfortable than humid air. When moisture in the atmosphere comes in contact with the cold evaporator, it condenses into water droplets (like water condensing on a glass of cold water). The process removes excess moisture, allowing it to drain from the air conditioner. When you see water dripping from the roof of your RV while the air conditioner is operating, this is the moisture that has been removed from the interior of the RV.

Working on an air conditioner system involves certain potential hazards. RV owners should be especially careful before proceeding with any type of maintenance or repair on one of these systems because high-pressure refrigerant and 120-volt AC power are involved. For the sake of safety, the sealed compressor/refrigerant system should not be opened or tampered with by the owner. This is a complex job best left to the experts. However, there are certain procedures that owners should follow to detect problems, or better yet, prevent them from occurring, through proper maintenance.

Operation During Cool Nights

When the outside temperature drops to below 75°F, the air-conditioner thermostat should be set to a midpoint between "warmer" and "cooler" to prevent ice buildup on the evaporator coil.

If ice-up occurs, it is necessary to turn off the air conditioner to allow the coil to defrost before resuming normal operation. During the defrost period, operate the fan in the maximum airflow position. Airflow will be reduced by the blockage of the ice

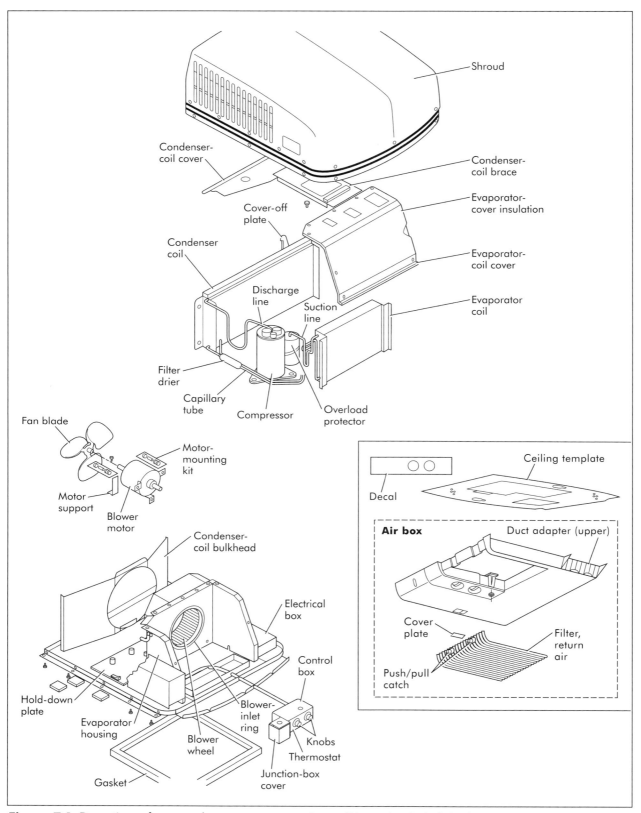

Figure 7.1 Dometic roof-mounted compressor-type air conditioner (exploded view)

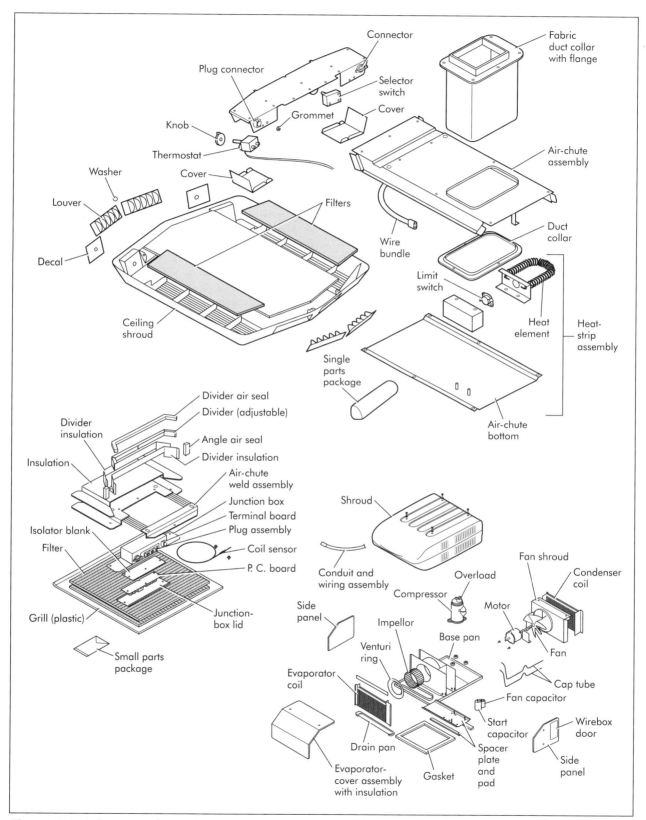

Figure 7.2 Coleman roof-mounted compressor-type air conditioner (exploded view)

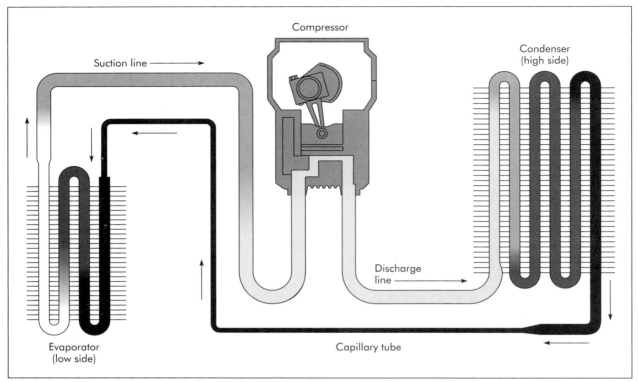

Figure 7.3 Operation and path of Freon in RV compressor type air conditioners

during this period. When the ice has melted from the coil, airflow will return to normal.

Servicing Compressor Air Conditioners

Other than insuring that the AC voltage supply is proper, keeping the roof-mounted air conditioner unit clean is the most important routine service procedure the owner can perform. To help maintain a clean air conditioner, the roof-top unit should be kept covered in the off-season to prevent dirt, debris, and small animals from getting inside.

Once a year, remove the cover shroud (Figure 7.4) and, using compressed air, blow the dust, bugs, leaves, and other debris out of the unit. Another effective cleaning method is to give the air conditioner the once-over with a shop vacuum or other hose-type vacuum cleaner.

Moving to the inside, remove the ceiling cover frequently (Figures 7.5 and 7.6) and wash or replace the intake filter pads. A recommendation from most roof air manufacturers is that the intake filters should be cleaned or changed at least every two weeks during periods of continuous use. It is critical that the air con-

ditioner not be operated without a filter in place. To do so invites problems, as lint, dirt, grease, and other airborne contaminants accumulate in the cooling coil. This can lead to loss of air volume and possible icing-up of the cooling coil and can result in serious damage to the unit's operating components.

Figure 7.4 The cover shroud should be removed once a year in order to blow out the unit with compressed air.

■ TROUBLESHOOTING ■
THE COMPRESSOR AIR CONDITIONER

Problem	Possible Cause	Correction
Unit will not run	No 120-volt AC power	Connect to power source
	Tripped 120-volt breaker	Reset circuit breaker
	Defective on/off switch	Replace switch
	Loose connector plug	Check connection integrity
	Defective on/off switch	Replace main switch
Fan runs too slowly	Poor electrical contact	Check all connections
	Low line voltage	Check supply voltage
	Undersized power cord	Replace with proper size
	Tight motor shaft	Check shaft
	Blower/fan misaligned	Check alignment
	Intake filters clogged	Clean or replace filters
Fan runs but compressor will not engage	Low voltage	Inspect supply output
	Undersized power cord	Replace with correct size
	Starting capacitor	Replace capacitor
	Improper temperature setting	Reset thermostat
	Defective thermostat	Replace thermostat
	Defective time delay	Replace delay switch
	High compressor pressure	Defective time-delay switch
	Defective compressor	Replace compressor
Compressor will not cycle off	Thermostat set too low	Set to warmer temperature
	Clogged condenser coils	Clean condenser
	Excess heat gain	Reduce heat gain areas
	Iced-over evaporator	Turn system off to melt ice
	Stuck thermostat switch	Replace switch
	Low refrigerant charge	Recharge unit

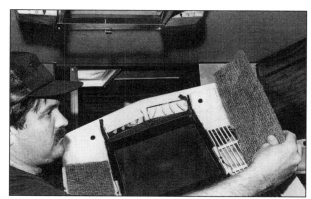

Figure 7.5 Intake filter pads are easily accessed from inside the RV and should be cleaned every two weeks during continuous use.

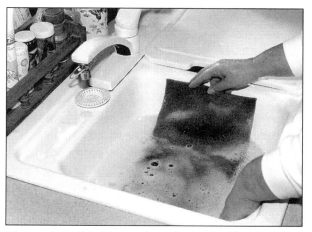

Figure 7.6 Wash or replace the intake filter pads.

Cleaning and/or Replacing Filters

To service the filters inside the control shroud:

1. Remove the selector switch and thermostat knobs from the ceiling assembly.
2. Remove the screws that hold the shroud to the ceiling assembly.
3. Lower the shroud and carefully slide it off the control knobs.
4. Remove the filters and either clean them or replace them with new filters.
5. Reverse the procedure to replace the shroud and control knobs.

To service the filters, accessible from the outside of the ceiling shroud:

1. Apply pressure on the grill tabs and remove access cover.
2. Remove rubber-band retainers holding the filter.
3. Remove the filter.
4. Clean filter with soap and water and let air dry—do not wring out.
5. Reverse procedure when filter is dry.

Checking for Air-Conditioner Operating Failures

All air conditioners operate on 120-volt AC power and certain models with electronic controls require 12-volt DC wired to the control board. If you are experiencing no or poor air-conditioner performance, the first thing you should do is verify that the power requirements are being satisfied. The operating range for the control boards is between 10 and 16 volts DC; if voltage is below 10 volts, you could experience problems with the operation of the components within the main board. Models using a separate thermostat normally use a 12-volt DC power supply for control operation. Check for 12-volt DC power first. If power here is verified, the next step is to check the incoming AC power supply.

CAUTION: Any 120-volt AC power source can be dangerous and can deliver a fatal shock. If you're not certain of the procedures for working with 120-volt AC, seek qualified help.

Safe Procedures Checklist

■ Check 120-volt AC voltage by using a multimeter that has been set to monitor 120-volt AC. Insert the probe into any convenient outlet inside the RV (see page 1.4). It's always a good practice to check the incoming voltage from the available hookups or the onboard AC generator after arriving in the campground. The proper operating range is between 103 and 126 volts AC. Most air conditioners are equipped with thermal-overload protection systems that will shut down the compressor if it becomes overheated. Overheating is caused by low voltage. As voltage drops, current rises, creating abnormal heat. Most thermal-overload controls will shut down the compressor by the time voltage drops to between 100 and 103 volts AC. The newer electronically controlled air conditioners have electronic-threshold protection built into the circuit that automatically shuts down the compressor when voltage drops to between 103 and 107 volts AC. If voltage is hovering in the 108- to 110-volt AC area while hooked up, monitor the multimeter periodically because the voltage may drop further when other users get on the line. If the compressor is still running at 105 volts AC, the air conditioner should be turned off until proper voltage is restored.

WARNING: Most common extension cords are inadequately sized for their length and should not be used in conjunction with the RV's power cord (Table 7.1).

■ If there is no power present when using the onboard AC generator (if your RV is so equipped), make sure the power cord is

Table 7.1 Extension Cord Amperage Ratings

Gauge	Length (feet)	Maximum amps
12	1–50	20
12	51–100	15
14	1–50	15
14	51–100	13
16	1–50	13
16	51–100	9.8
18	1–50	9.8
18	1–100	5.8

plugged into its proper receptacle. Usually this receptacle is located inside the same compartment as the AC generator. Check the main breaker and the individual breaker for the air conditioner. If either is tripped, reset and try the air conditioner again. Continual tripping of the breakers is an indication of either excessive amperage draw by the air conditioner itself, low voltage, or a defective breaker. If the AC generator is the source of power, check the circuit breaker in the AC-generator control panel. If no power is coming from the campground outlet, check the breaker in the power receptacle box at the campground. If there is a problem here, contact campground personnel for assistance.

■ If it is determined that 120-volt AC power is available and no breakers are tripped, the problem may be at the connector terminal under the air-conditioner ceiling shroud. To check this connection, turn off all power and remove the screws that hold the control/ access panel to the ceiling. Pull the panel down. Check that the wires are connected properly and that the connector (if so equipped) is plugged in and tight. Turn on the power. If the unit will not start at this point, seek help from a qualified air-conditioner service technician (Figure 7.7).

■ If the main on/off switch is a manual type and not a solid-state electronic switch, it can be checked with a multimeter–ohms as

Figure 7.7 Loss of 120-volt AC power to the air conditioner may be attributed to a loose connector terminal under the ceiling shroud.

Figure 7.8 A manual-type main on/off switch can be checked with a multimeter.

shown in Figure 7.8. To check the switch, turn off the 120-volt AC power and remove the ceiling-shroud assembly and wires from the on/off switch. Make a note of the proper wire location. With a multimeter, check the continuity from one side of the switch to the other. When the switch is in the off position there should be infinite resistance between the two points. When the switch is turned to the on position, the resistance should be zero. If not, a new switch should be installed.

■ A new switch can be installed by removing the retaining nut and connection wires from the switch and pulling it free from its mount. Note the location of the wiring. Install a new switch in the reverse order.

■ If all these checks fail, then the cause may be a shorted or burned-out motor. Seek qualified electrical help to determine the condition of the motor and compressor assembly.

Checking for Fan-Operating Problems

If the fan runs at a speed that is too slow, check these points:

■ Low voltage will cause slow running speed. Measure the voltage present, as detailed on page 7.6.

■ The fan-motor shaft may be too tight. A tight fan-motor shaft can be tested by removing the outside cover shroud and spinning the

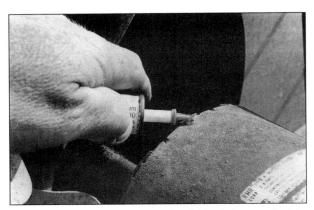

Figure 7.9 The fan motor should be lubricated with SAE 20-weight oil once a year.

fan by hand with the power turned off. Many fan motors have a small oil cup on the top of the motor. Remove the plastic plug from the cup and place three or four drops of SAE 20-weight nondetergent oil in the cup once a year (Figure 7.9). Do not over-oil. If the motor continues to be slow and tight, the bearings have failed and should be replaced by a qualified service technician.

■ Dirty intake filters will reduce airflow. Periodic cleaning or replacement of the filters is necessary, as described on page 7.4.

Checking for Compressor Failure

It is possible that the fan motor will operate correctly, but the compressor will not engage and no cooling will result. This can be caused by several factors.

To check the compressor:

1. Turn off the circuit breaker for the air conditioner.
2. Remove the cover from the air conditioner.
3. Disconnect the wires from the Common, Start, and Run terminals (Figure 7.10).
4. Using an ohmmeter at the lowest scale, check for continuity between all three terminals. A lack of continuity between these three terminals indicates faulty windings and the compressor should be replaced.
5. If there is continuity between the terminals, the next test requires that you scrape some paint from the side of the compressor and check for continuity between each terminal and the casing. A reading indicates that the windings are shorted to the casing and the compressor must be replaced.

The overload protector (Figure 7.11) will open the AC volts circuit to the compressor if it has overheated

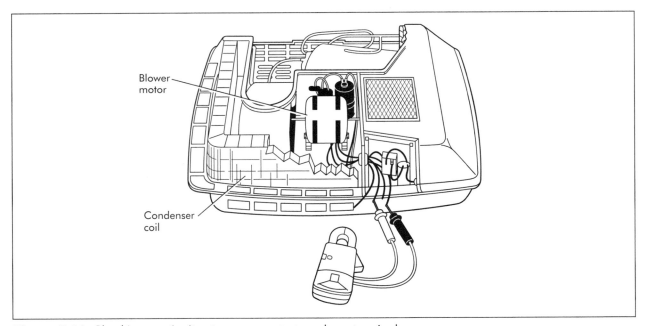

Figure 7.10 Checking continuity at common, start, and run terminals

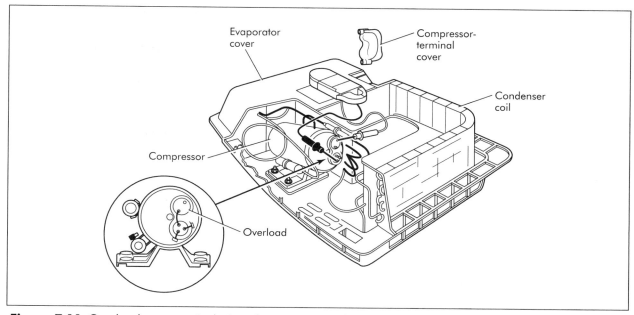

Figure 7.11 Overload protector is designed to open AC-volts circuit when the compressor becomes overheated

due to an electrical problem. A weak overload protector will cause the compressor to start and stop rapidly or short cycle. This can be a very difficult problem to test and identify. To test, turn off the circuit breaker for the air conditioner. Let the unit cool to ambient temperature and measure the continuity across its terminals. If open, the unit must be replaced. Make sure to use an exact replacement.

Check the following if the compressor fails to turn on:

- The time-delay circuit may be defective. This circuit prevents the compressor from coming on before the head pressure is depleted. Failure to deplete the head pressure can damage the compressor. The time-delay circuit/switch should only be repaired by a qualified service technician.
- The freeze switch may be inoperative. This would tell the control board that the evaporator is frozen and not allow the compressor start relay to operate.
- The air-conditioner thermostat determines when the compressor will start. Make sure the thermostat is set to a sufficiently cool temperature.

- If these steps fail to restore cooling, the temperature-sensing-bulb mechanism that sends a signal to the thermostat may be defective or improperly placed. The thermostat may also be defective. Seek a qualified service technician to test these components.
- If the motor does not start easily and quickly, the capacitor (an electrical storage device) may be defective. When a signal is sent from the thermostat, calling for more cooling, the capacitor dumps its stored power to the motor, providing an extra boost for a few seconds to get it going. Seek authorized service to check the capacitor circuits.

  NOTE: The electric power stored in these starting capacitors is enough to provide a severe shock. Use extreme caution when working around them (Figure 7.12).
- When the air-conditioning unit has been operating for a while, but the compressor fails to restart, the problem may be in the start-delay circuit. This circuit permits the compressor to rest for a few minutes between cycles, allowing pressure in the system to equalize. If the compressor tried to start immediately after shutting off, there would be excessive pressure against the pistons, which would make starting difficult. The delay cir-

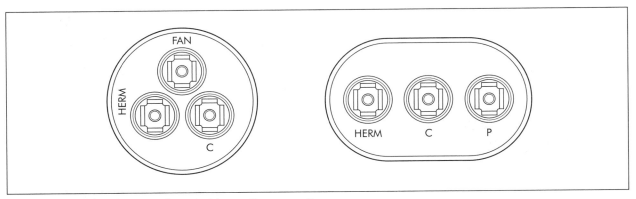

Figure 7.12 Electric power is stored in starting capacitors

cuit allows this pressure to subside after each cycle. If the switch is defective, it may not close again when a signal from the thermostat calls for cooling. Seek authorized service for this difficulty.

■ The compressor motor could be burned out. Seek qualified help to determine the condition of the compressor assembly.

Checking for Failure of Compressor to Shut Off

The opposite problem occurs when the compressor refuses turn off. Several areas can be checked for this condition:

■ Check to see that the thermostat is not set too low. If it is set on maximum cold, the unit will run excessively.

■ Make sure the condenser coils are clean and unclogged. If not, the unit will be unable to cool to its full potential. This causes the unit to run excessively to compensate for the inefficiency. Remove the exterior cover shroud and vacuum or blow out the coils to remove dirt (Figure 7.13). Carefully straighten the cooling fins if they are bent (Figure 7.14). They are delicate, but the job can be done with a dull pocketknife blade or using a fin comb (available at RV supply stores).

■ Continuous running may be the result of excessive heat gain. That is, the rate that the RV absorbs heat is faster than the air conditioner can remove heat. In this case, the unit will

never shut down. Make sure all windows and doors are closed. Sunlight causes a great deal of heat gain, so if the RV is parked in direct sunlight, move it to a shady spot, if possible. If the condition persists, the ambient temperature is simply too hot for the air conditioner to overcome—the air conditioner is not large enough to deal with the volume of heat it is receiving.

■ During extended operation in hot, humid weather, the evaporator coils may actually freeze up. This will cause the compressor to run continually but fail to cool adequately because the airflow over the coils is blocked by ice. To correct this situation, keep RV doors and windows closed as much as possible, so that no additional heat and humidity is allowed inside. Take care not to release large amounts of heat and steam while cooking. If these things cannot be avoided, set the air-conditioner thermostat to a slightly warmer temperature, permitting the compressor to cycle off more frequently, which will melt ice buildup on the compressor coils. If the buildup is very heavy, the air conditioner should be shut down for a period of time until the ice melts (thirty minutes is usually adequate).

■ Thermostat switch contacts can become stuck together, which will cause the compressor to continue running even though the thermostat is dialed to a warmer setting. If this is suspected, seek qualified assistance in testing and replacing the thermostat assembly.

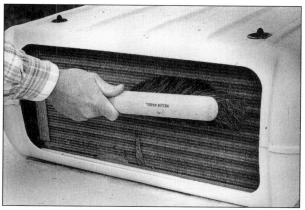

Figure 7.13 The condenser coils in an air conditioner must be kept clean to insure optimum efficiency

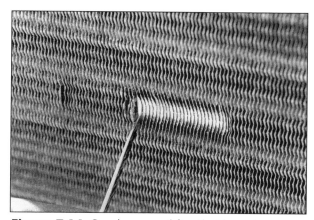

Figure 7.14 Condenser coil fins that have become bent should be carefully straightened with a knife or screwdriver.

■ Another possible cause of compressor run-on is a lack of R-22 type refrigerant. This can only be determined with a pressure test by qualified service personnel. If the system is low on refrigerant, there is probably a leak in the system, requiring repair before recharging takes place. The Clean Air Act of 1990 set guidelines regarding the recapturing and disposition of refrigerants. An authorized air-conditioner service facility should be contacted to deal with these problems. Make sure the technician knows that refrigerant can permanently damage a rubber roof (see page 15.4).

Checking for Mechanical Integrity

Periodically inspect the air conditioner to make sure the bolts and nuts that hold the unit to the roof of the RV are tight and in good condition. Inspect the shroud to make sure it is being held securely to the unit and is not developing cracks or has not been damaged.

The drain hole in the drain-pan area should be inspected periodically. This must be kept clean, or the water removed from the inside of the RV will not be able to drain off properly.

The evaporator bulkhead in the rear section of the air conditioner, which contains the compressor, the blower motor, and the condenser coil, is designed to dispose of any water that may enter. A watertight seal must exist along the entire bulkhead that separates

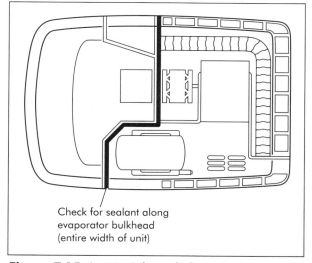

Check for sealant along evaporator bulkhead (entire width of unit)

Figure 7.15 A watertight seal along the evaporator bulkhead separates two compartments.

the two compartments (Figure 7.15). Check for sealant along this section and add sealant to any area where none is visible. Note that the sealed portion extends up the sides of the unit.

Basement-type Air Conditioners

The basement air conditioner (Figure 7.16) sequence of operation and general maintenance is the same as the roof-mounted type. Basement air conditioners come in two basic models: a single-stage system, which

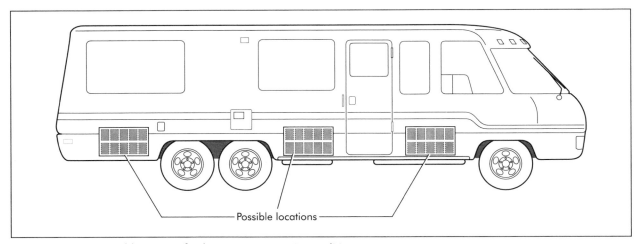

Figure 7.16 Typical locations for basement-type air conditioners

is very similar to the roof-mounted counterpart, and a two-stage cooling unit.

The largest difference between the roof and basement systems is the location of the unit and the air-distribution system. The basement unit is mounted in the lower section of the RV in an accessible compartment. Preventive maintenance must be performed to insure that components remain free of dirt and trash that could potentially block the vents around the unit (Figure 7.17). The air filter must be changed every three months and checked monthly during use.

Two-stage Cooling Units

Two-stage basement air conditioners, incorporating a dual-compressor refrigeration system that provides the cooling capacity of two roof-mounted air conditioners into one efficient and compact package, are designed for RVs with 50-amp service. In a two-stage air conditioner, the first compressor and refrigeration circuit are referred to as *first-stage cooling*. The second compressor and refrigeration circuit are called *second-stage cooling*.

The first- and second-stage cooling units are connected to separate electrical circuits. The ability to operate the second-stage unit depends upon the electrical power source available. When the RV is hooked up to only 30-amp 120-volt AC power, the system will automatically limit operation to the first stage.

If 50-amp hookup power is available, or the RV is being powered by an onboard AC generator, the system automatically allows for operation of both first- and second-stage cooling units.

Air-Conditioner Heat Strips

Some compressor-type air-conditioning units are equipped with, or can be optionally equipped with, heat strips. These are grids of electrical wiring connected to a thermostat temperature-control system within the air conditioner (Figure 7.18). When the heat strip is turned on, the fan in the air conditioner circulates air; the heat strips warm the incoming air before routing it to the RV interior. Heat strips require 120-volt AC power. It must be noted that heat strips are not intended to replace the use of an RV furnace for general comfort heating purposes, but they are capable of taking a minor chill out of the air in the morning.

Servicing Heat Strips

To diagnose the heat strip, you must first turn off the air-conditioner circuit breaker and then remove the cover inside the RV. Next, unplug the heater strip and using an ohmmeter take a reading across the two wiring terminals of the heat strip. You should have an ohm reading of 9.5 ohms plus/minus 10 percent. If

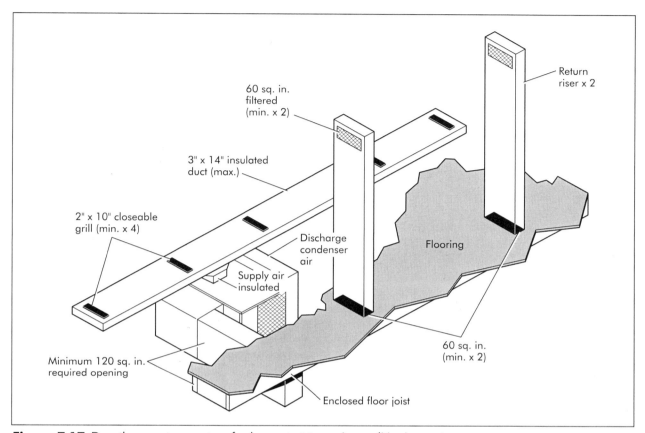

Figure 7.17 Duo-therm return system for basement-type air-conditioning systems

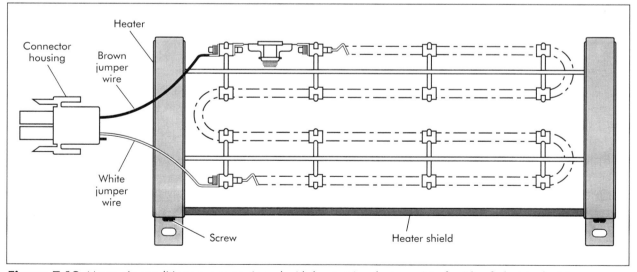

Figure 7.18 Many air conditioners are equipped with heat strips that consist of grids of electrical wiring.

the readings are outside these parameters, you need to replace the heat strip. To test the heater-limit switch, check for continuity across the limit-switch terminals with the limit switch at room temperature. If you have an open-limit switch, you will need to replace it. Also check the heater plug to make sure the heat strip is properly connected to it.

CAUTION: Remember, 120-volt AC power can be dangerous. It is best to seek qualified help when in doubt.

Heat-Pump Systems

A heat pump (Figure 7.19) is designed to work in geographically mild areas in temperatures above 40°F. During the heating mode, heat is removed from the outside air and released into the inside of the RV. When the temperature falls below 40°F, there's not enough heat in the air that can be removed.

The heat-pump system works best utilizing a wall thermostat so that it can work in series with the RV's furnace. When the outdoor ambient temperature drops below 40°F, the RV's primary heating system is activated. If the heat pump did not cut off at 40°F, it would begin to accumulate frost and the coils would eventually ice up. The heat pump would con-

tinue to run if the coils iced up, but it would no longer produce heat. The Comfort Control Center has a defrost system that allows continued operation in outdoor ambient temperature as low as 24°F.

A heat pump works in two modes: heating and cooling. Refrigerant is reversed depending on the cycle. The system utilizes a compressor, evaporator and condenser coils, reversing valve, capillary tubes, an air-movement system (fan), and, of course, refrigerant. The evaporator and condenser act as either the inside or outside coils, depending on the operation cycle. When heat is called for, the compressor sends a high-pressure vapor to the reversing valve that routes the vapor to the inside coil, which in the heating mode is the condenser coil.

High-pressure vapor enters the condenser, where it is cooled and condensed to liquid as it passes through the coil. Heat removed from the refrigerant is expelled to the inside air via the fan. Refrigerant leaves the condenser as high-pressure liquid. When the high-pressure liquid leaves the condenser, it passes through small capillary tubes, acting as the metering device in the sealed system.

A controlled amount of high-pressure liquid refrigerant enters the evaporator from the capillary tube. When this liquid reaches the low-pressure at-

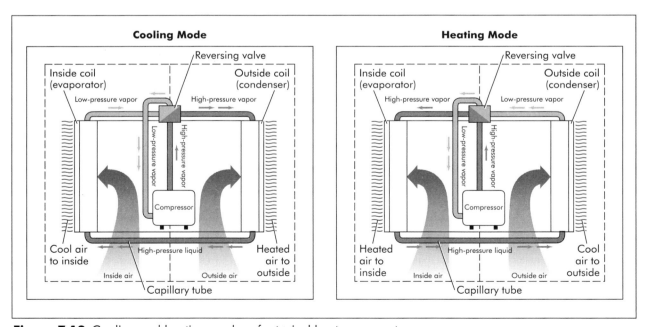

Figure 7.19 Cooling and heating modes of a typical heat-pump system

■ TROUBLESHOOTING ■
THE HEAT STRIP

Problem	Possible Cause	Correction
No heat	No 120-volt AC power	Check for power
	Tripped breaker	Reset breaker
	Low voltage	Check voltage level
	Loose connection	Inspect connections
	Defective switch	Replace switch
	Defective thermostat	Replace thermostat
	Burned-out strip	Replace strip

mosphere of the evaporator, it turns into vapor. During this process, heat is removed from the air flowing through the evaporator, and the cool air is returned to the ambient air via the blower assembly.

Low-pressure vapor from the evaporator returns to the reversing valve that routes the low-pressure vapor to the compressor through a suction line, starting the heating process again.

Maintenance for the heat-pump system is basically the same as for standard air-conditioning units, with the major difference being the control system.

■ EVAPORATIVE COOLERS ■

One of the laws of physics is that evaporation causes cooling. Evaporative coolers operate on the principle that air passes through a water-soaked mat or screen, which cools the air as the water evaporates. The evaporative-cooler fan is usually powered by a 12-volt DC electric motor. A 12-volt DC pump is used to distribute water to the absorbent evaporation mat while the fan blows air across the mat.

The cooler's reservoir is filled either by a connection to the RV's water pump via a float-control valve, or by manually filling with a hose from an outside water source. Most reservoirs hold enough water for a day's cooling—about five gallons. Evaporative coolers are best suited to dry climates where the humidity is low. In areas of high humidity, the cooling effect of an evaporative unit is substantially reduced.

Servicing Evaporative Coolers

Periodic cleaning of evaporative coolers is necessary to prevent operational difficulties. Algae can build up in the water pump, reservoir, and distribution lines. Dirt may accumulate on the evaporative mat, severely reducing airflow. It is good maintenance practice to keep the cooler covered during the off-season and when it is not in use. This prevents dirt and grime from entering. Periodic replacement of the absorbent evaporation mats is to be expected.

Checking for Failure of Cooler to Operate

If the evaporative cooler fails to operate properly, consult the Evaporative-Cooler Checklist on page 7.16.

Checking for Failure of Unit to Cool

Another condition that results in failure to cool is when the fan operates, circulating air through the unit, but resulting in no cool air. Here is a list of possible causes for this situation.

■ If the outdoor temperature (over 85°F) and humidity (50 percent or more) are high, it is likely the evaporative cooler is doing its best. The air simply does not feel very cold as it leaves the cooler because the evaporation

---

■ **CHECKLIST** ■
THE EVAPORATIVE COOLER

- ■ Check the condition of the RV battery. If the voltage is low, the unit may fail to run.
- ■ Locate the 12-volt DC fuse panel in the RV, and check the condition of the fuse in the circuit supplying power to the cooler. Use a multimeter to check the fuse.
- ■ Check the condition of the wiring connections; gain access by removing the ceiling cover on the cooler. The cooler wires are usually tied together with wire nuts. Make sure they are tight and free of corrosion. Check these connections with a multimeter to insure that current flows to this point. Make sure there is a good ground and the electrical polarity (positive to positive, negative to negative) is correct.
- ■ Locate the on/off switch and determine with the multimeter if power flows to that point. Then turn on the switch and check to see if power is available at the motor side of the switch. If power is not available, the switch needs replacing.
- ■ If power is confirmed, check to see that the motor shaft is free to turn. If it is not, try to free it by hand (Figure 7.20). If the shaft is stuck, the motor may need replacement.
- ■ If the pump is clogged or jammed and will not rotate, it could be drawing enough amperage to prevent the fan motor from running. With the switch in the on position, make sure 12 volts are present at the pump motor. If there is power to the pump motor and it will not rotate, it is probably seized and will require replacement. These pumps are usually a one-piece assembly with no provision for repair.

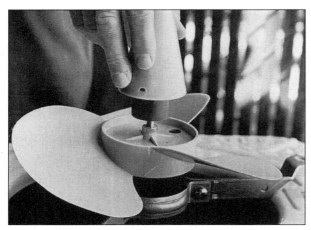

Figure 7.20 The fan-motor shaft in evaporative coolers can be freed by hand to turn in most cases.

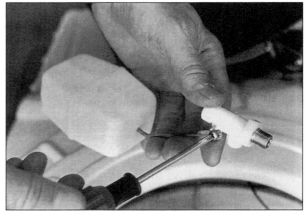

Figure 7.21 Evaporative coolers use a float to open the water reservoir valve. If the float valve is stuck, a few drops of penetrating oil may free it.

rate is low during high-humidity weather, thus reducing the system's effectiveness.

- ■ Check the water level in the reservoir. If it is low, cooling will be reduced.
- ■ If the cooler is equipped with a float-valve control for the reservoir's water level, remove the outside cover from the cooler and check to see that the float drops, opening the water valve (Figure 7.21). A small amount of penetrating oil applied to the float-valve pivot usually will free it.
- ■ The cooler will not function unless adequate

water is supplied to the absorbent pad by the pump. Remove the exterior cover and insure that there are 12 volts DC present at the pump motor when the switch is in the on position. If the pump does not operate, it should be replaced.

- ■ If the pump runs normally, it may fail to pump adequately if any of the associated plumbing or hoses are kinked or choked with debris or mineral deposits. When checking the pump, scrutinize the passages that the water must travel through to get to the pad. If

■ TROUBLESHOOTING ■
THE EVAPORATIVE COOLER

Problem	Possible Cause	Correction
Unit will not run	Blown 12-volt fuse	Test and replace fuse
	Loose wiring connection	Check connection tightness
	Dead battery	Charge or replace battery
	Stuck fan shaft	Rotate by hand to free
	Stuck pump shaft	Remove and clean pump
Unit will not cool	High-humidity condition	No correction possible
	Low water level	Replenish water supply
	Stuck float valve	Free float valve
	Inoperative pump	Check pump condition
	Clogged water passages	Clean unit
	Dirty evaporative mat	Clean or replace
	Inoperative fan	Check fan motor

there is any sign of clogging, the outlet hose from the pump can be removed and pressure-flushed with a garden hose to remove debris.

■ Failure to cool could be due to a dirty absorbent pad. The accumulation of dirt on the pad reduces its ability to hold water and allow air to pass through, resulting in reduced cooling. Most pads can be cleaned by washing with a pressure (garden) hose to remove dirt. These pads are not expensive, so it is a good idea to replace them every few years. Pads are easily changed by removing the cover-retaining screws and the cover, then lifting the pad out of the cooler. Reverse the order to install the new pad (Figure 7.22).

Figure 7.22 Evaporative cooler pads must be kept clean and should be replaced every two years.

■ CHAPTER 8 ■
REFRIGERATORS

Refrigerators in RVs operate using an absorption system which incorporates a completely different set of principles than are employed in compressor-driven household units. The RV is far more demanding than the relatively static residential environment. For example, RV refrigerators are required to operate on a variety of energy sources and withstand all the jostling and vibration of highway travel. In order for these appliances to endure well, they must be given special care. However, even with the best of care, it is possible to suffer a variety of malfunctions.

The most common complaint from owners of RV refrigerators is that the unit simply doesn't perform very well, allowing the temperature inside the food compartment during hot weather to approach or exceed 50°F. This is not sufficiently cool to protect the contents from spoilage. Food must be kept at a maximum temperature of around 40°F.

To understand all the potential problems associated with RV refrigerators, it is essential to be familiar with how absorption refrigeration works (Figure 8.1). In absorption refrigeration, heat is absorbed from the interior of the refrigerator. The theory is that where there is an absence of heat, there is cold. This is distinctly different from the way a compressor-driven household refrigerator operates; it applies cold directly to the refrigerator cavity.

There are no moving parts in an absorption refrigerator. The cooling process is based on laws of chemistry and physics rather than mechanics. Here's how it works. Water, ammonia, hydrogen gas, and sodium chromate are combined under pressure in a containment vessel, sometimes known as a *generator* or *boiler*. Each of these elements plays an important role in the process of cooling or in the preservation of the equipment. The water, ammonia, and hydro-

gen gas are directly involved in the cooling process, but the function of the sodium chromate is to prevent the heat from corroding the pipes.

As an electrical heating element or gas burner brings the solution to a boil, the liquid percolates up the pump tube. The ammonia is distilled out of the solution and continues to rise up the tube as a gas. A short way up the tube, the water and ammonia gas part company, and the water returns to the reservoir via a circuitous system of pipes. During the water's return, it is recombined with the ammonia at the far end of its voyage.

Meanwhile, the ammonia gas continues upward until it reaches the condenser, where it dissipates its heat and returns to a liquid form. As the drops of pure liquid ammonia fall, they trickle into the evaporator (freezing unit) where they combine with hydrogen gas. This chemical marriage causes very vigorous evaporation, which results in cooling. Because this rapid evaporation process takes place in the freezer unit, that's where most of the cooling occurs, as the heat is absorbed from the unit.

As a result of the evaporation process, the liquid ammonia again becomes a gas and travels to a secondary evaporator in the refrigerator unit (the shiny fins inside) where it absorbs more heat. Then the gas enters a return pipe on its way back to rejoin the water and start the process again.

■ THE ELECTRONIC REFRIGERATOR ■

The electronic refrigerator does not operate any more effectively than a manual type; however, the electronic types do work more efficiently. All control functions are passed from the human operator to the

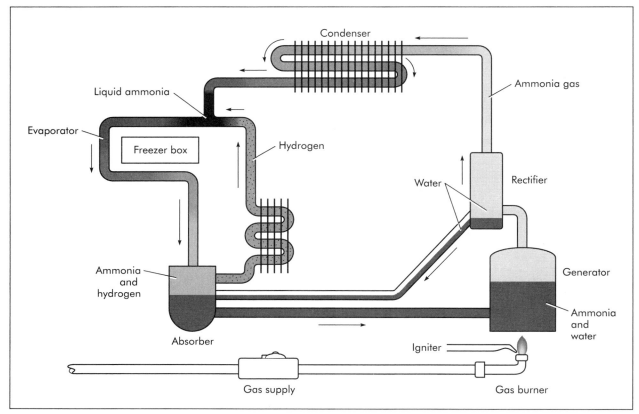

Figure 8.1 RV absorption refrigerators use ammonia, hydrogen, water, and sodium chromate under pressure to produce a cold food compartment.

control systems. The cost for this ease of operation is the complexity of the system. The main difference seen by the user is the display (eyebrow) panel, which allows the user to select the basic parameters, such as how cold and what mode of operation to use, and lets the system do the rest of the work.

Basic Modes of Operation

Auto Mode

In automatic mode, the control system will select the best method of operation and power selection. The control system will automatically select between "AC," "Gas," and in three-way systems, "DC power." AC power has priority over Gas. Gas has priority over 12-volt DC. If the control system does not detect AC power, the system will automatically shift to the Gas mode. If no AC or LP-gas is detected, the system will turn off in the case of two-way systems or shift to the

DC mode in the case of three-way systems. In auto mode, the Auto light will activate to show the operating mode.

Gas Mode

In the Gas mode, the system will activate the Gas indicator lamp, the ignition system, and will attempt to light the burner for a period of approximately forty-five seconds. If unsuccessful, the Check indicator lamp will illuminate and the Gas-mode indicator will turn off. To restart Gas operation, you need to press the main power on/off button to the off position and then back to the on position. The control system will attempt a new forty-five-second ignition sequence. If the refrigerator has not been in use for an extended period of time, or if the LP-gas supply has just been refilled, air may have been trapped in the lines, requiring you to purge the air. This means that you will have to perform the restart sequence three to four times until the air is removed from the lines. If this does not prove successful, first check the propane supply and make sure all the manual shut-off valves are open. If this does not work, then start the troubleshooting process by following the checklist on page 8.11.

DC Mode

Some systems can also be powered by DC current. When this power source is selected, the DC-mode light will be illuminated. All the other lights will be off. The DC mode will override all other operating modes until either AC or Gas is again provided to the system.

CAUTION: Never operate the refrigerator in the DC mode for any longer than absolutely needed—or without the engine running—as it is a severe drain on the batteries.

Bypass Operation

Both Dometic and Norcold have a system feature that allows the refrigerator to continue to operate in the event of a major component failure. If the display module fails, the system will go to the fully automatic mode of operation. The second bypass will function in the event a temperature-sensing device or associated electronic-circuitry failure occurs. If this happens, the cooling unit will run continuously on the selected energy source.

Control Panels

Dometic

The Dometic control panel (Figure 8.2) provides information on the power mode and the level of cooling and is fitted with an on/off switch and a check light in case of an equipment fault.

Norcold

Norcold provides a diagnostic-code feature on its control panels. Models 962, 963, 982, and 983 use the front panel shown in Figure 8.3 and the diag-

nostic codes in Table 8.1. Models 9162, 9163, 9182, and 9183 use the control panel shown in Figure 8.4 and the diagnostic codes in Table 8.2.

Dirty DC Power

A common problem with electronically controlled refrigerators is dirty DC power. Refrigerators that rely on a 12-volt DC source to operate must have clean current. In many cases, the 12-volt DC power from the converter will have an AC ripple, which can affect refrigerator operation. Most of the time, the problem is associated with erratic operation of the eyebrow panel. Dirty DC voltage can lead to relay chattering and an erratic check light in the eyebrow panel. Using a digital multimeter set on AC volts, check the voltage at the DC-terminal block. You should not read more than 6 volts AC (see Figure 8.21, page 8.19). Also, make sure the connections are free of corrosion and that the ground is secure.

If you find too much AC voltage at the DC-terminal block, make sure the power lead is hooked up to the clean side of the converter or is hooked up directly to the battery.

Low or High DC Voltage

Most refrigerators will experience operational problems when the power falls below 10.5 volts or when it goes above 15.5 volts. A faulty power converter, where the 12-volt DC power becomes unregulated, is the culprit most of the time. Dirty connections or faulty connectors can also be at fault. The 12-volt DC power should be checked at the refrigerator-terminal block and at the batteries and power converter; if there is a voltage loss, suspect the wiring and connections.

■ LEVELING EARLY-MODEL ■ REFRIGERATORS

Overall, refrigerators are simple and relatively trouble free. There are no pumps or motors to move the ammonia around inside the unit; simple gravity does the job. One serious problem is related to operating the refrigerator off-level, causing the fluid in the gen-

Table 8.1 Norcold 900 and 9100 Series Diagnostic Fault Indicators, Meanings, and Corrective Actions

9100 Series LED	Meanings	Corrective actions
No LEDs	Control voltage unavailable to display panel	**Check:** 10.5 to 15.4 volts DC being supplied to refrigerator? Battery charging equipment Converter DC connection to the refrigerator Refrigerator's DC fuse (3-amp control fuse) Refer to Norcold's service manual.
Flashing LP-gas LED (flash, pause, flash, pause, etc.)	LP-gas-ignition fault (initial startup)	**Check:** 10.5 to 15.4 volts DC being supplied to refrigerator? Have gas lines been purged? LP supply valve on? LP supply empty? LP supply pressure 11" water column? Refrigerator's manual shut-off valve open? Refer to Norcold's service manual.
Flashing Battery LED (flash, flash, pause, flash, flash, pause, etc.)	Fault external to refrigerator controls; DC-input voltage too low	**Check:** Battery(ies) supplying DC to refrigerator Battery-charging equipment Converter DC connection to the refrigerator Refer to Norcold's service manual.
Flashing Battery LED (flash, flash, pause, flash, flash, pause, etc.)	Fault external to refrigerator controls; DC-input voltage too high	**Check:** Battery(ies) supplying DC to refrigerator Battery-charging equipment Converter DC connection to the refrigerator Refer to Norcold's service manual.

NOTE: For more information refer to the operator's guide or contact an authorized Norcold service center.

erator to pool on one side and leave part of the chamber dry. If the heating element or flame heats the vessel while there is not enough liquid in the right place, the heat may "cook" the sodium chromate. When that happens, the sodium chromate gets hard and brittle and can flake and float around until it finds a place to lodge in tiny passages of the pump tube. Eventually, this can result in refrigerator failure.

Another problem caused by operating the refrigerator off-level is that the liquid in the system can accumulate into pockets that can impair or completely block gas circulation. When this happens, cooling will stop permanently, in most cases.

Normally, when an RV is stationary, it is parked and leveled as much as possible to provide comfortable living conditions. If the refrigerator is properly installed (the freezer compartment parallel with the RV floor), the refrigerator will then operate properly. To check this, use a bubble level and adjust the level of the RV front to rear and side to side until at least one-half of the bubble is within the center portion of the level.

When the RV is in motion, the continuous rolling and pitching movement will not affect the refrigerator as long as the movement breaks the plane of level. But whenever the RV is parked, even temporarily, the vehicle should be leveled to protect the refrigerator from damage during operation.

In those situations where the refrigerator cannot be leveled, such as in an inclined parking lot, regardless of how short the time, turn off the refrigerator until it can be leveled or until you are traveling again. The damage that occurs is cumulative, and each time the refrigerator is operated off-level, the blockage becomes more serious, until finally the obstruction is complete and the cooling unit is no longer functional.

In the mid 1980s, the refrigerator manufacturers incorporated a safety shut-off feature designed to prevent serious damage or operational failures when the refrigerators are used in a severe off-level posi-

Table 8.2 Diagnostic Codes, Meanings, and Actions

Code	Meaning	Action
	No display on control panel	**Check:** 10.5 to 15.4 volts DC being supplied to refrigerator? Battery-charging equipment or converter DC connection to the refrigerator Refrigerator's DC fuse (3-amp control fuse) Consult your dealer or a Norcold service center.
A1	LP-gas-ignition fault (initial startup)	**Check:** 10.5 to 15.4 volts DC being supplied to refrigerator? Have gas lines been purged? LP supply on? LP supply empty? LP supply pressure 11" water column? Consult your dealer or a Norcold service center.
A2	LP-gas-reignition fault (during normal operation)	**Check:** 10.5 to 15.4 volts DC being supplied to refrigerator? LP supply valve on? LP supply empty? LP supply pressure 11" water column? Consult your dealer or a Norcold service center.
A3	Door ajar and interior light on for more than two minutes	**Closing door will deactivate alarm and remove the code**
A4	Fault external to refrigerator controls AC mode selected but AC power not available	**Check:** Is refrigerator plugged into a functional AC outlet? Has the vehicle fuse or circuit breaker blown? Vehicle generator functioning (if applicable)? Refrigerator's AC fuse (5 amp) blown? Consult your dealer or a Norcold service center.
A5	Fault external to refrigerator controls AC input voltage too low	**Check:** AC input to refrigerator (108 volts AC minimum)? Generator (if applicable) If AC problem cannot be located, consult your dealer, campground administrator, or a Norcold service center.
A6	Fault external to refrigerator controls. AC input voltage too high.	**Check:** AC input to refrigerator (132 volts AC minimum)? Generator (if applicable) If AC problem cannot be located, consult your dealer, campground administrator, or a Norcold service center.
A7	Fault external to refrigerator controls DC input voltage too low	**Check:** DC supply to refrigerator (10.5 volts DC mininum)? Battery-charging equipment or converter DC connection to the refrigerator Consult your dealer or a Norcold service center.
A8	Fault external to refrigerator controls DC input voltage too high	**Check:** Battery(ies) supplying DC to refrigerator (15.4 volts DC maximum) Battery-charging equipment or converter DC connection to the refrigerator. Consult your dealer or a Norcold service center.
C1	Fault within refrigerator controls	Not owner serviceable; consult your dealer or a Norcold service center
C2	Fault within refrigerator controls	Not owner serviceable; consult your dealer or a Norcold service center
C3	Fault within refrigerator controls	Not owner serviceable; consult your dealer or a Norcold service center
C4	Fault within refrigerator controls	Not owner serviceable; consult your dealer or a Norcold service center
C5	Fault within refrigerator controls "Back-up Operating System Mode"	Not owner serviceable Temporary operating mode; read "Back-up Operating System" Seek service as soon as possible Consult your dealer or a Norcold service center.
C6	Fault within refrigerator controls	Not owner serviceable; consult your dealer or a Norcold service center
C7	Fault within refrigerator controls	Not owner serviceable; consult your dealer or a Norcold service center
C8	Fault within refrigerator controls	Not owner serviceable; consult your dealer or a Norcold service center
C9	Fault within refrigerator controls	Not owner serviceable; consult your dealer or a Norcold service center
D1	Fault within refrigerator controls	Not owner serviceable; consult your dealer or a Norcold service center

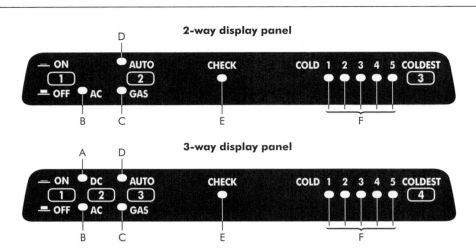

Models include: S1521. S1531, S1621, S1631, S1821, S1831, RM2607, RM2611, RM2807, RM2811

Auto Mode When operating in the Auto mode, the Auto mode indicator lamp (D) will illuminate. The control system will automatically select between AC and Gas operation with AC having priority over Gas. Either the AC indicator lamp (B) or the Gas indicator lamp (C) will illuminate depending on the energy source selected by the control system. If the control system is operating with AC energy and it then becomes unavailable, the system will automatically switch to Gas. As soon as AC becomes available again, the control will switch back to AC regardless of the status of Gas operation.

Gas Mode When operating in the Gas mode, the Auto mode indicator lamp (D) will not be illuminated. This mode provides LP gas operation only. The control system will activate the ignition system and will attempt to light the burner for a period of approximately 45 seconds. If unsuccessful, the Check indicator lamp (E) will illuminate and the Gas mode indicator lamp (C) will turn off.

To restart Gas operation, press the main power On/Off button (1) to the Off and then On position. The control system will attempt a new 45-second ignition sequence.

If the refrigerator has not been used for a long time or the LP tanks have just been refilled, air may be trapped in the supply lines. To purge the air from the lines may require resetting the main power On/Off button (1) three or four times. If repeated attempts fail to start the LP gas operation, check to make sure that the LP gas supply tanks are not empty and all manual shutoff valves in the lines are open.

If the control is switched to AC or DC operation while the Check indicator lamp is on, it will function properly, but the Check indicator lamp will not go off until the main power On/Off button is pressed to the Off then On position.

DC Mode (3-Way Models Only) When operating in the DC mode, the DC mode indicator lamp (A) will be illuminated. All other mode lamps will be off. The DC mode overrides all other operating modes. If one of the other operating modes is desired, the DC selector button (2) must be in the Up (Off) position.

Special Features of Operation This control system contains a feature where it will continue to operate the cooling system in the event of a failure of a major operating component. Two different modes of operation can occur in this category.

Figure 8.2 Typical Dometic two- and three-way eyebrow panels.

tion. This feature allows the refrigerators to operate properly as long as the RV is comfortably level. The rule of thumb: If you are comfortable inside your RV, the refrigerator is happy. You can also use the refrigerator door as a barometer: if it stays in place when opened, the rig is probably level enough. Keep in mind that when the refrigerator shuts down to protect the system, your food will become spoiled if the off-level condition is not corrected in a reasonable amount of time.

Testing for Safety Shut-off

To determine if the refrigerator has a self-protecting design, use the following information:

Dometic

A quick way to tell if your refrigerator has this safety feature is to simply look at the boiler-tube cover in

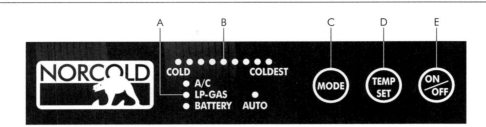

1. **Auto Mode** Push the On/Off button (E) to start the refrigerator in the fully automatic mode. Push the Set Point (thermostat) button (D) to a mid-range setting. If 120-volt AC is available, Auto LED and AC LED will illuminate, indicating AC operation. After ten seconds, the AC LED will turn off and only the Auto LED will remain illuminated. If 120-volt AC is not available, Auto LED and LP-Gas LED will illuminate. After ten seconds, LP-Gas LED will turn off and only the Auto LED will remain illuminated. Press and release any button to display operating mode. Push the Set Point (thermostat) button (D) to a mid-range setting.
2. **Manual Mode** Press and hold Mode selection button until Auto LED disappears and LP-Gas LED is the only LED illuminated. LP-Gas LED will remain illuminated until an

alternate mode is selected or the refrigerator is turned off.

Note: If the gas does not ignite within thirty seconds, the refrigerator's gas valve will automatically close and the operating controls will select an alternate energy source (Auto Mode) or revert to a stand-by-mode in which the LP-Gas LED flashes, indicating flame ignition fault. If burner flame does not ignite after several attempts, refer to "Diagnostics" for corrective actions.

3. To turn the refrigerator "Off", push and hold the "On/Off" button (E) for two seconds.

Note: 12-volt DC must be available for both the Auto and Manual modes.

Figure 8.3 The Norcold control panel

the rear, on the right side. (Figure 8.5). Square covers indicate the old model; round covers are used on the new type.

Norcold

Norcold specifies that refrigerators built since 1977 can be operated as long as they are not more than 3 degrees off-level in a side-to-side axis, and/or 6 degrees off-level in a front-to-back axis (Figure 8.6).

NOTE: The vehicle may be perfectly level, but the refrigerator may be off-level due to improper installation. Make sure the refrigerator is

level with the RV. Normally, if the RV is leveled so that the occupants are comfortable, the newer-model refrigerators will work properly.

■ REFRIGERATOR PROBLEMS ■

Correcting Blockage in a Dometic Unit

Blockage of the unit in the liquid circuit is most often made evident by signs of overheating on the vapor pipe leading from the boiler to the condenser (refer to Figure 8.1, page 8.2). The paint on this pipe may be blistered and the metal discolored. To test a Dometic refrigerator for blockage, bypass the control system and apply 120-volt AC power directly to the heater and let it run for twenty-four hours. After the twenty-four-hour period, the inside temperature should be approximately 30°F. If this is not the case, the refrigeration unit must be replaced.

CAUTION: This should only be done by a qualified technician.

This problem could be remedied in some older units by turning the unit upside down several times so that the liquid in the absorber vessel can be mixed with the liquid in the boiler. Make sure the refrigerator has ample time to cool down first. This proce-

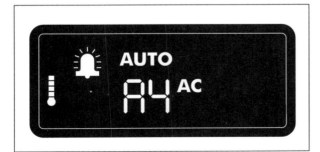

Figure 8.4 Norcold control panel diagnostic readout alerts user to operational problems

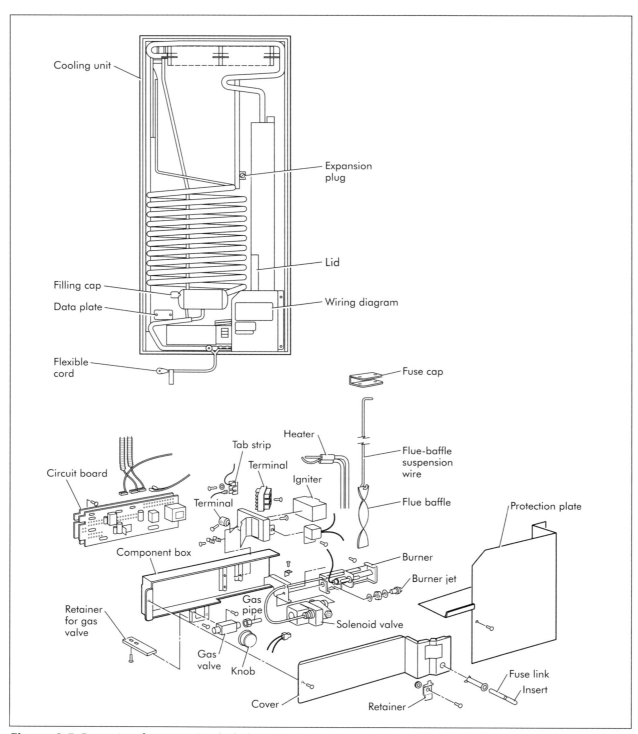

Figure 8.5 Dometic refrigerator (exploded view)

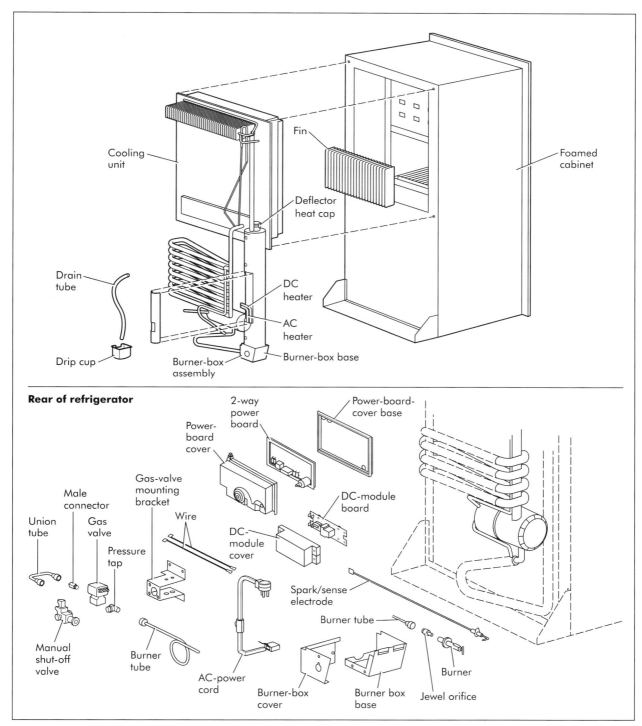

Figure 8.6 Norcold refrigerator (exploded view)

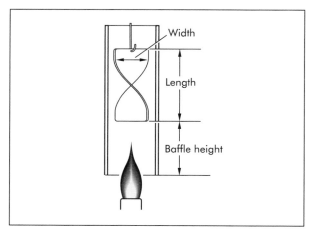

Figure 8.7 Baffle position for Dometic refrigerators

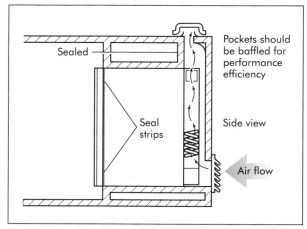

Figure 8.8 Baffle position for Norcold refrigerators

dure will restore the liquid balance to the unit. Sometimes a vigorous drive around the block will restore minor blockages.

Correcting Blockage in a Norcold Unit

If a Norcold refrigerator suffers loss of cooling ability due to operation for extended periods of time in an off-level condition, there is a special procedure that may or may not restore function. There are no guarantees. The refrigerator must be removed from its compartment and placed on its left side for a minimum of one hour. This will allow the ammonia and water to mix with one another. After an attempt has been made to relieve the system of its blockage, the unit should be allowed to stand upright for one hour to allow the remainder of the refrigerant to return to the boiler. Operation on AC should once again be initiated for a maximum of one hour to determine if the refrigerator's cooling capability has been restored. After a one-hour period of operation the left rear of the freezer compartment should be cold; if it is not, the blockage has not been remedied, and the cooling unit must be removed and replaced.

■ HELPFUL HINTS ■ FOR REFRIGERATOR OPERATION

Leaving aside the technical details of absorption refrigerator operation, there are many simple tricks that help an RV refrigerator deliver better service.

Some of the procedures described here require a periodic visit to a service center, where technicians can test components with instrumentation if erratic refrigerator performance is noticed. But most of these tips are just common-sense techniques.

■ Precool the refrigerator by starting it the night before the camping trip. This should be done with no food in the refrigerator.

■ Wait until the refrigerator is thoroughly cold before placing food inside.

■ Precool food in your home refrigerator. Prefreeze foods to be kept in the freezer. This gives the unit a break by adding cold to it rather than adding heat and demanding more work to cool it down.

■ Proper refrigeration requires free air circulation within the food storage compartment. Restricted air circulation within this compartment will cause higher cabinet temperatures. To remedy this situation, simply rearrange the foodstuffs. It is essential that the shelves not be covered with paper or large storage containers, because this inhibits free air circulation.

■ To reduce frost buildup, cover stored liquids and moist foods, and do not leave the door open longer than necessary.

■ When buying food on the road that is intended for storage in the refrigerator, buy the coldest packages available, and get them into the refrigerator as quickly as possible. This prevents the refrigerator from having to work extra hard to chill warm packages.

- Always wipe moisture off the outside of containers before putting them in the refrigerator. If cold items are taken from the unit, they will have a tendency to sweat as they warm. Dry them off before putting them back into the refrigerator. This will help prevent frost buildup, which consumes cooling power and insulates against efficient heat transfer.
- Periodically clean out the burner unit. LP-gas has a garlic or rotten-egg odor that becomes especially strong as the cylinders/tank run low. This scent attracts spiders, which will build nests in the burner.
- Special care must be taken when cleaning burner orifices; these parts are delicate. They must not be cleaned by simply inserting a pin or thin wire. They must be removed, cleaned in alcohol, and then blown dry with compressed air. When reinstalling, make sure the burner flame is centered directly below the flue.
- Clean out the refrigerator's roof-exhaust vent. Bird nests, leaves, twigs, or other debris can lodge there, choking the refrigerator's efficiency. In extreme cases, they can even cause a fire. A "spider-web" brush works very well for this.
- Do not overfill the LP-gas cylinder(s) or tank. This can damage the regular diaphragm, causing irregular delivery of the propane and resulting in erratic operation of the refrigerator.
- In the Gas mode, the burners are designed for a specific Btu rating. The LP-gas pressure must remain constant or the refrigerator will operate erratically (see Troubleshooting, page 8.12).
- If you have noticed erratic cooling when operating on gas, check for kinks or clogs in the gas line.
- Check LP-gas pressure at the refrigerator when other appliances are operating. Using

■ TROUBLESHOOTING ■
THE ABSORPTION REFRIGERATOR

Problem	Possible Cause	Correction
Insufficient cooling	Wrong thermostat setting	Adjust thermostat to higher setting
	Restricted air circulation over cooling unit	Remove any restrictions
	Refrigerator not level	Adjust RV to level refrigerator
	Air leakage into cabinet	Check door gasket; adjust or replace if necessary
	Heavy coating of frost on evaporator	Defrost unit frequently
	Faulty heater, wrong voltage or type	Install new heater of appropriate voltage
	Intermittent power	Check for loose connections; repair as necessary
	Voltage drop	Maintain voltage at full rate
	Break in electric circuit	Check fuses, switch wiring; repair as necessary
	Faulty thermostat	Replace thermostat
	Failed cooling unit	Replace cooling unit
Excessive cooling	Wrong thermostat setting	Adjust thermostat to lower setting
	Incorrectly located end of thermostat capillary tube	Reinsert capillary end of thermostat fully into the sleeve under the ice-tray compartment
	Faulty thermostat	Replace thermostat
	Improperly wired heater	Rewire heater according to unit wiring diagram

---

■ TROUBLESHOOTING ■
REFRIGERATOR OPERATING ON LP-GAS

Problem	Possible Cause	Correction
Insufficient cooling	Restricted air circulation over cooling unit	Remove any restrictions
	Refrigerator not level	Adjust RV to level refrigerator
	Insufficient LP-gas	Refill LP-gas tanks
	Feeler point of thermocouple flame-failure device not heated enough by flame	Adjust position of feeler point in flame
	Clogged bypass screw, clogged burner head, clogged burner-jet orifice	Clean bypass screw with alcohol and by blowing through with air; if necessary, replace burner jet; clean the head with a brush or toothpick
	Flue baffle not inserted into central tube of cooling unit	Position baffle correctly; consult manufacturer's specs.
	Baffle too low in flue	Position baffle correctly. Consult manufacturer's specs (Figures 8.7 and 8.8).
	Improper LP-gas pressure	Have pressure checked; pressure must not fall below 11 inches water-column pressure when thermostat is set on "max"
	Loose burner assembly	Refit burner assembly
	Improper thermostat setting	Increase thermostat setting
	Failed cooling unit	Replace unit
Refrigerator too cold	Improper thermostat setting	Lower thermostat setting
	Incorrectly located end of thermostat capillary tube	Reinsert end of capillary tube in clamp on fresh-food compartment
	Incorrect size of bypass screw	Replace bypass screw
	Dirt in thermostat valve	Clean valve and valve seat in thermostat

a test manometer, pressure should read 11 inches of water-column pressure. This should be done by a qualified technician.

■ Periodically have the LP-gas regulator replaced, to insure maximum efficiency. The diaphragm can load up with a waxy substance after a great deal of use, which changes the way the pressure is controlled. If the pressure vacillates, the refrigerator will suffer irregular operation.

■ Don't put filters, covers, or plastic bags over the vents to the refrigerator unit. They are designed to be operated as they come from the factory, with nothing covering the vents. If the ventilation is restricted, a buildup of excess heat results, and the refrigerator cannot function properly.

■ Don't open the refrigerator or freezer doors more often than necessary. Cold air in the refrigerator is like a pile of sand. It falls to the bottom, and when the door is opened, the cold air runs out onto the floor. Every time the door is opened, the refrigerator gains a few degrees of heat. If it is opened six or eight times on an extremely hot day, it may lose much of its cold.

■ In extremely hot weather, a small battery-powered fan (Fridgemate) in the refrigerator will help circulate the air faster than occurs by natural convection.

■ Make sure an adequate electric cord is used when operating in the 120-volt AC mode. An extension cord of inadequate gauge, used with the RV power cord, will cause inefficiency of the refrigerator heating element and result in a reduction of cooling capacity.

■ Install a surge suppresser where the electric cord from the refrigerator plugs in, to prevent a power spike from destroying the equipment.

■ The flue, which is located directly above the burner flame, should be cleaned periodically to remove rust, scale, and soot. How often this is done is determined by frequency of use, LP-gas quality, and region of the country. If the refrigerator is operated in areas with high humidity or salt air, it will require more frequent cleaning.

■ After removal of the flue tube, the spiral baffle inside the tube must be carefully removed. Then a shotgun-bore brush or a special brush available from the refrigerator manufacturer is used to clean the tube. When everything is clean, the baffle must be replaced exactly as it was originally. In order to perform this operation, it may be necessary to remove the refrigerator from its recess. To get total efficiency, this cleaning is critical. Generally, however, its benefits will only be noticed in extremely hot weather when maximum refrigerator cooling is needed.

■ If possible, park so the refrigerator side of the coach is shaded.

■ Clean the absorber coils and condenser fins to remove any buildup that can act as a heat-transfer insulator.

■ The electric heating element should be checked periodically for proper resistance. It will deteriorate with age, leaving the refrigerator with a slowly diminishing capacity for cooling when used in the electric mode. Generally, owners have this test performed at a repair facility because of the instruments required.

■ Defrost the unit regularly. A frost buildup insulates against thermal exchange, preventing the refrigerator from absorbing heat from its interior and contents. Do not use a hairdryer or high-heat source to speed defrosting because this can warp the cooling fins. Instead, use a pan of warm water and wait patiently for the defrosting to take place.

■ Because the interior refrigerator light (if so equipped) produces some heat, check to see that it goes out when the door is closed. To do this, use a thin butter-knife blade to spread the door gasket back a bit when the door is closed. This will allow you to look inside at night when the door is closed to see if the light is on.

■ High humidity can cause condensation to freeze on the interior fins. There is usually a catch tray and/or a drain hose inside the refrigerator that removes ice melt from the unit. This water is ducted to a hose that exits the refrigerator or is designed to use a drain hole behind the unit. You must insure that the water drain hole is kept clear of debris.

■ Inspect the door gasket for proper sealing ability. Use the dollar-bill trick. Shut the refrigerator door with a dollar bill halfway inside, then tug on the other half to see how difficult it is to remove. It should offer some resistance. Or you can place a lighted flashlight inside the refrigerator at night and shut the door to see if light escapes.

■ Install a fan in the compartment behind the refrigerator to speed the removal of hot air. This will significantly enhance the performance of your refrigerator. These fans can be powered by 12-volt DC or a small solar panel.

■ If your refrigerator can be operated in the 12-volt DC mode, make sure the connection uses an adequate gauge of wire and that there is no corrosion or damage to the wire.

CAUTION: Do not operate the refrigerator on 12-volt DC unless the vehicle's engine is running. The 12-volt DC mode only acts as a temperature-holding system; always cool the refrigerator on 120-volt AC power or LP-gas first.

Checking for Overfreezing

If your manual-control refrigerator freezes food in the lower compartment, follow these steps:

1. Make sure the gas thermostat knob is not stripped. If it is, replace it.
2. Turn the knob up and down, and watch for the flame to change. If it does not change, the thermostat is defective and must be replaced.
3. Make certain the end of the thermistor (sensing tube) is seated properly inside the refrigerator against the cooling fins.

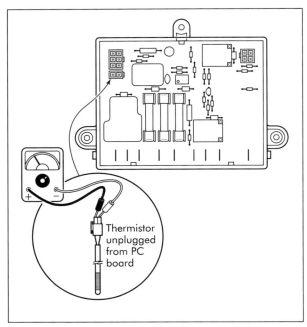

Figure 8.9 To test the thermistor, remove the cover from the lower circuit board, disconnect the thermistor harness from the P2, 2-pin terminal and check with a multimeter.

4. If it changes from "high" to "low" (or vice versa) and still freezes in the lower section, change the bypass screw (shut off the gas). Remove the existing screw in the thermostat and replace it with a new one that has a lower number stamped on top. Finish by checking for gas leaks using soapy water or perform a manometer test (see LP-Gas, Chapter 2).

If your automatic-control refrigerator freezes food in the lower compartment, follow these steps:

1. The most common cause of lower-compartment freezing in refrigerators with improved control systems is a faulty thermistor. To test this temperature sensor, remove the cover from the lower circuit board (Figure 8.9) and disconnect the thermistor harness from the P2, 2-pin terminal.
2. Place the thermistor in a glass of ice water and wait two to three minutes.
3. Use a multimeter to obtain a reading of approximately 7,000 to 10,000 ohms. Nor-

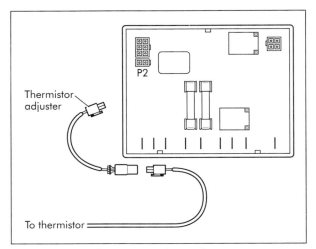

Figure 8.10 Thermistor adjuster for Dometic refrigerator

mally, a thermistor that has failed will have a very high resistance. If the resistance is more than 11,000 ohms, replace the thermistor; if not, the control system may be at fault and should be checked by an RV technician.

Dometic refrigerators operating in warm weather may need to use a thermistor adjuster (Figure 8.10) to bring the interior temperatures below the normal 35°F to 46°F readings. A thermistor adjuster (not supplied with the refrigerator) is a resistor-type part that attaches between the thermistor and the lower board. The thermistor adjuster is operating properly when the resistance across the terminals reads 23,200 ohms (± 10 percent).

Checking a Cooling Unit

Failure of refrigeration doesn't necessarily indicate that the cooling unit is defective. Other factors governing its operation must be checked.

If the refrigerator has been operating on LP-gas and a loss of cooling is noted, switch over to electric operation. If the unit has been operating on AC power, switch over to LP-gas. This will determine if component failure in the electric or LP-gas system is causing the cooling fault. After the refrigerator has been switched over from one power source to another, allow sufficient time to assure that the unit is cycling properly. The freezer plate should start to cool. Check the following items before suspecting that the refrigeration cooling unit is faulty.

- Evaporator plate is level in each direction
- Controls have been properly set for the power source being utilized
- Power source is at the correct rating (11 inches water-column pressure for LP-gas, 120 volts for AC)
- 12-volt DC supply is present for the mode-selector control
- Upper and lower vents are clear and unobstructed
- Refrigerator is properly leveled
- Good ventilation is available
- Clean proper-size burner orifice
- Clean proper-size bypass screw
- Clean thermostat valve
- Correct flame
- Correct position of baffle in boiler tube
- No burned-out element
- Heating element in correct position
- Correct size and wattage of heating element
- Supply voltage corresponds to voltage stamped on the heating element
- No fluctuation in voltage supply
- No loose electrical connections
- Thermostat intact

- No unit leaks
- Safety valve intact

CAUTION: If you have a 3-way power refrigerator, do not attempt to operate the system on 12-volt DC power when analyzing the system performance because this power source is designed for short-period operation only and does not power the system at its full cooling capability.

■ GENERAL MAINTENANCE ■

Once or twice a year, depending upon frequency of use, it is recommended to clean and adjust the burner assembly. This includes the burner jet, the burner barrel, and the flue system (Figure 8.11). On all LP-gas appliances, the cleaning solution used on the jets and associated parts should be one that dries without any residue. Rubbing alcohol and wood alcohol are appropriate cleaning agents.

CAUTION: Do not use a cleaner with a petrochemical base, because it will leave a film on the inside of these parts and reduce burner efficiency. Never use a wire or pin when cleaning the jet. This will enlarge the orifice opening, damage the refrigerator, and cause a fire hazard.

LP-gas pressure being delivered to the appliances should be checked annually by a qualified dealer or propane agency. Correct LP-gas pressure is 11 inches of water-column pressure. This should be checked at the test point in the refrigerator compartment.

When replacing a jet with a new one, make sure

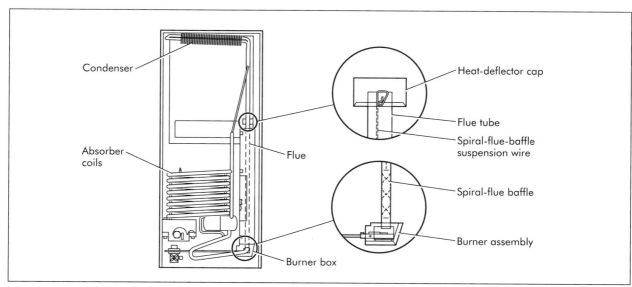

Figure 8.11 Burner assembly and flue system

the replacement is correct for your refrigerator model. A jet that is too large or too small can ruin the cooling unit. A jet that is too small will also result in failure to maintain desired temperatures.

It is important to always check for LP-gas leaks after repair work has been performed. Do this with soapy water (see LP-Gas, Chapter 2).

Replacing or Cleaning the Burner

The efficiency of the refrigerator is highly dependent on the correct burner flame, which provides energy for the refrigerator's cooling. The efficiency of the burner flame is dependent on the gas-supply pressure, air input, and burner-orifice cleanliness. For routine cleaning or replacement of the burner (Figure 8.12), follow this procedure as it applies to your particular unit:

1. Turn off the LP-gas supply at the cylinder(s)/ tank and/or electric power.
2. Disconnect the gas pipe from burner assembly. To prevent damage, use two wrenches.
3. Disconnect the thermocouple from the safety valve.
4. Disconnect the ignitor lead (if applicable) and loosen the screw.
5. Remove the burner housing.
6. Remove the orifice from the burner tube.
7. Clean both with alcohol and compressed air only.
8. Clean the burner tube and especially the gauze or slots with a brush. Blow out with compressed air (80 psi maximum).

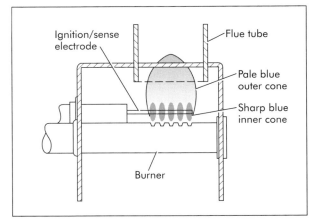

Figure 8.13 Proper burner flame in a Norcold refrigerator

9. Check the flue baffle to see that it is clean and free of soot. Heavy soot formation indicates improper functioning of the burner.
10. Clean the baffle and the flue.
11. Clean the cooling unit and the floor under the refrigerator.
12. Reassemble in reverse order. Be very careful to avoid crossthreading when connecting the gas-supply line. To prevent damage, use two wrenches when loosening or tightening the gas-line connection.
13. Turn on the LP-gas supply.
14. The entire gas installation should be checked for leaks. Test all pipes and fittings with soapy water.

   NOTE: Do not use a solution that contains ammonia, because ammonia will attack brass fittings of the burner and gas valve assemblies.

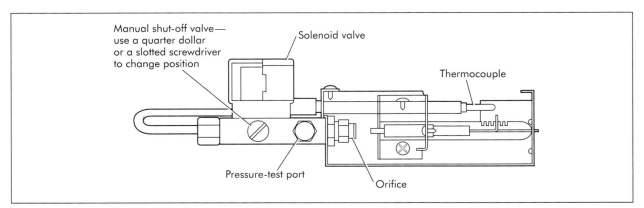

Figure 8.12 Routine cleaning or replacement of the burner is necessary for effcient refrigerator operation.

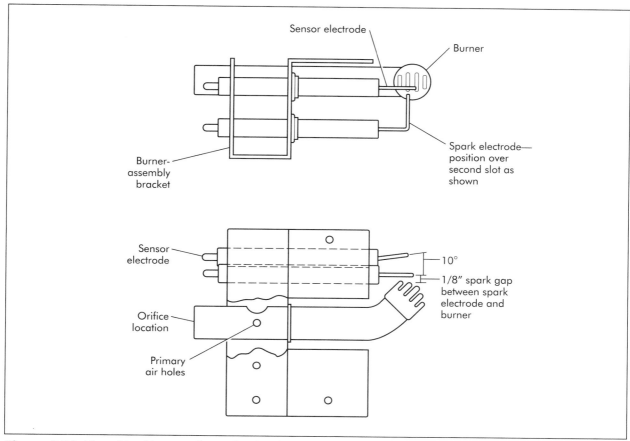

Figure 8.14 Norcold refrigerator has a fixed orifice; flame should be sharp blue with no yellow color.

15. Check the burner with full flame (Max) and with bypass flame (0). The thermostat will not close to bypass on setting 0 unless the refrigerator has been working a few hours and the thermostat bulb is cooled to at least 40°F.

Setting the Norcold Burner Flame

Norcold refrigerators employ burners with nonadjustable, fixed orifices using primary air holes that control the flame (Figure 8.13). A properly set flame in the burner of a Norcold refrigerator should be sharp blue with no yellow color. If there is a constant yellow flame or if the flame appears erratic, the burner and burner orifice must be cleaned.

The ignition/sense electrode for the Norcold refrigerator must be properly aligned. Alignment of the electrode should be between ⅛ inch to ³⁄₁₆ inch from the top of the burner (Figure 8.14).

Setting the Dometic Burner Flame

Dometic refrigerators have employed several different types of burners over the years, and a different procedure is used for each when setting the proper flame.

- The Bunsen B-type burner has a ceramic head and a Klixon safety valve (Figure 8.15). When the thermostat dial is turned to Max, the flame must form a crown around the burner's inner cone and have upright streaks through its center holes. When properly set, the flame will be blue and soft and may have a slightly luminous tip. Air-adjustment rings on the burner are turned to adjust the flame.
- The cylindrical H-type burner has adjustable primary air inlets combined with the Junker-type thermoelectric flame-failure safety device (Figure 8.16). Air-adjustment rings are used for regulation of the flame. The correct flame

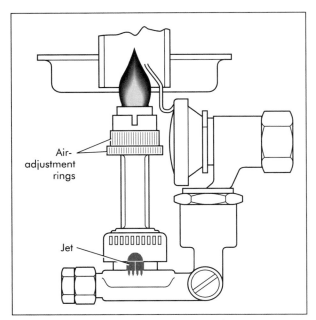

Figure 8.15 Dometic Bunsen B-type burner is set properly when the flame is blue and soft.

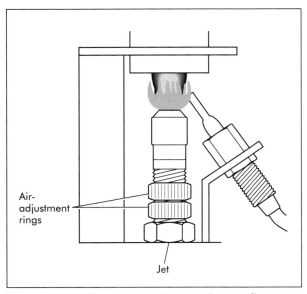

Figure 8.16 The Dometic "H" type burner flame should have a bright-blue crown at the base of the flame and emit a slight buzzing noise.

at Max setting should have a bright-blue crown at the base of the flame and emit a slight buzzing noise.

■ The E-type burner is designed with the jet and adapter horizontally located, and the burner mixing tube is formed as a bend with a verti-

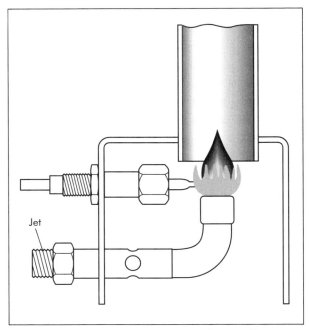

Figure 8.17 The Dometic "E" type burner flame should have a bright-blue crown at the base of the flame and emit a slight buzzing noise.

cal outlet (Figure 8.17). The primary air inlets are preset and therefore not adjustable. The burner is combined with the Junker-type thermoelectric flame-failure safety device. When adjusted properly, the flame at Max setting should have a bright-blue crown at the base of the flame and emit a slight buzzing sound.

■ The AMES and AES refrigerators (Figure 8.18), Silhouette models (Figure 8.19), and the Royale and Elite systems (Figure 8.20) use a horizontal burner, orifice, and thermocouple. This is combined with a manual gas-shut-off valve and a solenoid valve, which are controlled by the electronic system control board. A gas-pressure test port is also provided.

Power-Module Replacement for Dometic Electronically Controlled Refrigerators

Before replacing the power module (circuit board), perform the following tests:

■ Test for dirty DC power by using a digital voltmeter set on the AC scale. Probe the leads to the main terminal block (Figure 8.21). A read-

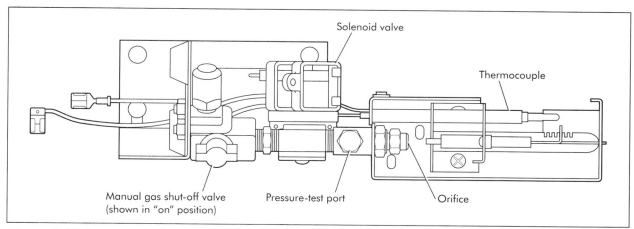

Figure 8.18 Dometic AMES and AES refrigerators

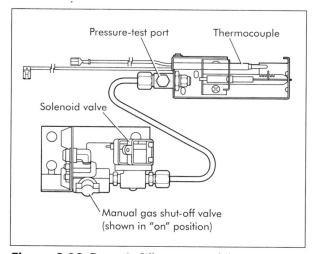

Figure 8.19 Dometic Silhouette model

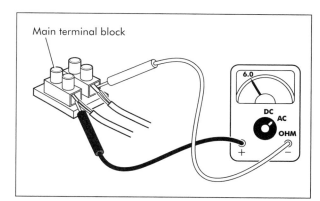

Figure 8.21 Probe leads to the main terminal block when testing for dirty DC power.

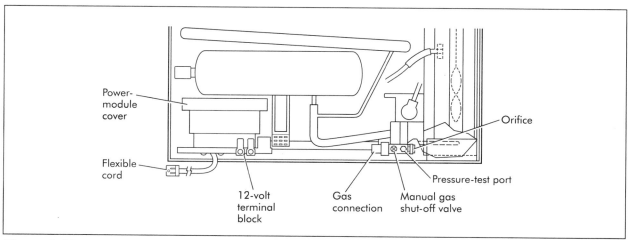

Figure 8.20 Dometic Royal and Elilte models

ing of 6 volts AC or less is acceptable. If the reading is more than 6 volts AC, check the connections, wiring, and/or power converter.

NOTE: A brief interruption of the DC power while the refrigerator is operating on LP-gas can cause the check light to illuminate.

- Test the thermocouple; it should produce 24 to 30 millivolts DC (MVDC). If the DC power is interrupted and then restored, the thermocouple may not have sufficient time to cool. If the power module sees more than 6 MVDC, it will assume there's a problem in the LP-gas mode when the power is restored and immediately turn on the check light. Any reading less than 18 MVDC could relate to erratic LP-gas operation. Improper mounting and location of the thermocouple can cause an erroneous reading.

- To check for proper LP-gas pressure (11 inches water-column pressure), make sure half of all the propane-fired appliances are on during the test. The pressure at the refrigerator should not exceed 12 inches of water-column pressure with all the appliances off. Test LP-gas pressure at the test port, after the solenoid, with the refrigerator operating.

- Make sure the burner assembly, the horizontal metal tube with slots or holes located below the flue tube of the cooling unit, is clean. The burner should be cleaned periodically or at least once a year. To clean the burner, soak it in an alcohol-based solvent and allow to air dry.

NOTE: Be sure to test for gas leaks after reinstalling the burner or any of the other components.

- Verify that there is DC power at the re-ignitor (the electronic device that produces high voltage to create a spark to ignite a flame at the burner when the refrigerator starts on LP-gas). Using a multimeter (DC volts) to check power at the re-igniter (Figure 8.22), confirm that reading is within 1 volt of the voltage at the main terminal block in the back of the refrigerator when the unit is performing an ignition operation. On some units, if the DC voltage is below 12.5, the re-igniter will lockout the ignition cycle until reset.

- Check the electrode (where the spark is produced) for cracks and melting on the ceramic insulator. The proper mounting of the elec-

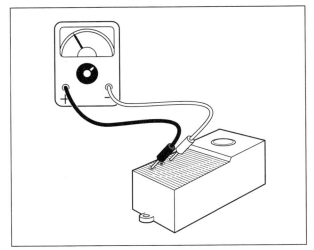

Figure 8.22 Use a multimeter (DC volts) to check power at the re-igniter.

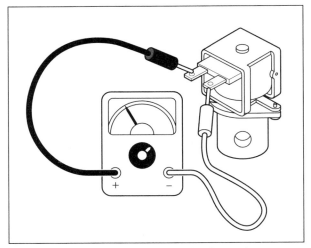

Figure 8.23 Check the solenoid valve with a multimeter set on the ohms scale.

trode should be directly over the burner with a ³⁄₁₆-inch gap.

- Check the solenoid valve with a multimeter set on the ohms scale. Remove one of the connectors (Figure 8.23) from the solenoid and measure the resistance across the terminals. The proper reading should be 44 to 53 ohms.

- Check for continuity of the fuses (Figure 8.24) in the power module (under the cover). Never replace a fuse with a larger one than specified by the manufacturer. A special tester (PAL tester) is needed to test the power module it-

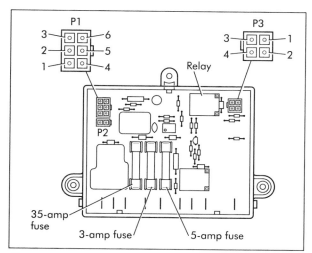

Figure 8.24 Remove the cover to check for continuity of fuses in the power module.

DC voltage between J4 and J10 on the lower circuit board; if the fuse is good and no DC voltage is determined, replace the lower circuit board.

■ Check for DC voltage at plug 1, terminal 1 on the circuit board; the main switch in control panel must be on. Voltage should be within 1 volt of the supply to the refrigerator. If no voltage is present, the switch is faulty, and the control panel should be replaced. If DC voltage is present, check for DC voltage at plug 1, terminal 3. If there is no DC power present, the circuit board is defective and should be replaced.

NOTE: Always confirm circuit-board condition with an appropriate tester (dealer).

self. If all other tests fail to determine the cause of a malfunction, take the power module (circuit board) to a dealer who has the testing equipment and technical experience.

■ Check for DC voltage at plug 1, terminal 4 at the lower circuit board (see Figure 8.24); the main switch in the control panel must be off. If no voltage is present, check fuses. Check for

Improper or dirty electrical grounds are one of the biggest problems with refrigerators. A quick and easy way to test for ground problems can be done with a digital multimeter (millivolts). Probe the multimeter to terminals J3 and J10 of the power module (Figure 8.25). Remove one of the connection wires from the gas solenoid valve. The millivolt reading should be 1 to 2 millivolts or less. Replace the wire on the solenoid valve and, with the re-ignitor spark-

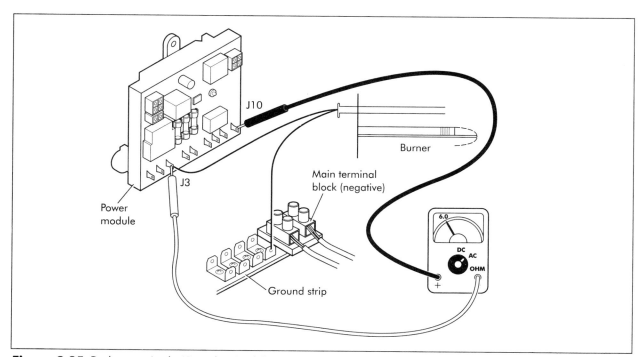

Figure 8.25 Probe terminals J3 and J10 of the power module with a multimeter to test for ground problems.

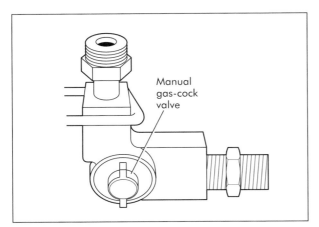

Figure 8.26 Manual gas-cock valve

ing, the meter should read 5 millivolts or less. If the meter shows more than 6 millivolts, there may be a ground problem. Your dealer can install a special wiring harness to solve this problem. With the refrigerator running on gas (flame burning), there should be a 25- to 30-millivolt reading. Shut off the manual gas-cock valve (Figure 8.26) and watch the millivolt reading as it drops.

NOTE: The millivolt reading when the re-ignitor starts sparking should read 7 to 13.

Check all connections on the 6-terminal ground bus bar for tightness and corrosion. The connections at the 4-pole main DC terminal block must be clean and tight. Check connections at the battery and the converter.

NOTE: Never replace the board—even after performing the above checks—without having it tested by a qualified dealer with proper instruments.

Cleaning the Refrigerator

The interior of the refrigerator should be thoroughly cleaned on a regular basis. Remove the shelves and wash the interior walls with a solution of lukewarm water to which a small amount of baking soda or dishwashing detergent has been added. Dry the surfaces thoroughly, especially around the door frame and the door gasket. Warm water only should be used to wash the cooling evaporator, ice trays, and shelves.

CAUTION: Never use strong chemicals or abrasive materials on any part of the refrigerator interior.

Defrosting the Refrigerator

Before defrosting the refrigerator, move food to another refrigerator, if possible, to prevent spoilage during defrosting. To defrost the refrigerator, turn the power-selector switch off. Fill trays or pans with hot water and place them in the freezer compartment. After all the frost has melted, empty the drip tray from beneath the finned evaporator (if not drained to the outside) and wipe up the excess moisture with a clean cloth. Replace the drip tray and all the food. Turn on the refrigerator, and turn the thermostat to Max for a few hours for maximum cooling before returning it to its normal position.

Refrigerator Odors

Odors inside the refrigerator are caused by improper food storage. They may also be caused by infrequent cleaning of the food compartment or if the refrigerator has been shut off for some time with the door closed. Odors can be removed by careful cleaning of the interior, using only a solution of warm water combined with a small amount of either baking soda or dishwashing detergent. Use no harsh chemicals or abrasives.

Checking for Gas Leaks

Odors outside the refrigerator may be caused by gas leaks. LP-gas is blended with a rotten-egg (sulfur) aroma to alert owners to leaks. To check for leaks:

- Make sure all gas appliances are turned off. Test gas connections and all joints in the gas line with soapy water, up to and including the gas valve.
- Never look for a leak with an open flame. Use a flashlight when necessary to look for soap bubbles caused by leaks.
- Turn on the gas valve and light burner, then test connections between the gas valve and the burner carefully with soapy water.
- Do not use a solution that contains ammonia, because ammonia will attack brass fittings of the burner and gas-valve assemblies.

- Odors outside the refrigerator may be caused by improper burner flame. If the flame touches the side of the boiler due to improper location of the burner, relocate the burner. Burner dislocation may also cause smoke and discoloration of walls and ceiling. Remember:

  - If the burner is damaged or faulty, replace it.
  - If the flame touches the flue baffle, correct the position of the baffle.
  - If the flue is dirty, clean it.

Cleaning the Flue Tube

The purpose of the flue system is to provide a draft that will pull the burner flame into the central tube and supply sufficient primary and secondary air to the flame. The baffle is inserted in the central tube to distribute the heat produced by the burner to the boiler system. In order to obtain the best cooling performance, it is important to use the correct size of baffle and to position it properly.

A variety of problems may be caused by obstructions in the flue. If there are obstructions, they will reduce or stop flue draft, cause odors in the refrigerator, slow the freezing process, and raise the temperature inside the refrigerator. Flue stoppages may also cause the flame to burn outside the central tube.

To clean the flue tube, loosen the burner assembly, drop it down, and cover it with a rag so no debris from the flue will fall into it. Lift out the spiral baffle on its support wire from the flue top. Working from the top of the flue, clean the tube with a suitable brush. Also clean the baffle before reinstalling it.

In some refrigerators, it is not possible to reach the top of the flue tube to remove the spiral baffle. In this situation, cover the burner with a rag and then use air pressure from the bottom of the flue to loosen rust.

In the 1200 LR, 900, and 9100 series Norcold refrigerators, the procedure for cleaning the flue involves removal of the refrigerator from its enclosure. This entails disconnecting 12-volt DC, 120-volt AC, and gas-supply lines from the refrigerator. Remove the front- and rear-mounting screws and slide the unit forward and out of its enclosure. When the unit

is cool to the touch, remove the heat-deflector cap from the flue. Then remove the spiral baffle from the flue tube. Using a wire brush or fine emery cloth, clean the spiral baffle of debris. Cover the burner, and clean inside the flue tube with a flue brush. Reinstall the flue baffle, insuring that the baffle is securely in place. Finally, reinstall the refrigerator in its enclosure.

Flame Blow-out

If the flame blows out under especially windy conditions, try to position the RV to avoid the wind blowing against the wall where the vent outlets are located. Make sure the metal shields around the burner box are in place and secure. Confirm that the burner and flame are adjusted correctly. If the problem persists, set the thermostat to Max. This measure can only be temporary because, after a few hours, items in the refrigerator compartment will freeze. Do not cover the vents to prevent flame blow-out. Circulation of air is necessary for proper and safe refrigerator operation.

The Thermoelectric Flame-Failure Safety Device

The reason for incorporating an automatic flame-failure device in the burner assembly is to prevent unburned gas from escaping from the burner and to avoid a fire if the flame has been extinguished or blown out (Figure 8.27).

The device operates in this manner: By pressing the button, the gas valve is opened and gas can pass on to the burner. The thermocouple is located at the burner. When the gas flame of the burner is ignited, heat is transferred to the thermocouple feeler. This heats the hot junction of the thermocouple feeler, and an electric current is generated. This current passes through the copper wire to the electromagnet.

As soon as the electric current is generated, the electromagnet attaches the armature to the valve. The button can then be released. As long as current is flowing, the valve is kept open, allowing gas to pass to the burner. When the flame is extinguished, the heat transfer to the hot junction is interrupted and no electric current is generated. The armature to the valve is then forced back by a spring, and the gas flow through the valve ceases.

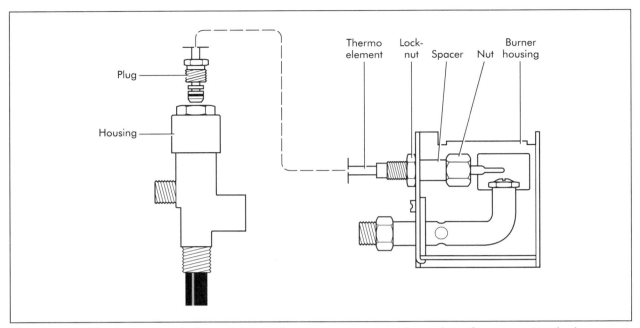

Figure 8.27 The thermocouple flame-failure safety device prevents unburned gas from escaping the burner.

Replacing the Thermoelectric Flame-Failure Safety Device

Replacement of the thermoelectric flame-failure safety device is simple:

1. Unscrew and remove the end of the thermo-electric unit from the valve housing of the LP-gas-supply line.
2. Unscrew and remove the thermo-element from the burner housing.
3. Bend the new thermo-element to match the shape of the old one and screw the new unit into place on the burner. Make sure the feeler is located properly over the burner.
4. Check that there are no burrs inside the valve housing that may cause leaks. Then install the end of the thermo-element into the valve housing of the LP-gas-supply line. The plug must be properly tightened into the valve housing to insure contact between the thermo-element and the magnetic coil within the housing.

Replacing the Safety-Valve Magnet

If the safety-valve magnet is defective, it must be replaced (Figure 8.28):

1. Unscrew the connecting plug on the thermo-element from the housing nut.
2. Unscrew the housing nut and remove the defective safety-valve magnet from the housing.
3. Fit a new magnet valve and insure that it is properly inserted in the housing.
4. Fit the housing nut and the connection plug and check that a good contact between the contact plug on the thermo-element and the contact on the safety-valve magnet is obtained.

The Thermostat

If the thermostat-control assembly loses its charge, it will become inoperative. To test for a lost charge, while the flame is reduced to a minimum and the temperature control is set at a numbered position on the dial, remove the thermistor from its clamp in the evaporator and warm the capillary end with a hand. If the flame fails to increase in size, the thermostat has lost its charge and must be replaced (Figure 8.29).

To replace the thermostat:

1. Shut off the gas supply.
2. Remove the capillary from its clamp on the evaporator fins.
3. Remove sealing plugs on the outside and

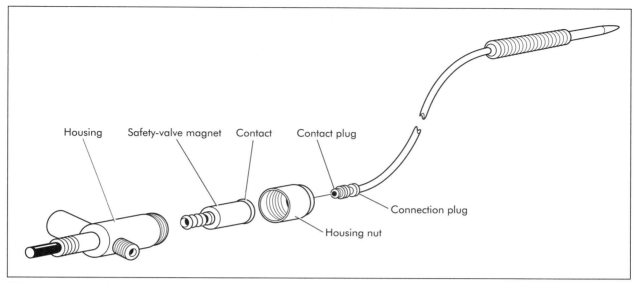

Figure 8.28 Replacing the safety valve magnet in the thermocouple flame-failure safety device

Labels: Housing, Safety-valve magnet, Contact, Contact plug, Connection plug, Housing nut

inside of the cabinet.

4. Straighten the capillary and pull it through the cabinet.
5. Remove the thermostat by unscrewing it from the gas filter and the flame-failure safety device.
6. Install a new thermostat by reversing the order of removal.

The Heater Element

Some refrigerators are equipped for both 120-volt AC and 12-volt DC operation. The heat necessary for operation of an absorption-cooling unit is supplied by an electric cartridge heater mounted in a pocket in the boiler system. If the heater is faulty, it must be replaced. Be certain that the replacement heater is of the proper wattage for your model refrigerator. If a unit of too low or too high wattage is used, the refrigerator will not cool efficiently.

Replacing the Heater

To replace the heater:

1. Unplug the unit from the 120-volt AC power supply and disconnect the wires leading to the 12-volt DC power supply.
2. Open the lid or door on the boiler cover.

3. Remove as much of the boiler insulation as necessary to give access to the heater unit.
4. Remove the defective heater unit.
5. Install the new heater unit and replace the insulation material.
6. Close the lid or door to the boiler cover.
7. Reconnect the 12-volt DC power supply wires and plug in the 120-volt AC power cord.

The Igniter

The igniter is an electronic device that produces high voltage to create a spark at the burner when the refrigerator is in Gas mode. To test the igniter, you must first verify that the 12-volt DC power is within 1 volt of the supply voltage at the main power block during the trial-for-ignition phase of the starting sequence. A drop of more than 1 volt indicates a loose connection or a circuit-board problem. Next, disconnect the DC power at the main 12-volt power block, remove the high-voltage cable from the igniter, and reconnect the 12-volt DC power. The refrigerator will go into the trial-for-ignition phase of the starting sequence, and you should hear a sparking sound coming from the igniter block. The igniter will need to be replaced if there is no sound.

The piezo-electric igniter for all automatic Dometic models (Figure 8.30) is part number 2931132019 (RV gas model 679). This is a self-contained 50 MA

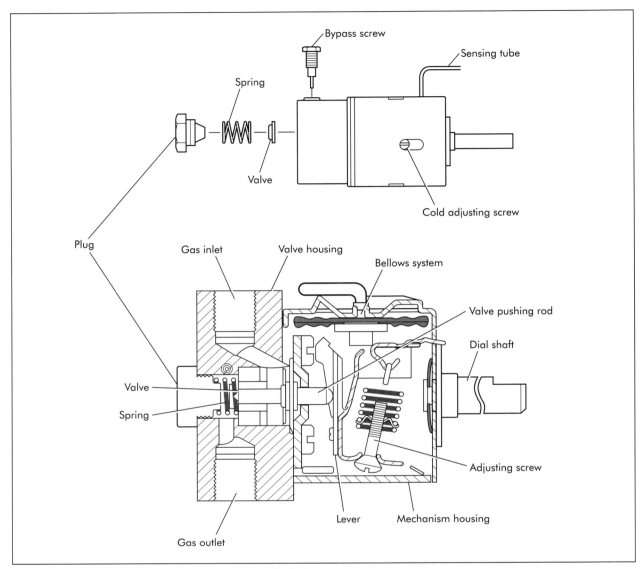

Figure 8.29 Thermostat control assembly (exploded view)

unit that generally does not need maintenance. Nor-cold igniters are a part of the control system and must be matched to the refrigerator. For manual models, a spring-loaded striker creates a spark as the sparker button is pushed. If there is no resistance when pressing the button, the unit is defective and must be replaced. If there is an audible "snap," or the unit has resistance when the button is pushed, but there is no spark, the problem is in the electrode.

To replace the igniter you must:

1. Disconnect DC power at the terminal block.
2. Remove high-voltage cable from the igniter.

3. Reconnect DC power. The igniter should produce a sparking sound.
4. If not, replace the igniter.

Replacing the Flint-type Igniter

Refrigerator models equipped with flint-type igniters require periodic replacement of the flint itself (Figure 8.31). To replace the flint, follow these steps:

1. Remove the outer burner shield.
2. Remove the lighter by loosening the screw

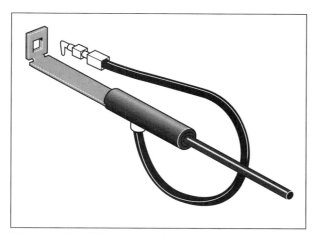

Figure 8.30 Piezo-crystal igniter used to light burner in Dometic refrigerator

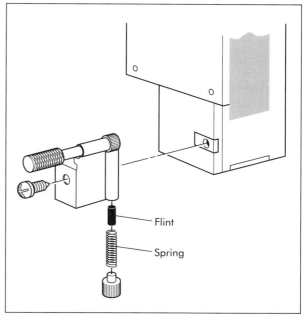

Figure 8.31 Flint-type igniters used in some refrigerator models require periodic flint replacement.

retaining the lighter.

3. Remove the cap and spring and tap out any remaining piece of flint.
4. Install a new flint and reassemble in reverse order.

Replacing the Igniter Wheel

If, after several years of use, the flint-type lighter fails to function properly even after a new flint has been installed, the serrated wheel may be worn and need replacement. Follow these steps:

1. Remove the lighter as described for flint-type igniter replacement.
2. Unscrew the rod from the serrated wheel and install a new wheel.

Dometic Electrode Replacement

To check the electrode:

1. Do a visual inspection for cracks or breaks on the ceramic insulator.
2. Make sure the mounting bracket is attached properly to the electrode.
3. If either of the above conditions is found, replace the electrode.

If the electrode requires replacement, follow these steps:

1. Unscrew the burner outer shield.
2. Loosen the fastening screw holding the electrode against the side of the burner housing.
3. Loosen the electrode from its cable by unscrewing the electrode counterclockwise.
4. Install a new electrode. When attaching the electrode to the burner housing, make sure the insulation plate is properly fitted between the burner housing and the electrode.
5. Adjust the spark gap. It must be set at $\frac{3}{16}$ inch, and the tip of the electrode must be positioned directly above the slots in the burner.

Norcold Electrode Replacement

If the electrode must be removed, follow these steps:

1. Remove the burner assembly.
2. Remove the ignition-electrode mounting screw.
3. Remove the ignition electrode.
4. Remove the sensing-electrode mounting screw.
5. Remove the sensing electrode.
   NOTE: Always check the spark gap after removing or replacing the ignition electrode. The spark gap between the electrode and the burner must measure $\frac{1}{8}$ inch.

■ CHAPTER 9 ■
OVENS AND RANGES

anges and ovens in RVs function quite similarly to household gas stoves and ovens, providing reliable and easy cooking capability to travelers. But the rigors of highway travel, with vibration, changing climates, and extensive usage can take its toll on these stoves and ovens. Most maintenance and repair procedures that will keep these units in tip-top operating condition are certainly within the capability of their owners.

Top burners on RV ranges operate when LP-gas is routed via the supply line to the manifold that is located in the top-burner section. This manifold is continually pressurized as long as the LP-gas-tank valve is open. When a burner valve is opened, the gas is injected through the burner orifice into the venturi (mixing tube), where it mixes with primary combustion air and flows to the burner.

Then the gas-air mixture is evenly discharged through the ports in the burner cap. Ignition occurs either by use of a lighted match, a pilot light, or electronic ignition, if applicable. Combustion characteristics may be modified on some stoves by adjusting the amount of primary combustion air available.

The oven burner takes its fuel supply from the manifold in the top section of the range. The supply tube leading from the manifold extends down and into the automatic-oven safety valve.

When this valve opens, gas passes through to the burner orifice. The orifice mixes the gas flow into the burner venturi, where it mixes with primary combustion air and enters the burner. The oven pilot or electronic-ignition system ignites this mixture, resulting in flame evenly spread around the burner.

■ OVEN AND RANGE COMPONENTS ■

Pilot Burner (Magic Chef)

On Magic Chef units, the pilot burner is actually two pilots in one. The standby pilot is the portion of the pilot light that burns constantly, provided that the LP-gas tank and manifold valve (if applicable) are open. The pilot light ignites the gas-air mixture at the burner when the oven valve opens. It also provides the base for the heater pilot.

The heater pilot is an extension of the standby pilot. It is on only when the oven thermostat calls for heat. The purpose of the heater pilot is to open the oven safety valve, thereby enabling gas to flow to the oven burner.

Thermostat

The thermostat is probably the most important component in the functioning of the oven. It regulates the oven to maintain the desired cooking temperature. The thermostat senses the oven temperature by means of a thermal bulb located in the top of the oven. This bulb is filled with gas and connected to a bellows in the thermostat by a capillary tube. When the oven is on, the bulb heats up and the gas expands, causing the bellows in the thermostat to expand. A mechanical linkage within the thermostat shuts off the flow of gas to the pilot burner. When this happens, the pilot flame ceases to burn at the heater position but continues at standby. As the temperature decreases in the oven, the bulb cools, and the gas

---

■ TROUBLESHOOTING ■
THE MAGIC CHEF OVEN AND RANGE

Problem	Possible Cause	Correction
No gas to oven pilot	Improper control-knob setting	Set oven-control knob to "oven pilot on". position
Oven slow to heat; poor baking; poor ignition of burners; pilots won't stay lit; popping sound from top burners; carbon on pilot shield; burner flame too low or too high	Defective gas pressure regulator	Have regulator tested
Oven pilots won't light or stay lit	Incorrect pilot adjustment; damaged pilot tubing; defective pressure regulator; incorrect oven-control-knob setting	Adjust pilot; check pilot tubing for kinks or clogs; have pressure regulator checked; be sure oven control knob is not in "pilot off" position.
Top burners won't light	Top burners and flash tubing out of position; no pilot flame; air shutter improperly adjusted; clogged burner ports	Check and adjust position of burners and flash tubing; check and adjust pilot flame; adjust air shutter; clean burner ports with a toothpick
Gas smell	Leaky gas line	Check all connections with soapy water; repair if necessary
Cake rises higher on one side than other	Uneven heat	Pans set too close to side of oven; allow 2 inches from side. Level range.
Cake burns on bottom	Improper circulation	Oven too full for proper circulation; remove item; do not use pan with a dark bottom
Oven will not operate	Pilot not lit	Relight pilot
Oven door not closing properly	Misaligned door	Open oven door and slightly loosen four sheet-metal screws holding the door panel to the liner
No constant pilot	No gas to range	Check gas supply; turn on LP-gas tank
	Constant-pilot-selector key turned off	Adjust constant-pilot-selector key to LP position
	Blocked tubing supply line	Disconnect tubing at source and at pilot end and blow out to clear passageway
	Blocked orifice	Single tube pilot; disconnect tubing from pilot and blow out to clear orifice
	Blocked pilot	Disconnect tubing from pilot; remove orifice from pilot and clean out blockage or replace pilot
	Pilot too close to oven burner flame	Adjust position of pilot assembly
No heater pilot	Thermostat turned off	Turn thermostat knob to setting above oven temperature
	Blocked tubing supply line	Disconnect tubing at source and at pilot end and blow out to clear passageway
	Blocked orifice	Single tube pilot; disconnect tubing from pilot and blow out to clear orifice
	Blocked pilot	Disconnect tubing from pilot; remove orifice from pilot and clean out blockage or replace pilot.

■ TROUBLESHOOTING ■
THE MAGIC CHEF OVEN AND RANGE, continued

Problem	Possible Cause	Correction
Oven will not maintain proper temperature	Oven bulb not in proper location	Secure oven bulb in clips that hold it in proper location; oven bulb should not touch any surface; place approximately ½ inch away from surface of oven drum top
	Oven bulb coated with foreign material	Use fine steel wool or scouring pad to gently clean surface of bulb
	Oven bottom covered with aluminum foil	If foil blocks holes or slots in oven bottom, heat distribution will be affected; remove foil
	Pilot flame not cycling off	High pressure can cause the constant-pilot flame to act as a heater-pilot flame; check pressure and adjust as necessary if that fails to solve the problem, replace the thermostat
	Safety device not closing; flame-responsive element is being heated by oven burner flame due to either improper location or an overrated oven burner	Check flame-responsive element for proper location on burner pilot; pilot burner must be properly located on bracket bracket must be in proper location check oven burner rate
	Safety device not closing when flame-responsive element is not being heated	Replace safety device
No main burner flame	Thermostat set lower then oven temperature	Reset knob to higher temperature
	Closed oven burner orifice	Readjust to rated input
	Flame-responsive element not hot enough	Check position of flame-responsive element; it must be enveloped in the heater-pilot flame; check gas pressure; check pressure regulator; repair if necessary
	Defective thermostat	Replace thermostat
	Defective safety valve	Replace safety valve
Yellow tips on burner flames	Improper gas-air mixture	Open the air mixture on units having adjustable air shutters; orifice hoods may be out of alignment (Figure 9.1)
Flames blowing off ports	Excessive gas pressure; air shutter opened too much	Close air shutter slightly; check gas pressure regulator
Flames flashing back in mix tube	Gas-air mixture too lean	Reduce air shutter opening; check for sufficient gas pressure

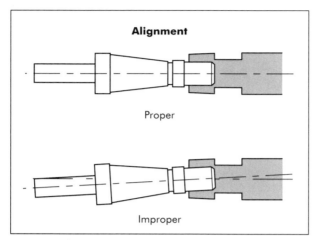

Figure 9.1 Oven air-shutter-orifice hoods must be aligned properly to produce a good gas-air mixture.

and the bellows in the thermostat contract. The mechanical linkage in the thermostat then causes an increasing amount of pilot gas to flow, and the pilot goes to the heater-flame position.

On some newer ranges, the thermostat will have an off position (full clockwise rotation), where all gas is shut off to the oven main-burner safety valve and to the oven pilot. At the pilot-on position, standby pilot gas is admitted to the oven pilot.

Oven Safety Valve

The oven safety valve (Figure 9.2) controls gas flow to the main burner. The valve is operated by a thermal bulb in the heater-pilot flame. This bulb is connected to a bellows in the valve by a capillary tube. When the

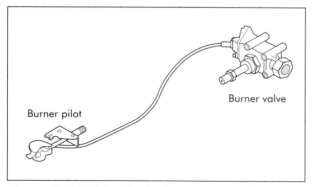

Figure 9.2 Safety valve in the oven controls gas flow to the main burner.

bulb is heated, the mercury within it expands, in turn expanding the bellows and opening the valve. The opposite occurs when the heater-pilot flame subsides.

■ RANGE AND OVEN ■
COMPONENT OPERATION AND MAINTENANCE

Lighting and Extinguishing Pilots

Magic Chef Top Burner and Oven Pilots

To light or extinguish the pilot(s) on Magic Chef ranges:

1. Turn off all burner valves. The oven-thermostat dial should be in the pilot-off position.
2. Turn on the top-burner gas-supply valve (Figure 9.3).
3. Lift the main cook-top panel and light the top burner pilot with a match or portable ignitor (if so equipped).

Figure 9.3 Magic Chef top-burner gas-supply valve

4. Depress and turn the thermostat dial to the pilot-on position.

5. Open the oven door and light the pilot. A small flame will be noted at the top of the pilot burner. If the range has not been operating for a long period of time, a longer waiting period for ignition of the pilot may be necessary due to air in the gas lines.

6. To extinguish top range and oven pilots, turn the thermostat dial to the pilot-off position and turn off the gas-supply valve.

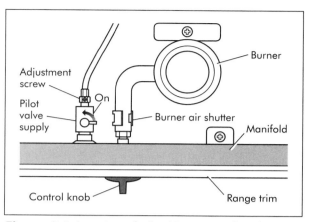

Figure 9.4 Location of pilot LP-gas supply valve in Wedgewood ovens

Wedgewood Top Burner and Oven Pilots

To light the pilot(s) on Wedgewood ranges:

1. Verify that the gas supply is sufficient.
2. Turn all controls to the off position.
3. Lift or remove the range top.
4. Turn the pilot-supply valve on—if so equipped (Figure 9.4).
5. Light the top-burner pilot.

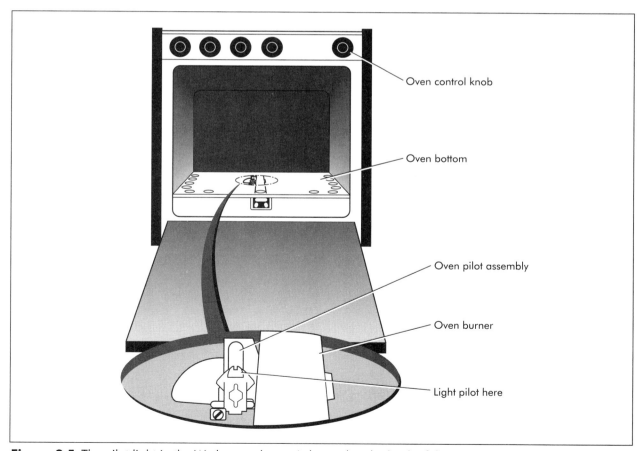

Figure 9.5 The pilot light in the Wedgewood oven is located at the back of the oven.

■ TROUBLESHOOTING ■
THE WEDGEWOOD OVEN AND RANGE

Problem	Possible Cause	Correction
Pilot won't light or stay lit	Closed supply valve	Turn valve on
	Insufficient gas supply	Check gas supply
	Insufficient gas pressure	Check for gas leaks and check regulator
	Blocked pilot orifice or blocked flash tubes	Clean pilot orifice with toothpick; clean flash tubes
	Pilot flame too high or too low	Adjust pilot flame
	Pilot-flame cover out of position and/or coated with carbon	Reposition pilot-flame cover and/ or remove carbon buildup
	Pilot flame blow-out	If range is installed near an open window, the pilot may not stay lit on a windy day. **CAUTION:** Turn off gas and wait five minutes before relighting.
Burner won't light or stay lit	Insufficient gas pressure	Check for gas leaks and check regulator
	Incorrect gas-air mixture	Adjust air shutter
	Blocked burner ports, flash tubes, and/or burner-orifice hood	Clean as necessary
Burner lights but flame is too small	Improper gas pressure	Check for gas leaks and check regulator
	Improper gas-air mixture	Adjust air shutter
	Restriction in gas line	Check gas line for kinks or blockage; replace if necessary
Burner flame lifts off burner head	Gas pressure too high	Check regulator
	Incorrect gas-air mixture	Adjust air shutter
Oven burner won't light or stay lit	Insufficient gas pressure	Check for gas leaks and check regulator
	Incorrect gas-air mixture	Adjust air shutters
	Blocked burner ports	Clean as necessary
	Clogged oven-pilot orifice	Clean oven-pilot orifice
	Defective oven safety valve or sensing element out of position	Check position of sensing element; replace safety valve if necessary
	Defective thermostat	Replace thermostat
Oven burner lights, but flame remains very small and oven heats very slowly	Improper gas pressure	Check for gas leaks and check the regulator
	Restriction in gas line	Check gas line for kinks or blockage; replace if necessary
Oven-burner flame lifts off burner and oven cycles too frequently	Gas pressure too high	Check regulator
Oven cooks unevenly and/or food burns	Poor oven ventilation	Oven too full for proper circulation and/or the ventilation holes in oven bottom are covered; take steps to improve oven ventilation.

6. To light the oven pilot, push in the oven-control knob and rotate counterclockwise to the pilot-on position.

7. Light oven pilot, located at the back of the oven to the left of the oven burner (Figure 9.5).

Spark-Ignition Range Models

To light spark-ignition range models:

1. Verify that the gas supply is sufficient.
2. Turn on the desired top burner.
3. Wait approximately seven seconds and push the red ignitor button or turn the ignitor knob clockwise.
4. To light the oven pilot, turn the thermostat knob to the pilot-on position and light the pilot inside the oven.
5. To extinguish the oven pilot, turn the thermostat knob to the off position.

Pilot Adjustment

Magic Chef

To adjust Magic Chef top-burner pilots, remove the thermostat knob and turn the adjustment screw in the thermostat body with a screwdriver (Figure 9.6). The top pilot flame should be about ⅛ inch above the lower edge of the flash tube (Figure 9.7).

For ranges without the pilot-off or pilots-off position on the thermostat knob, raise the main top and turn the adjustment screw with a screwdriver.

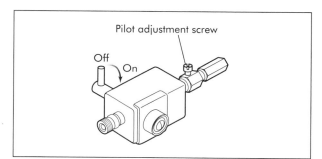

Figure 9.6 Location of pilot adjustment screw for Magic Chef top-burner pilots

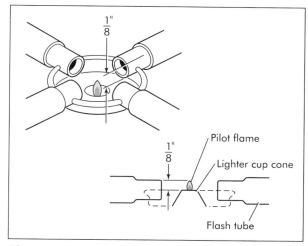

Figure 9.7 Adjusting the top-pilot flame in a Magic Chef top burner

NOTE: The Magic Chef oven pilot has been preset and no adjustment is possible.

Wedgewood

To adjust Wedgewood top-burner pilots, the adjustment can be made with the brass screw on the pilot-supply valve. Turn the screw clockwise to decrease flame, counterclockwise to increase flame. The pilot flame should extend ⅜ inch above the pilot assembly cup.

The oven pilot has been factory adjusted and requires no further adjustment.

NOTE: The oven pilot may be slow in lighting due to initial air in the gas lines.

Burner Adjustment

The burner flame is adjusted by means of air shutters. If the air shutters are set too far open, the flame will lift away from the burner head and will be difficult to light. If the air shutters are set too far closed, the flame will look hazy and the distinct cone will be missing.

Open the air shutters to increase the air-to-gas-mixture ratio until the flame has yellow tips but does not lift away from the burner head. Then close the air shutters until the yellow tips of the flame are eliminated. This provides the maximum flame efficiency without flame blow-off.

NOTE: Top burner flames are preset at the factory on all Wedgewood models without optional range pilot.

Maintenance

Combustion problems are sometimes caused by an accumulation of dirt, grease, dust, or spider webs in the venturi or burner. Periodic inspection and cleaning of the range and oven components will help prevent reduced operating efficiency.

When cleaning the burners or any orifice, care must be taken to prevent damaging or enlarging the openings. Never use a wire or other metallic implement to clean an orifice or burner port. Any enlargement of an orifice or the burner ports will affect the gas flow and burner function. Use a toothpick to clean orifices and burner ports.

Clean all surfaces as soon as possible after spills. Use only warm, soapy water. Never use abrasive or acid-type cleaners. Avoid the use of lye or caustic solutions on aluminum parts.

Chrome parts may be cleaned with a chrome cleaner to remove stubborn stains. In regions of high humidity and salt-air conditions, the chrome range top may show signs of rust on the underside directly above the pilot. To help eliminate this condition, the underside of the range top should be kept as dry as possible. If signs of rust are detected, spray the underside with a coat of high-temperature rust-inhibiting or silicone paint. Remove the range top and spray the paint in a well-ventilated area.

Always allow porcelain surfaces to cool before washing. Always clean stainless-steel surfaces as soon as possible after a spill. Pitting and discoloration will result on stainless steel if spills are allowed to remain for any length of time.

Use an oven cleaner on the oven interior, following instructions on the product container. If a commercial oven cleaner is used, protect aluminum gas tubing, the thermostat sensing bulb, and electrical components from the cleaner (masking tape is good for this). After cleaning, thoroughly rinse the oven with a solution of one tablespoon of vinegar to one cup of water.

Periodically, have the LP-gas system checked to insure that the pressure regulator is functioning prop-

erly and delivering LP-gas at a pressure of 11 inches water column to the regulator at the oven. Modern RV oven gas pressure is regulated to 5 inches water-column pressure for safety reasons.

CAUTION: It should take close to one minute for the burner to light. If the burner lights immediately (after setting the thermostat knob with the pilot lit), then the safety valve is stuck open. Repairs should be made immediately by a qualified service technician.

■ MAGIC CHEF COMPONENT REPLACEMENT ■

Magic Chef Oven Thermostat

To replace the Magic Chef oven thermostat, follow these steps (Figure 9.8):

1. Shut off the gas.
2. Remove the main top and grates.
3. Disconnect the pilot fuel lines and the ¼-inch main fuel line at the thermostat.
4. Remove the two screws mounting the thermostat to the manifold pipe.
5. Open the oven door and remove the capillary-bulb clips in the top of the oven.
6. Pull the capillary bulb up through the top of the stove and remove the thermostat.
7. To install, reverse the procedure. Be sure the thermostat gasket is in place before installing the thermostat.
8. Using soapy water, check for gas leaks at all connections.

Magic Chef Oven Automatic-Shutoff Valve

To replace the Magic Chef oven automatic-shutoff valve:

1. Shut off the gas.
2. Remove the oven racks and the oven bottom. The oven bottom is removed by pushing it toward back of the oven. Then lift up the front of the oven bottom to release the catches and pull the oven bottom forward.
3. Remove mounting screw from oven burner and remove burner.

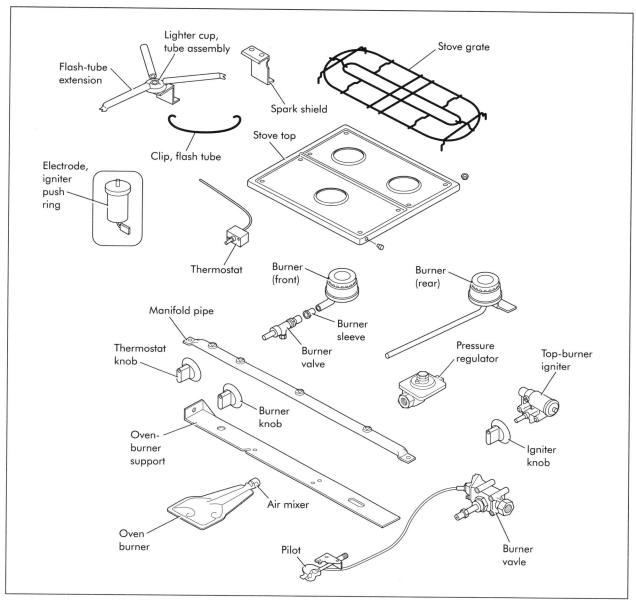

Figure 9.8 Magic Chef top-burner assembly (exploded view)

4. Disconnect the ¼-inch supply tube from the shutoff valve.
5. Loosen the screw holding the sensing bulb to the pilot-light assembly.
6. Remove the sensing bulb.
7. Remove the two screws attaching the automatic oven shutoff valve support and remove the automatic oven shutoff valve.
8. To install, reverse the procedure.
9. Using soapy water, check all connections for gas leaks.

Magic Chef Range Top-Burner Valve

To replace the Magic Chef range top-burner valve:

1. Shut off the gas supply at the tanks.
2. Remove the knobs.
3. Remove the burner grates, the main top, and the top burners.
4. Remove the two bolts from the thermostat and raise slightly to permit the removal of the manifold.

5. Remove the gas-inlet tube from the half union and move the tube out of the way.
6. Remove the two screws, one from each end of the manifold assembly.
7. Remove manifold assembly from the range.
8. Remove the defective valve (screw counter-clockwise).
9. To install, reverse the procedure.
10. Before installing the new valve, apply pipe sealant to the threads.
11. Using soapy water, check all the connections for gas leaks.

CAUTION: Some of the Magic Chef range tops have a weight/size limit to prevent damage to the stove top. Do not use skillets larger than ten inches in diameter. If the cookware extends more than one inch beyond the grate top, rests on two grates, or touches the cooktop, the resultant buildup of heat can damage the burner valve, the burner, the burner grate, and the cooktop. It's also better not to use heavy cast-iron pots and pans; these types of cookware help retain heat, which can be transferred to the burner valve. Make sure the flames from the top burners extend past the stove top or excessive heat can result. If the burner valve becomes difficult to turn or seizes (if this happens, turn off the propane at the cylinder/tank and let the flame burn out), it should be replaced immediately.

Magic Chef Range-Top Pilot-Light Adjustment

To adjust the Magic Chef range-top pilot light:

1. Remove the thermostat knob to provide access to the adjusting screw. The adjusting screw is located at the bottom right corner of the thermostat. (Some models require raising the main top to turn the adjustment screw with a screwdriver.)
2. Adjust so that the tip of the flame is just over the edge of the inner cone and the top burners light within four seconds.

Magic Chef Oven-Door Replacement

To replace the Magic Chef oven door (Figure 9.9):

1. Open the oven door and insert a nail or rod into the hole in each arm that connects the

door to the range. The nail head should not rest on the front frame.
2. Use your thigh to push against the door top.
3. Pull out on bottom portion of the door, exposing the hinge-stop mounting screw.

NOTE: Do not remove the nails or rods from the connecting arms until the door is replaced and the arms are engaged. The arms are spring loaded and will retract into the range if the nails or rods are prematurely removed. If this should happen, the entire range must be removed from the cabinet enclosure and the side panels are removed to get the arms back in place.

4. Remove the hinge-stop mounting screw.
5. To install the door, set the door in position so the hinge stop can be screwed in place.
6. Raise the door up and rehook the connecting arms into the door frame.
7. Make sure both connecting arms are securely rehooked, then remove nails.

Magic Chef Oven-Burner Replacement

To replace the Magic Chef oven burner:

1. Shut off the gas.
2. Remove the oven racks and the oven bottom.
3. Remove the mounting screw from the oven burner and remove the burner.
4. To install, reverse the procedure.

Magic Chef Oven Pilot-Light-Assembly Replacement

To replace the Magic Chef oven pilot-light assembly:

1. Shut off the gas.
2. Remove the oven racks and the bottom.
3. Remove the screw holding the sensing bulb to the pilot assembly.
4. Remove the sensing bulb from the pilot assembly.
5. Remove the pilot fuel tube.
6. Remove the nut and bolt attaching the pilot assembly to the support.
7. Remove the pilot assembly.
8. To install, reverse the procedure.
9. Using soapy water, check all the connections for gas leaks.

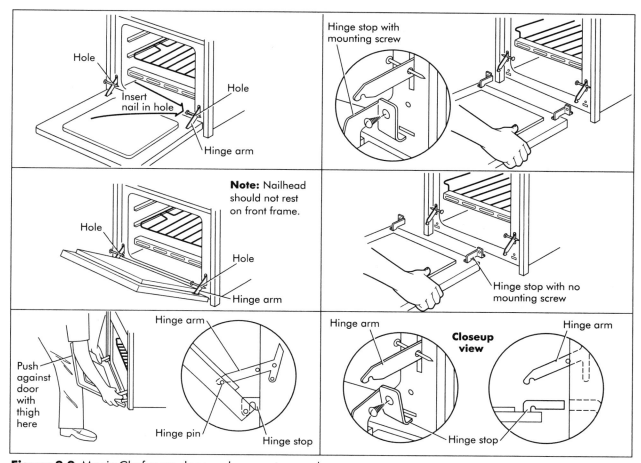

Figure 9.9 Magic Chef oven-door replacement procedure

■ WEDGEWOOD COMPONENT REPLACEMENT ■

Wedgewood Range-Top Replacement

To replace the Wedgewood range top (Figure 9.10):

1. Remove all the burner grates.
2. Lift the top upward by the front end and pull out and away from the rear vent trim.
3. To replace, insert the lip on the rear edge of the range top beneath the rear vent trim.
4. Lower the range top into place.
5. Apply a slight downward pressure on both sides to engage the retaining clips.
    CAUTION: On models with a range pilot, be sure burner-pilot flash tubes are in place and the pilot is burning before replacing the top.

Wedgewood Top-Burner Replacement

To replace the Wedgewood top burners (Figure 9.11):

1. Remove the range top.
2. Remove the burner retaining screw.
3. Lift the burner up and away from the burner orifice.
4. To replace, reverse the procedure.
    NOTE: When cleaning the top burners, be sure all ports are open before using. A toothpick is good for this purpose.

Wedgewood Top-Burner Valve Replacement

To replace the Wedgewood top-burner valves:

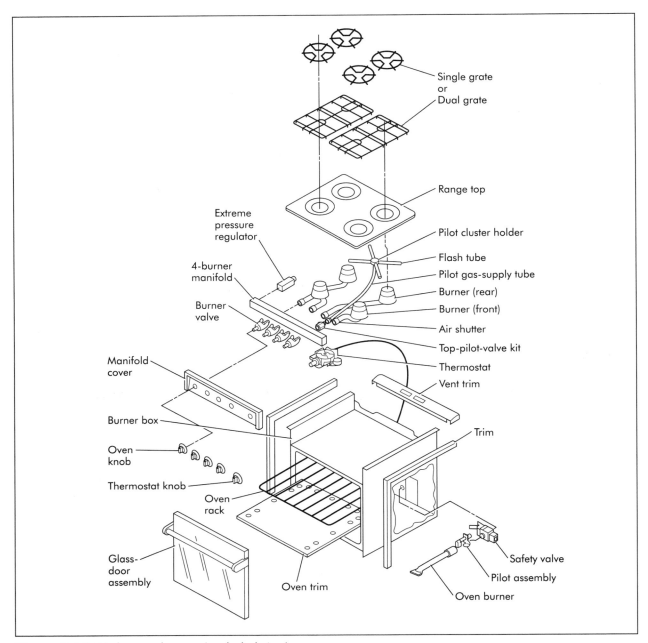

Figure 9.10 Wedgewood range (exploded view)

1. If the range has an oven, set the oven control to off.
2. Turn off the gas supply at the tanks.
3. Remove the range top and all the top burners.
4. Unscrew the gas-line-input connection to the manifold.
5. Remove all control knobs.
6. Remove retaining screws that secure the manifold to the burner box.
7. Raise the manifold just enough to remove the defective burner valve.

   CAUTION: Do not raise the manifold more than necessary because the interconnecting gas lines to the pilot(s) can be damaged.

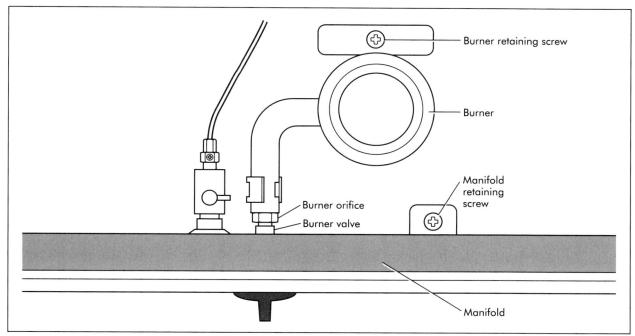

Figure 9.11 Wedgewood range top-burner assembly

8. Remove the bolts securing the burner valve to the manifold.
9. Install the new burner valve. Torque to 20 to 25 inch-pounds.
10. Replace the manifold and the top burners. Reconnect the gas-supply line.
11. Using soapy water, check all connections for gas leaks.

Wedgewood Oven-Door Replacement

To replace the Wedgewood oven door (Figure 9.12):

1. Open the oven door and insert a nail or rod into the hole in each arm connection.
2. Push inward on the door, as if trying to close it.
3. Using pliers, grasp the connecting arms close

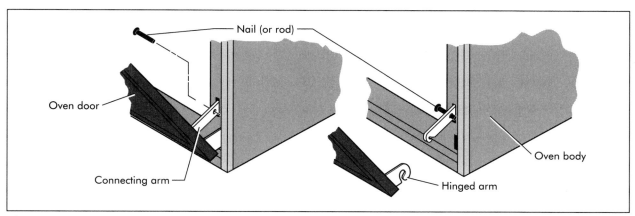

Figure 9.12 A nail or rod may be used to facilitate removal of the Wedgewood oven door.

to the door liner and raise them upward. This will unlock the arms from the door.

> **NOTE:** Do not remove the nails or rods from the connecting arms until the door is replaced and the arms are engaged. The arms are spring loaded and will retract into the range if the nails or rods are prematurely removed. If this should happen, the entire range must be removed from the cabinet enclosure and the side panels removed to get the arms back in place.

4. Pull the door outward until the hinged arms clear the openings in the frame. Due to tight tolerances, removal of the door requires a moderate amount of pressure.
5. To install the door, set the door in position with the hinged arms placed into the slots in the front frame.
6. Raise the door up and rehook the connecting arms into the door frame.
7. Make sure both connecting arms are securely rehooked, then remove nails or rods.

Wedgewood Oven-Burner Replacement

To replace the Wedgewood oven burner:

1. Set the oven control to off.
2. Turn off the gas supply.
3. Remove the oven rack and the oven bottom.
4. Remove the screw that secures the burner to the front support bracket.

> **NOTE:** Observe the position of the oven-pilot assembly and routing of the sensing element (capillary tube) around the oven burner and into the pilot assembly. Return them to the same position when replacing the oven burner.

5. Lift and turn the oven burner just enough to enable removal of the screw anchoring the oven-pilot assembly to the oven burner.
6. To replace, reverse the procedure.

Wedgewood Safety Valve

The Wedgewood safety valve is located in the rear of the oven behind a galvanized shield. To determine if it is defective:

1. Light the oven pilot.
2. While watching the pilot, turn the oven control to the broil position.

3. The pilot flame should increase in size and cover the sensing bulb located at the front of the pilot assembly. If the flame doesn't increase, clean the pilot orifice and check the thermostat.

> **CAUTION:** If the flame increases and the oven burner lights before thirty to sixty seconds, the safety valve is defective and must be replaced.

Wedgewood Safety-Valve Replacement

To replace the Wedgewood safety valve (Figure 9.13):

1. Turn off the gas supply, and remove the oven burner.
2. Remove the safety-valve sensing element (capillary tube) from the oven-pilot assembly (Figure 9.14). The element is held in place by a single screw on the side of the oven pilot assembly.
3. Remove the safety shield from the rear of the oven interior.
4. Remove the mounting screws holding the safety valve to the rear panel of the oven unit.
5. Pull the safety valve forward into the oven interior and remove the gas input line on the safety valve assembly.

> **CAUTION:** The safety valve can be pulled forward only a few inches. Use care to avoid damaging the gas input line.

6. Connect a new safety valve to the gas-input line.

> **WARNING:** Do not replace sensing element into the oven-pilot assembly while testing for leaks.

7. To verify that the connection is properly seated and will not leak:
   a. Turn on the gas supply.
   b. Set the oven control to pilot on.
   c. Light the pilot(s).

   > **WARNING:** When lighting the oven pilot, be sure the safety-valve sensing element cannot be heated by the pilot flame. This will prevent the safety valve from opening and allowing gas to flow through the oven-burner orifice.

   d. Set the oven control to 400°F.
   e. Apply soapy water to the safety-valve gas-input-line connections to check for leaks.
   f. When you are certain that the connections are properly seated, turn the oven control to off.

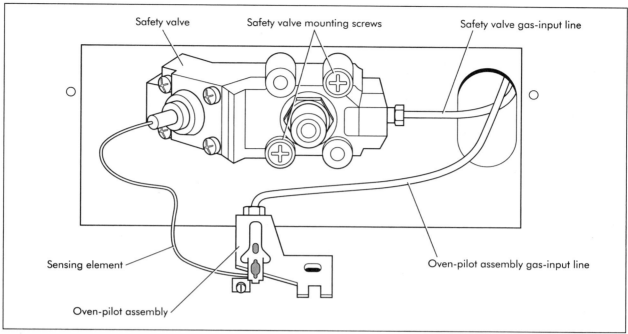

Figure 9.13 Wedgewood range safety-valve assembly

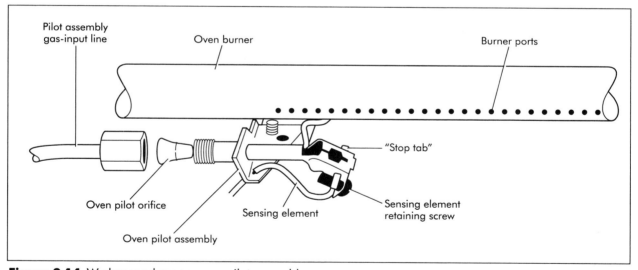

Figure 9.14 Wedgewood range oven-pilot assembly

g. Shut off the gas supply.

8. After performing the leak test, replace the various components by reversing the removal procedure.

> **NOTE:** When replacing the safety-valve sensing element, be sure it has been inserted through both holes and is resting against the stop tab of the oven-pilot assembly before tightening the retaining screw. If the sensing element (capillary tube) is kinked or out of place, it will not function properly. Any damage to the sensing element will require replacing the entire safety valve. Individual parts of the safety valve cannot be repaired or replaced.

Cleaning the Wedgewood Pilot Orifice

The Wedgewood oven-pilot orifice is a common area of blockage and should be cleaned periodically. To do this:

1. Set the oven control to off.
2. Turn off the gas supply.
3. Remove the oven rack and the oven bottom.
4. Disconnect the oven-pilot-assembly gas-input line.
5. Remove the oven burner.
6. Using a small screwdriver (inserted through the hole in the back of the pilot assembly), pop the orifice out of the pilot assembly.
7. Thoroughly clean soot and other foreign matter from the orifice. Use a toothpick to clean the small hole in the orifice and any clogged ports in the oven burner.
8. Make sure the pilot-assembly gas-input line is clean and free of obstructions.
9. Replace the orifice in the pilot assembly.
10. Replace the burner.
11. Reconnect the pilot-assembly gas line.
12. Turn on the gas supply.
13. When you are certain no leaks exist, check the operation of the oven.

Wedgewood Thermostat Replacement

The Wedgewood thermostat is quite difficult to replace. Check the safety valve and oven-pilot orifice before deciding to change the thermostat. If the thermostat must be replaced as shown in Figure 9.10, page 9.12):

1. Set the oven control to off.
2. Turn off the gas supply.
3. Remove the range top and all top burners.
   NOTE: On models with a range pilot, remove the two screws that secure the pilot assembly to the burner box.
4. Disconnect the gas-supply-line input connection to the manifold.
5. Remove all screws that secure the range to the cabinet or wall.
6. At the manifold, remove both gas lines to the thermostat.
7. At the rear wall of the oven interior, just under the flue opening, remove the thermostat capillary tube from the tension clip.
8. Slide the range forward enough to feed the capillary tube through the entry hole in the oven's rear wall up through the rear vent trim of the burner box.

9. Remove the manifold from the burner box.
10. Remove the bolts securing the thermostat to the manifold.
11. Connect the new thermostat to the manifold. Torque to 20 to 25 inch-pounds.
12. Reinstall the manifold in the burner box.
13. Carefully feed the capillary tube back into the oven and replace in the tension clip so that it is directly centered beneath the flue opening.
    NOTE: If the capillary tube is kinked or out of place, it will not function properly. Any damage to the capillary tube requires replacing the whole thermostat. Individual parts of the thermostat cannot be repaired or replaced.
14. Continue reassembling the range by reversing the removal procedure.
15. After reconnecting the gas-supply line to the manifold, replace all the top burners.
16. Turn on the gas supply.
17. Set the thermostat control knob to pilot on.
18. Light the pilot(s).
19. Coat all connections with a soapy-water solution. Be sure to include the thermostat to manifold, the pilot(s), and the oven safety-valve gas lines, as well as the gas-supply-input connection.
20. Using soapy water, check for indication of leaks.
    WARNING: If leaks occur at any connection, turn the thermostat control knob to off and shut off the gas supply before tightening or reseating any connection. Then repeat the leak test after repairs have been completed.
21. When you are certain there are no leaks, check oven operation.

Wedgewood Piezo Field Repair

If the piezo unit fails to operate, it may require a field repair. This should take about twenty minutes.

1. Determine whether or not the piezo knob should be replaced. The correct knob (part number 56095) has either white or black directional arrows molded in. If the knob does not have these arrows, remove the knob and steel insert and discard both; replace with the proper knob. If the knob does have

the proper markings, remove it and set it aside for reinstallation later.

2. Remove the two screws that hold the piezo unit to the back of the panel.

3. Push the piezo unit into the burner box.

4. If the oval decal partially blocks the round hole in the panel, use a utility knife to trim the decal to the same size as the hole in the panel.

5. Inspect the piezo unit. If the shaft falls through the piezo housing, install a new "C" clip (part number 56903) by snapping it onto the slot in the shaft. Make sure the shaft cannot fall through the piezo housing.

6. Reinstall the piezo housing on the rear of the control panel, using the two screws previously removed. Do not overtighten the screws, because it is possible to strip the threads in the housing.

7. Replace the piezo knob, aligning the flat on the shaft with the flat in the knob.

8. Turn the piezo knob through a full rotation (six clicks) to test for proper operation of the unit.

Additional Oven and Range Safety Cautions

1. In the event you smell gas:
   a. Evacuate all persons from the RV.
   b. Close the gas valve at the cylinder(s)/tank.
   c. Extinguish any open flame.
   d. Open all windows.
   e. Don't touch any electrical switches.
   f. Find and correct the source of the leak.
2. Never use the stove or oven as a space heater.
3. Make sure a window or exhaust vent is open when using the stove.
4. Do not modify any of the stove components.
5. Insure that pilot lights are turned off before moving the RV.

■ RANGE HOODS ■

Range hoods are fairly basic appliances, made of sheet metal, with a 12-volt DC light and ventilation-fan-assembly components as the only parts requiring periodic attention (Figure 9.15). Simple as the system may be, it is one of the areas of the RV that quickly becomes dirty with greasy cooking residue. Frequent cleaning is important.

Hood Cleaning

All surfaces of the hood should be thoroughly cleaned on a regular basis, with special attention given to the corners and more inaccessible recesses. As grease from cooking builds up, it attracts dust and dirt like a magnet, and soon the hidden nooks and crannies of the hood become very dirty.

Warm, soapy water and a soft cloth or sponge are usually sufficient for cleaning. But if grease has been

---

■ TROUBLESHOOTING ■
THE RANGE-HOOD FAN AND LIGHT

Problem	Possible Cause	Correction
No power to fan or light	Blown fuse	Check the fuse; replace if necessary
	Faulty switch	Check switch for continuity; replace if faulty
Power to fan, but still won't work	Faulty fan motor	Replace fan motor
Power to light, but still won't work	Faulty light bulb	Replace bulb

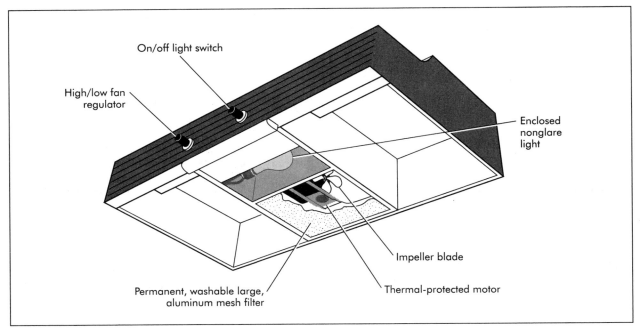

On/off light switch

High/low fan regulator

Enclosed nonglare light

Impeller blade

Permanent, washable large, aluminum mesh filter

Thermal-protected motor

Figure 9.15 Range hoods are usually equipped with a 12-volt DC fan, a light, and a filter.

permitted to build up over time, it may be necessary to use a stronger solution, such as a grease-cutting ammonia cleaner. After cleaning is completed, follow with a soft cloth to dry the hood. This will help remove water spots and any residue that may be left.

The part of the hood that collects the greatest amount of grease is the aluminum mesh-filter element designed to trap grease as the ventilation fan is expelling steam, smoke, odors, and greasy air from the cooking area. To clean the filter, remove it from the hood and soak it in warm, soapy water. Swish the filter back and forth in the soapy water to encourage the grease to dissolve. Don't try to scrub the grease from the filter since this will only damage the aluminum screen. A soft brush may be of benefit, if used very gently. After washing, rinse thoroughly under a stream of clean water, shake dry, and then replace.

If, despite your best efforts, the filter is too clogged with grease and dirt to be cleaned, replace it with a new element. It is inexpensive and available at most RV supply stores.

While the filter element is out of its holder, wipe the fan clean. This is a 12-volt DC appliance, so there is no possibility of electric shock hazard.

Fan-Motor Replacement

If the fan motor is faulty, buy a new one before removing the old one. This will help prevent confusion during the replacement procedure because you can study the original and keep it fresh in your mind as you install the new unit.

1. Disconnect 12-volt DC power to the fan by either removing the fuse from the fan circuit or removing the cable from the battery positive terminal.
2. Remove the grease filter from the hood, exposing the fan.
3. Remove the screws holding the fan in place.
4. Disconnect the fan lead wires (cut if necessary).
5. Connect new fan wires. If the original wires were cut, use high-quality butt connectors to reinstall.
6. Install the new fan by reversing the procedure.

CHAPTER 10

MICROWAVES
AND ICE MAKERS

Small appliances, such as microwave ovens and ice makers, have made life so much easier at home that it made sense for the RV industry to pick up on this trend. The microwave oven has become almost as common as the kitchen sink in RVs. Although microwaves and ice makers require little maintenance, there are a few problems that can arise. Microwave-oven maintenance is a very sophisticated science and should be left to a qualified service technician.

Microwave ovens are very sensitive to voltage spikes due to erratic AC generators or surges in campground-hookup power and should be safeguarded by a high-quality electronic surge protector similar to those used for computers. Because microwave ovens mounted in RVs are in a much harsher environment than in homes and are subject to vibrations and bouncing, they should be checked frequently for leakage. Commercial meters are available for this purpose.

Convection ovens are normally integrated with the microwave, but can be found as gas-oven replacements in some RVs. A convection oven contains an electric heating element similar to those found in electric ovens. A high-speed fan circulates the heated air within the oven to provide cooking temperatures. One of the benefits of a convection oven is the ability to "brown" foods for a more appetizing appearance. The convection heating element and fan unit are not user serviceable.

Ice makers can be integrated with the refrigerator or purchased as separate appliances. They should be equipped with an in-line water filter to protect the system from harsh chemicals and the bad taste associated with treated water. Unless the RV has a high-amperage power inverter, ice makers will only operate when the AC generator is running or when the rig is hooked up to campground power.

■ MICROWAVE OVENS ■

Theory of Microwave Cooking

Microwave ovens operate on radio frequency (RF). When the correct frequency is directed at food or liquid, it causes the molecules of food to oscillate, which produces heat. The radio frequency employed in a microwave oven is 2,450 mHz, which falls within the radio broadcast band, not the X-ray band.

Food is cooked when the RF energy strikes molecules of food and causes them to agitate as the molecules try to align themselves with the 2,450 mHz RF energy. Because the energy of 2,450 mHz changes polarity every half cycle due to its half-wave double/rectifying circuit, the food molecules also change every half-second. This makes the food molecules oscillate 4,900,000 times per second. Oscillation causes friction, which creates a substantial amount of heat energy for cooking.

Microwaves are reflected by metal (which is why the walls of the oven cavity are metal), but they pass through materials such as paper, glass, plastic, and ceramic. Food and liquids absorb microwave energy. Microwaves penetrate about ½ to 1½ inches of food, depending upon the food's density. Heat to complete the cooking process is transferred throughout the remainder of the food by conduction. Heat buildup takes place only within the food, but the oven cavity or the cookware may warm up as heat transfers from the food.

The oven cavity is made of metal so that it can contain and reflect microwaves back to the food. With a glass cooking shelf positioned above the oven floor on which food can be placed for cooking, microwaves can reflect from the oven floor to the underside of the food as well.

Microwave Components

Components typically found in a microwave oven include the following (Figure 10.1):

- A cabinet to enclose all working parts of the oven
- A door that swings either on a hinge system or on pins. The door must be precisely aligned and adjusted to prevent microwave leakage.
- A timer and cooking-level (temperature) control panel
- A magnetron, which produces the radio frequency for cooking
- A blower to cool the magnetron
- A stirrer to assure even distribution of microwave energy within the oven cavity
- Interlocks to prevent the oven from operating when the door is open
- Various electrical components—a transformer, a relay, a diode, a fuse, and a capacitor

Troubleshooting and Service

Because of the highly technical nature of microwave ovens, owners should seek professional service when problems with the oven arise.

CAUTION: The training and equipment necessary to properly troubleshoot and service microwave ovens are generally beyond the reach of the average owner; improper service can be very dangerous. The information in this book is designed to educate the owner to the various repair procedures so that he or she can better communicate with the service technician. The microwave-oven case should never be tampered with. Owner maintenance should be limited to cleaning, checking for leakage, lubricating the door hinge, and changing the light bulb.

All procedures described and illustrated in this section apply to Magic Chef microwave ovens. Although the procedures may be similar for other brands, for specific details regarding the servicing of these other brands, please refer to the respective manufacturers' service manuals.

Maintenance

Cleaning

Always unplug the oven before cleaning. Clean the outside and inside of the oven using a soft cloth and nonabrasive detergent and warm water; rinse well. With a soft cloth, dry the inside top, side, and back walls of the oven cavity, as well as the cooking shelf. Never use chemicals, such as commercial oven cleaners or alcohol, and avoid the use of abrasives, such as cleansing powders, steel wool, or plastic scrubbing pads. Wipe spills off the interior components with a damp cloth as soon as they occur. If left unattended, accumulated spills will dry and become difficult to clean up. Spilled food can cause damage to some components. For example, the door-seal plate and polypropylene cover in the oven cavity can burn if excess grease or food has carbonized on them.

Most foods can be removed easily with glass cleaner or soap and warm water. To remove dried-on foods, place ½ cup of water in the oven and heat it on high for three to five minutes. The steam will soften dried-on foods, and they will wipe away more easily.

The glass oven floor can become scorched from the high temperature generated from the bottom of a browning dish. These stains can be removed by using Bar Keeper's Friend or Bon Ami cleanser. After using these products, rinse and dry thoroughly. Do not use cleansers on any other surface of the oven.

The probe should be cleaned by wiping it with a damp cloth as soon as possible after using. If food is baked on, rub very gently with a plastic scouring ball. Rinse and dry.

Lubrication

Twice a year, it is recommended the door hinge be sprayed lightly with WD-40 or some comparable

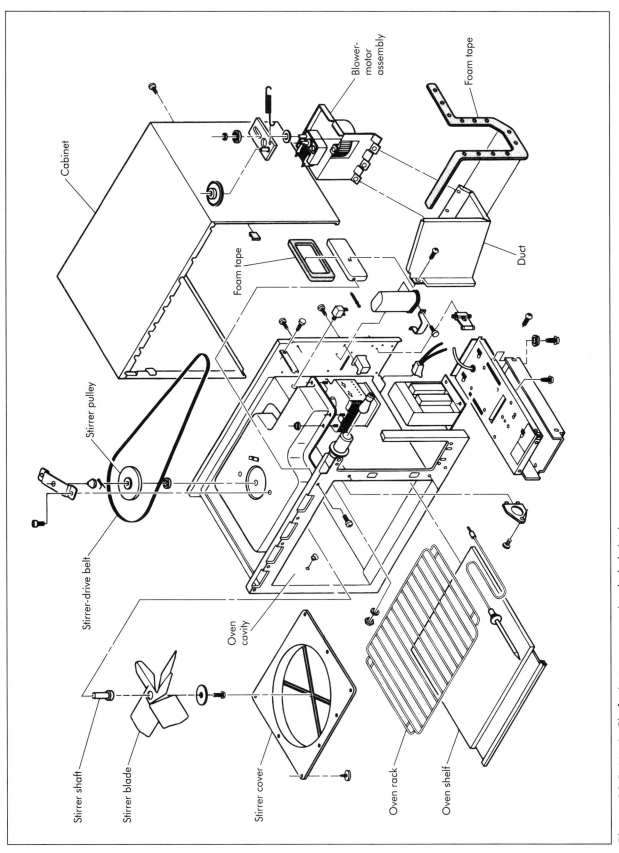

Figure 10.1 Magic Chef microwave oven (exploded view)

Cabinet

Blower-motor assembly

Foam tape

Foam tape

Duct

Stirrer pulley

Stirrer-drive belt

Oven cavity

Stirrer shaft

Stirrer blade

Stirrer cover

Oven rack

Oven shelf

product. Also at this interval, the tip of the oven door latch should be lightly coated with Lubriplate. Apply lubricant sparingly and wipe up any excess. Never use any lubricant that contains silicone (Figure 10.2).

Oven Light Replacement

On all Magic Chef and many other brands of microwave ovens, the oven lamp is accessible through an access cover in the upper section of the oven cavity; it's in the upper right rear of the oven cavity in the Magic Chef microwaves (Figure 10.3). To replace the bulb:

1. Unplug the oven.
2. Remove the access cover.
3. Remove the light bulb.
4. Replace with any similar 25-watt bayonet-base bulb rated for 115–130 volts.
5. Replace the access cover and secure with a ¼-inch hex screw.

Removing the Oven Cabinet

To remove the oven cabinet, follow these steps (Figure 10.4):

1. Be certain the oven is unplugged.
2. Remove the screws from the back panel.
3. Spread the sides slightly from the bottom edge.
4. Slide the cabinet back to free the notched front edge from the front frame.
5. Lift the cabinet off.

Testing for Microwave Leakage

By using one of the following RF survey meters, you can test the oven periodically for microwave leakage.

Holiday Industries Model 1500
Holiday Industries Model 1501
Holiday Industries Model 1700
Holiday Industries Model 1800
NARDA Model 8100
NARDA Model 8200
Simpson Model 380
Radio Shack Microwave Meter

To test for leakage, follow this procedure:

1. Fill an eight-ounce Styrofoam cup with water and place it in the center of the oven cavity.
2. Close the oven door; turn the oven on to a full (100 percent power) cooking mode.

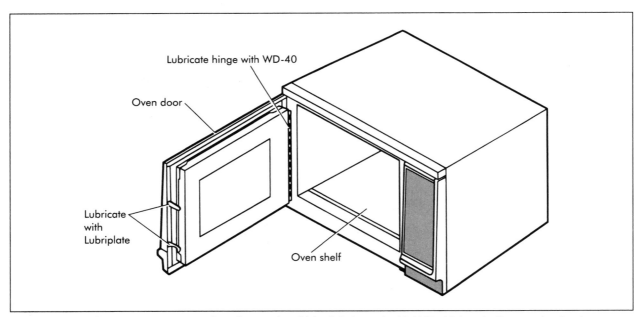

Figure 10.2 The microwave-oven door hinge should be lubricated with WD-40 (or similar product) twice a year; Lubriplate is used on the latch.

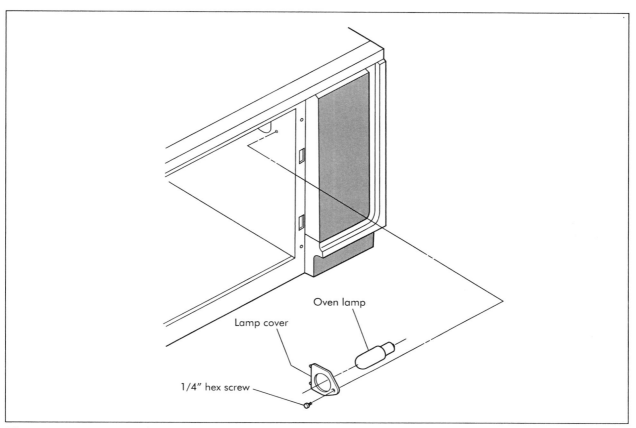

Figure 10.3 Removing the microwave-oven interior light bulb

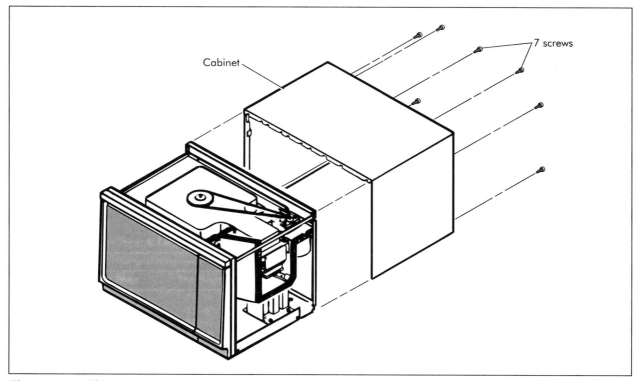

Figure 10.4 The microwave-oven cabinet should only be removed by a qualified service technician.

3. While the oven is operating, check around the perimeter of the oven door and in the window area with the meter's probe. Move the probe at a rate of about one inch per second.
4. When the point of maximum leakage is located, rotate the probe until a peak reading is obtained. Then apply pressure to the door edge to see if the peak reading increases. The peak reading should not exceed 5 mw/cm².
5. If the test indicates that the leakage is lower than the 5 mw/cm² level, the oven is operating normally and no repairs or adjustments are necessary.
6. If the test indicates that the leakage is greater than the 5 mw/cm² level, the oven should be repaired by an authorized service technician before any further use.

Door Adjustment

To adjust the microwave oven door (Figure 10.5):

1. Place the oven on its back.
2. Loosen the top- and bottom-hinge bracket nuts/hinge screws.
3. Align the top, bottom, and left edges of the door with the front frame.
4. Jiggle the door slightly to be sure it is lying flat against the front frame and that the secondary seal is not riding up on the sides of the choke.
5. Tighten the hinge-bracket nuts/hinge screws.
6. Test for microwave leakage.

If the door leaks at or near a corner on the latch side, loosen the hinge-bracket nut and hinge screws across the door diagonally from the leak and slide that pinned or hinged corner outward slightly, then retighten.

If the leak is on the pinned or hinged side of the door, loosen the hinge-bracket nuts/hinge screws and adjust the door slightly closer to the front frame in that area, then retighten.

If the leak is on the latch side of the door, add a latch-bracket shim of appropriate thickness between the interlock-switch bracket and the front frame. Recheck for leaks.

Replacing the Stirrer Cover

To replace the stirrer cover:

1. Open the door fully.
2. Use a small flat-blade screwdriver to pry the plastic inserts loose from the stirrer cover through the oven cavity front opening.
3. Remove the stirrer cover through the oven cavity front opening.
4. To replace the stirrer cover, reverse procedure.

Replacing the Stirrer

The stirrer is located in the top of the oven between the stirrer cover and the top of the oven cavity (Figure 10.6).

1. Unplug the oven.
2. Remove the oven cabinet.
3. Remove the stirrer cover.
4. Remove the drive belt from the pulley and fan-motor shaft.
5. Remove the cotter pin holding the stirrer in the oven cavity from the stirrer shaft.
6. Remove pulley and shaft, noting the positions of the washer, the spacers, and bushings.
7. When replacing the stirrer, make certain the blades are not out of line, causing them to hit the top of the oven or cover.
8. Be sure the stirrer and the pulley turn freely.
9. To replace any component in the stirrer assembly, follow the procedure in reverse.

Replacing the Oven Shelf

Most often, shelf breakage is a result of improper use of the oven. This can occur if the oven is operated without being properly cleaned. Grease and food deposits can carbonize, causing the oven to arc. This results in extreme heat on some areas of the oven shelf, causing the glass to melt or crack. The same problem can be caused by improper use of aluminum foil or use of metal pans or containers in the oven.

To replace the oven shelf, follow these steps (Figure 10.7):

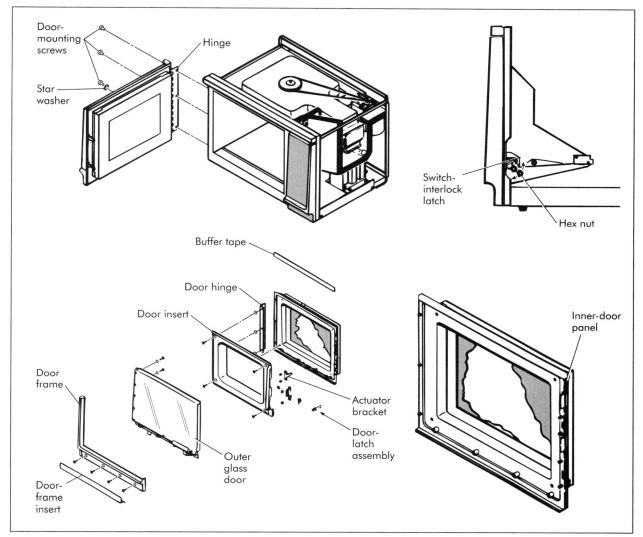

Figure 10.5 The Magic Chef microwave oven-door adjustment

1. Using a hook-type knife, such as a linoleum knife, cut the sealant all around the oven shelf.
2. Remove the old shelf and clean out all chips and debris that have fallen to the oven floor.
3. It is not necessary to remove all the old sealant from inside the oven.
4. Hold the edge of the deeply grooved plastic trim strip (supplied with the new shelf) over the turned-back flange on the edge of the oven front. Position the beveled edge up and toward the front.
5. Lay a small bead of RTV-102 White Silicone Rubber Adhesive behind the beveled edge of the plastic trim strip; then put the edge of the new shelf behind the beveled edge, forcing the RTV up along the edge, making a good seal.
6. Lower the new shelf onto the support studs in the back of the oven cavity.
7. Seal the shelf in place by applying a bead of RTV-102 White Silicone Rubber Adhesive on the back and side edges of the oven shelf.
8. Wipe away any excess adhesive with a damp cloth so that a smooth fillet is formed between the shelf and the walls of the oven cavity on the sides and the back. Wipe away any excess adhesive on the front edge.

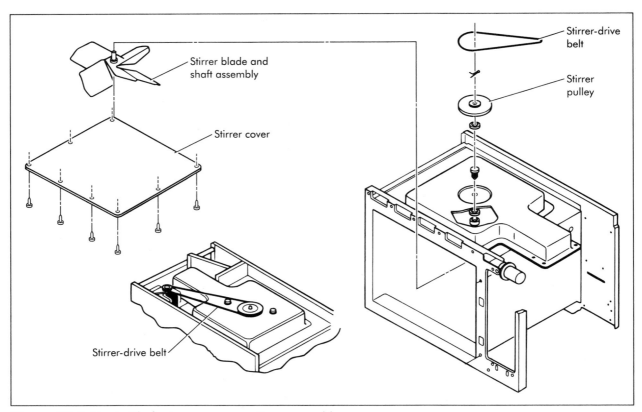

Figure 10.6 Magic Chef microwave-oven stirrer assembly

■ ICE MAKERS ■

Automatic ice-cube makers are designed to provide a continuous supply of ice cubes. Ice makers can be found inside the freezer compartments in a number of models of refrigerators or can be freestanding. Normally, these machines require very little attention, but routine care will insure that they function at maximum efficiency (Figure 10.8).

General Operation

The ice maker must be installed level with the vehicle floor; otherwise the cubes will be larger at one end of the trough than the other and will take longer to eject into the ice bucket. Also, if the unit is tipped toward the rear, a condition known as *frostback* occurs on the suction line and the cubes will not be able to eject. To insure a level installation, the unit (freestanding models; those in the freezer compart-

ments should be okay as long as the refrigerator is installed fairly level) must be checked with a level gauge placed along the inside of the ice-maker mold itself, not on top of the cabinet.

The stand-alone unit must have ventilation. If a free flow of air is not permitted through the grill, the compressor may run all the time, the cubes may stick together excessively, the unit may produce too few ice cubes, and the machine may demand frequent defrosting. Do not limit air circulation by installing the unit behind closed doors.

Because the ice-cube maker is connected to a water-supply line, it is possible that particles of scale or dirt may be dislodged from the line. This will produce dirty or discolored cubes. For this reason, it is recommended that all the cubes produced during the first two or three hours of initial operation of a new machine be discarded.

When the cube bin is full, the ice maker will automatically shut off, but the refrigeration unit will continue to operate to prevent the cubes from melt-

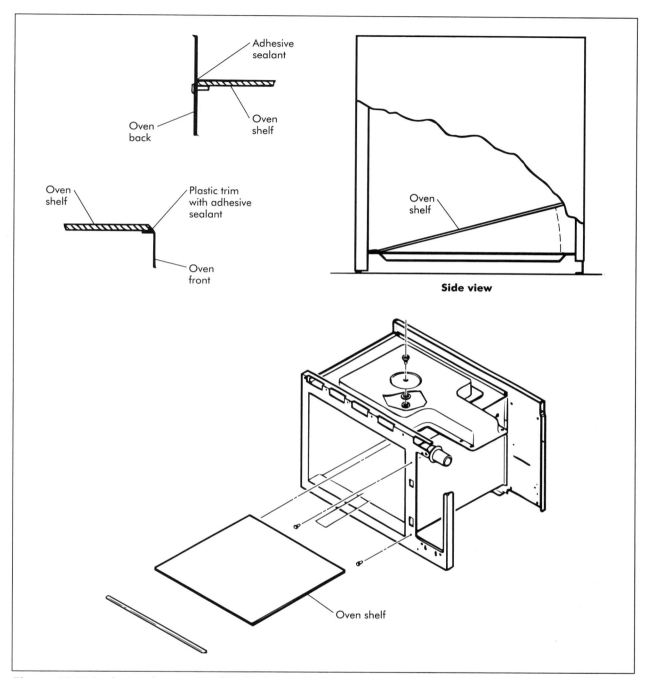

Figure 10.7 Replacing the oven shelf in the Magic Chef microwave oven

ing. Even though it is common for cubes to stick together, they are easy to separate by hand or by striking with a blunt object.

CAUTION: Do not use a sharp object such as an ice pick or knife to separate the cubes, since damage to the plastic interior of the machine could result.

Maintenance

When cleaning the ice maker, do not use solvents or abrasive cleaning agents that can impart an odor or flavor to the cubes. The exterior may be treated with mild cleaners and furniture polish. Clean the interior

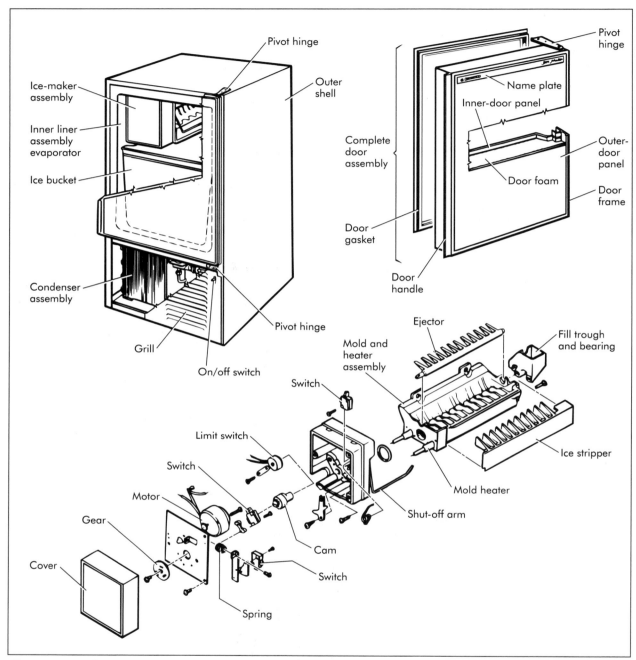

Figure 10.8 The Dometic automatic ice maker (exploded view)

with a soft, damp cloth. The ice bucket may be washed with warm, soapy water, but should be rinsed thoroughly and then dried to prevent the taste of soap in future cubes. Do not use hot water; this causes cubes to stick.

The condenser (stand-alone units), behind the grill, should be cleaned three to four times a year.

If the ice maker is not used regularly, empty it periodically (every week to ten days) to maintain a supply of fresh cubes.

The ice maker should be defrosted periodically. When defrosting, leave the door propped open a few inches to permit air circulation.

When the ice maker is shut down after a trip, the

on/off switch should be turned to the off position. All remaining ice should be removed and the interior wiped dry. The door should be propped open a few inches to allow air to circulate inside the ice maker to prevent odors, mold, or mildew.

Once a year, or more often if necessary, shut off the water supply and remove the brass nut on the water-inlet valve. Use a toothbrush to clean sediment from the inlet screen. This will help prevent sediment and impurities from clogging the water line.

Ice-Maker Adjustments

To set a colder temperature, move the adjustment screw one-quarter turn clockwise. To set a warmer temperature, turn the adjustment screw counterclockwise. When the temperature is colder, ice cube production slows down.

To adjust the amount of water permitted to enter the mold where the ice cubes are made, turn the water-fill adjusting screw (Figure 10.9). One full turn clockwise diminishes the amount of water allowed into the mold by 18 cubic centimeters. One full turn counterclockwise increases the amount of water allowed into the mold by 18 cubic centimeters. In this manner, cube size can be regulated. If the ice cubes do not eject easily from the mold, they may be too large; turn the water-fill adjusting screw to decrease the amount of water in the mold to a total of 120 cubic centimeters or 4.5 ounces.

Component Replacement

Before working on the ice maker, disconnect the appliance service cord from the power supply, or turn off the refrigerator.

Ice-Stripper Replacement

To replace the ice stripper:

1. Remove the ice maker from the cabinet.
2. Remove the retaining screw at the back of the mold.
3. Pull the stripper back to disengage from the front of the mold.
4. Replace in reverse order.

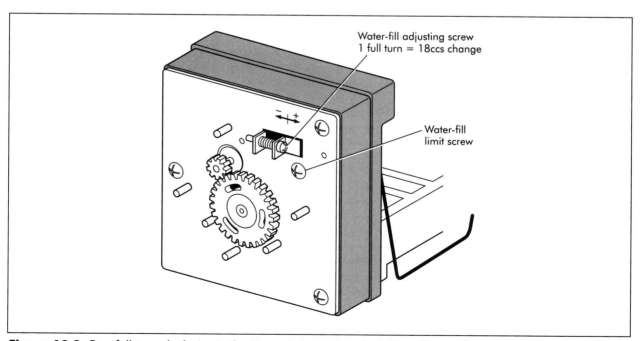

Figure 10.9 One full turn clockwise in the Dometic ice maker diminishes the amount of water entering the mold by 18 cubic centimeters.

■ **TROUBLESHOOTING** ■

THE ICE MAKER

Problem	Possible Cause	Correction
Machine fails to operate	Lack of power	Check power supply
	On/off switch	Check on/off switch for continuity in "on" position. Replace if defective.
Compressor fails to start	Temperature control	Check temperature control for continuity when cube maker contains water only.; replace if defective.
	Relay or overload	Bypass relay and overload by using test cord on compressor, replace if defective.
	Control	Check control; replace if defective.
Cube maker fails to fill with water	Water supply	Check water supply at inlet of solenoid water valve
	Solenoid water valve	Check screen and clean if needed; also check valve coil by energizing terminals with test cord
	Water-valve switch	Check switch for continuity
Ice maker will not eject frozen cubes	Cubes too large	Defrost machine; remove some water from tray; adjust water fill to 120 cubic centimeters or 4.5 ounces
	Faulty limit switch	Test switch for continuity. Replace if necessary.
	Faulty control	Test control for continuity; replace if defective.
	Frost buildup	Defrost; remove some water from cube tray with cloth; check door gasket seal.
	Mold heater	Check for continuity; replace if defective.
	Holding switch	Check for continuity; replace if defective.
	Cube-maker motor	Use test cord to energize motor leads; replace if motor is dead or internal gear is stripped
	Shutoff-arm switch	Check for continuity; replace if defective.
	Cam	Check if loose wire has jammed in cam
Water fails to freeze	Fan motor	Check fan motor; replace if not working while compressor is running.
	Temperature control	Test continuity through terminals 2 and 3 on control; clean internal contacts or replace control
	Refrigeration system	Have system serviced by authorized shop
	Dirty condenser	Clean lint and dust from condenser
Water in ice bucket	Unit not level	Level unit
	Poor gasket seal	Check door gasket for proper seal
	Water-valve switch	Check switch; replace if defective.

■ TROUBLESHOOTING ■
THE ICE MAKER, continued

Problem	Possible Cause	Correction
Ice maker freezes up	Poor door seal	Check door gasket for proper seal
	Water splashing out of mold into bucket	Turn down water-fill adjusting screw
	Leak through electric solenoid valve	Replace electric solenoid valve
Failure to make ice	Frozen ejector blades	Defrost machine
	Power supply off	Check power supply, including power cord to wall socket
	Water supply off	Check water supply
	Defective cold control	Check and replace if necessary
Failure to stop making ice	Shutoff-arm switch	Replace switch if defective; free switch arm if frozen in ice or if stuck under the freezing tray.
Not making enough ice	Improper cold control setting	Lower the cold-control setting
	Cubes too large	Turn down water-fill adjusting screw
	Inoperative fan motor	Check and replace if necessary
	Dirty condenser coil	Clean coil
Excessive water	Water-valve switch	Adjust downward
	Faulty control	Check and replace if necessary
	Leak through solenoid valve	Check solenoid valve and replace if necessary
Water keeps running	Faulty water valve switch, solenoid valve, cold control	Check components and replace any that are defective
Compressor knocks	Machine not level	Level unit
	Faulty compressor	Replace compressor
	Fan motor not running	Check fan motor; replace if necessary
Compressor runs continually	Control setting too cold	Reset cold control to warmer setting
	Dirty condenser	Clean condenser coils
	Improper ventilation	Insure that grill is not blocked; relocate ice maker if necessary.
Ejector motor runs, but ejector blades do not turn	Stripped gear in ejector motor	Replace ejector motor
Ejector motor and blades turn continually	Defective cold-control or holding switch	Check and replace control or switch as necessary

Fill-Trough and Bearing Replacement

To replace the fill trough and the bearing:

1. Remove the ice stripper.
2. Push the retaining tab away from the mold.
3. Rotate counterclockwise until the trough is clear.
4. Pull from the back to detach from the mold and ejector blades.
5. Replace in reverse order.

Ejector-Blade Replacement

To replace the ejector blades:

1. Remove the ice stripper.
2. Remove the fill trough and bearing.
3. Force back and up to detach from the front bearing.
4. Place a small amount of silicone grease on the bearing ends of the replacement.
5. Replace in the reverse order, insuring the blades are in the same position as they were-originallly.

Front-Cover Replacement

To replace the front cover:

1. Place a coin in the slot at the bottom of the mold support and pry the cover loose.
2. To replace, be sure the retaining tabs inside the cover are located on top and bottom, then snap into place.

Mounting-Plate Replacement

To replace the mounting plates:

1. Remove the front cover.
2. Remove the 3 retaining screws that hold the plate in place.
3. Carefully remove the plate, disengaging the end of the shut-off-arm, noting the relative position of the shut-off-arm spring.
4. Before replacing the plate, be sure all wiring is in order and the shut-off arm-spring is in place.
5. Replace in reverse order.

Motor Replacement

To replace the motor:

1. Remove the front cover.
2. Remove the mounting plate (3 screws).
3. Disconnect the wiring.
4. Remove the 2 screws holding the motor.
5. Replace in reverse order.

Water-Valve-Switch Replacement

To replace the water-valve switch:

1. Remove the front cover.
2. Remove the mounting plate (three screws).
3. Disconnect the wiring.
4. Remove the switch (2 screws).
5. Replace in reverse order, making sure the switch insulator is in place.
6. Check the water fill and adjust if necessary.

Holding-Switch Replacement

To replace the holding switch:

1. Remove the front cover.
2. Remove the mounting plate (3 screws).
3. Disconnect the wiring.
4. Remove the switch (2 screws).
5. Replace in reverse order, making sure the switch insulator is in place.

Shutoff-Switch Replacement

To replace shut-off switch (Figure 10.10):

1. Remove the front cover.
2. Remove the mounting plate (3 screws).
3. Raise the shut-off arm.
4. Disconnect the wiring.
5. Remove the switch (two screws).
6. Replace in reverse order.

Limit- (Thermostat) Switch Replacement

To replace the limit- (thermostat) switch:

1. Remove the front cover.
2. Remove the mounting plate (3 screws).
3. Loosen the limit-switch-clip mounting screw.
4. Disconnect the wiring and remove the limit switch.
5. Apply Thermalastic (special gray putty sub-

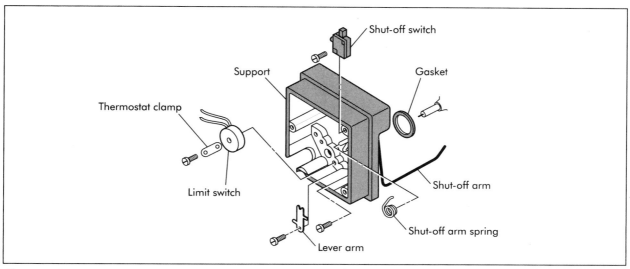

Figure 10.10 Dometic automatic ice-maker-shutoff switch assembly

stance) to the sensing surface of the replacement-limit switch and bond to mold.

NOTE: Do not use regular gray putty tape or similar compounds. Contact appliance manufacturer for availability.

6. Replace in reverse order.

Mold-Heater Replacement

To replace the mold heater:

1. Remove the stripper (1 screw).
2. Remove the front cover.
3. Remove the mounting plate (3 screws).
4. Detach the limit switch from the mold.
5. Detach the heater leads.
6. Remove the mold from the support (4 screws).
7. With a flat-blade screwdriver, pry the defective heater from the bottom of the mold.
8. Clean all Thermalastic from the groove in the bottom of mold.
9. Apply new Thermalastic to the groove in the mold.
10. Install the replacement heater, using 4 screws in the holes adjacent to the heater groove.
11. Replace the parts in reverse order of removal.

Control (Thermostat) Replacement

To replace the control in a stand-alone unit:

1. Remove the rear panels from the cabinet.
2. Remove the mounting plate (2 screws).
3. Remove the control from the plate (2 screws).
4. Remove the wires (3 terminals).
5. Remove the control element from the upper rear cabinet.
6. Straighten 12 inches of the element on the new control to insert it into a small-diameter aluminum tube control well. The control will not work if it is not inserted in the control well.
7. Assemble in reverse order.

Solenoid Water-Valve Replacement

To replace the solenoid water valve:

1. Shut off the water supply.
2. Remove the water connections from the valve.
3. Remove the mounting screws (2 screws).
4. Remove the electrical connector.
5. Replace in reverse order.

Timing-Cam Replacement

To replace the timing cam:

1. Remove the front cover.
2. Remove the large white plastic gear.
3. Remove the mounting plate.
4. Remove the plastic timing cam.
5. Lubricate the new cam with silicone grease.
6. Assemble in reverse order.

Ice-Maker Replacement

To replace the ice maker:

1. Remove the formed rear panel.
2. Disconnect the 6 wires.
3. Use an Allen wrench to remove the 2 screws holding the ice maker to the left-side wall.
4. Remove the 3 hex head screws from the bottom of the ice maker.
5. Carefully pull the ice maker out of the cabinet.
6. Apply Thermalastic and assemble in reverse order.

CHAPTER 11

TRAILER BRAKES

The function of trailer brakes is to safely reduce trailer speed at the same time the tow vehicle brakes are applied, or when the driver activates the brake-controller manual switch. Properly functioning trailer brakes, acting in concert with the brake system of the tow vehicle, help prevent overheating of the tow-vehicle brakes while maintaining speed control on long, downhill stretches. Independent use of trailer brakes, by the driver activating the brake-controller manual switch, can reduce trailer sway caused by side wind or passing trucks.

Two types of trailer-brake systems are in use today: electric and surge. Surge brakes, typically used on boat trailers, are rarely found on RVs. Although both systems perform similar functions, they operate differently and require specific installation, maintenance, and repair procedures.

■ ELECTRIC BRAKES ■

Electric brakes are the standard of the RV industry (Figure 11.1). They are engineered to operate simultaneously with the tow-vehicle brakes and are activated by the application of the tow-vehicle brake system. Electric trailer-brake assemblies employ a revolving armature located in the brake drum. An electromagnet pivots on an arm with a cam that is attached between the brake shoes. When the magnet is energized, current flows through it, causing a magnetic attraction between it and the armature. The magnet attempts to follow the rotation of the armature. This causes the cam to rotate, forcing the primary brake shoe against the drum and energizing the secondary shoe, resulting in resistance to the rotation of the drum. When the brakes are released,

the current ceases to flow through the magnet, releasing it from the armature, and the return springs pull the shoes away from the brake drum.

Electric current is directed from the tow-vehicle battery via the brake controller and modulated (in varying amounts) to the trailer brakes. The controller is usually mounted on the lower edge of the vehicle's dashboard within easy reach of the driver. Two types of controllers are used with electric brake systems: electronic and electric hydraulic. In either case, the controller is the first place to begin troubleshooting whenever there is difficulty with an electric brake system.

■ SURGE BRAKES ■

Surge brakes (Figure 11.2) operate through an actuator that is attached to the A-frame of the trailer. The system is hydraulic and includes its own master cylinder. As the tow-vehicle brakes are applied, the trailer pushes against the slowing tow vehicle, and the hydraulic actuator pushes a piston in the master cylinder. This, in turn, supplies hydraulic pressure to the brakes, and automatically synchronizes the trailer brakes with the tow-vehicle braking action.

■ HOW BRAKE CONTROLLERS WORK ■

The Electronic Brake Controller

Some electronic brake controllers should be mounted in a position that is as level as possible because they incorporate a swinging pendulum inside. If perfectly level installation is not possible, adjustment can be

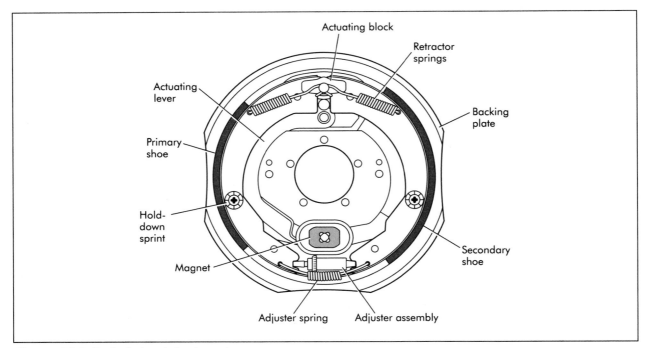

Figure 11.1 Typical electric brake unit

made to compensate for the out-of-level situation (see "Controller Adjustment," page 11.12). However, the Tekonsha Sentinel and those electronic units that incorporate no moving parts can be installed in any position without respect to being level.

One such electronic unit made by Draw-Tite utilizes a circuit that applies power to the brakes by a timed increase of power. This ramped timing circuit applies voltage to the brakes in a linear response to the position of the sync dial located on the left front side of the controller. The power output is also adjustable by use of the dial located on the top right of the unit. Because there are no moving parts, the unit can be installed in any position without regard to being level, even upside down. A manual-override bar on the front of the controller allows the driver to apply the trailer brakes without activating the tow-vehicle service brakes. Some models of the Draw-Tite feature a digital display that indicates the precise amount of amperage selected by the driver as the unit is adjusted.

The Tekonsha Voyager electric controller is an example of a controller that is sensitive to the degree of level and can be adjusted for level by turning the

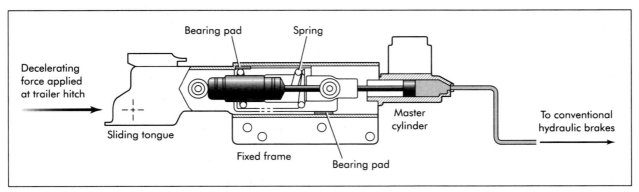

Figure 11.2 Trailer surge brakes

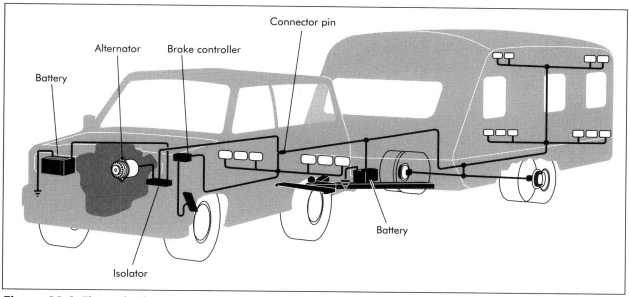

Figure 11.3 Electric brakes in travel trailers are activated by 12-volt DC current fed from the tow-vehicle's battery activated by the brake controller mounted under the dash.

wheel located on the left side. A housing that contains a lamp and a light-sensitive device is connected to the adjustment wheels. Also inside the housing is the pendulum weight with a separating tab. When the pendulum is at rest, the separator tab is positioned between the lamp and the light-sensitive device, blocking illumination.

As the tow-vehicle brake pedal is applied, the electric controller red wire is energized through the tow-vehicle stoplight switch. This activates the brake controller (Figure 11.3). The act of deceleration causes the pendulum weight to move forward, allowing light from the lamp to illuminate the light-sensitive device. The amount of light that is permitted to strike the light-sensitive device establishes the resistance in the brake controller and activates the trailer-brake magnets. More light equals more resistance and thus more braking effort. The force of deceleration moves the pendulum automatically in direct proportion to the amount of braking applied to the tow vehicle by the driver. Whether the tow-vehicle brakes are applied smoothly or abruptly, the trailer brakes should respond similarly because of the pendulum movement.

Tekonsha's latest entry, the Sentinel, has an advanced design which allows the unit to be mounted in virtually any position.

The Tekonsha Sentinel brake controller (Figure 11.4) has been called the most user-friendly unit

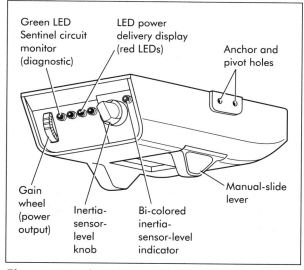

Figure 11.4 The Tekonsha Sentinel brake controller

on the market. It is microprocessor based and inertia activated. Sentinels come with built-in diagnostics and LED displays that show braking force and the correct level positions. They also automatically adjust for 2-, 4-, or 6-axle trailers.

The Sentinel can be mounted between 20° and 90° (Figure 11.5) without affecting the performance of the unit. This makes the physical mounting very easy even in today's crowded truck cabs.

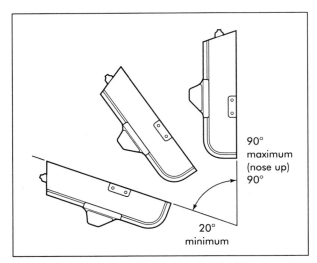

90°
maximum
(nose up)
90°

20°
minimum

Figure 11.5 You can mount the Sentinel brake controller at positions between 20° and 90°.

The Kelsey electronic brake controller utilizes a pendulum leveling arm and a system of magnets, a hall device, and a detector assembly. During braking, when the tow-vehicle stoplights come on, the control module electronic circuit is activated by current on the red wire connected to the tow-vehicle stoplight switch. As the tow vehicle decelerates, due to increased pedal effort, the magnet in the pendulum pulls away from the hall device and sends an electrical signal to the control module to increase amperage to the trailer brakes. The trailer brakes apply in direct proportion to the tow-vehicle braking effort. The control-module indicator light illuminates from dim to bright during the stop and goes dim at the end of the stop. When the tow-vehicle pedal is released, the control module is turned off and the indicator light turns off.

Because electric current travels and activates the trailer brakes faster than the hydraulic-brake system of the tow vehicle, the trailer should feel as if it is braking just slightly before the tow vehicle.

The Electric-Hydraulic Brake Controller

An electric-hydraulic brake controller utilizes an integral hydraulic cylinder to control the amount of braking effort directed to the trailer brakes. As the brake pedal of the tow vehicle is depressed, hydraulic-fluid pressure from the vehicle's master cylinder moves the piston inside the brake controller hydraulic

cylinder. Movement of this piston pushes the controller's manual control arm toward the unit's wire-wound resistor assembly, activating the control automatically. Electric-hydraulic controllers are usually not used on vehicles with antilock braking systems, unless specified by the vehicle manufacturer.

Jordan Brake Controllers

Jordan Research Corporation's current-model electronic controller, the Mark IV, is activated by a small current delivered from the stoplight switch. Because there are no moving parts, the unit can be installed in any position without regard to being level. A red manual override bar on the front of the controller allows the driver to apply the trailer brakes without activating the tow-vehicle brakes. Once it is properly wired, the only modification is a slide adjustment according to the number of brakes on the trailer. The Mark IV is recommended for trailers with no more than four brakes in the system.

The Quantum is a switchable electronic unit for use with trailers equipped with two, four, six, or eight brakes. In addition to selectability for the total number of brakes on the trailer, the controller is also adjustable for the intensity of braking desired. The Quantum features a digital display that indicates the precise amount of amperage selected by the driver as the unit is adjusted. As a fully electronic controller with no internal moving components, it can be installed in any position within easy reach of the driver. A red manual override button gives the driver the option of activating the trailer brakes independently of the tow-vehicle brakes.

Kelsey Micro Control Brake Controller

The computer era has had its effect on trailer brake controllers, as evidenced by the Kelsey Micro Control HD Plus, a microprocessor-equipped controller. Once properly installed and adjusted, this unit can be operated automatically or manually. In the automatic mode, the control module continuously monitors the vehicle's brake-light switch. When the brake pedal is pressed, the pendulum sensor provides a direct measurement of tow-vehicle deceleration, and the microprocessor converts the deceleration value to an output current for the trailer brakes. All this happens in direct proportion to the tow vehicle's braking effort.

The driver can override the automatic mode and actuate the trailer brakes without activating the tow-vehicle service brakes. The manual button allows the driver to fully apply the trailer brakes at any time, and, as a safety feature, when the trailer brakes are applied in manual mode, both the tow-vehicle and the trailer-brake lights will come on to alert other drivers.

This controller also features a remote manual switch, which can be held in one's hand, allowing the driver to activate the trailer brakes without removing his or her hands from the steering wheel.

■ TESTING PROCEDURES ■ FOR TRAILER BRAKES

Testing the Electrical Circuit

When testing the electric-brake circuit and components, use a multimeter (amps). The following procedure indicates if current is flowing from the battery to the trailer brakes.

CAUTION: To prevent damage to the multimeter, connect one lead, then touch the other lead. It the needle moves in the opposite direction on the scale, the polarity is reversed. To correct, simply reverse the leads.

1. Connect the trailer's electrical plug to the tow vehicle.
2. Connect the multimeter (amps) in series with the wire leading from the controller to the electric brakes.
3. Actuate the controller.
   a. *Electronic*: Set gain control to maximum. Move the manual lever to the applied position.
   b. *Hydraulic*: Apply the tow-vehicle brake pedal.

The amperage reading will vary as you apply more brake-pedal pressure or move the manual control arm to the fully applied position. The minimum low current will be 1 to $1\frac{3}{4}$ amperes. The maximum amount of amperes depends on the size and number of brakes on the trailer (Table 11.1). Each electromagnet can draw about 3 to 4 amperes.

Table 11.1 Minimum Current Values in Amperes

Brake Drum Diameter	Two Brakes	Four Brakes	Six Brakes
7-inches	3.8–4.4	7.6–8.8	11.4–13.2
10–12-inches	6–6.5	12–13	18–19.5

Checking for Low Maximum Current

If a low maximum current is registered, use a multimeter (voltage and continuity) to check the following:

■ Check the complete electric brake system for faulty wire connections.
■ Check the trailer plug and tow-vehicle receptacle for corrosion. If there are any signs of bad contact points, replace the plug or receptacle as necessary.
■ Check the electromagnets for wear or shorting.
■ If no current registers on the multimeter, test the controller.

Testing the Hydraulic Controller

To test the hydraulic controller:

1. Using a multimeter, check for open wires to the stoplight switch, the battery, and the service circuits.
2. Remove the controller from the vehicle:
   a. Remove the cover from the unit (Figure 11.6).
   b. Check the resistor coil for burnout, using a multimeter (continuity).
   c. Check the hydraulic cylinder that actuates the lever for leakage. Replace if necessary.

Testing the Electronic Controller

Check for open wires to the cold side of the stoplight switch, the battery, the ground, and the service circuits with the multimeter (Figure 11.7).

NOTE: If a short circuit exists in the trailer-brake wire (blue), the electronic controller is designed to shut off. After the short is corrected, the brake controller should function normally.

■ TROUBLESHOOTING ■
THE ELECTRIC BRAKE SYSTEM

Problem	Possible Cause	Correction
Weak brakes	Loose connections	Check that all connections are clean and tight
	Inadequate trailer ground	Check for proper grounding
	Short circuit	Check electrical circuit
	Incorrect variable resistor setting	Check for proper setting to avoid too much resistance
	Worn or defective magnets	Replace magnets
	Poor brake adjustment	Adjust brakes
	Bent backing plate	Check backing plate flange; correct if necessary
	Contaminated lining	Check and replace contaminated linings
	Inadequate gauge of wire	Refer to manufacturer's wiring recommendations
	Stoplights connected in brake circuit	Stoplights must not be connected in the brake circuit; the graduation of the current changes as it passes through the controller, resulting in weak or grabbing brakes; wire a separate circuit for the stoplight switch
	Improper linings	Replace with proper linings
	Worn linings	Reline with new linings
	Worn brake drums	Inspect the brake-drum surface; it should be free of scoring and excessive wear; machine or replace drums as necessary
	Out-of-round drums	Machine brake drums
	Loose axle on springs or frames	Inspect and make necessary repairs
	Loose lining on rivets	Replace brake shoes
	Excessive load on trailer	Check to be sure trailer is not underbraked; check the brakes on each axle to make sure they are working
	Using trailer brakes only	Use of trailer brakes only can cause brake fade or loss of friction due to excessive heat
No brakes	Open circuit	Check for broken wires, loose connections, improper grounding, or faulty connector plug
	Improperly wired or inoperative controller	Rewire controller; check controller operation.
	Poor brake adjustment	Adjust brakes
	Defective variable resistor	Check for loose or broken connections
	Worn or defective magnet(s)	Replace magnets
	Short circuit	Check electrical circuit
	Defective connector plug	Check plug between tow vehicle and trailer for loose connections, dirty or corroded blades, or broken Bakelite insert in socket, shorting blades or pins
	Burned-out resistor	Check resistor for continuity; replace if necessary.

■ TROUBLESHOOTING ■
THE ELECTRIC BRAKE SYSTEM, continued

Problem	Possible Cause	Correction
Intermittent or surging brakes	Out-of-round drums	Turn or replace drums
	Inadequate trailer ground	Check for proper grounding **NOTE:** A ground through the coupler and ball is inadequate.
	Broken magnet lead wires	Bench-check magnets and replace if necessary
	Loose wheel bearings	Check and adjust bearings
Noisy Brakes	Excessively worn lining	Check and replace shoes if necessary
	Weak or broken springs	Check for weak or broken springs; replace if necessary
	Improperly located flange; bent backing plate	Check and repair if necessary
	Contaminated linings	Check and replace contaminated linings
	Improper bearing adjustment	Check and adjust wheel bearings; check for worn or damaged bearings; replace if necessary.
	Incorrectly adjusted brakes	Check brake adjustment
	Improperly adjusted shoes	Adjust starwheel until there is a heavy drag, then back off adjuster slightly
	Grease on linings	Replace leaky seal and linings
	Worn magnets	Check for excessive or uneven wear; replace if necessary
Breakaway switch fails to function	Weak or dead battery	Replace with new 12-volt DC battery; if brakes fail to function, replace breakaway switch.
	Faulty breakaway-switch wiring	Check breakaway-switch circuit for broken or frayed wires; replace wire where necessary. Each splice must have a good connection
	Faulty breakaway switch	Check breakaway switch by pulling pin and attempting to tow trailer; if switch works, brakes will engage.
	Only one brake working	Check the amperage at each brake; where no amperage is indicated, check the wires leading to brake; if no defect is found, remove magnet from backing plate and check for amperage capacity, ground, or short; if brake is okay electrically, check for mechanical defects.
	Poor electrical connections	Check wiring for loose connections, broken wires, or worn insulation; rewire as necessary.

■ TROUBLESHOOTING ■
THE ELECTRIC BRAKE SYSTEM, continued

Problem	Possible Cause	Correction
Grabbing or locking brakes	Improperly installed flanges	Check flange locations; refer to axle manufacturer
	Contaminated linings	Check and replace badly contaminated linings
	Controller too sensitive	Adjust brake controller
	No variable resistor	A variable resistor is required when brakes have greater stopping power than is necessary for the weight on the axle; install variable resistor when necessary. **NOTE:** Not required on electronic controller
	Weak or broken springs	Check for weak or broken springs; replace if necessary.
Dragging brakes	Incorrectly adjusted brakes	Check brake adjustment
	Insufficient gap between hydraulic controller	Replace controller contact pins and coil
	Excessive residual pressure in the tow-vehicle hydraulic system or "gummed up" hydraulic controller cylinder	Purge tow-vehicle hydraulic lines; replace fluid; replace controller
	Improperly installed flanges	Check flange location; refer to axle manufacturer
	Badly corroded brake assembly	Check brake assemblies for corrosion; be sure magnet levers operate freely; clean and lubricate brake assemblies
	Weak or broken springs	Check for weak or broken springs; replace if necessary
	Worn or bent magnet lever arm	Replace magnet and lever arm

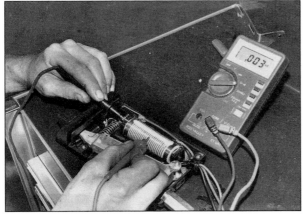

Figure 11.6 The resistor coil in the hydraulic brake controller is tested for burnout using a multimeter.

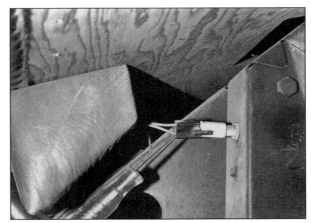

Figure 11.7 The cold side of the brake-light switch can be determined by using a multimeter or test light.

■ CONTROLLER INSTALLATION ■

The Electronic Brake Controller

The controller must be installed on a solid surface, normally beneath the dashboard, with the rear of the controller toward the front of the tow vehicle (Figure 11.8). Ideally, position the controller within easy reach of the driver.

For those controllers that must be leveled prior to final installation, hold the controller in the intended location (after complete wiring is made) and check to see that the pendulum can be adjusted properly. If the pendulum cannot be adjusted properly due to excessive controller angle, another location must be selected that is more level.

All electronic controllers are designed for use with 12-volt DC, negative-ground systems only. Reversing polarity or miswiring can cause permanent damage to the controller.

NOTE: Electronic controllers should be wired directly to the positive and negative terminals of the battery. In many cases, using the chassis for a ground can cause erratic (and unsafe) operation of the electronic controller.

It is recommended that all connections be made with insulated, solderless, crimp-style connectors.

Figure 11.8 The brake controller must be within easy reach of the driver.

Use a rubber grommet where wires pass through the firewall for protection of the wiring and to seal against air leaks.

Wiring the Electronic Brake Controller

Wiring should be done in the following order (Figure 11.9):

1. White wire to the negative terminal of the battery. Do not use a frame ground.
2. Black wire to the positive side of the battery. When routing this wire, keep it away from

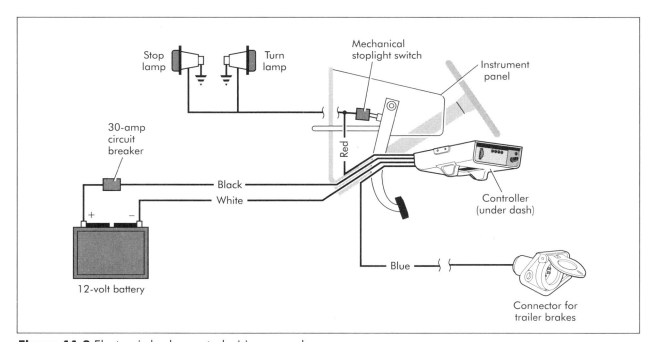

Figure 11.9 Electronic brake-control wiring procedure

the radio antenna (or other radio transmitters) to reduce possible RF interference. Use 10- or 12-gauge stranded wire.

CAUTION: Do not use a fuse. A 20- or 30-amp automatic-reset circuit breaker (depending on model) should be used to protect this wiring.

WARNING: Do not reverse the white and black wires. Reversal will destroy the brake control.

3. Red wire to cold side of stoplight switch. Note that the cold side of the stoplight switch is only energized when the brake pedal is pushed.

CAUTION: Some vehicles are equipped with separate switches for the transmission converter and the cruise control. Be sure the red wire is connected to the nonpowered side of the stoplight switch. If not properly connected to the stoplight switch, the indicator light and trailer brakes will not operate in conjunction with the vehicle brake pedal. To locate the nonpowered wire, use a multimeter or 12-volt DC test light. Connect one test lead to the ground and the other lead to one of the two stoplight switch terminals. The nonpowered wire is the one that turns on the test light or registers voltage when the brake pedal is depressed and registers no voltage or is off when the brake pedal is released.

4. Blue wire to trailer brakes. This wire has electronic short-circuit protection. Note that some makes and models of tow vehicles are wired in such a manner that the wire coming from the four-way-flasher circuit is connected to the cold side of the brakelight switch. This causes the trailer-brake controller to turn on every time the four-way flasher flashes and results in brake pulsation. Some trailer-brake systems are so sensitive that this pulsing may become objectionable. To overcome this problem, install a Tekonsha Pulse Preventer (part number 2180-S) or a Draw-Tite Pulse Preventer (part number 5501) to isolate the brake-light current from the four-way-flasher current. With a Pulse Preventer in place, brake-switch current can flow to the brake lights, but four-way-flasher current cannot flow to the brake-light switch or the brake controller.

The Kelsey 81741 control module allows the four-way-flasher lights to operate without affecting the trailer brakes, but the pendulum and load control knob must be adjusted properly. If the control module is not properly adjusted, the trailer brakes

may pulse when the four-way-flasher lights are activated.

NOTE: Always use the factory wiring when vehicle is equipped with a towing package.

The Electric-Hydraulic Brake Controller

CAUTION: Electric-hydraulic trailer-brake controllers are not intended for use with some small vehicles because the brake master cylinders are too small. Installation of a hydraulic brake controller in these vehicles will result in the manufacturer voiding the warranty. For these vehicles, install an electronic brake controller that does not tap into the tow vehicle's hydraulic brake system. Hydraulic brake controllers may not be used on certain vehicles with antilock braking systems (ABS). Check the vehicle owner's manual for recommendations concerning trailer-brake controllers.

Install the controller mounting bracket at a solid location (normally beneath the dashboard).Connect the hydraulic line from the brake controller to the tow-vehicle master cylinder. Late-model vehicles feature dual or divided master-cylinder systems with two outlets: one for front brakes and one for rear brakes. Select the proper brake-control-adapter T-fitting for your particular vehicle. This T-fitting should be inserted at the outlet on the master cylinder serving the rear brakes. Be sure the rear brake outlet is properly identified by referring to the vehicle owner's manual or by following the hydraulic line from the rear brakes to the master cylinder.

CAUTION: Use only cadmium-plated adapter T-fittings on aluminum master cylinders. Cadmium plating prevents electrolytic corrosion, which can severely damage the threads in the master cylinder over a period of time. When working with a cast-iron master cylinder, use either a cadmium-plated or a standard brass T-fitting. Do not use a compression fitting to connect the hydraulic line to the master cylinder. A compression fitting has only a quarter of the design strength of an automotive brake line. Compression fittings will not provide the proper gripping force on steel brake lines.

To make the hydraulic connection:

1. Assemble the tube fitting to the T-connector.
2. The tube fitting should be turned hand tight.
3. Tighten the assembly with a wrench until it feels solid.
4. Apply ⅙ turn more. Do not overtighten since it may damage the fitting and/or threads.

IMPORTANT: Do not run the tubing in a straight line. Put a small loop in the line (to permit flexing) before running it through the firewall (Figure 11.10).

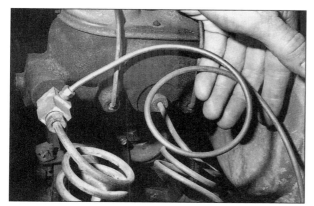

Figure 11.10 A loop in the hydraulic tubing between the master cylinder and firewall must be used when installing a hydraulic brake controller.

Bleed the hydraulic line by loosening the fitting at the brake controller. Press the brake pedal to allow the line to fill with fluid and expel all air. Hold a small container or a rag below the fitting to catch escaping brake fluid. Keep the brake pedal depressed

until fluid flows continuously without sputtering. Tighten the fitting before allowing the brake pedal to be released. Check for leaks by depressing the pedal again several times while observing the connections at the master cylinder and at the brake controller. Check master cylinder fluid level and fill if necessary.

Wiring the Electric-Hydraulic Brake Controller

Use 12-gauge automotive grade wire or larger for wiring the electric-hydraulic brake controller (Figures 11.11 and 11.12).

1. Connect the black wire to the positive terminal of the battery.
2. To protect the brake controller and vehicle wiring, an automatic-reset circuit breaker should be installed in the black wire between the battery and the brake controller. Use a 15-amp circuit breaker for two-brake trailers,

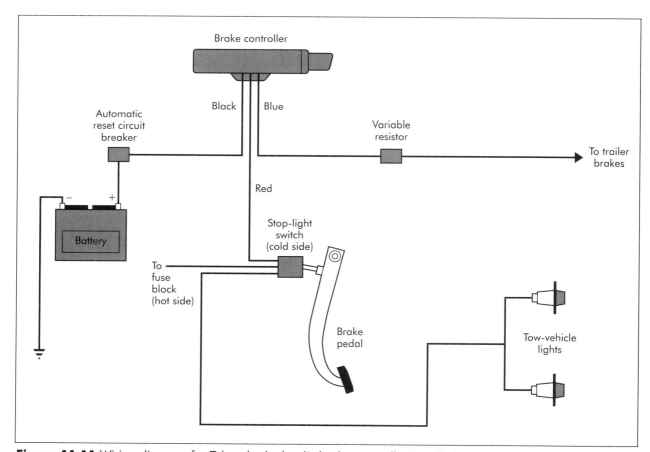

Figure 11.11 Wiring diagram for Tekonsha hydraulic brake-controller installation

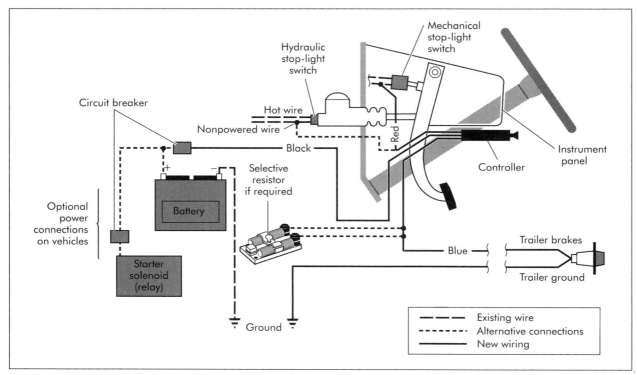

Figure 11.12 Wiring diagram for Kelsey-Hayes hydraulic brake-controller installation

a 20-amp circuit breaker for four-brake trailers, and a 30-amp circuit breaker for six-brake trailers.

3. Connect the blue wire to the brake-system pin in the tow vehicle/trailer connector plug. If the brake controller provides too much braking—regardless of the adjustment-knob position—install a variable resistor in the blue wire. This resistor should be installed in an unobstructed location under the hood.
4. Connect the red wire to the cold side of the stoplight switch.

■ CONTROLLER ADJUSTMENT ■

Electronic Controllers

It may be necessary to adjust the brake controller to compensate for an out-of-level mounting position. This is accomplished by rotating the level-adjustment wheel/knob (for older Tekonsha units, it's located underneath the controller; newer models have this adjustment on the left side or on the

front panel), or the pendulum leveling arm (for Kelsey, it's on the left side of the controller).

Tekonsha Brake-Controller Adjustment

On some models, if the front of the Tekonsha controller is tipped too far upward, the pendulum may be out of position. When this happens, the indicator light on the face of the controller will glow brightly, indicating that the brakes are being activated even though there is no pressure on the tow-vehicle brake pedal. To correct this condition, the tow vehicle must be resting on level ground with the engine running. The trailer plug does not have to be connected for older models, but will have to be connected for later versions, except for the Sentinel. Although the control positions may be in different locations on the Tekonsha controllers, the steps for making the adjustment are relatively the same.

To level the Sensor, Tekonsha Voyager:

1. Make sure the trailer and tow vehicle are on level ground.

2. Plug the trailer harness into the tow-vehicle receptacle. The LED will only glow green when the trailer is connected to the tow vehicle.
3. Set the gain control (right side) to the maximum position by turning the knob clockwise (total rotation is only 270 degrees).
4. Depress the brake pedal and hold.
5. Rotate the level-control knob (left side) counterclockwise until the LED starts to change from green to red.
6. Carefully rotate the level-control knob clockwise until the first shade of orange appears. The LED will glow dim orange for a typical setting and a brighter orange for a more aggressive setting. Use caution when turning this knob; zero to full output is less than 20 degrees or a ⅛-inch turn.
7. Release the brake pedal.

To level the Sensor, Tekonsha Sentinel:

1. Make sure the tow vehicle is on level ground.
2. The trailer harness does not need to be plugged in.
3. Set the gain wheel (front panel, left side) to maximum (rotate upward until three bars inscribed on the wheel show).
4. With the brake pedal depressed, the bi-colored LED (right of level knob) should glow red (controller is shipped from factory at maximum clockwise position).
5. Rotate the level knob counterclockwise until the bi-colored LED glows green.
6. Slowly turn the knob until the red light just shows, then turn counterclockwise until solid green is visible.
7. Release the brake pedal.

If the controller has been previously adjusted and the LED is clear, rotate the level knob (with brake pedal depressed and gain set to maximum as per above) clockwise until bi-colored LED turns green. Unit is now adjusted correctly.

To level the Sensor, older Tekonsha models:

1. Make sure the tow vehicle is on level ground.
2. The trailer harness does not have to be connected.

3. Set the gain control to minimum; depress the brake pedal and hold.
4. Rotate the adjustment wheel (on bottom panel) toward the rear of the controller as far as it will go. As the wheel is being turned, the indicator light will begin to flicker.
5. Rotate the adjustment wheel toward the front of the unit until the indicator light glows steadily.
6. Again, rotate the adjustment wheel back toward the rear of the unit until the indicator light just begins to flicker.
7. Release the brake pedal. The adjustment wheel is now set.

The only other adjustment to be made is to set the gain control. This is done after the level control has been set. When making this adjustment, the trailer must be connected. Proper gain-control adjustment is just before trailer-brake lock-up.

1. Set gain to about the halfway position.
2. Tow the trailer at low speed (20 MPH) on a level, hard, dry surface.
3. Slowly move the manual lever on the controller to the full-on position.
4. If the trailer brakes don't lock up, increase the gain control.
5. Repeat the procedure until the maximum gain-control setting (decrease or increase as necessary) without trailer-wheel lock-up is found. Leave the gain control set to that position.
6. To check automatic operation, use the tow-vehicle foot brake at low speed. The tow-vehicle and trailer should make a smooth, straight stop.
7. The gain-control setting is adjustable and should be varied to compensate for great changes in trailer weight.

Adjusting the Kelsey Brake Controller

Adjustment of the Kelsey controller involves setting the pendulum leveling arm and the load-control knob.

1. Hitch the trailer to the tow vehicle for this adjustment. If an equalizing hitch system is

used, it should be operational and ready to go on the road. Make sure the tow vehicle and trailer are resting on a flat, level surface. Check to see if the tow vehicle stoplights are operating correctly, then disconnect all electrical connections between the tow vehicle and the trailer.

2. Adjust the load-control knob to its maximum brake position.

3. Depress the brake pedal far enough to activate the tow-vehicle stoplights. Hold this position.

4. Pull the pendulum leveling arm toward the indicator light. The indicator light should illuminate brightly.

5. Push the pendulum-leveling arm away from the indicator light until the light just reaches minimum brilliance (or just goes off). The leveling arm should be approximately straight down. Repeat this step several times to make sure the indicator light has reached minimum brilliance.

6. Release the brake pedal. The pendulum assembly is now initially adjusted. A readjustment may be necessary if the loading of either the tow vehicle or trailer causes a considerable change in the tow-vehicle front-to-rear attitude.

7. Move the control-module manual lever to the left and observe the control-module indicator light become increasingly brighter as the lever is moved.

8. If the indicator light does not illuminate, the tow vehicle has a short to ground in the trailer-brake circuit. Check and repair as necessary.

9. Connect the trailer to the tow vehicle and check the trailer to see if the stoplights are operating properly. Move the control-module manual lever to the left. If the indicator light does not illuminate, check the trailer-brake magnets and trailer-brake circuit (including trailer-to-tow vehicle connection) for a short. If a short occurs in the trailer brakes, plug, or wiring, the control-module circuitry will shut down and the indicator light will not illuminate or will glow extremely dimly. Locate and correct short.

NOTE: It is normal to hear the trailer-brake magnets hum while testing the controller, or whenever the trailer brakes are activated.

10. Move the control-module manual lever to the left and observe the trailer stoplights come on. The trailer stoplights must illuminate when the manual lever is moved to the left. If they do not, check circuit and bulbs. Also check to see if the red wire connection at the brake controller is connected to the nonpowered side of the stoplight switch.

Road Testing and Readjusting the Kelsey Controller

To road test and readjust the Kelsey controller, follow this procedure:

1. Adjust the load-control knob to the mid-range setting (center of knob travel).

2. At a moderate speed (20 MPH or less), push the tow-vehicle brake pedal in a normal manner. With the load-control knob set in the mid-range setting, a firm braking action should occur. If more trailer braking is required, turn the load-control knob clockwise. If less trailer braking is required, turn the load-control knob counterclockwise. The indicator light should illuminate from dim to brighter during the stop, and back to dim after the stop is completed.

3. At a moderate speed (20 MPH or less), activate the manual lever slowly to the left. A much harder stop can always be obtained since the manual lever is not affected by the load-control setting. The indicator light should illuminate from dim to bright during the stop.

4. The pendulum leveling arm may be readjusted forward if the indicator light fails to glow, if there is delayed braking, or if there is no braking.

5. The pendulum leveling arm needs to be readjusted backward if the indicator light glows steadily, if the trailer brakes grab, or if the trailer brakes pulse when the four-way flasher is activated.

6. The pendulum leveling arm is properly ad-

justed if the indicator light glows dimly when the vehicle is stopped on the level and the indicator light glows increasingly brighter as the pedal is pressed while stopping. There should be smooth braking action.

When properly adjusted, the Kelsey control module will allow a slightly greater amount of trailer braking when going downhill and slightly less trailer braking when going uphill. Normally, no control-module readjustment is needed for towing in hilly terrain.

Adjusting the Electric-Hydraulic Controller

An adjustment spring on electric-hydraulic brake controllers allows the driver to alter the amount of fluid displacement required to move the hydraulic piston and activate the trailer brakes. When the adjustment spring is altered, the amount of brake-pedal pressure required changes slightly, increasing or decreasing actuation of trailer brakes. This adjustment is made either with a fingertip-adjustment wheel or by turning the knob on the manual control arm, depending upon the unit brand and model.

Adjusting the Kelsey Micro Control HD Plus Controller

Pendulum setup must be performed when the controller is initially installed and after the control module loses its power connection to the battery. If the module loses power, stored data will be lost.

To level the pendulum, the leveling-adjustment procedure should be made with the vehicle parked on level ground. Position the pendulum arm so it points straight down, perpendicular to the ground. This is the reference point for all pendulum adjustments.

With the pendulum level, the microprocessor must mark this position as zero. The zero-adjust is only needed once to capture the reference starting point. If the control module loses its memory as a result of power disconnection, the zero-adjust routine must be performed again. To perform the zero-adjust, push and hold the gain-select button for approximately five seconds. The LED display will flash when the zero-adjust is complete.

The gain setting is used to adjust the intensity of trailer braking, and it is set according to the load weight and axle capacity. The gain setting is adjusted by the driver and is automatically stored in the microprocessor memory. When the controller is powered up for the first time, the gain setting defaults to a value of 1. Current gain settings can be displayed by pressing and releasing the gain button. Each additional push of the button increases the gain setting by a value of 1. If a gain setting is too soft or too hard, it can be adjusted up or down until the desired braking effort is set.

To use the gain setting chart (Table 11.2):

- Determine the total axle capacity for the trailer.
- Determine the total loaded-trailer weight.
- Compute the load-weight-to-axle-capacity ratio by dividing the total trailer weight into the total axle capacity. For example, if the trailer has a total axle capacity of 10,000 pounds, and the total weight of the loaded trailer is 7,500 pounds, the ratio is 0.75:1 or 75 percent of the total axle capacity.
- Using the chart, choose a gain setting that represents this ratio. This will be the starting point from where you may make additional adjustments.
- To fine-tune the gain setting, perform several stops under normal brake-pedal pressure at moderate speed (25 MPH or less) on a flat, hard, dry surface. A firm braking action should result. If more or less trailer braking is desired, increase or decrease the gain by a value of 1.

Table 11.2 Gain Setting Chart

Gain Setting	Load-Weight-to-Axle-Capacity Ratio	LED Display			
		1	2	3	4
1	20–30% (Light)	On	Off	Off	Off
2	30–40% (Light)	Off	On	Off	Off
3	40–50% (Medium)	Off	Off	On	Off
4	50–60% (Medium)	Off	Off	Off	On
5	60–70% (Medium)	On	Off	Off	On
6	70–80% (Heavy)	Off	On	Off	On
7	80–90% (Heavy)	Off	Off	On	On
8	90–100% (Heavy)	On	Off	On	On

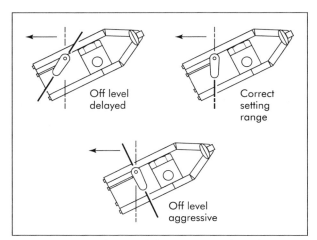

Figure 11.13 The pendulum arm can be adjusted for smoother breaking response.

The normal operating mode is with the pendulum in the level position. But once the gain setting has been adjusted, the pendulum leveling arm is used to adjust the smoothness of the brake response (Figure 11.13). Moving the pendulum arm away from level will activate a delayed or aggressive mode of trailer braking.

To adjust for more aggressive action, move the pendulum leveling arm approximately 2 to 3 degrees back toward the rear of the tow vehicle. To adjust for more delayed braking action, move the arm 2 to 3 degrees toward the front of the tow vehicle.

The pendulum is a deceleration sensor and can momentarily energize the brakes under bumpy or adverse road conditions. The controller can be desensitized by adjusting the pendulum leveling arm to a slightly delayed position.

Adjusting the Jordan Controller

Adjustment of the Jordan Mark IV controller is done by beginning with a rough initial setting of the slide adjustment, ¼ of the way toward minimum, down from the maximum setting. Adjusted to this point, make a few slow-speed stops on dry, level pavement. Slide the control toward maximum to increase braking firmness. Slide the control toward minimum for lighter braking. Final adjustment is a matter of personal preference, but it should always be less than full lock-up.

The Quantum is adjusted by first hitching up the trailer and then pressing and holding the tow-vehi-

cle brake pedal down for approximately ten seconds or until the digital readout on the controller stabilizes. Continuing to hold the brake pedal down, reach around to the rear of the controller and move the output adjustment to the left (minimum) and note the digital readout. Then slide the adjustment to the right and note the readout. If the unit is working properly, the readings should be as follows:

- Two-brake system: minimum 2 to 3 amps; maximum 5 to 6 amps
- Four-brake system: minimum 3 to 4 amps; maximum 11 to 13 amps
- Six-brake system: minimum 4 to 5 amps; maximum 14 to 16 amps
- Eight-brake system: minimum 5 to 6 amps; maximum 21 to 23 amps

These readings are typical and may vary depending on the length and gauge of the wire used to make the connections and the battery condition.

This test checks for magnet operation. Failure to reach maximum readings indicates a problem with bad magnets, broken wires, or bad connections. Repair the malfunction before continuing.

Set the output adjustment to the initial setting prescribed for the number of brakes on the trailer. Slide the adjustment to the left for less current and to the right for more current.

- Two-brake system: 3.5 amps
- Four-brake system: 7.0 amps
- Six-brake system: 10.0 amps
- Eight-brake system: 13.0 amps

After making this initial adjustment, test the system by making a few slow-speed stops on dry, level pavement to determine if further adjustment is needed. Slide the adjustment control to the left or right until the trailer brakes are applied firmly but do not lock up. This is the optimum adjustment.

Adjusting the Draw-Tite Controller

There are two sets of adjustments that control the Draw-Tite unit. One is the output control, and the other is the sync control. The output control establishes the maximum amount of power available to the trailer brakes. To increase the amount of available power to the trailer brakes, the output control is rotated upward. Rotating the control downward decreases the power to the trailer brakes. The output control setting is shown on the digital display at the front of the controller when the trailer is hitched and the tow-vehicle brake pedal is pressed. Settings are shown as 0 through 10, with 0 being the minimum and 10 the maximum setting.

The sync control adjusts the aggressiveness of the trailer brakes, and this control is located on the left side of the control module, forward of the mounting bracket. The trailer brakes become more aggressive as the control is moved toward the front of the tow vehicle. To view the sync-control setting on the digital display, press the brake pedal and move the control slightly. The display will change to the sync mode. The setting is displayed as 1o through 9o, with 1o being least aggressive and 9o being the most aggressive. The sync control should be adjusted to meet driver preference or changing road conditions.

■ THE VARIABLE RESISTOR ■

Braking may be excessively harsh and aggressive while using an electric-hydraulic controller during slow stops. The use of a variable resistor will normally correct this problem (Figure 11.14). The variable resistor permits adjustment of the amount of resistance in the circuit feeding the trailer brakes. The unit is installed by wiring it directly into the wire leading from the brake controller to the trailer brakes. Ad-

justment is made by sliding a metal bridge toward one end or the other of the device to achieve more or less resistance.

■ INSPECTING ELECTRIC BRAKE COMPONENTS ■

When inspecting the electric-brake system, check the breakaway switch, the magnet assemblies, and the brake drums.

Testing the Breakaway Switch

To test the breakaway switch, follow these steps:

1. Connect a multimeter (amps) or test light between the breakaway switch and the trailer brakes (Figure 11.15).
2. Pull out the breakaway pin. The multimeter should register current. If no current flows:
    a. Check for open wires.
    b. Check the battery for full charge.
    c. If the wires and batteries are okay, replace the switch.

Checking the Magnet Assembly

To check the magnet assembly:

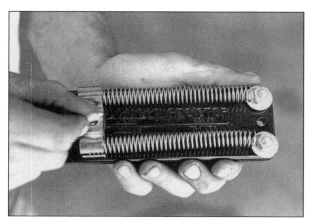

Figure 11.14 A variable resistor in the line to the trailer brakes can correct overbraking at slow speeds.

Figure 11.15 The breakaway switch on a trailer can be tested by pulling the pin and checking the current with a multimeter or test light.

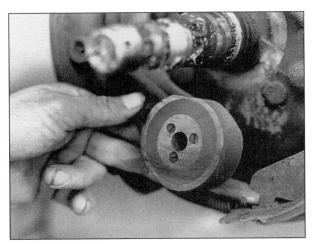

Figure 11.16 Check the brake magnet for wear.

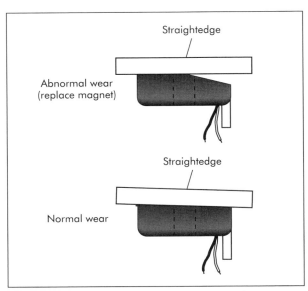

Figure 11.18 The most common cause of uneven magnet wear is a worn lever pivot allowing the magnet to contact the armature at an angle.

- Check the magnet for wear (Figure 11.16). Replace the magnet if the brass screws that hold the friction element show wear.
- Check the magnet-wearing surface for flatness by using a straightedge (Figure 11.17). The magnet should show normal wear (Figure 11.18). If the magnet wearing surface is worn abnormally, replace the lever arm, the armpins, and the magnet assembly.

Testing the Magnet

To test the magnet, follow these steps:

1. Test for short circuits and open circuits by connecting the magnet in series with an ammeter and a battery (Figure 11.19).
2. Test for short circuits within the magnet coil by connecting it in series with an ammeter and a battery. When grounding the battery to the magnet case, the magnet should show no

Figure 11.17 The trailer-brake-magnet wearing surface can be inspected for flatness by using a straightedge.

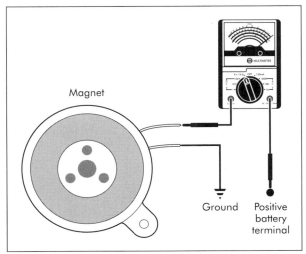

Figure 11.19 Short circuits and open circuits can be checked by connecting the magnet in series with an ammeter and battery.

amperage value. If it does, a short circuit exists and the magnet must be replaced:

    a. Connect a test lead wire to a magnet wire.

    b. Take the other test lead wire to the positive post on the battery.

    c. Connect the other magnet wire to the negative post on the battery or ground the magnet case directly to the negative post and leave the remaining magnet wire open.

3. The average reading on the ammeter will vary with the magnet size (Table 11.3).

Testing the Brake Drum and Mechanical Components

Inspect the mechanical components of the electric brake system (Figure 11.20). Brake shoes, drum, the bearings, grease seals, and the brake hardware all require periodic service.

1. Inspect brake drums and armature surfaces for grooves.

Table 11.3 Magnet Amperes Chart

Brake Size	Amps/ Magnet	Two Brakes	Four Brakes	Six Brakes
7 × 1¼	2.5	5.0	10.0	15.0
10 × 1¼	3.0	6.0	12.0	18.0
10 × 2¼	3.0	6.0	12.0	18.0
12 × 2	3.0	6.0	12.0	18.0
12¼ × 2¼	3.0	6.0	12.0	18.0
12¼ × 3⅜	3.0	6.0	12.0	18.0

    a. Replace the brake-drum armature if it indicates excessive scoring due to contamination from mud, small stones, and sand. Armatures are either part of the drum or will separate easily from the drum.

        NOTE: A one-piece drum/armature can be machined on the lathe .030 inch. The magnets must be replaced whenever the armature is refaced. It is not recommended to machine the two-piece armature.

    b. Inspect the brake-drum surface for heavy scoring. If the drum is worn more than .020 inch oversized, or the drum has worn out of round by more than .015 inch, the drum surface should be turned. If scoring or other wear is greater than .090 inch, the drum should

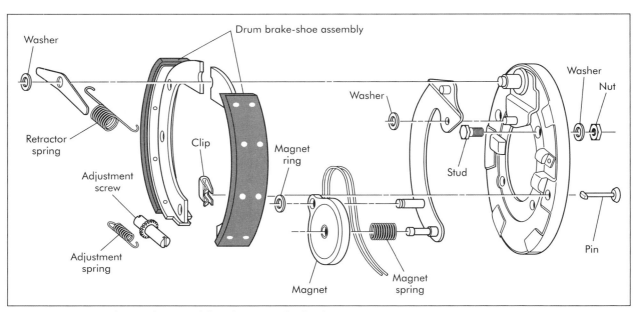

Figure 11.20 Mechanical parts of the electric trailer brake

be replaced. When turning the drum, the maximum diameter must not exceed the following:

- 7-inch drum—7.090 inches
- 10-inch drum—10.090 inches
- 12-inch drum—12.090 inches
- 12¼-inch drum—12.340 inches

   CAUTION: If a drum is machined beyond .045 inch of its original diameter, use .030-inch oversize brake shoes. This maintains the correct shoe arc to the brake drum.

2. Replace linings if they are worn to within ¹/₃₂ inch of the rivet heads, or if they are contaminated with grease or oil.

Inspecting the Wheel Bearings

Wash the bearings with a suitable solvent, making sure that all the grease and oil is removed from the bearing cone and rollers. Dry the bearings with a lint-free cloth and inspect each roller and cage closely. If

Figure 11.21 Wheel bearings from the trailer should be thoroughly cleaned and dried before repacking with new grease.

any pitting, spalling, or corrosion is present, then the bearing must be replaced (Figure 11.21). It is very important that bearings be replaced in sets of a cone and a cup.

CAUTION: Be sure to wear safety glasses when removing or installing force-fitted parts; the possibility of metal chipping is very real and may result in eye damage.

The bearings can be reused if they are in good condition. Proper lubrication is essential to the reliability and longevity of the bearings. *Bearings should be repacked every 12 months or 12,000 miles.*

Install the wheel seal into the backside of the drum. Using a torque wrench, tighten the spindle nut to the factory torque specification (see bearing service starting on page 11.22).

■ ADJUSTING THE BRAKES ■

For efficient braking, an electric-brake assembly must have the correct brake shoe-to-drum clearance. Brake adjustment must be performed regularly because it is not automatic.

1. Using a brake-adjusting tool or a large flat-blade screwdriver, remove the plug in the backing plate (Figure 11.22).

   NOTE: Some hubs have an adjuster slot in the front of the hub, which makes the adjustment much easier and safer. If so, there is no need to get under the trailer.

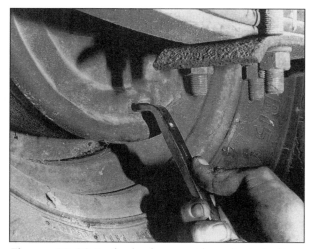

Figure 11.22 Trailer brakes must be adjusted after service by turning the starwheel that is accessed through the backing plate.

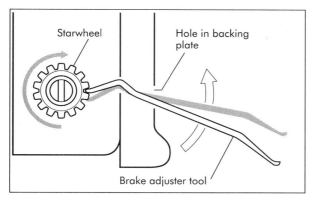

Figure 11.23 A brake-adjuster tool works best for turning the starwheel between the linings, but in a pinch a screwdriver will work.

2. Insert the brake tool or screwdriver and locate the adjuster starwheel. This is a toothed wheel (Figure 11.23).
3. While spinning the wheel and the tire, turn the adjuster starwheel up or down to adjust the brakes. Generally, moving the brake tool up loosens the brakes and moving the tool down tightens them. Continue adjusting until a heavy drag results.
4. Back off the adjuster until there is no drag (enough to allow the tire/wheel to spin freely).

■ INSTALLING THE WHEELS ■

To properly install the wheels:

1. Clean the threads of the wheel lugs and apply a light coat of anti-seize compound (available at most auto-supply stores).
2. Make sure the wheels are centered precisely on the axle flange.
3. Using the proper tightening pattern (Figure

Table 11.4 Wheel Torque Requirements

Torque Sequence			
Wheel Size	1st Stage	2nd Stage	3rd Stage
12″	20–25	35–40	50–75
13″	20–25	35–40	50–75
14″	20–25	50–60	90–120
15″	20–25	50–60	90–120
16″	20–25	50–60	90–120

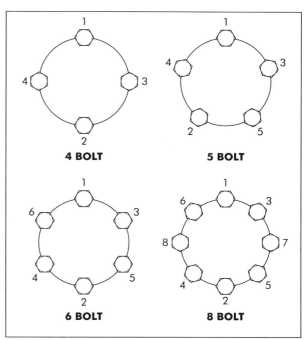

Figure 11.24 Tightening pattern must be followed to insure proper seating of the nuts and the wheels.

11.24), tighten the lug nuts/bolts to the proper torque reading (Table 11.4).
4. Wheel nuts/bolts need to be torqued before first-road use and after each wheel removal. Check and retorque after the first ten miles, twenty-five miles, and at fifty miles to insure the wheel nuts/bolts are fully seated. Check them monthly thereafter.

■ SERVICING TRAILER BRAKES ■

Servicing trailer brakes is within the capability of most do-it-yourself RVers. The job is messy but simple if all the proper tools and replacement parts are on hand.

Brake service requires removal of the trailer wheel, so begin by jacking up the trailer and supporting it on jack stands. It is best to dismantle the trailer brakes one side at a time for two reasons: First, it is safer to have one side supported by wheels while the opposite side is up on jack stands; and second, if you become confused about the brake reassembly, you still have at least one completely intact assembly to refer to.

Removing the Bearings

Begin trailer-brake service by removing bearings as follows:

1. Remove the tire and wheel.
2. Remove the bearing dust cap (Figure 11.25).
3. Straighten and remove the cotter pin.
4. Remove the castle nut. It should be only finger tight (Figure 11.26).

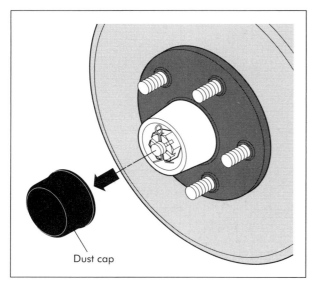

Figure 11.25 The bearing dust cap is removed to access the castle nult and cotter pin.

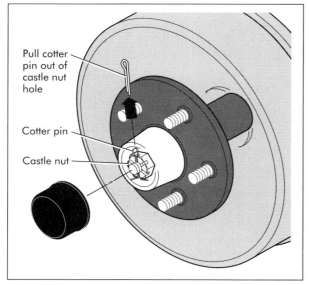

Figure 11.26 After removing the cotter pin, the castle nut should be only finger tight.

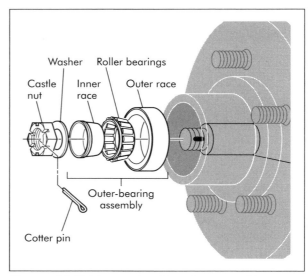

Figure 11.27 Outer wheel bearing assembly

5. Remove the washer and lay it aside on a clean newspaper or rag.
6. Pull the brake drum toward you about an inch, wiggling it side to side slightly. This tends to force the outer wheel bearing toward the end of the spindle where it can be grasped easily.
7. Pull the outer wheel bearing off the spindle and lay it aside on a clean newspaper or rag (Figure 11.27).
8. Remove the brake-drum assembly by pulling it straight out, and place it open side up on a clean newspaper or rag. You may have to back off the adjuster, if the drum will not pull off.
9. Remove the inner wheel bearing by running a wooden shaft through the hub interior until it contacts the grease seal. A gentle tap usually pops the seal out, and the bearing is then free to be removed (Figure 11.28).
   NOTE: Always wear a protective surgical-type breathing mask when working on brake drums, and use water to clean the dust from the drums, linings, and hardware. Never use compressed air to blow dust from the drums.

Cleaning the Bearings

In preparation for reinstallation in the hub, all the old grease should be removed from the bearings before repacking with new grease.

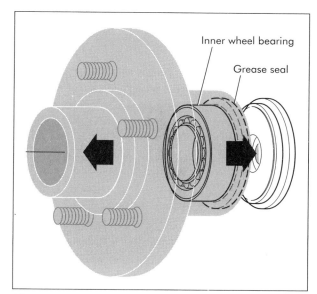

Figure 11.28 A gentle tap is all that is needed to pop out the seal so the bearing can be removed.

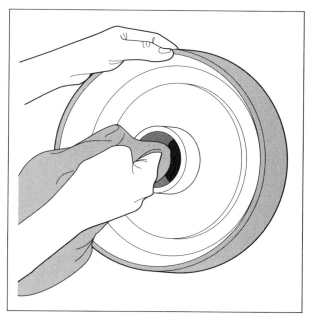

Figure 11.29 The spindle and hub interior must be cleaned of all old grease before reassembly.

CAUTION: For cleaning the bearings and all associated components, use parts-cleaning solvent rather than gasoline, which leaves a dangerous residue.

Clean the bearings thoroughly, until all the old grease is removed. Clean the bearing dust cap, the castle nut, and the bearing washer. When these components are completely free of old grease, set them aside to dry. Do not use compressed air to dry bearings because the stream of air can spin them at a dangerous speed. Tap the bearings on a cloth in the palm of your hand to remove excess solvent, then dry all the rollers with the cloth. Remove all the solvent before repacking with new grease.

While waiting for the bearings to dry, clean the spindle and the hub interior of all old grease (Figure 11.29). This is a messy job, so keep a roll of paper towels handy.

Inspecting the Bearings

Inspect the bearings and races with a critical eye. There is no sense reinstalling worn or damaged bearings—this would only invite failure.

Signs of pitting, scoring, heat damage (indicated by discoloration), or uneven wear patterns are good reasons to discard a bearing and race set. If any of the rollers are imperfectly round, replace the bear-

ing. If there are any signs of cracking, discoloration, or shiny spots (excessive wear) on the race, replace it. Always replace bearings and races as a set.

If you plan to reuse the old bearings, be sure to keep track of which race they mate with, so you don't mismatch the bearings and races upon reinstallation. If new bearings and races are to be used, have a professional shop press the races into place.

Inspecting the Brake Drum

Before reinstalling bearings in the hub, inspect the brake drum. If it has been badly worn or damaged, it may need to be replaced or turned to renew the face of the drum. Damage is evident when the drums show cracks, scoring, excessive wear, or are out of round.

If oil or grease contamination has fouled the drums, use brake-parts solvent to clean the face of the drums. If heavy scoring is evident, the cause may be excessively worn brake linings, loose lining rivets, or particles embedded in the linings.

Out-of-round drums have the appearances of uneven wear—as if the lining had not been contacting the face of the drum at some point. Drums in this condition need to be turned (bored) by a professional brake shop or replaced. If the drums have been

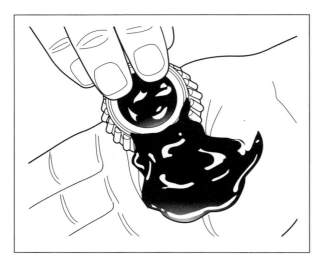

Figure 11.30 Wheel bearings can be packed by hand using a good grade of high-temperature grease if a wheel-bearing packer is not available.

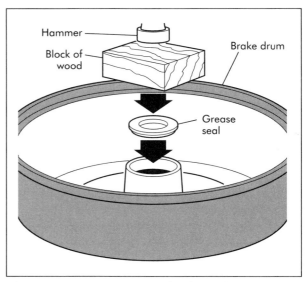

Figure 11.31 New grease wheels can be pressed into the wheel by using a straight block of wood and a hammer.

turned before or are so badly damaged that turning them will remove too much material, the new linings may not contact the drum when the brakes are applied. In such cases, new drums should be installed. Inside-drum measurements taken by the brake shop will determine if new drums are necessary or if the old ones can be reused. Linings should be arced at the same time the drums are turned, but many shops no longer do this because of the dangers related to brake-lining dust.

The drum inspection should include the drum-assembly bolts. If the bolts are loose, they may shear under hard-braking conditions. Replace any bolts that are suspect.

Proceed with the next section only if the original drums are deemed usable.

Packing the Bearings

Use high-temperature wheel-bearing grease to repack the bearings. Unless you have a wheel-bearing packing device, you will have to do the job by hand (Figure 11.30).

Place a blob of grease about the size of a golf ball in the palm of one hand. Grip the bearing with the other hand. Force the side of the bearing (where there is an opening between the roller cages) down onto the grease. Do this repeatedly until the grease starts

to ooze from the top of the bearing and out the bearing face between the rollers. Continue forcing grease through the bearing until it is apparent that grease has filled every cavity between the rollers. Then rotate the bearing to a new spot and begin the process again, forcing grease through the bearing. Continue with this process until you have rotated the bearing all the way around. Lightly coat the races with grease and spread some grease inside the hub.

Reinstalling the Inner Bearing

Follow these steps to reinstall the inner bearing:

1. Lay the drum with the open (inner) side facing up.
2. Position the inner bearing on its race.
3. Place the new grease seal (never reuse an old seal) in position at the spindle opening on the inner side of the hub (Figure 11.31).
4. Place a block of hardwood over the seal and gently tap it with a hammer to drive the seal into the hub. Make sure the seal fits in the hub evenly all around. Drive the seal in until it is beyond flush and below the level of the surrounding hub.

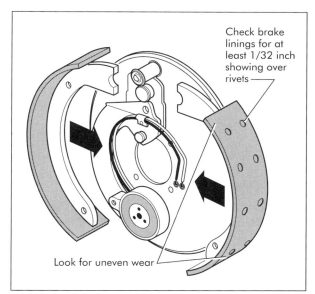

Figure 11.32 Brake linings must be replaced if they have less than ¹⁄₃₂ inch of material showing over the rivets.

Inspecting the Brake Linings

Before proceeding, clean your hands of all grease. Grease or oil contamination will destroy the integrity of brake linings.

If the linings are worn down to within ¹⁄₃₂ inch of the shoe, they should be replaced (Figure 11.32). If the linings have worn unevenly, look for the cause rather than simply replacing the linings. The uneven wear may be caused by a broken return spring, out-of-round drums, grease contamination, or a shoe that has slipped out of position due to failure of a hold-down spring.

If the linings are due for replacement, replace the linings for all the brakes on that axle at the same time.

NOTE: Never replace the linings on only one side of the axle, because this will cause erratic braking.

Removing the Brake Shoes

To remove the brake shoes follow these steps:

1. Remove the shoe-return springs (Figure 11.33) using a brake tool or locking pliers. Be careful, because the springs are under tension.
2. Remove the shoe hold-down springs (Figure 11.34).

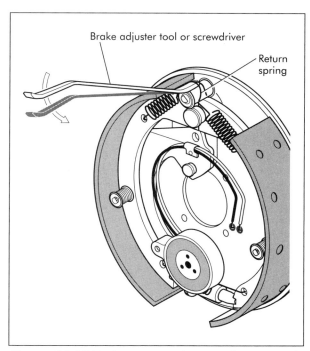

Figure 11.33 Brake return springs can be removed with a brake tool or a screwdriver.

   a. Reach behind the backing plate and hold the head of the hold-down pin to prevent it from turning.

   b. Grasp the hold-down spring retainer (cup) with pliers. Push the retainer in against spring pressure and turn 90 degrees in either direction to align the end of the pin with the slot in the retainer. The retainer and spring will now separate from the pin.

3. Grasp the brake shoes at the top and pull them away from each other. Remove them along with the adjuster mechanism and spring (Figures 11.35 and 11.36).
4. Remove the adjuster mechanism and adjuster spring from the shoes. If these parts are to be reused, clean them thoroughly. Give the adjuster a light coating of lubricant as recommended by the manufacturer.

Inspecting the Magnets

The magnet can be inspected by placing a straight-

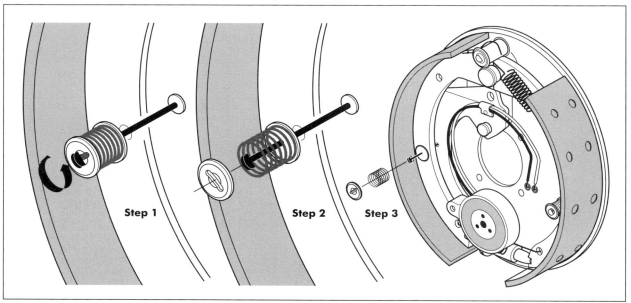

Figure 11.34 Removing the brake-shoe hold-down springs

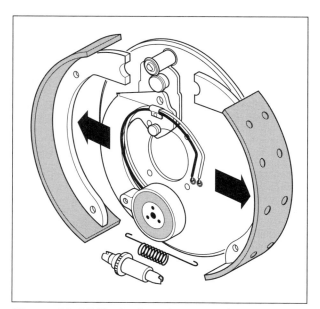

Figure 11.35 The brake-adjuster mechanism and spring must be removed with the linings.

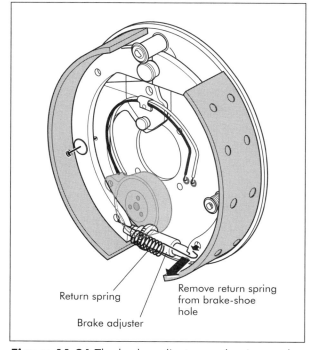

Return spring

Brake adjuster

Remove return spring from brake-shoe hole

Figure 11.36 The brake-adjuster mechanism and spring should be thoroughly cleaned and lubricated before reinstalling.

edge across the magnet's rubbing surface (Figures 11.17 and 11.18 on pages 11.18). If the rubbing surface is flat all the way across, it is contacting the armature correctly.

If the friction element isn't worn too thin, and if there is not excessive scoring from contaminants, the unit need not be replaced.

If the magnet is wearing unevenly, find the cause and correct it before installing a new magnet. The most common cause for uneven magnet wear occurs when a worn lever pivots, allowing the magnet to contact the armature at an angle. If this is the case, replace the entire lever assembly.

When replacing a magnet on one brake, it is necessary to balance the brake system by replacing the counterpart magnet on the opposite end of the axle.

CAUTION: Replacement of magnets on only one side of the trailer will result in erratic braking.

Installing New Magnets

The magnet lead wires usually run through the backing plate to a position behind the brake assembly (Figure 11.37). Reach behind the backing plate to detach the wires, or cut them, whichever applies.

If a grommet protects the wires as they pass through the backing plate, remove it with pliers before pulling the wires through. A new grommet will be needed

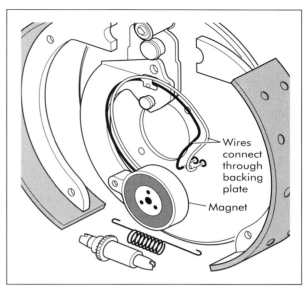

Figure 11.38 New grommets should be used when replacing the wires from the magnet through the backing plate.

in the same location on the wires of the new magnet, prior to magnet installation (Figure 11.38).

The magnet can be replaced with the lever arm in place or removed (Figure 11.39). To remove the lever arm, first carefully remove the clip that holds it in position. Slide the lever off the stud. On Kelsey

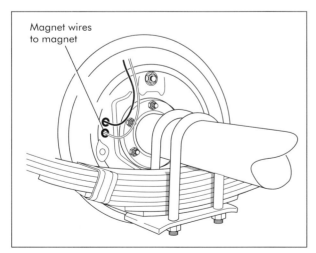

Figure 11.37 Wires to the magnet that are routed through the backing plate must be disconnected or cut before removal.

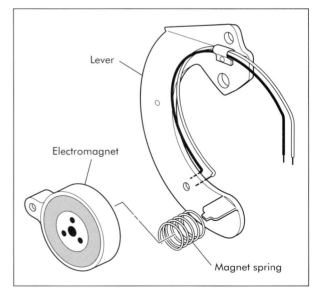

Figure 11.39 Brake magnets are attached to the lever arm, which can be removed to facilitate magnet removal.

brakes, it is necessary to first remove the small spring clip from the positioning stud. On other systems, there is a detent ring inside the magnet assembly. This will slip off easily if the magnet is pulled toward you using a gentle rocking motion. Pay close attention to how the follow-up spring is positioned behind the magnet. The spring pushes against the magnet to maintain proper contact with the armature. This spring will frequently be wider at one end than the other. It must be reinstalled in the proper position. Normally, the wider end is toward the installer.

Install the new magnet, using the new clip included in the magnet kit. If necessary, squeeze the clip with pliers until it fits. Reinstall the lever mechanism if it was removed. Route the magnet lead wires and make the connections. If the wires plug into a socket, clean the socket prior to installation. If the wires were cut, make the connection either by soldering or by using quality crimp connectors. Use heat-shrink material or silicone to protect and strengthen the connection (see page 1.10).

Installing Brake Shoes

With the magnets installed, brake shoes can be reinstalled. When installing new shoes, the primary shoe must be installed toward the front of the trailer and the secondary shoe to the rear.

1. Install an adjuster and adjuster spring on each set of new shoes. Make sure the adjuster nut is on the left side.
2. Position shoes and adjuster mechanism on the backing plate.
3. Install the shoe, the hold-down spring, and the retainer.
4. Install shoe-return springs.

Inspecting the Armature

Armatures (the inside surface of the drum to which the magnet is attracted) generally last the life of the trailer, but they are subject to rusting and scoring.

Light scoring is normal and is caused by contaminants getting between the magnet and the arma-ture. To remove mild rust or scoring, use a solvent and steel wool. If the scoring is substantial, the armature may need to be replaced.

Replacing the Armature

When replacing the armature, it is not necessary to also replace the counterpart armature on the other end of the axle. However, it is wise to inspect all the armatures and their magnets, because they probably have all been exposed to the same damaging conditions.

If the assembly is unicast, the entire unit must be replaced. If the assembly was riveted, drill out the rivets and replace them with nuts and bolts to install the replacement unit.

Reinstalling the Drum Assembly

Follow these steps in reinstalling the brake-drum assembly:

1. Carefully slide the drum over the spindle, taking care to avoid damage to the new grease seal as it slides over its mating ledge on the inner end of the spindle. Push the drum as far as it will go. The drum should entirely cover the shoes.
2. Install the outer wheel bearing over the spindle and press it up into the hub until it meets the bearing race.
3. Slide the bearing washer onto the spindle so that it fits snugly against the bearing.
4. Install the castle nut and finger-tighten it as far as possible.
5. While slowly rotating the drum counterclockwise, tighten the castle nut (to preload the bearings) with a wrench until it is snug, or torque to 50 foot-pounds. Stop spinning the drum. Loosen the nut. Hand-tighten the nut and line up the holes in the spindle with the castle nut; install and bend a new cotter pin.
6. Spin the drum to see that it spins freely; if it doesn't, the shoes may be too tight against the drum. If so, back them off with the brake-adjusting tool until the drum can spin freely.

Final Reassembly

Follow these steps in the final reassembly :

1. Reinstall the bearing dust cap, taking care not to crush it against the nut when tapping the cap down tightly. If the cap is crushed against the nut, a hole will wear in the cap and allow dirt and water to enter.

2. Reinstall the wheels, and torque the lugs according to manufacturer's specifications. Retorque the lugs as specified in Table 11.4, on page 11.21.

■ CHAPTER 12 ■
DINGHY TOWING

Towing a vehicle behind a motorhome, commonly referred to as "dinghy towing" is very popular among RVers. The convenience and the freedom of economical transportation when you arrive at your destination are the main reasons so many motorhome owners have opted to tow.

The equipment used to tow small cars or trucks behind motorhomes typically does not need extensive maintenance. A bit of grease on the hitch ball usually will suffice when a tow bar is used. Wheel bearings should be repacked every year on a tow dolly or trailer, and if the dolly or trailer has brakes, they should be inspected annually. The most important aspects for safe towing are the necessary equipment, installed and used properly, along with vigilance.

A prerequisite for safe towing is use of a proper combination of vehicles. Although a relatively small motorhome may be able to tow a heavy car, the questions are, how far? how well? and how safely? Weight limits prescribed by manufacturers of motorhome chassis are intended to insure adequate performance and braking for the motorhome. Applying these limits to one's personal situation requires knowledge of the motorhome's curb weight and the chassis manufacturer's gross combination weight rating (GCWR). The GCWR is the maximum total weight of the motorhome, towed vehicle, and all their contents (Table 12.1). With knowledge of the motorhome's weight loaded for travel (including passengers), it's possible to calculate the weight allowance for a towed car or truck.

These weight factors encourage motorhome owners to choose compact or subcompact vehicles weighing in the neighborhood of 3,000 pounds. Even when the gross vehicle weight is within the manufacturer's limits, the ability to keep speed in check on steep downhill grades may require more braking than the motorhome can produce from the combined effect of downshifting the transmission (engine-compression braking) and the application of service brakes. Additional discussion of braking will be included later in this chapter. It's also important to consider special requirements of the individual motorhome-chassis manufacturers. Although Ford and Chevy chassis have decent GCWRs, towing may be restricted to only 1,500 pounds if brakes on the towed vehicle or trailer cannot be activated in concert with the motorhome's braking.

A variety of compact cars, sport-utility vehicles, and trucks, including those with front-wheel drive and power steering, are approved by their manufacturers for towing over long distances without speed restrictions (Figure 12.1). In order to determine whether a vehicle is suitable to be towed behind a motorhome, check the owner's manuals of the models you're considering; this is the only way to be sure the vehicle can be towed without drive-train modifications. The owner's manual will have specific written instructions on how to tow behind a motorhome, if it is approved. *Do not* accept a verbal "sure, it's okay to tow" from a dealership salesperson.

The instructions will tell you how to shift the transmission to the correct gear, how fast, and how far you may travel. Some vehicles have very simple instructions like "shift transmission to neutral" while others have somewhat complicated shift procedures that *must* be followed in order to prevent drive-line damage. Manufacturers may specify distance limits before stopping; a common requirement is to stop every 200 miles and run the dinghy vehicle's engine for a few minutes to circulate oil throughout the transmission.

Table 12.1
Gross Combination Weight Ratings (1998 Models)

Model	Weight (lbs.)
Chevrolet	
P Cutaway	19,000
P12 Class A	26,000
P32 Gas/Diesel	17,000–21,000
P72, P92 Rear diesel	20,000–40,000
Country Coach	
Dynomax	36,000–42,700
Ford	
F-Super Duty Class A	26,000
E-350 Class C	18,500
E-Super Duty Class C	20,000
Freightliner	
XC Line	23,000–36,000
VC Line	31,000–36,000
MC Front engine	25,500
Powerliner	40,000
GM	
GM-600 Cutaway	13,500–17,000
Safari Magnum	
Blue Streak	29,000
Blue Max	33,000
Blue Diamond	41,220
Remco	
F2000 Rear diesel	26,000
Roadmaster by Monaco	
Windsor R2800	39,000
Dynasty R2900, R3100	39,500–41,500
Executive R3500-E	45,000
Navigator	39,200
Signature	45,000
Imperial	41,000
Spartan	
Alpine	23,000–28,000
K2	40,000–41,200
Mountain Master	31,000–36,000
Highlander	28,000–31,500
EXP 2001	23,000–28,000
HVC	24,000

Most vehicles that are not approved by their manufacturers for towing on all four wheels can still be towed using aftermarket accessories such as a cable-operated driveshaft-disconnect device (rear-wheel-drive vehicles only), a driveshaft-disconnect device, or free-wheeling hubs (front-wheel drive), a dolly, or a trailer. Yet another option is an automatic-transmission-lubrication-pump system. Such systems, operated by 12-volt DC power from the motorhome, circulate the towed vehicle's transmission fluid to prevent bearing damage; they are available for many models of conventional automatic-transmission cars.

■ TOWING EQUIPMENT ■

Beyond maintaining a realistic weight situation, the choice of towing equipment is important for safety and convenience. Vehicles can be successfully and legally towed three ways: on their own four wheels utilizing a tow bar, with two wheels on a dolly (Figure 12.2), or with the entire vehicle on a trailer (Figure 12.3).

Many owners find that the extra weight of a dolly (310 to 600 pounds, depending on brand and model) or trailer (900 to 2,000 pounds) will not add enough weight to exceed the motorhome chassis manufacturer's GCWR. Proper choice and installation of equipment is especially important when using tow bars since they are mechanically attached to the towed vehicle.

Hitch Platforms and Ball Position

Whether the towing method is a tow bar, dolly, or trailer, height of the hitch ball is important for proper handling and safety. Ball height will vary with the road clearance of the vehicle or trailer, which means that there is no precise ideal ball height, but the average will be around 18 inches. The proper ball height is one that places the tow bar or coupler of the dolly or trailer in a level attitude (Figure 12.4). *This is very important!*

When the ball position is too high or too low, coupler damage is possible if the motorhome is driven in an unusually high or low position relative to the towed vehicle. This high or low position can also cause problems during braking and turning. It's possible that the coupler can be "forced" off the ball during certain conditions. Obviously, this can be a dangerous situation.

A proper hitch setup for a motorhome includes a receiver assembly (Figure 12.5) that does not reduce the motorhome's rear-ground clearance any more than necessary. The receiver should be positioned only slightly below the bumper and securely mounted to the frame of the motorhome. If the ball is positioned at the level of the receiver, it may be too high or too low, depending on the towed vehicle's height. Ball mounts of different configurations are used to create proper ball height regardless of the position of the receiver (Figure 12.6).

Figure 12.1 A variety of compact cars, sport utility vehicles, and trucks are approved for towing over long distances without speed restrictions.

Figure 12.2 Towing with two wheels on a tow dolly

The hitch receiver attached to the motorhome must be clearly rated for the total weight of the towed vehicle and car/dolly or trailer you will be towing. (Ratings are stamped on receivers and on ball mounts.)

Likewise, the tow-bar, the dolly, and the trailer couplers must be clearly stamped with a load rating that is sufficient for the weight being towed.

In addition to heeding the ratings, use a mechanic's creeper to get under the motorhome and check the integrity of the hitch attachment to the motorhome frame. The hitch receiver should be bolted securely with grade 5 or higher bolts and lock washers or lock-

ing nuts. Also, Loctite thread sealant should be used. Check all nuts for tightness. Welding of the receiver to the motorhome frame is *not* recommended.

When the motorhome chassis is not long enough to extend fully to the bumper of the motorhome, the coach builder usually adds chassis extensions. It is these frame extensions, sometimes hastily welded on the chassis, to which the hitch platform is attached. Inspect the quality of the welds that attach the extensions to the chassis.

Hitch balls are available in various quality levels and types. The ball should be stamped with a load rating equal to or in excess of the entire weight of your towed vehicle plus the dolly or trailer, if applicable. If the ball is not stamped with a rating, discard it and buy one that is. The ball should have a stem to allow the coupler full flexibility of movement (Figure 12.7). Don't use a ball without a stem because it restricts the range of movement of the coupler on the ball and in some situations can force the coupler off the ball. When tightening the nut securing it to the mount, make sure you use a lock washer and that there are a number of threads protruding past the end of the nut.

Figure 12.3 Towing with entire vehicle on a trailer

Figure 12.4 Proper ball height places the tow bar or coupler of the dolly or trailer in a level attitude.

Figure 12.5 Hitch-receiver assembly

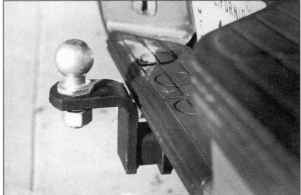

Figure 12.6 Ball mounts of different configurations are used to create proper ball height regardless of receiver position.

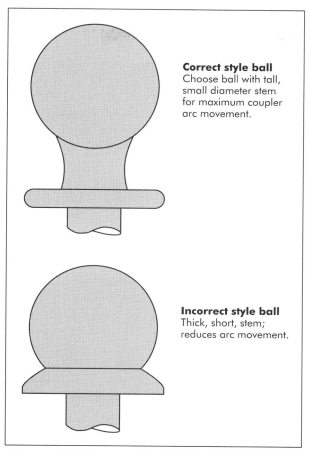

Correct style ball
Choose ball with tall, small diameter stem for maximum coupler arc movement.

Incorrect style ball
Thick, short, stem; reduces arc movement.

Figure 12.7 Coupler movement flexibility depends on the type of ball. In all cases, a ball with a stem should be used.

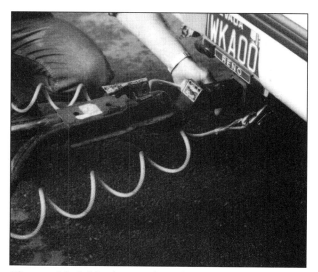

Figure 12.8 Vinyl-coated steel cable can be used instead of chains.

Safety Chains

Federal law requires use of safety chains, regardless of the towing method. Two chains should be used, rated for the equipment involved, either class 2 or class 3 chain rated for 3,500 or 5,000 pounds, respectively. Vinyl-coated steel cable can also be used and is more convenient, with less weight and bulk than chain (Figure 12.8).

The chains or cable should be attached to loops provided in the tow-bar baseplate and in the hitch platform. The chains or cables should be arranged in an X-pattern under the coupler and ball with enough slack so that they do not crimp the pivoting of the coupler on the ball but not with so much slack that they drag in driveways. The purpose of crossing the chains under the ball is so the tow bar or dolly/trailer A-frame will be held off the ground if the coupler should ever become disengaged from the ball.

Tow Bars

Selecting and Installing the Tow Bar

Although rental yards offer tow bars that are designed for temporary installation using chains and partially relying on vehicle bumpers for support, we will limit this discussion to tow bars that are bolted to the frames of towed vehicles—the arrangement most commonly used by motorhome owners.

A variety of tow bars is available, ranging from universal, removable bars, to telescoping, self-align-

Figure 12.9 Tow bar designed to be folded against the front of the car

Figure 12.10 Tow bar designed to be folded against the back of the motorhome

ing bars that offer additional flexibility while positioning the car or truck for hitching. All tow bars should be identified with ratings for maximum vehicle weight. Make sure your towed vehicle's curb weight does not exceed the tow-bar rating.

Locking pins make many tow bars easily removable; they're stowed in the vehicle or with the motorhome until needed. Special tow bars are designed so they can be either folded against the front of the car (Figure 12.9) or the back of the motorhome (Figure 12.10) and locked while the vehicle is driven.

All tow bars utilize a triangular structure for rigidity, whether the structure is steel tubing, flat steel bar, or two lengths of chain that form triangular support for a telescoping center bar. Rigidity is necessary because heavy stress can be exerted on a tow bar during sharp turns or when traveling over uneven terrain.

Many small trucks and 4-wheel-drive vehicles present no significant installation challenges for tow-bar manufacturers. These vehicles typically have a body-on-frame design, offering a system of steel girders in the front of the vehicle for attachment of the tow-bar baseplate (mounting platform). Ideally, the tow-bar manufacturer supplies a baseplate designed specifically for the vehicle so that few, if any, addi-

tional holes must be drilled in the vehicle's frame. The baseplate usually is bolted into place, using grade 5 or higher bolts, lock washers, and Loctite thread sealant as added insurance against loosening, or self-locking nuts may be used.

The design of baseplates for cars with unitbody construction presents a real challenge because such cars do not have conventional frames. The sheet-metal body itself provides the vehicle's rigidity, and designs do not allow stress loads of engine and suspension mounts to concentrate too heavily at single points. Unfortunately, front ends of unitbody cars are not designed with tow-bar attachments in mind, and the tow-bar baseplate designer must take care to distribute stress loads properly. Failure to do so can result in the baseplate-mounting bolts being pulled out of the body, or, in extreme cases, major sheet-metal components may be torn off the car.

In rare situations, where a prefabricated baseplate is not offered by the tow-bar manufacturer, a local welding or hitch shop may be used to build a custom-designed baseplate. Master welders have an excellent understanding of stress loads and can come up with designs that offer acceptable durability. However, mediocre welders have been known to create unsafe designs. Unfortunately, the typical motorhomer may not be knowledgeable enough to choose a competent welder. It's best to choose a tow bar that is supplied with a prefabricated baseplate. If that's not practical or possible, at least choose a welding shop that does a large volume of tow-bar installations or hitches for vehicles that tow large trailers.

Visually Checking the Tow Bar

While traveling, it's important that the motorhome owner visually inspect the tow bar every time the vehicle is stopped. The owner should perform a walk-around that includes these visual inspection points:

- Coupler secured on hitch ball
- Pin (or bolt) securing coupler in locked position
- Hitch ball nut tight
- Ignition key positioned so steering column is unlocked
- Transmission shift lever and/or transfer case

shift lever (4-wheel-drive only) still in the position recommended by the manufacturer for towing

- Hand brake in off position
- All bolts, nuts, and pins on tow bar and baseplate tight
- Wiring harness connected
- Tires inflated properly

Although it includes several points, this inspection takes less than a minute. The walkaround inspection should also include the motorhome's tires and a quick look underneath the chassis for signs of oil or coolant leakage.

Failure to see obvious problems developing is a primary cause of mishaps and costly damage that could be prevented. Many motorhome owners who do not regard themselves as mechanically adept do not take the time to check their equipment, assuming they probably won't recognize a problem. However, owners who take the time to make mental notes of how their rigs are set up may be able to notice when something changes. They may not know if the change presents a problem, but they could find out and possibly prevent an accident or being stranded in a remote location.

It's also best to check tail- and stoplights and directional signals once a day, preferably in the morning before setting out for a day of driving.

Mechanically Checking the Tow Bar

A more detailed mechanical inspection should be performed periodically, as common sense dictates, or once every week while traveling. It should cover these points:

- Inspect all bolts underneath vehicle or otherwise out of sight that are used to attach the tow-bar baseplate to the vehicle.
- Inspect the vehicle body or frame for deformation caused by stress on the bolts.
- All such bolts should have several threads protruding from the nuts when installed. A lower number of threads protruding will be a danger signal without having to retorque each nut with a wrench. Deformation of

metal components indicates improper design of the baseplate.

- Inspect the bolts securing the hitch platform to the motorhome..
- Check the wiring for chafing or damage.
- Inspect all tow-bar pivot points for any excessive wear.

Tow-Bar Cleaning and Lubrication

Generally, tow bars require very little maintenance other than cleaning and lubrication. Tow bars are constantly subjected to road debris and particles of grit and dirt. Clean the entire surface with WD-40 or an equivalent product; use a generous amount and make sure you cover all the wear points. Wipe clean with a dry cloth and allow the wear points to drain, then wipe again. Spray the entire surface with a silicone lubricant, such as Roadmaster's LUBEmaster 100% Pure Silicone Spray. Silicone spray will provide a protective film without attracting dirt. Proper cleaning and lubrication will help prevent corrosion. The cleaning and lubrication procedure is especially important for tow bars with sliding bars or tubes.

If your tow bar has stainless-steel arms that have become scratched or corroded, clean the surface with extra-fine steel wool (#0000) or a fine pad like the one made by 3M under the Scotch Brite label.

Dollies and Trailers

Dollies (Figure 12.2, page 12.3) first became popular with motorhome owners when only a few manufacturers of small, front-wheel-drive cars approved of their cars being towed. Many motorhome owners prefer dinghy vehicles with automatic transmissions. There are a few manufacturers that approve of towing with all four on the ground with an automatic transmission without drivetrain modifications as listed earlier in this chapter. A dolly immobilizes the front (drive) wheels of the car, eliminating any concern about transmission damage while towing. Obviously, it does no good to tow a rear-wheel-drive vehicle on a dolly.

Dollies are basically small trailers equipped with ramps that haul one axle of a vehicle. While it is possible to tow with the rear axle on the dolly, it is generally not recommended, since towing a vehicle backward can present problems with tracking and stability. One of the most significant advantages of a dolly or a trailer is availability of brakes, either hydraulic surge-type or electric, which can make a sizable difference in braking capacity while traveling mountainous terrain.

Trailers are used by a small number of motorhomers who want the ultimate protection of the car against damage to the drivetrain as well as to the paint while towing—motorhome owners who don't mind the inconvenience of parking a trailer after arrival at a destination. Trailers of various weight capacities can be purchased for towing a wide range of car sizes and weights. The weight of a towed car on a trailer is more apt to exceed the motorhome manufacturer's GCWR, which is still an important factor, even though braking may not be a limitation. Gasoline-powered motorhomes usually are not capable of climbing steep mountain grades at acceptable speeds when gross combined weight approaches or exceeds the chassis manufacturer's GCWR.

Dolly Loading and Tie-down

Tie-down systems of several designs are used to hold the vehicle rigidly in place on the dolly or trailer. The owner should be sure that the tie-downs are not too large or too small for the tires of the towed vehicle. A tie-down that is too large will not hold the tire securely, and one that is too small may not be properly fastened. Be sure that nylon or other fabric tie-downs do not come in contact with metal parts that can cut fabric.

Stop and recheck tie-downs after five to ten miles of driving to make sure road vibration has not loosened any components. Regular rechecking about every 200 miles is advisable. Check the coupler locking mechanism as well.

Lubricating the Dolly

Some dollies have few lubrication points other than the hitch ball, while others have pivoting platforms that require oil. In all cases, repack wheel bearings

every 10,000 miles or every two years under normal conditions.

Dolly- and Trailer-Brake Maintenance

Electric or surge brakes should be adjusted approximately every 3,000 miles of travel or as needed to maintain good brake effectiveness. Since electric brakes can be actuated independently of motorhome brakes (via the brake controller), it's possible to independently test dolly- or trailer-brake effectiveness periodically. However, effectiveness of surge brakes may be difficult to measure accurately because surge brakes function only in concert with the motorhome's brakes. Thus it is necessary to adjust brakes on a regular basis.

Dolly- and Trailer-Brake Adjustment

Dolly and trailer surge or electric brakes require manual adjustment of brake-shoe position, the same procedure used on cars and light trucks before the advent of automatic adjusters. To adjust brakes:

1. Hitch dolly or trailer to motorhome and set motorhome emergency brake. Block wheels.
2. Jack up one wheel of the dolly or trailer so the wheel can be spun freely.
3. Remove the rubber plug from the brake adjustment slot at the bottom center of the brake-backing plate.
4. Using a flashlight, locate the round, toothed wheel (starwheel) just inside the slot. To determine which direction to turn the starwheel for tightening, use a brake-adjusting tool (available at auto-supply stores) to turn the starwheel while spinning the tire. If after turning the starwheel at least half a turn you don't hear the brake shoes begin to drag on the drum, reverse the direction.
5. Tighten the starwheel adjustment until the brake shoes make it impossible to spin the tire. Then loosen the adjustment until the brake shoes drag very lightly.
6. Reinsert the plug in the adjustment slot and adjust remaining brakes the same way.

Remove the jack and all the tools when completed.

Checking Dolly and Trailer Hitching

Check the dolly and the trailer for the following:

- The coupler is secured on the hitch ball. Lift the coupler to make sure. Install the coupler locking pin or bolt. Check the coupler fit. The coupler adjusting nut should be tightened to make firm contact with the ball, but it should not be so tight that latching the coupler is difficult.
- Safety chains are attached (arranged in an X under the ball).
- The license plate is in place.
- The wheel platforms are tilted into position; the pivot platform is in proper position (if applicable).
- The car/truck is properly positioned on the wheel platforms.
- The wheel tie-downs are tightened and locked.
- The steering wheel is locked with wheels straight ahead.
- The wheel platforms are locked (if applicable).
- The electrical plug is connected; lights function properly?
- Check the wheel lug nuts. Torque to 90 pounds or to the rating provided by the dolly or trailer manufacturer. Recheck once a week while traveling.
- Check the tire pressure; inflate to dolly or trailer manufacturer's recommendation, if different from the maximum inflation pressure stamped on the tire sidewall.

Lights and Wiring

All states require towed vehicles to have legal brake-, tail-, and turn-signal lights actuated by the motorhome's lighting system. Dollies and trailers are fitted with appropriate lights by their manufacturers, and a 4- or 6-wire receptacle can be installed at the rear of the motorhome to make the connection to the towed vehicle.

The motorhome owner who tows a vehicle on its own wheels with a tow bar must either use the towed vehicle's taillights or add an independent tail/signal light system. When using the towed vehicle's lights, the common wiring method is to splice three wires from the motorhome (tail, left turn, and right turn) into the wiring harness leading to the towed vehicle's rear lights. The splice point should be close to the taillight/stoplight housings.

Electrical feedback problems can occur with late-model vehicles. Current from the motorhome may feed back through the towed vehicle's lighting system into ignition components or other control systems. This can be prevented by using a taillight wiring kit that includes diodes that are one-way electrical valves (Figure 12.11). Most systems require the use of two diodes. If the motorhome and towed vehicle have separated brake and turn signals, then you'll need to use four diodes (Figure 12.12). These electrical devices are available from a variety of sources, including most RV supply stores. Light bars require a simple 4-wire hookup that is identical to the system used for a dolly or trailer (Figure 12.13).

Motorhomes that use turn signals that are separate from brake lights (Figure 12.14) require use of a solid-state converter (in addition to the diodes) to provide compatibility with the conventional lights of a dolly or trailer in which the same light is used for brakes and turn signals. Such converters are available from RV supply stores. Conversely, many towed cars and trucks now use turn-signal lights that are separate from the brake-light system. If your motorhome does not have a compatible turn-signal system, you will need an adapter to split the motorhome's turn-signal circuit to feed the towed car's dual-bulb system (Figure 12.15). Pay close attention to the packaging for these converters and match the one needed by your system.

Problems with intermittent loss of power to taillights and turn-signal lights involve poor ground connections, improperly crimped electrical connectors, and deterioration of wiring due to vibration when solderless connectors are used. The connectors can become loose and cause intermittent open circuits.

An independent lighting system that's permanently installed in the towed vehicle can also be utilized. Auto-bulb-type sockets with wire leads can be mounted inside the taillight fixtures of the towed vehicle, providing there's enough room. These sockets

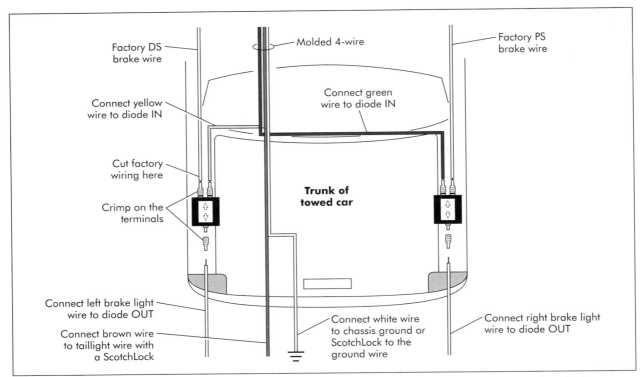

Figure 12.11 Electrical feedback problems are eliminated by using diodes when wiring a dingly vehicle.

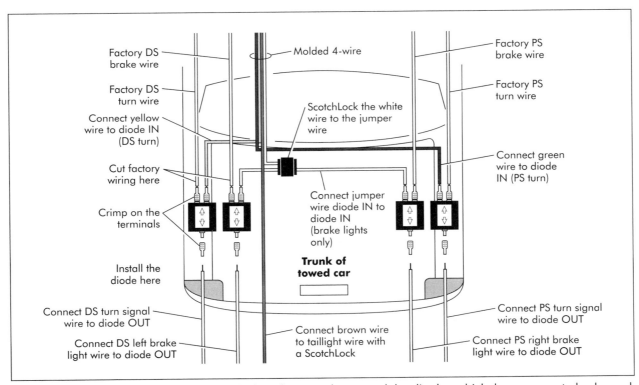

Figure 12.12 Four diodes must be used when the motorhome and the dinghy vehicle have separate brake and turn-signal bulbs.

Figure 12.13 Light bars are simple to use but can be unsightly if not removed from the vehicle.

are available at most auto-parts stores. Use 16/4 automotive wire and route it from the front of the towed vehicle, along the chassis, and to the taillight fixtures. Make sure one of the wires is used as a ground.

Plugs and Receptacles

Four-wire systems can use a molded flat connector or the 4-pin round-type connector. If you are using the molded flat connector, make sure that the hot wires (from the motorhome wiring) are spliced into the side with the shielded terminals (Figure 12.16).

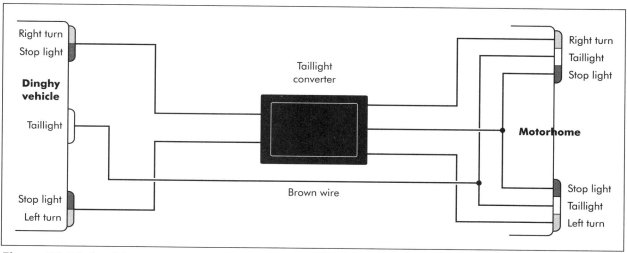

Figure 12.14 A solid-state converter is used when the motorhome has turn signals that are separate from the brake lights.

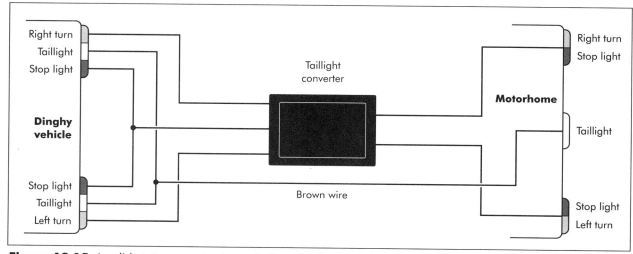

Figure 12.15 A solid-state converter is used when the dinghy vehicle has separate turn signals and brake lights.

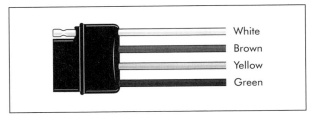

Figure 12.16 Half of a 4-pin molded connector used on a motorhome

- Universal Wiring Code, 4-Wire, flat and round connectors:
- White: Chassis ground
- Brown: Taillights
- Yellow: Left brake/turn
- Green: Right brake/turn

A better method for wire connection is to use the 4-pin plug/receptacle (Figure 12.17). The receptacle can be mounted on the motorhome's bumper or a convenient location and the plug on the end of a cable that connects the towed-car's lighting system. A more custom setup includes a receptacle mounted on the motorhome and front of the towed vehicle, using a coiled cable with plugs on each end (Figure 12.18). With this system, the wiring can be disconnected and stored when not towing. Six-wire connectors must be used when the motorhome and towed vehicle have separated brake and turn-signal lights. Typically, five of the six positions will be used to connect the appropriate wiring (Figure 12.19).

Using the Brakes

With extra weight tagging along behind, it's always wise to allow an extra margin of stopping distance than normally would be required. Any motorhome

Socket Pin #	Wire Color	Motorhome	Car
3	Green	Right turn	Right turn
1	Yellow	Left turn	Left turn
4	Brown	Taillight	Taillight
2	White	Ground	Ground

Figure 12.17 It's best to use a 4-pin round plug/receptacle when wiring a motorhome and dinghy vehicle.

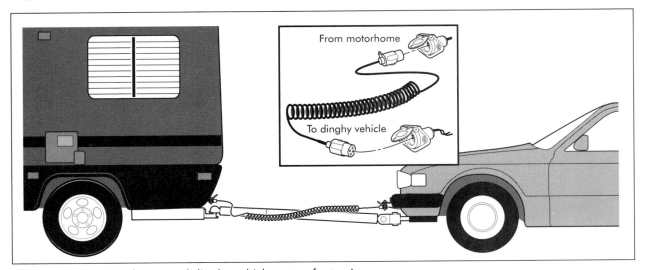

Figure 12.18 Motorhome and dinghy vehicle set-up for towing

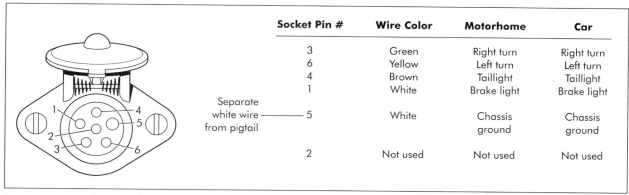

	Socket Pin #	Wire Color	Motorhome	Car
	3	Green	Right turn	Right turn
	6	Yellow	Left turn	Left turn
	4	Brown	Taillight	Taillight
	1	White	Brake light	Brake light
Separate white wire from pigtail	5	White	Chassis ground	Chassis ground
	2	Not used	Not used	Not used

Figure 12.19 Six-pin plug/receptacle must be used when motorhome and dinghy vehicle have separate brake lights and turn signals.

towing a vehicle should always have the capability of making an emergency stop on a downhill grade, even though service brakes have been used intermittently to retard speed. It's usually necessary to use service brakes frequently to retard speed on downhill grades in mountainous terrain, sometimes to the extent that partial brake fade occurs. Fade is caused by overheating of brake pads, rotors, shoes, and drums to the point where friction between the two is partially or fully lost. Although the brake pedal may feel firm, little or no reduction of speed occurs.

The RVer who is towing a vehicle on its own wheels must use lower gears to retard speed and minimize use of service brakes. If weight is too high to avoid excessive use of service brakes, additional braking in the form of a brake-equipped dolly, a brake actuating tow bar, an engine-braking system, or a driveline retarder for the motorhome is needed.

There are several manufacturers offering products that apply the towed vehicle's brakes in response to motorhome braking. The complexity of today's braking systems, ABS (antilock braking system), and computer-controlled braking makes actuating the dinghy's brakes a real challenge. Technology in this area is advancing rapidly. Expect several good dinghy-braking systems to be on the market in the next few years.

There are many engine-braking systems available for diesel-powered motorhomes. Exhaust brakes work very well with diesels, providing extra compression resistance when coasting. These types of brakes are also available for gasoline engines. Diesel owners also have the option of a compression brake, sometimes know as a "Jake" brake, named after its manufacturer, Jacobs. This device is extremely effective as it alters the engine's valve timing, turning it into an efficient air compressor, providing heavy resistance when coasting downhill. Another option for diesel owners is a retarder built into the automatic transmission. A torque converter-like device uses the transmission's hydraulic fluid to provide resistance. This system works very well but must be carefully matched to the individual transmission. The heat generated is dispersed through the transmission-oil cooler.

Driveline retarders have become popular because they require no modification to the motorhome's engine. These devices are installed on the driveshaft and operate electrically. A rotor, surrounded by an electrical coil, is connected to the driveshaft. When current (12-volt DC) is passed through the surrounding coils, a strong magnetic field is formed, which slows the rotor. Braking force is controlled by the amount of electrical current passing through the coils. Heat is generated in the coils and is dissipated to the surrounding air.

Remco Lube Pump

The lube pump allows towing automatic-transmission vehicles on all four wheels without damaging the transmission. It uses a $\frac{1}{8}$-hp self-priming pump that provides lubrication for the transmission while the vehicle is being towed without the engine running. The motorhome is connected to the towed vehicle with a single cable that operates the pump, the monitor, and the towed-vehicle taillights. A fail-safe electronic alarm system is built into the monitor, providing a visual and audible signal if the pump is not delivering an adequate amount of oil to the transmission. When you plug in your towed vehicle to the motorhome with the motorhome ignition on, the red light and alarm will operate until the monitor switch is turned on and the pump is operating.

If the red light/alarm comes on with the motorhome engine running, the monitor switch on, and the towed vehicle connected, check the following:

- Make sure the 10-amp fuse is in the blue wire at the fuse holder.
- Check the connection of the blue wire to the motorhome battery.
- Make sure the connections on the coiled cable between the motorhome and towed vehicle are secure at the sockets.
- Assure proper ground on both vehicles is okay.
- Check that power is at the red wire at the socket of the motorhome.

If the pump is running, check the following:

- Transmission-fluid level in the towed vehicle.
- Damage of the socket wiring and the lube pump hoses.
- Use a test light to check power across both terminals of the pressure sensor at the selector valve.
- Flow of transmission fluid from pump before and after the pump filter. It should pump a quart of fluid in ten to twelve seconds. If not, replace the filter.
- Make sure there are no grounding/shorts of the red wire of the 2-conductor cable running back from the monitor to the socket of the motorhome.

If the motorhome engine is on, the monitor switch is off while not towing the vehicle, and the monitor red light/alarm comes on intermittently while driving the motorhome or comes on continuously, check for a short to ground in the red wire between the monitor and the rear socket.

If the motorhome engine is running with the towed vehicle connected and monitor lights are off (red and green), check the following:

- Fuse in the orange wire (1-amp fuse), with the engine switch on.
- Connection to ignition accessory terminal.
- White ground connection from monitor.

■ MISCELLANEOUS TOWING TIPS ■

Motorhome owners who tow a vehicle on its own wheels find that the miles on the odometer of the towed vehicle accumulate rapidly, reducing the resale value of the vehicle. Speedometer-tampering laws of recent years have made it very difficult, illegal, or impossible to disconnect a speedometer drive. There are several products on the market that disconnect the cable when the wiring harness is plugged into the motorhome. Be aware that these devices are only "legal" when operated as prescribed in the owner's manual. A number of late-model vehicles use an electronic-odometer system, which does not add miles when the ignition key is turned to the off position (which it is when you are towing). You may want to consider this factor when shopping for a tag-along for your RV.

Some compact cars and trucks track better than others while being towed due to differing steering geometry. If a vehicle does not track well, have an alignment shop set the front-wheel caster to the maximum factory-recommended setting. Always maintain maximum air pressure in tires to help reduce tire wear.

If the towed vehicle's front wheels have a tendency to reverse-steer (crank all the way in the wrong direction when turning sharply) it may be necessary to use a stretch-type cord to anchor the steering wheel to a point on the driver's seat so the wheel cannot make a full revolution. This is not ideal because it will accelerate tire wear, but it will prevent an annoying lockup situation in driveways and on other uneven terrain. A little experimentation with cord tension and you'll find the right setup that minimizes tire wear and prevents the wheel from going full crank.

Avoid sharp turns at slow speeds. Motorhomes have long rear overhangs, and sharp turns cause rapid lateral movement of the hitch ball. This tends to drag the towed vehicle sideways.

CAUTION: While towing with a tow bar or dolly, don't back up. The car or dolly will not steer in the motorhome's intended direction and the car will be dragged sideways.

CHAPTER 13

DRIVETRAIN SYSTEMS

An RV engine is the heart of the drivetrain, which consists of an engine, a transmission, a driveshaft, a differential, axles, and wheel bearings. The engine is a complex piece of machinery that requires proper lubrication and tune-up intervals to live up to its performance potential.

The types and varieties of engines range all the way from a small 1.5-liter four-cylinder type found in a compact car to a 8.0-liter gasoline V-10 to a thundering 525-horsepower diesel in a high-line motorhome. Because each type requires a systematic approach to both maintenance and troubleshooting, every RV owner should become familiar with the requirements of his or her particular engine. To identify the engine, check the emissions sticker attached under the hood or on the engine's valve cover. Most heavy-duty diesel engines have a stamped metal plate riveted directly to the engine block or to one of its cover housings. If the sticker or plate is missing, check with the vehicle manufacturer to make positive identification of the engine. It is vital to know the engine type, displacement (size), and sometimes the serial number, so that the proper parts and accessories can be purchased.

■ ENGINE SERVICE AND REPAIR ■

Most vehicles will be difficult to start without a fully charged battery that is in good condition. Make sure that connections are clean and tight. A battery can be charged with a trickle charger over a period of hours or by using a fast charger that can boost the battery in about thirty minutes (see page 1.14).

Fuel-Filter Replacement

Engines have a fuel filter installed in the system to prevent dirt and debris from reaching the carburetor (or fuel injectors). Periodic maintenance of this element can prevent many roadside difficulties. Depending on the vehicle, fuel filters are found in a variety of locations.

The Inlet The filter is located either behind the fuel-inlet nut on the carburetor or enclosed in a small canister that screws on the front of the carburetor bowl (Figure13.1).

The In-line Filter A metal or plastic canister is located between the fuel pump and the carburetor (Figure 13.2). This type of filter is easily replaced by removing the hose clamps and replacing with a new ele-

Figure 13.1 The carburetor inlet filter is usually located behind the fuel-inlet nut.

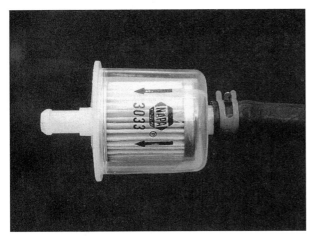

Figure 13.2 In-line filters can be made of plastic or metal; all these filters are flow-directional.

ment. In-line filters used for fuel-injection systems are under a great amount of pressure and can pose a serious danger if the pressure is not relieved before removing. Make sure that the flow-direction arrow is pointed toward the carburetor so that the filter will function correctly.

On the Fuel Pump Many older RVs use a filter located on the bottom of the fuel pump, housed in a screw-on container. By simply removing the container, a new element can be installed in minutes.

In-Tank Filters Many newer vehicles, especially those with fuel injection, utilize an intake filter that consists of a fine-mesh screen formed like a sock on the end of the fuel pickup. These screens require no periodic maintenance; however, if dirty fuel blocks the screen, fuel pressure will be low and performance poor. In some cases, a blocked filter sock can create symptoms similar to vapor lock. In most models, the fuel tank must be drained and dropped to facilitate cleaning of the screen.

Diesel engines usually have two (a primary and a secondary) filtering systems that remove particles much smaller in diameter than are caught by gasoline filters. This is necessary because diesel-injection systems require extremely clean fuel. Diesel-fuel systems also have a water trap; diesel fuel has an affinity for water. Unlike gasoline engines, which can pass water relatively easily through the combustion chambers of the engine, water will not pass through the small holes in the diesel-injection nozzles.

When fuel filters for a diesel engine are changed, it is necessary to bleed the system of air. The injection system will not function properly with air in the filters or lines. Depending on the type of diesel engine you are dealing with, the filter change/bleeding operation will vary. Check the owner's manual for your particular application.

Air-Filter Service

Changing the air filter is probably the easiest maintenance operation to perform on any vehicle (Figure 13.3). Be sure to check for the correct type and size air-cleaner element. The wrong air-cleaner element can allow air to pass over instead of through the element, where dirt particles can be removed. Tests have shown that an engine's life is only about a third of what it could be when it is operated without an air-cleaner element. To change the air-cleaner element:

1. Purchase the correct size air filter for the make and model of your RV's engine.
2. Open the air-cleaner housing and lift or pull out the old element.
3. Do not attempt to clean the old element. Air filters are relatively inexpensive; use a new one.
4. Make sure the new element you are installing is exactly the same type as the old one.
5. Drop the new element into the housing and replace the cover. Tighten the cover securely.

Figure 13.3 Clogged air cleaners can decrease performance and shorten engine life.

Oil and Filter Changes

Changing the engine oil and filter, one of the most important maintenance procedures to prolong the life of an RV engine, is also easy and inexpensive to do in your own backyard. Use only top-quality oil and filters; bargain-basement lubricants may do more harm than good in the long run. Use only SH- or SJ-rated oils for gas engines and CG4-rated oils for diesels. Follow the manufacturer's viscosity recommendations for the ambient outdoor temperatures you expect to encounter. Generally, for gasoline engines, 20W-50 works well for summer use and 10W-30 for cold (consistently below 32°F) winter driving. If you have a diesel engine, carefully check the oil requirements. Most heavy-duty diesels require a 15W-40 viscosity rating meeting the CG4 standards, while lesser-duty types may have different requirements.

Engine oil and filter changes can be accomplished by following these simple steps:

1. Check the owner's manual for the engine-oil capacity with a filter change. Purchase the correct quantity of oil and the correct oil filter for the engine.
2. Operate the engine until it is fully warmed. It will require seven to ten miles of driving to fully warm the engine.
3. With a proper-fitting wrench or socket, loosen the drain plug in the oil pan (Figure 13.4).
4. Drain the oil into a suitable container for proper disposal. Used oil is accepted at most service stations for recycling.
5. While the oil is draining, remove the oil filter with a filter wrench (Figure 13.5).
6. Clean the oil-filter base on the engine block with a rag. Make sure that the oil filter's O-ring gasket came off with the old filter and did not stick to the filter base on the engine.
7. Wipe a thin film of clean oil on the gasket of the new filter and screw it into place. Fill the oil filter with fresh oil first if it mounts vertically to the engine, and hand tighten with a three-quarter turn after the gasket contacts the filter base.
8. Next, replace the drain plug in the oil pan and tighten snugly.

Figure 13.4 A proper fitting wrench or socket must be used to remove the oil-pan drain plug, or the plug head might be stripped.

Figure 13.5 There are many tool configurations for removing oil filters.

9. Fill the crankcase with the proper amount of oil and replace the fill cap.
10. Start the engine. Watch the oil-pressure gauge or light: If pressure is not attained after fifteen to twenty seconds, shut off the engine before damage can be done. If pressure does not build, check for leakage. It is rare that the oil pressure fails to return to normal after an oil change, but if it does fail, have a professional check the system before running the engine.
11. Once the oil pressure is confirmed, check for any external leaks around the drain plug and filter gasket while the engine is running to

■ TROUBLESHOOTING ■
THE ENGINE

Problem	Possible Cause	Correction
Will not start	Low battery	Charge or replace
	Out of fuel	Refill
	Clogged fuel filter	Clean or replace
	Faulty ignition	Repair
	Wet ignition components	Dry ignition with hair dryer
	Flooded carburetor	Wait fifteen minutes, retry
	Inoperative carb choke	Adjust and clean
	Vapor lock	Let engine cool
	Defective starter	Replace
	Bad starter solenoid	Replace
Hard to start	Inoperative carb choke	Adjust and clean
	Damp ignition parts	Dry parts
	Weak battery	Charge or replace
	Incorrect timing	Check and reset timing
	Dirty air filter	Replace with new filter
	Worn spark plugs	Replace with new plugs
	Faulty ignition cables	Replace with new cables
	Contaminated fuel	Fill with fresh fuel
	Clogged fuel filter	Clean or replace filter
	Wrong oil viscosity	Replace with proper type for climate
	Overheating engine	Check cooling system
Lack of power	Clogged air cleaner	Replace
	Worn spark plugs	Replace
	Poor fuel delivery	Check fuel pressure
	Wrong ignition timing	Check and reset timing
	Incorrect fuel mixture	Repair or recalibrate carburetor
	Poor engine compression	Check cylinder compression
	Restricted exhaust	Examine exhaust components
	Dragging brakes	Examine brake system
	Worn cam timing chain	Replace
Low oil pressure	Low oil level	Fill to proper level
	Inaccurate gauge	Compare with good gauge
	Incorrect oil viscosity	Replace with proper oil for climate
	Aerated, level too high	Confirm dipstick reading
	Worn engine bearings	Overhaul engine
	Defective oil pump	Replace with new pump
	Clogged pickup screen	Clean and replace
	Diluted oil	Inspect for coolant contamination

■ TROUBLESHOOTING ■
THE ENGINE, continued

Problem	Possible Cause	Correction
Burning excessive oil	Clogged PCV or hose	Replace
	Worn piston rings	Overhaul engine
	Defective bearings	Overhaul engine
	Worn valve guides	Valve job with new guides
	External engine leaks	Replace defective gaskets
	Vacuum leak	Replace intake-manifold gasket
	Defective valve seals	Replace with new seals
Overheating	Loose fan belt	Check belt tension
	Low coolant level	Inspect for level or leaks
	Dirty radiator fins	Clean radiator
	Obstructed radiator	Remove obstruction
	Clogged radiator core	Clean or replace radiator
	Failed water pump	Replace
	Bad radiator cap	Check holding pressure
	Wrong ignition timing	Check and reset timing
	Lean fuel/air ratio	Calibrate or adjust carburetor
	Collapsed radiator hose	Replace soft hoses
	Stuck thermostat	Replace thermostat
	Broken fan shroud	Replace
	Faulty thermostatic fan	Check for engagement
	Improper coolant	Verify 50-50 ratio
	Leaking head gasket	Perform cylinder-leak test
	Blocked exhaust system	Inspect for obstruction
	Cracked head or block	Perform cylinder-leak test

assure that the job is leak-free.

12. Repeat this oil-changing routine every 3,000 miles or according to the schedule in your owner's manual for severe service.

Ignition Systems

Service and repair of ignition systems are becoming increasingly complex with the extensive use of electronic computer-controlled circuitry. Expensive specialized testing equipment is needed to analyze most electronic-ignition systems; this is best left to a repair facility. When these electronic systems go down, there is little that can be done by the average do-it-yourselfer except to replace suspected parts. If your RV utilizes a replaceable control unit (sometimes known as a "black box" or module), you can purchase and carry a spare. This may prove, however, to be expensive with some models of ignition systems. Replacement instructions vary widely; follow the replacement-part manufacturer's instructions exactly.

Checking the Ignition System

There are very few RVs on the road that utilize a points ignition system; in the past few years electronic-ignition systems have been supplied by vehicle manufacturers as original equipment. If your rig has a points system, you can easily carry spare parts for roadside repair.

To check the ignition system, follow these steps:

1. Remove a spark-plug cable and hold it about ½ inch from a ground source (Figure 13.6).
2. Crank the engine and look for a spark jumping from the cable to the ground surface.
3. No spark or a short yellow (weak) spark indicates ignition trouble.
4. With a points-ignition system, remove the distributor cap and check to see that the points open and close when the engine is cranked.
5. Points should open about .020 inch (about the thickness of five or six sheets of paper). If not, open them using a feeler gauge between the contacts when the point-rubbing block is on the peak of one of the distributor cam lobes.
6. If you have a test light or a multimeter (DC volts) make sure there is power to the movable contact of the points. Open the points and turn on the ignition switch. Place the positive test lead on the movable contact and the other lead to ground: There should be about 9 volts to the point's movable contact. If voltage is present, but there still is no spark, the problem is narrowed to the ignition coil or the condenser. The condenser can be tested with the points open using a multimeter (ohms). There should be infinite resistance between the body of the condenser and the pigtail lead leaving the condenser. If not, the condenser is internally grounded and must be replaced.
7. If replacing the condenser does not result in spark from the coil, the coil should be replaced.
8. Sometimes failure to start is caused by moisture in the coil or distributor. The only solution is to remove the moisture. Remove the distributor cap and dry the inside. A dry paper towel or rag works well. Or if you have an RV equipped with an AC generator, use an electric hair-dryer to dry components quickly, especially in those hard-to-get-at locations.

Figure 13.6 Hold the spark-plug cable about ½ inch from a ground source and crank the engine to check for ignition spark.

Ignition Timing

Proper ignition timing is vital to engine performance and economy (Figure 13.7). Timing can be set accurately with a precision timing light. Timing settings vary widely among engine types, sizes, and year of manufacture. The correct setting can be found on the underhood emission sticker or by checking the service manual for the model year and displacement of engine. In electronic fuel-injected engines, timing is controlled by the on-board computer and should not be set by the vehicle owner.

It is often necessary to use a specially shaped tool, called a distributor wrench, to loosen the hold-down bolt because of poor accessibility to the bolt (Figure 13.8). One rule to remember: Rotating the distributor in the same direction that the distributor shaft turns will retard the timing; rotating the distributor in the opposite direction of the shaft rotation will advance the timing (Figure 13.9).

Setting the Timing

To set engine timing:

1. Make sure the crankshaft pulley is clean and timing marks are visible.
2. Connect the timing light to the battery and number 1 spark-plug cable.
3. Loosen the hold-down bolt until the distribu-

Figure 13.7 Accessibility of timing marks in some vehicles is sometimes poor, but here the timing mark is fairly easy to view.

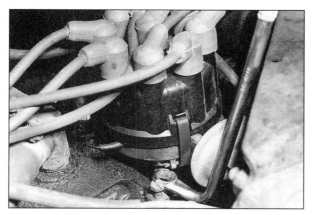

Figure 13.8 A distributor wrench is the best tool for loosening the hold-down bolt on the distributor.

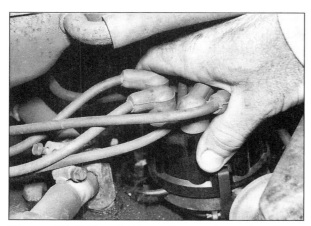

Figure 13.9 The distributor is turned to adjust the timing; rotation in the same direction of the distributor shaft retards the timing.

tor moves under moderate pressure. Remove the vacuum hose leading to the distributor-advance diaphragm and plug it (most engines).

4. Make sure the timing-light wires are clear of the belts and fan; start the engine and allow it to idle at factory-recommended speed (off choke).

5. Aim the light at the timing marker. Make small corrections by moving the distributor slightly until the correct timing setting lines up with the marker (Figure 13.10).

6. Tighten the distributor hold-down bolt and check setting again; repeat if the setting changed when the hold-down bolt was tightened.

Carburetor Flooding

Engine flooding is caused by an excessive amount of fuel entering the cylinders, resulting in an engine that is difficult or impossible to start. The situation also causes oil to be washed from the cylinder walls, causing rapid wear of piston rings. Ultimately the oil in

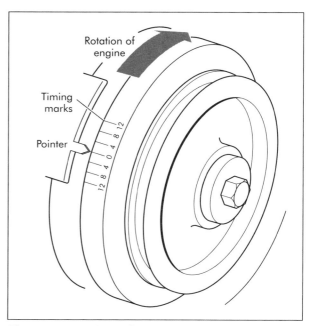

Figure 13.10 Once the timing setting marks line up with the pointer, the distributor must be tightened and the timing rechecked.

the crankcase can become diluted, leading to early engine-bearing failure. Flooding is sometimes a problem at high altitudes, where gasoline boils more easily. This causes fuel to bubble over into the intake manifold. The most common causes are defective or improperly adjusted carburetor floats, defective needle and seat assemblies, dirty air-cleaner elements, and poorly adjusted carburetor chokes. EFI (electronic fuel injection) systems have nearly eliminated engine flooding with their precise control of fuel delivery, whether conditions are hot or cold. Here are the procedures to start a flooded engine:

1. Wait fifteen minutes before attempting to start a flooded engine. This time will allow some of the fuel in the cylinders to dissipate.
2. Do *not* pump the accelerator pedal. This only worsens the situation by inducing additional fuel into the engine.
3. After fifteen minutes, press the accelerator to the floor and hold the throttle wide open while cranking the engine. This allows the maximum amount of air to enter the cylinders while adding a minimum amount of fuel.
4. If the engine still does not start, remove the air-cleaner cover and check the carburetor choke plate. When the engine is warm, the choke plate should be open, standing in a vertical position. If it is not open, it can be manually propped open and the engine then cranked over. Caution should be exercised here not to crank the engine with the air-cleaner cover off, which can result in a fire should the engine backfire upon starting. If it is stuck closed, the most likely cause is dirty or bent linkage or a defective choke-control unit. Commercially available carburetor cleaners can be used to clean dirty linkage. If this does not cure the problem, the control unit should be replaced and the choke readjusted.

Vapor Lock

Vapor lock is the opposite of flooding: no fuel is reaching the carburetor. This condition is common during warm weather when the fuel in the pump or lines becomes so hot that the fuel vaporizes and fails to reach the carburetor in sufficient amounts to allow the engine to function. Some RV engines have chronic vapor-lock problems. In the past few years, with the proliferation of electronic fuel-injection (EFI) systems, vapor-lock complaints have been reduced considerably. The fuel in these systems is under a higher pressure (30 to 50 psi versus 4 to 7 psi in carbureted systems) and these systems have a closed-loop-plumbing design, which always keeps a fresh, cool supply of fuel going to the injection manifold. Whether it's a carburetor or EFI, there are some basic things that can be done to prevent or reduce vapor lock:

1. Make sure all fuel lines are routed away from heat sources, especially exhaust components. If it is impossible to route lines away from heat sources, they should be protected by a shield.
2. An auxiliary electric fuel pump (for carbureted systems) mounted as near the fuel tank as possible and fitted with ⅜-inch hose barbs will keep the engine's mechanical pump supplied with sufficient fuel to reduce the incidence of vapor lock.
3. If vapor lock does occur, pull well off the road and allow the engine to cool. Pouring cool water over the fuel lines and the pump will cause the fuel to condense back to liquid form.
4. Fuel tanks must be properly vented, either through the filler cap or by the evaporative emission system, to allow air to enter the tank as fuel is drawn from it. If the tank cannot vent, the resulting vacuum will cause the engine to starve for fuel.

Electric Fuel Pumps as a Remedy for Vapor Lock

Vapor-lock problems can be difficult to correct but the installation of an auxiliary fuel pump at the rear of the vehicle (in carbureted vehicles) near the fuel tank is often an effective solution (Figure 13.11). Since the engine-mounted fuel pump must draw fuel by suction from the fuel tank at the rear and lift it to the carburetor, the slightest bit of vapor developing in the fuel lines due to excessive heat will cause the pump to lose suction and fail to pump. An electric pump mounted near the tank is not as susceptible to heat absorption and will force a steady column of

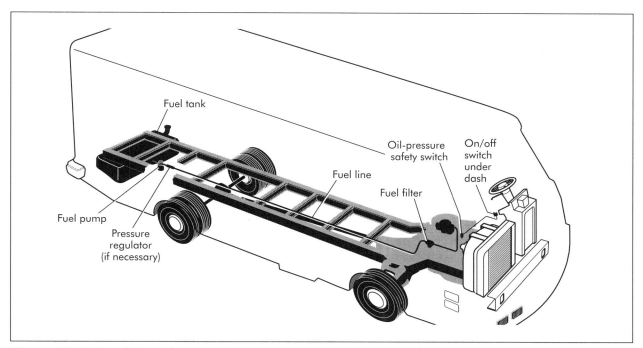

Figure 13.11 Installation of an electric fuel pump should be as close to the fuel tank as possible. An on/off switch located under the dash and an oil-pressure safety switch should be included in the installation.

fuel to the suction side of the engine's mechanical fuel pump. Selection of a quality electric pump that will provide sufficient volume without restricting fuel flow is important. Installation should include a ⅜-inch (inside diameter) fuel hose and connection barbs, an oil-pressure safety switch that will not allow the pump to operate if the engine stops running, and a pressure regulator that will not allow the pump pressure to exceed 5 psi.

Installing Electric Fuel Pumps The installation procedure for electric fuel pumps is as follows:

1. Select a suitable mounting location as close as possible to the fuel tank. The pump must be mounted below the level of the tank.
2. Make sure the pump and any fuel lines are not near any exhaust component that would induce heat into the fuel.
3. Drill mounting holes in the vehicle frame as recommended in the electric-pump manufacturer's instructions.
4. The vehicle's existing fuel line must be cut and the pump spliced in, using a ⅜-inch fuel hose and connection barbs. If a pressure

regulator is used, it should be installed at the electric pump's outlet.
5. An oil-pressure-sensitive switch must be installed in the vehicle's engine. The switch must be a "normally open" type that closes the contacts when oil pressure is detected. This feature will shut the pump off when the engine has stopped, even though the ignition key may be in the on position, as might occur in an accident.
6. Connect a wire of the proper gauge, as recommended by the pump manufacturer, to one contact of the switch.
7. Connect another wire with an in-line fuse of the proper amp rating from the other contact of the oil-pressure switch to a 12-volt DC circuit that is energized when the ignition switch is turned to the on position.
8. If a pressure regulator is used, a fuel-pressure gauge connected at the suction side of the mechanical pump should be used to set pressure at 5 psi. Follow the regulator manufacturer's procedure for setting pressure. It is important to check pressure at the mechanical pump; checking pressure at the electric pump and

regulator will give a false reading. There will be a pressure drop due to line friction between the electric and mechanical pumps.

9. Start the engine and check for leaks at all connections.

Defective Starter and/or Solenoid

Starters seldom are the cause of failure to start, although some engines have been known to ruin starters on a regular basis due to exposure to excessive heat, mainly from the exhaust system. If the starter is suspected, here are the steps to diagnose the problem:

1. Make sure the battery is fully charged and all terminal connections are clean and tight. A starter draws a very high amperage load; a marginal battery or poor terminal connections may not produce enough power to crank the engine.
2. If the starter motor spins but the engine does not turn over, the problem is in the starter-drive mechanism or the flywheel ring gear.
3. If the engine cranks slowly, and it is determined that the battery is fully charged and has clean, tight terminal connections, the problem could be caused by excessive engine-oil viscosity in cold weather. Other causes may be starter drag caused by a worn starter motor or a defective starter solenoid.

Troubleshooting the Starter

As underhood temperatures soar, the starter and the starter solenoid absorb heat. When electrical components soak up heat, their internal resistance increases. If the battery cables and connections are not in perfect condition, the initial power requirement of a hot starter and solenoid may be more than the system can deliver. The problem is called, fittingly enough, "hot start." Battery cables should be the heaviest gauge possible, terminals should be kept clean, and if hot starts have been a problem, the starter should be replaced with a heavy-duty type that is free of aluminum parts, which conduct heat at a faster rate than cast iron and steel.

General Motors vehicles utilize a starter solenoid relay that is mounted on the starter (Figure 13.12). This design is especially susceptible to the hot-start problem. One remedy is to bypass the solenoid and install a fenderwell-mounted Ford-type relay (Figure 13.13). This removes the relay from the high-heat condition on the starter to a cooler location so that it is not affected by excessive heat gain.

Installing Spark Plugs

An engine's fuel economy and power potential are only as good as the spark plugs' ability to ignite the fuel in the cylinder. Spark plugs are inexpensive, and their installation is not beyond the abilities of the do-it-yourselfer, although some engines are shoe-horned into a very tight compartment, making plug changing a bit of a chore. Here are the necessary steps:

1. Purchase name-brand plugs that are recommended for the engine year and displacement. Many times this can be found on the engine emission sticker in the owner's manual or by asking an auto-parts dealer.
2. The engine should be cool.
3. Use only a proper size spark-plug socket to remove plugs (Figure 13.14).
4. Pull off spark-plug cables by the boots; do not pull on the cables (Figure 13.15). A tool called a *boot puller* is available at auto-parts stores. Don't use pliers; they will cut the plug-cable boots, causing electrical leaks. It's

Figure 13.12 General Motors solenoid relay mounted on starters

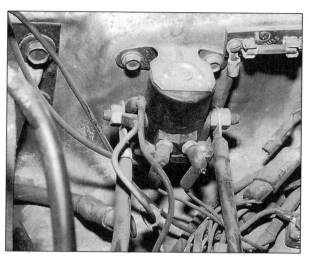

Figure 13.13 Fenderwell-mounted Ford-type relay

Figure 13.14 Use only the proper size spark plug socket.

a good idea to mark each cable as to its proper cylinder location. Failure to return plug cables to their respective spark plugs will cause the engine to run roughly or fail to start.

5. Using compressed air, blow off dirt from around the spark-plug base (Figure 13.16). If you don't have a compressed-air source, a short length of vacuum hose can be aimed at the plug base while you blow through it.

6. Spark plugs should be gapped to manufacturer's specifications. If there is a range of gap openings recommended, set them to the narrower setting; the gaps tend to open as the plugs wear.

7. Inspect the plug seating surface on the cylinder head; any dirt, grease, or debris should be removed.

8. Thread new plugs into the cylinder head. Be careful that cross-threading does not occur.

9. Torque plugs as specified by the manufacturer. Ford recommends 5 to 7 foot-pounds for its 5.8L (351 cid) and 7.5L (460 cid) engines; Chevrolets require 17 to 27 foot-pounds for the 5.7L (350 cid) and 7.4L (454 cid) engines; Dodge recommends that 26 to 30 foot-pounds be used for its 5.9L and 8.0L engines.

10. Install spark-plug cables to the proper spark plugs.

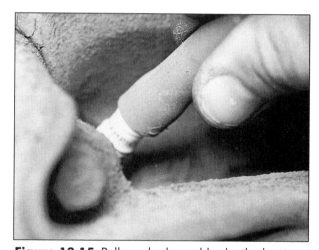

Figure 13.15 Pull spark-plug cables by the boot, not the cable.

■ COOLING-SYSTEM SERVICE ■

The cooling system must be in top shape to perform properly. With frequent inspection of hoses and belts and a regular coolant-change program, overheating is not likely to occur. Belts and hoses should be inspected frequently and replaced every four years or 50,000 miles. For most gasoline engines, coolant should be changed every other year or at 20,000 miles. If your RV is diesel-powered, refer to your owner's manual for specific information on other additives that may be required to prevent cooling-

Figure 13.16 Before removing spark plugs, clean the area with compressed air to avoid dirt dropping into the cylinder.

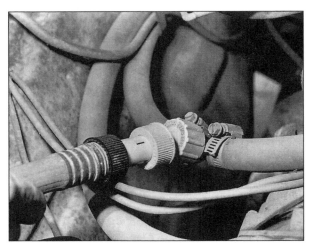

Figure 13.17 Simple backflushing devices that utilize garden hoses are available in most auto-parts stores.

system damage. These additives are needed in some applications to prevent pitting of the cylinder liner walls. Most heavy-duty diesel applications also use a cooling-system filter. Often the filter element will have the chemical additives necessary to keep protection up to the required levels. By simply changing the filter at the recommended intervals, the cooling system is protected. Here is how to drain, flush, and refill the cooling system:

1. Purchase and install a simple backflush device in the heater hose. This device is found at most auto-parts facilities and makes cooling-system maintenance easy. It is inexpensive, can be installed permanently in a heater hose in just a few minutes, and enables a garden hose to do the flushing.
2. Open the petcock on the bottom of the radiator and allow coolant to start draining. Collect the coolant for recycling; most service stations will accept used coolant.
3. Remove radiator cap (coolant will drain faster) and inspect the rubber gasket for defects. If the rubber seal is not soft and pliable, the cap should be replaced with one having the proper pressure rating for your application.
4. Remove the lower radiator hose from the radiator.
5. Connect a garden hose to the backflush device and flush the engine block (Figure 13.17).

6. Run clean water through the radiator to flush.
7. Connect the lower radiator hose and remove the garden hose from the backflushing device.
8. Consult the owner's manual to determine the total capacity of the cooling system.
9. Fill 50 percent of the system's capacity with ethylene glycol coolant; top off to capacity with water.
10. Run the engine until it reaches full operating temperature, and recheck the level of the coolant in the system. Sometimes it is necessary to "burp" the system to remove trapped air. This can be done by loosening the heater-hose clamp at the fitting immediately behind the thermostat housing. Allow any air to escape. When you see coolant appear, retighten the clamp. Add a 50/50 mixture of water/coolant if you need to top off the system.

■ THE TRANSMISSION ■

The transmission conducts the entire drive force exerted by the engine to the rear differential assembly and ultimately to the rear wheels. RV service should be extensive; whether it is in a motorhome or a tow vehicle, the transmission undergoes a tortuous routine.

Description and Identification of Transmission Configurations

Transmission configurations found in today's RV applications include three-speed automatic, four-speed overdrive automatic, five-speed automatic, six-speed automatic, four-speed standard shift, five-speed overdrive standard shift, and six-speed overdrive standard shift. The vehicle owner's manual will contain information about the type of transmission, service requirements, oil change intervals, and type of oil that should be used.

Because RVs place such heavy demands on the transmission, the oil should be changed at least every 25,000 miles, whether the transmission is standard or automatic. Heat is the main enemy of the automatic transmission. An automatic transmission should be outfitted with either a factory or aftermarket external oil cooler that is properly sized according to the gross vehicle weight of the motorhome or gross combined weight of a tow vehicle/trailer. Standard transmissions do not require oil coolers because they do not generate excessive heat. Automatic transmissions should not be allowed to run at temperatures that exceed approximately 250°F. This is the highest short-duration temperature under the worst conditions: heavy loads and hill climbs.

Transmission repair should be left to experts, although the average RVer can perform service routines at home with a little effort.

Transmission Service and Repair

Although transmission repairs are beyond the capabilities of the backyard mechanic, service is definitely not. Service neglect is the single largest cause of transmission failure. By changing the oil and filters frequently (25,000-mile intervals), transmission life can be improved significantly.

Be sure to consult the owner's manual to find the correct type of lubricant for each particular transmission. There are many different requirements depending on the year, the make, and the model of the transmission. The use of incorrect fluid can have a detrimental effect on the operation and life of the transmission.

Changing Automatic-Transmission Fluid

The steps for changing automatic-transmission fluid are:

1. Determine the refill capacity of the transmission. Repair and owner's manuals include these specifications. Most transmissions do not have a provision for draining the torque converter. Even though the capacity may be more than 10 quarts, the most that can be drained from the pan in a fluid change is about 4 to 6 quarts.
2. Purchase the proper type and amount of oil required to do the job, plus an additional quart. This extra quart is "just in case" and can be carried in your RV as a spare.
3. Purchase a transmission-pan gasket and new filter element for the transmission. Many auto-supply stores sell transmission-oil-change kits that contain the gasket and filter plus a set of instructions.

   While the transmission is warm, drain by removing the pan and allowing the fluid to empty into a large container that will contain all of the spillage (Figure 13.18).

   NOTE: Dispose of used oil properly. Most service stations will accept used oil for recycling.
5. Remove the old filter element and clean both gasket surfaces on the pan and the transmission case (Figure 13.19).
6. Install the new filter element and gasket; tighten the pan bolts evenly in a crisscross pattern to prevent distortion of the pan.
7. Refill the transmission with all but one of the number of quarts recommended.
8. Start the engine and allow it to idle for a few minutes; shift the gear selector through all gear ranges, then return it to park.
9. Check the oil level on the dipstick. If any is needed, add only small amounts at a time until the correct level is attained. Overfilling the transmission will cause oil to foam and possibly spew from the dipstick/fill tube onto hot engine parts, which can cause a fire.

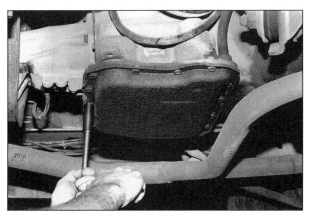

Figure 13.18 If the transmission pan does not have a drain plug, it must be removed to allow the fluid to empty into a bucket.

Figure 13.19 Remove the old filter element and clean the gasket surfaces on the pan and the transmission case.

Changing the Allison Automatic-Transmission Fluid

The Allison MD-3060 six-speed transmission for motorhomes requires a fluid-change interval of 5,000 miles for the first change and every 25,000 miles thereafter. Use only Dexron II or Dexron III automatic-transmission fluid unless otherwise specified by the manufacturer.

To check the fluid level:

1. Warm the transmission fluid by running the vehicle for twenty to thirty minutes.
2. Park on a level pad.
3. Place the transmission in park.
4. Use the dipstick to check the fluid level.
5. Fill in small amounts and wait for five minutes between fillings to insure that the transmission is not overfilled.

To change the transmission fluid:

1. Make sure you have a *large* catch pan for the fluid! If you only drain the apparent fluid, you will remove 15 to 16 quarts from the transmission. However, if you let the transmission drain for twenty to thirty minutes, you will remove 20 to 22 quarts because the torque converter will become partly drained.
2. Remove the drain plug from the bottom of the transmission.
   CAUTION: The transmission fluid will be extremely hot.

3. After the fluid has stopped draining from the transmission pan, remove the six bolts at the bottom front of the transmission and remove the filter cover. After removing the transmission and lube filters, several more quarts will drain from the transmission.
4. Install new filters and replace the filter cover and drain plug.
5. Remove the dipstick from the transmission and pour in 12 quarts of either Dexron II or Dexron III automatic transmission fluid.
6. Run the engine without driving the vehicle. Move the transmission gear selector through the gears several times to allow the torque converter and valve body to refill with fluid. Do this for about five minutes.
7. Place the transmission in park and continue filling the transmission with fluid, a small amount at a time, until the dipstick reads full.

Changing Standard-Transmission Fluid

The procedure for standard transmissions is much the same except that refilling will require an oil gun to force oil into the fill hole in the side of the transmission. These are available at auto-parts stores.

1. Purchase the correct amount and type of oil recommended in the owner's manual.
2. Operate the vehicle until the transmission is

warm. (Driving five to ten miles is adequate.)

3. Remove the drain plug in the bottom of the transmission, allowing the oil to drain into a container.

4. After draining is complete, install the drain plug and remove the fill plug on the side of the transmission.

5. Add the proper amount of oil until it runs out the bottom of the fill hole.

6. Tighten the fill plug in its hole.

Servicing the Gear Vendors Overdrive

Change the fluid at least every year or at 15,000 miles. Use only Dexron II or Dexron III automatic-transmission fluid. You may also use GL4-75/80 synthetic gear lubricant. This is MOPAR part number 4637579 or GM part number 1234-6190. Never use "synthetic" or "extreme pressure" ATF lubricants; never use additives such as moly or other "transmission improvers" in the Gear Vendors unit.

NOTE: It is up to the user to establish a schedule; it is not required by Gear Vendors.

To change the fluid:

1. Drive the vehicle for twenty to thirty minutes to warm the fluid.

2. Place a 2-quart drain pan under the overdrive unit.

3. Remove the drain plug from the bottom of the unit and wait about five minutes for all the fluid to drain.

4. Replace the drain plug.

5. Remove the fill plug located on the back (right side) of the main housing.

6. Using a plunger pump or a transmission pump, fill the unit with Dexron II or Dexron III fluid. The flat bottom unit will use 26 ounces and the deep sump model will use 38 ounces on the first filling and 32 ounces thereafter.

7. When the fluid is level with the bottom of the fill plug opening, the unit is full. Replace the plug.

To service the overdrive unit (this should be performed every year or at 10,000 miles):

1. Place a 2- to 3-quart drain pan beneath the overdrive unit.

2. Drain the fluid from the unit.

3. Remove the 6 bolts from the bottom of the unit and remove the sump. The sump gasket will usually stay on the overdrive unit.

4. Pull straight down on the suction filter to remove it. Wash the screen with solvent and allow it to air dry.

5. The high-pressure filter is located under the plug on the passenger side of the overdrive unit. To remove the high-pressure filter, use a spanner wrench or a small punch and hammer to turn the plug/cover counterclockwise.

6. Wash the filter in solvent and allow to air dry.

7. Install the high-pressure filter and washer. You may need to replace the washer if it has become damaged or scored.

8. Replace the plug and tighten to 16 foot-pounds

9. Install the suction filter; this is a press fit.

10. Inspect the sump gasket and replace it, if needed.

11. Install sump and secure it with the six bolts removed in step 3.

12. Replace the drain plug.

Servicing the U.S. Gear Overdrive/Underdrive

Change the fluid once a year with 80/90 weight gear lubricant. The use of synthetic fluid will allow the unit to run about 20°F cooler.

To change the fluid:

1. Drive the vehicle for twenty to thirty minutes to warm the fluid.

2. Place a 2-quart drain pan under the overdrive unit.

3. Remove the drain plug from the bottom of the unit and wait about five minutes for all the fluid to drain.

4. Replace the drain plug.

5. Remove the ⅜-inch fill plug from the passenger side of the unit near the serial number plate.

■ **TROUBLESHOOTING** ■
THE AUTOMATIC TRANSMISSION

Problem	Possible Cause	Correction
Transmission overheats	Low fluid level	Replenish fluid
	Foaming/overfill fluid	Lower fluid level
	Low engine coolant	Replenish coolant
	Inadequate oil cooler	Install larger cooler
	Blocked oil cooler	Clear debris
	Bent or crimped oil line	Repair restriction
	Overloaded vehicle	Reduce load
Transmission slips	Low fluid level	Replenish fluid
	Fluid level too high	Lower fluid level
	Dirty fluid and filter	Change fluid/filter
	Improper linkage adjustment	Seek professional help
	Improper internal adjustment	Seek professional help
	Defective internal parts	Seek professional help
Shift points incorrect	Low fluid level	Replenish fluid
	Incorrect linkage adjustment	Seek professional help
	Incorrect internal adjustment	Seek professional help
	Defective internal parts	Seek professional help
Gear fails to engage	Low fluid level	Replenish fluid
	Dirty fluid and filter	Change fluid/filter
	Improper linkage adjustment	Seek professional help
	Defective internal parts	Seek professional help

6. Use a plunger pump or a transmission pump to fill the unit with 80/90 weight gear lubricant or with synthetic 85/90 weight gear lubricant.
7. When the fluid is level with the fill plug opening, the unit is full.
8. Replace the plug.

■ **UNIVERSAL JOINTS** ■

Universal joints (U-joints) are the links between the transmission driveshaft and rear-axle assembly. U-joints provide a flexible connection and allow the rear suspension to move up and down, improving the quality of the ride. Many U-joints are permanently lubricated and require no service. If you need to replace a U-joint, be sure it is equipped with a grease fitting.

This fitting will allow clean grease to be added, extending the life of the joint.

Checking the U-Joint

If you suspect a U-joint may be defective, seek professional advice. U-joint replacement is not difficult, but if not done precisely, severe driveline vibration and possible damage can result. Here is a brief inspection/service routine you can perform:

• Every other engine-oil change, check the driveshaft's U-joints. Make sure the vehicle's wheels are blocked; grab the driveshaft near the U-joint, and, using a back-and-forth motion, check for any play in the assembly. There should be little or none. Many RVs, especially motorhomes and long-wheelbase pickup trucks, will have a two-piece driveshaft supported by a center bearing mounted in a rubber collar. The rubber collar will move, giving a floating action to the driveshaft. This is normal, but there should be no movement between the bearing itself and the collar or driveshaft.

- If the U-joints are fitted with a Zerk grease fitting, using a grease gun, pump enough approved chassis lubricant into the U-joint so that the old grease is expelled past the seals and fresh grease just starts to appear (Figure 13.20).
- If your U-joints do not have a grease fitting, they are not designed to be lubricated.

Figure 13.20 Lubing a Zerk fitting in a U joint with a grease gun

■ SUSPENSION COMPONENTS ■

In recent years, many of the familiar suspension components that required lubrication have been replaced with permanently lubricated parts (Figure 13.21). All rear-suspension pivot points are rubber mounted and require no periodic maintenance. Even in front suspensions, the grease fitting is becoming a thing of the past. However, most heavy-duty vehicles still equip the ball joints, tie-rod ends, and control-arm bushings with grease fittings. A good practice is to lube these components at 10,000-mile intervals (Figure 13.22). Most fittings are lubricated until fresh grease appears at the fitting. This practice forces out old grease, water, and road debris. You may discover that tie-rod ends and ball joints have rubber bellows seals that do not allow grease to escape. If the bellows seem to contain grease, do not lubricate the fitting; the bellows may rupture if they are too full. This will allow entry of water and dirt, causing early failure of the joint. The bellows should appear to have a slight bulge and feel spongy when depressed with a finger.

■ TROUBLESHOOTING ■
THE STANDARD TRANSMISSION

Problem	Possible Cause	Correction
Transmission slips	Improper clutch adjustment	Adjust pedal free-play to 1 to 2 inches
	Oil on clutch lining	Determine cause of oil
	Worn clutch lining	Seek professional help
Noise in neutral (clutch engaged)	Worn bearings	Seek professional help
	Low oil level	Replenish oil
Noise in neutral (clutch disengaged)	Defective throw-out bearing	Seek professional help
	Low oil level	Replenish oil
Noise while driving (all gears)	Defective gears/bearings	Seek professional help
Noise while driving (selected gear)	Defective single gear	Seek professional help
Hard shifting	Wrong oil in transmission	Replace with correct oil
	Improper clutch adjustment	Adjust clutch
Jumps out of gear	Worn syncro-mesh/gears	Seek professional help

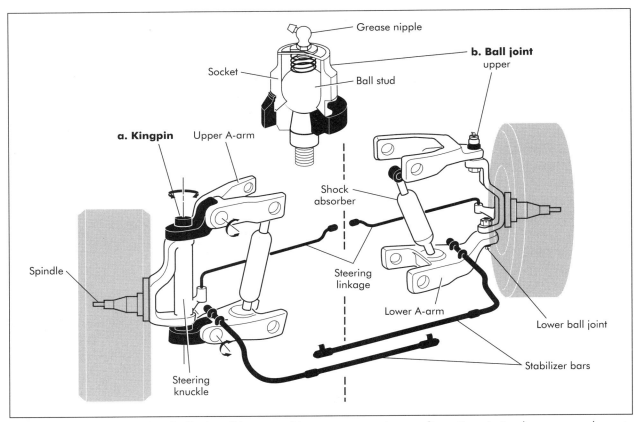

Figure 3.21 Kingpins (*a*) or ball joints (*b*) are used in most suspension configurations in trucks, vans, and sport-utility vehicles. Ball joints must be greased periodically.

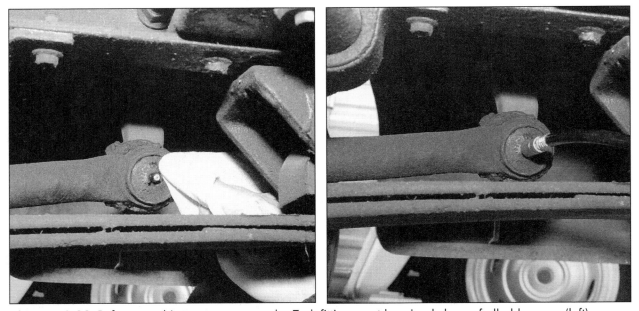

Figure 13.22 Before attaching a grease gun, the Zerk fitting must be wiped clean of all old grease (left). Lubricate fittings only if the bellows seem low on grease; allowing the bellows to rupture invites water and dirt contamination.

There are two types of grease suitable for chassis lubrication. One is a general-purpose chassis grease that has a lithium base. This dark brown, slightly translucent grease has a high resistance to water wash-off and an excellent load-carrying capacity.

A grease with slightly better characteristics is a lithium-based moly grease. The addition of molybdenum disulfide extreme-pressure additives and oxidation inhibitors makes this black-colored grease a good choice for heavily loaded components.

■ REAR DIFFERENTIAL ■

The rear differential assembly consists of a housing that holds the rear wheel bearings and drive axles, the ring and pinion gears, and the differential side gears. The pinion gear is connected to the driveshaft, and it, in turn, drives the ring gear that connects the differential side gears to the axles. The side gears allow one wheel to rotate faster than another during turning maneuvers so that the tires will not scrub.

The differential housing contains all these parts, as well as the gear oil that lubricates the entire assembly. Check your owner's manual for the type and viscosity of gear oil required. A gear oil with an API (American Petroleum Institute) rating of GL-5 will meet manufacturer's requirements.

If your vehicle is a pickup, it could be fitted with a limited-slip differential or "posi-traction." This type of differential uses a clutch assembly connected to the side gears to provide driving torque to both wheels when slippery conditions are encountered. These differentials normally require a special gear oil or additive to standard gear oil to maintain the proper coefficient of friction between the clutches. Check your vehicle's axle code carefully (found on the door panel) and compare it with the listing in the owner's manual to determine whether it is a limited-slip variety.

Changing the Differential Oil

Many manufacturers do not make a provision for draining the differential oil. The oil can only be removed by using a suction gun or by pulling the cover from the rear of the housing, if it is so equipped. For RV service, changing the differential oil every 50,000 miles is recommended. Here are the steps:

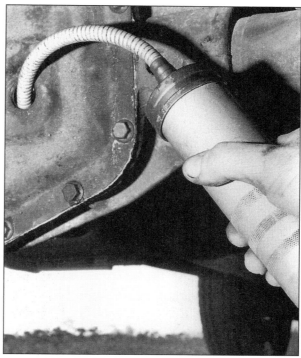

Figure 13.23 Suction guns are used to extract oil from differential housings without having to remove the cover.

1. Purchase enough of the correct grade and weight oil as noted in your owner's manual.
2. Drive the vehicle until the differential oil is warmed, about five to ten miles.
3. If there is no removable cover, the oil must be extracted through the fill hole by a suction gun. Remove all the oil possible (Figure 13.23).
4. If the cover is removable, you'll need to purchase a gasket to reinstall the cover so that leaks will not occur. Some manufacturers recommend sealing the cover with only a bead of silicone sealant. If this is the case, follow the sealant maker's instructions carefully.
5. Remove the cover and drain the oil thoroughly (Figure 13.24).
6. Clean the cover and housing surfaces so the new gasket will seal properly (Figure 13.25).
7. Replace the cover with the new gasket (or use silicone sealant) and tighten bolts evenly in a crisscross pattern.
8. If an additive for limited-slip is necessary,

Figure 13.24 Remove the differential cover and drain the oil thoroughly.

Figure 13.25 Clean cover and housing surfaces so the new gasket will fit properly.

add the proper amount and then refill the differential until oil is level with the bottom of the fill hole.

9. Replace the plug.

If you have a four-wheel-drive vehicle, don't forget to service the front differential.

■ WHEEL BEARINGS ■

Wheel bearings consist of precision-ground, hardened-steel, cylindrical rollers that are held together by a steel cage. These rollers rotate against a set of hardened-steel races. There is one race installed in the wheel hub (called the *outer race*) and one installed in the center of the roller/cage unit (called the *inner race*). It is upon these rollers and races that the entire weight of the vehicle is carried. The metallurgical quality of the steels used in bearing construction is of the highest quality. Combined with a clean, top-quality-bearing grease or oil, the lifespan of wheel bearings may exceed that of the vehicle itself (Figure 13.26).

Troubleshooting Wheel Bearings

The first sign that a bearing is failing is a distinct grinding sound from a wheel assembly. The noise is usually noticed at low speeds first; as the condition

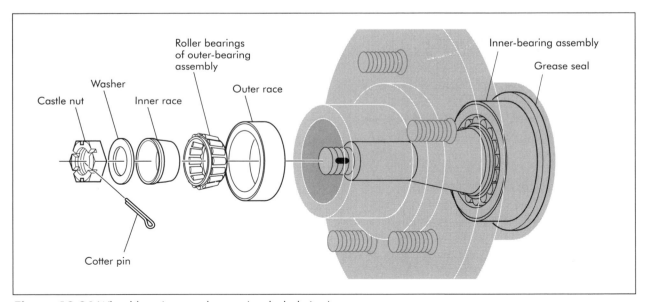

Figure 13.26 Wheel bearings and races (exploded view)

of the bearing worsens, the noise is also heard at higher speeds. Wheel-bearing noises can be isolated from other noises because the sound of a defective wheel bearing keeps time with the rate of wheel rotation. Some tire defects may also show similar symptoms; check the tires for defects before delving into the wheel-bearing assemblies.

If you suspect a defective wheel bearing, drive only far enough to have the bearing replaced. Trying to make it over a few more miles may destroy expensive wheel hubs, spindles, and brake components.

Servicing and Repairing Wheel Bearings

A good maintenance program should consist of periodic cleaning and lubrication (every 50,000 miles). It is most convenient to perform wheel-bearing maintenance at brake inspection or service intervals when the bearings are removed to service the brakes. Wheel-bearing service can be done at home by the do-it-yourselfer equipped with the proper tools. But be forewarned that access to bearings in motorhomes and heavy-duty pickups requires removal of heavy wheels, tires, brake drums, calipers, and rotors.

To service bearings:

1. Jack up the vehicle and use jack stands for safe support.
2. Remove the wheels and tires from the hub assembly.
3. If the vehicle is equipped with disc brakes, the caliper assemblies must be removed to allow the rotor to be slipped off the spindle.
4. Pull off the spindle dust cover to expose the bearing retainer nut and the locking cotter pin (Figure 13.27).
5. Remove the cotter pin and the castle nut, which will allow the outer wheel bearing and washer to be removed (Figure 13.28). Make sure you have a clean rag to put the bearing on after removal.
6. The brake hub and drum (with the disc brakes and the rotor) should now come off with a slight wiggling motion.
7. Turn the drum or rotor upside down on a clean rag or paper and drive the inner bearing and seal out of the hub with a hardwood dowel. (Using a metal device may

Figure 13.27 Spindle dust cover protects the bearing retainer nut and the locking cotter pin.

Figure 13.28 The cotter pin and castle nut allow the outer wheel bearing and the washer to be removed.

damage the bearing beyond repair.) Keep left-side and right-side bearings with their respective hubs. A wear pattern develops differently on each bearing and matching race; swapping bearings and races could lead to early failure.
8. Meticulously clean the bearings, the hub, the retaining washer, and the dust cap in cleaning solvent. It's best to clean the bearings separately, in solvent free of grit or grime (Figure 13.29).
9. Dry the components with a clean, lint-free rag. Make sure that all solvent is removed from the bearings since it will dilute the fresh grease that will be used to pack the bearings.

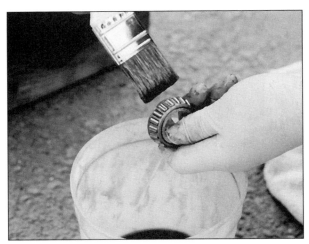

Figure 13.29 Clean bearings, hub, retaining washer, and dust cap in a cleaning solvent.

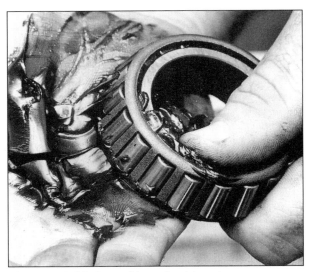

Figure 13.30 Repacking wheel bearings

10. Carefully inspect the bearings and hub races for any sign of defects. Chips, scratches, and discoloration warrant replacement of the bearings.
11. Bearings should be repacked with a top-quality wheel-bearing grease (Figure 13.30). Do not use standard chassis lubricants as they will liquefy at high temperatures generated by the braking system.
12. To pack the bearings, force grease between the rollers and the inner-bearing race surface. Place a small amount of grease in the palm of your hand and force the bearing side against the grease so that hydraulic pressure will push the grease between the rollers. Continue around the entire circumference of the bearing until grease oozes out the top side. All bearings should be packed in this manner.
13. Wipe a layer of grease on the inside of the hub, filling the cavity and covering the bearing races with a light coating. Place the inner bearing against its race and carefully install a new grease seal by tapping it against its seat; use a hardwood block to prevent damage.
14. Place a light coating of grease on the new seal lip and install the hub/bearing assembly on the clean spindle.
15. Push the outer bearing into place and install the retaining washer and nut.
16. Bearing-adjustment methods vary between manufacturers. If you use the following method (General Motors), it will work for virtually all vehicles:
    a. Tighten the castle nut to 12 foot-pounds while turning the wheel assembly forward by hand to fully seat the bearings. This will remove excess grease from between the rollers that could cause excessive wheel-bearing play later.
    b. Back off the castle nut until you reach the "just-loose" position.
    c. Hand tighten the castle nut. Loosen the castle nut until either hole lines up with a slot in the castle nut (no more than half flat).
    d. Install a new cotter pin. Bend the ends of the cotter pin against the castle nut. Cut off any extra length so the ends will not interfere with the dust cap.
    e. Measure the looseness of the hub assembly. There will be from .001 to .005 inches of end play when properly adjusted.
    f. Install the dust cap on the hub.
17. Reinstall the tires and wheels, torquing the lug nuts to the factory-recommended specification. After driving forty or fifty miles, check the nuts again; loose lug nuts can cause wheel damage and possible wheel loss.
18. Torque values for studs are generally as fol-

lows; check your owner's manual for specific torque recommendations and follow them precisely:

- ½-inch studs: 75 to 100 foot-pounds
- ⁹⁄₁₆-inch studs (single wheels): 115 to 130 foot-pounds
- ⁹⁄₁₆-inch studs (dual wheels): 110 to 140 foot-pounds
- ⅝-inch studs: 125 to 180 foot-pounds
- ¾-inch studs: 200 foot-pounds

■ TIRES ■

Tires are a marvel of today's engineering and manufacture. When you consider the job the tire must do—support weight, provide traction, stability, and a safe, smooth ride—it's a wonder they survive as well as they do. Tires are easy to maintain; you get a report of their condition every time you look at them. This allows you to spot trouble early.

Reading Your Tires

A tire's sidewall contains a wealth of information. Read the details that must appear on every tire by law to determine if the tire is right for your application. Tires are constructed in one of three ways: a bias ply, a bias/belted ply, and belted radial-ply construction. Nearly all tires fitted as original equipment today are of radial construction with steel belts.

Each type has its advantages and disadvantages. A bias-ply tire has a stiff, strong sidewall but has a higher resistance to rolling; it does not contribute to fuel economy. A bias/belted tire is an improvement over the straight bias version because belts of either polyester or steel add a protective layer to help protect against road-hazard damage. The belts also stabilize the tread surface, allowing for slightly better wear characteristics. Radial-belted tires offer less rolling resistance, which increases overall fuel economy and performance. The belts surrounding the plies serve to protect them from puncture damage. But radials lack the sidewall strength and stiffness of bias-ply tires, making the sidewalls more vulnerable to damage.

The following information is contained on the sidewall of every tire (Figure 13.31):

Tire Size: The section width, aspect ratio, speed rating for some automotive applications, construction type (radial or bias), and the wheel-rim diameter.

Load Range: A letter-identification system declares the load-carrying capacity; maximum recommended inflation pressure and maximum load in pounds are stated.

D.O.T Certification: This simply means that the tire is certified as being built to Department of Transportation standards. Adjacent to this is the tire's serial number, which, in code, describes the location and date of manufacture.

Tube or Tubeless: This section spells out whether the tire should be used with a or without a tube.

M+S rating: If the letters M+S are molded to the sidewall, this means the tire meets specifications that qualify it as combination highway, mud, and snow tire.

Figure 13.31 Load-rating designation and weight ratings in pounds and air pressure are marked on the sidewalls of all tires (*top*). Tire size is clearly marked on the sidewalls (*bottom*).

■ TROUBLESHOOTING ■
THE TIRES

Problem	Possible Cause	Correction
Wear bars showing	Tread worn to unsafe level	Replace tires
Wearing on inside	Negative camber alignment	Align, increase camber
	Worn ball joints	Inspect and replace
	Worn A-arm bushings	Inspect and replace
Wearing on outside	Positive camber alignment	Align, reduce camber
	Worn ball joints	Inspect and replace
	Worn A-arm bushings	Inspect and replace
	Underinflation	Increase tire pressure
Wearing in center	Overinflation	Reduce tire pressure
Cupping or scalloping	Worn shock absorbers	Replace
	Worn ball joints	Inspect and replace
	Worn A-arm bushings	Inspect and replace
	Worn steering components	Inspect and replace
	Out-of-round tire	Check and replace tire
	Out-of-round rim	Check and replace rim
	Imbalanced tire	Balance tires
	Grabbing brakes	Repair brakes
	Inaccurate wheel-bearing adjustment	Check and adjust
Feathering in wear pattern	Improper toe-in	Align front end
	Bent suspension component	Inspect and replace
Bulging in sidewall	Hitting road obstacles	Replace tire
	Manufacturing defect	Replace tire
Shaking	Improper balance	Balance tires
	Out-of-round tire	Replace tire
	Bent wheel rim	Replace rim
	Worn suspension parts	Inspect and replace
	Inaccurate wheel-bearing adjustment	Adjust bearings
	Worn shock absorbers	Replace shocks
Hard/uneven steering	Low tire pressure	Inflate to correct psi
	Incorrect front-wheel alignment	Align properly
	Worn suspension components	Inspect and replace
Vehicle wandering	Uneven tire pressure	Inflate to correct psi
	Incorrect alignment	Align properly
	Worn suspension parts	Inspect and replace
	Vehicle overload to one side	Balance vehicle load

■ **TROUBLESHOOTING** ■
THE TIRES, continued

Problem	Possible Cause	Correction
Squealing	Low inflation pressure	Inflate tires
	Misalignment	Align properly
	Differential problem	Inspect differential
	Wrong load-range tire	Check and correct
	Defective suspension parts	Inspect and replace
Losing air	Puncture	Inspect and repair
	Defective valve-stem seal	Replace valve stem
	Tire bead not seated	Reseat bead
	Corroded internal rim	Replace rim
	Flawed tire	Replace tire
	Dirty rim flanges	Clean or replace rim

Tire Service and Repair

Tire service and repair should not be attempted by the amateur; your safety is at risk with less-than-perfect tire repairs. But the do-it-yourselfer can perform two important tasks:

1. Regular tire inspections for irregular wear patterns, defects, and inflation pressures.
2. Perform tire rotation at 10,000-mile intervals.

Inflation pressures should be checked a least once a month, more often if the vehicle is used on a daily basis. The pressure in your tires should be matched to the load of the vehicle without exceeding the load rating or inflation pressure on the sidewall of the tires.

The best way to determine the load is by weighing your vehicle. Motorhomes often operate at near (and some over) the chassis gross vehicle weight rating (GVWR). If, in weighing the vehicle, one determines that a tire is overloaded, change to a tire of proper load range (the wheel must be rated to handle the capacity of the tire). If the tire is within its capacity rating, inflation should be set to match the load (See Tables 13.1 through 13.7, pages 13.27 through 13.31).

Inflation pressures should be checked and/or changed only when the tires are cold. A tire's pressure may climb 5 to 10 psi after driving some distance since heat causes the air to expand; measuring pressure in a hot tire will give erroneous readings. Never bleed air from a hot tire; it will then be operating in an underinflated condition. Light-truck tires with the LT designation stamped on the sidewall may be overinflated up to 10 psi over the manufacturer's recommendation.

A quick walkaround inspection should be made each day before the vehicle is driven. Check tires for odd wear patterns, sidewall defects, foreign objects that may be embedded in the tread, abrasions, and any other damage that may have occurred in the previous day's driving. By making this a regular habit, you'll avoid roadside tire failures.

Tire rotation is valuable in maximizing tire life. Different wear patterns develop, depending on the service the tire receives. (Drive tires develop patterns that differ from steering tires.) The rotation pattern will depend on the type of tire with which your RV is equipped. It's best to consult the owner's manual for your particular vehicle/chassis for specific recommendations regarding tire rotation (Figure 13.32).

Tire Maintenance

It's important to keep your tires clean and protected from the sun and other harmful elements. Although trailer tires, stamped with an ST (Table 13.1), have

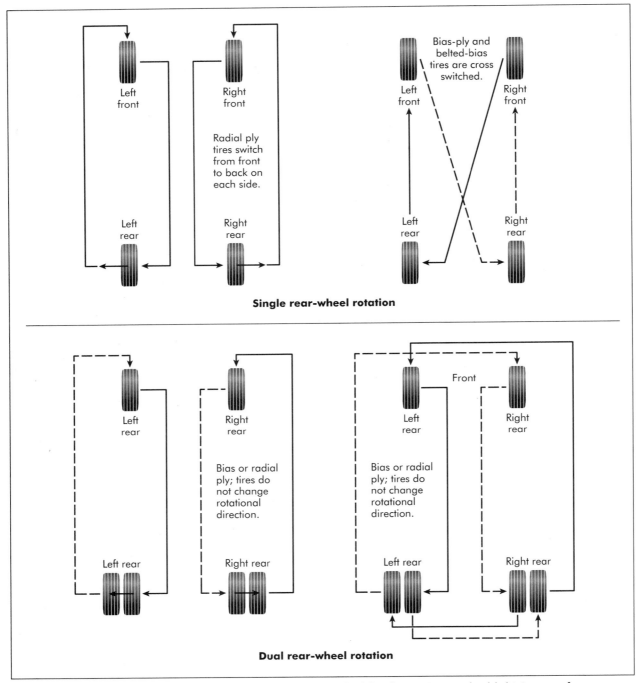

Figure 13.32 Rotating tires on a regular basis can extend the life of your tires and add driving comfort to your vehicle. Tires need not remain in their original direction of rotation.

compounds that protect the rubber from the elements, they should be covered when the trailer/fifth-wheel is in storage or parked in camp for an extended time. The same holds true for motorhome and tow-vehicle tires. If you are going to use a protectant on the tires, make sure the product does not contain petroleum distillates. Tires covered or treated with a protectant will have a longer service life and resist cracking or crazing. Tires older than seven years should be discarded, regardless of tread condition.

Table 13.1 Special Trailer Tire Load-Ratings for Normal Highway Service

TIRE SIZE	15	20	25	30	**35**	40	45	**50**	55	60	65
				Load Limits (pounds per tire) at Various Cold-inflation Pressures						
6.00-13 ST	570	675	765	855	**935(B)**	1010	1080	**1150(C)**			
6.50-13 ST	650	770	875	975	**1065(B)**	1150	1235	**1150(C)**			
7.00-13 ST	715	845	965	1075	**1065(B)**	1270	1360	**1150(C)**			
6.45-14 ST	630	745	850	945	**1065(B)**	1120	1200	**1150(C)**			
7.35-14 ST	755	895	1020	1135	**1065(B)**	1345	1440	**1150(C)**			
7.75-14 ST	830	980	1120	1245	**1065(B)**	1475	1580	**1150(C)**			
8.25-14 ST	895	1060	1210	1345	**1065(B)**	1590	1705	**1150(C)**			
8.55-14 ST	980	1155	1320	1465	**1065(B)**	1735	1860	**1150(C)**			
6.85-15 ST	690	815	925	1030	**1130(B)**	1220	1310	**1390(C)**			
7.35-15 ST	780	920	1050	1170	**1280(B)**	1385	1480	**1575(C)**			
7.75-15 ST	830	985	1120	1245	**1365(B)**	1475	1580	**1680(C)**			
8.25-15 ST	905	1070	1220	1355	**1485(B)**	1615	1720	**1825(C)**			
8.55-15 ST	990	1170	1330	1480	**1620(B)**	1755	1880	**2000(C)**	2115	2225	2330(D)
8.85-15 ST	1035	1220	1390	1550	**1695(B)**	1835	1965	**2090(C)**			

Note: Letters in parentheses indicate load range for which boldface loads are maximum.

Table 13.2 Tire and Rim Association Ratings, Flotation-Type Light-Truck Tires
Tire Load Limits (lbs) at Various Minimum Cold-Inflation Pressures (PSI)

TIRE SIZE	Radial Ply					
	25	30	35	40	45	50
	Diagonal (Bias) Ply					
	20	25	30	35	40	45
31×10.50*15LT	1400	1595	**1775(B)**	1945	2100	**2250**(C)
31×11.50*15LT	1455	1660	**1845(B)**	2020	2185	**2340**(C)
32×11.50*15LT	1575	1795	**1995(B)**	2185	2360	**2530**(C)
33×12.50*15LT	**1755**(B)	2000	**2225**(C)			
35×12.50*15LT	2015	2295	**2555**(C)			

*Indicates position where R (radial ply) or B (bias ply) designation will appear—i.e., 31 × 10.50R15LT.
Letters and **boldfaced** tire load values indicate tire load ranges B through C.

Table 13.3 Michelin Motorhome Tire-Load Ratings, Loads per Axle
Tire-Load Limits (lbs) at Various Minimum Cold-Inflation Pressures (PSI)2 Tires =Single; 4 Tires = Dual

TIRE SIZE		55	60	65	70D	75F	80F	85F	90F	95
*225/70R19.5	Dual	9290	9820	10,360	10,880	11,440	12,000	12,460	12,980	13,660
	Single	4950	5230	5510	5790	6080	6390	6630	6900	7280
**8R19.5	Dual	9150	9770	10,390	10,800	11,475	12,200	12,825	13,500	
	Single	4710	5035	5365	5600	5950	6340	6650	7000	

*XRV Tire
**XZA Tire

Table 13.4 Tire and Rim Association Ratings
Tire-Load Limits (lbs) at Various Minimum Cold-Inflation Presssures (PSI)

TIRE SIZE	USAGE	Radial Ply 35 / Diagonal (Bias) Ply 30	40 / 35	45 / 40	50 / 45	55 / 50	60 / 55	65 / 60	70 / 65	75 / 70	80 / 75
LT205/75*15	Dual	1145	1260	1365	**1520(C)**						
	Single	1260	1385	1500	**1655(C)**						
LT215/75*15	Dual	1225	1340	1460	**1610(C)**	**1680**	**1785**	**1930(D)**			
	Single	1345	1475	1605	**1765(C)**	**1845**	**1960**	**2095(D)**			
LT225/75*15	Dual	1315	1440	1565	**1710(C)**	**1800**	**1915**	**1985(D)**			
	Single	1445	1585	1720	**1875(C)**	**1980**	**2105**	**2205(D)**			
LT235/75*15	Dual	1390	1530	1660	**1820(C)**	**1910**	**2035**	**2150(D)**	**2265**	**2375**	**2535(E)**
	Single	1530	1680	1825	**1985(C)**	**2100**	**2235**	**2335(D)**	**2490**	**2610**	**2755(E)**
LT255/75*15	Dual	1575	1730	1880	**2040(C)**						
	Single	1730	1900	2065	**2270(C)**						
LT225/75*16	Dual	1365	1500	1630	**1765(C)**	**1875**	**1995**	**2150(D)**	**2220**	**2330**	**2470(E)**
	Single	1500	1650	1790	**1940(C)**	**2060**	**2190**	**2335(D)**	**2440**	**2560**	**2680(E)**
LT245/75*16	Dual	1545	1695	1845	**2006(C)**	**2125**	**2255**	**2381(D)**	**2515**	**2640**	**2778(E)**
	Single	1700	1865	2030	**2205(C)**	**2335**	**2480**	**2623(D)**	**2765**	**2900**	**3042(E)**
LT265/75*16	Dual	1740	1910	2075	**2270(C)**	**2390**	**2540**	**2755(D)**	**2825**	**2965**	**3085(E)**
	Single	1910	2100	2280	**2470(C)**	**2625**	**2790**	**3000(D)**	**3105**	**3260**	**3415(E)**
LT285/75*16	Dual	1940	2130	2310	**2535(C)**	**2660**	**2830**	**3000(D)**			
	Single	2130	2340	2540	**2755(C)**	**2925**	**3110**	**3305(D)**			
LT215/85*16	Dual	1360	1490	1625	**1765(C)**	**1865**	**1985**	**2150(D)**	**2210**	**2320**	**2470(E)**
	Single	1495	1640	1785	**1940(C)**	**2050**	**2180**	**2335(D)**	**2430**	**2550**	**2680(E)**
LT235/85*16	Dual	1545	1700	1845	**2006(C)**	**2125**	**2260**	**2381(D)**	**2515**	**2645**	**2778(E)**
	Single	1700	1870	2030	**2205(C)**	**2335**	**2485**	**2623(D)**	**2765**	**2905**	**3042(E)**
LT255/85*16	Dual	1745	1920	2085	**2270(C)**	**2400**	**2555**	**2755(D)**			
	Single	1920	2110	2290	**2470(C)**	**2635**	**2805**	**3000(D)**			
7.50*15LT	Dual	1190	1310	1420	**1520(C)**	**1620**	**1715**	**1800(D)**	**1870**	**1960**	**2040(E)**
	Single	1350	1480	1610	**1720(C)**	**1830**	**1940**	**2140(D)**	**2130**	**2220**	**2320(E)**
7.50*16LT	Dual	1430	1565	1690	**1815(C)**	**1930**	**2040**	**2140(D)**	**2245**	**2345**	**2440(E)**
	Single	1620	1770	1930	**2060(C)**	**2190**	**2310**	**2440(D)**	**2560**	**2670**	**2780(E)**

*Indicates position where R (radial ply) or B (bias ply) designation will appear—i. e., LT215/85R16.
Letters and **boldfaced** tire-load values indicate tire-load ranges C through E.

Table 13.5 Tire and Rim Association Ratings
Tire-Load Limits (lbs) at Various Minimum Cold-Inflation Presssures (PSI)

Radial Ply

TIRE SIZE	USAGE	65	70	75	80	85	90	95	100	105	110	115	120
225/70R19.5	Dual	**2600(D)**	2720	2860	**3000(E)**	3115	3245	**3415(F)**	3490	3615	**3750(G)**		
	Single	**2755(D)**	2895	3040	**3195(E)**	3315	3450	**3640(F)**	3715	3845	**3970(G)**		
245/70R19.5	Dual				3415	3515	3655	**3860(D)**	3940	4075	**4300(G)**	4345	**4540(H)**
	Single				3640	3740	3890	**4080(D)**	4190	4335	**4540(G)**	4620	**4805(H)**
265/70R19.5	Dual				3750	3930	4095	4300	4405	4415	**4675(G)**		
	Single				3970	4180	4355	4540	4685	4850	**5070(G)**		
305/70R19.5	Dual				4540	4670	4860	5070	5230	5410	**5675(H)**	5770	**6005(J)**
	Single				4940	5130	5340	5510	5745	5945	**6175(H)**	6340	**6610(J)**
255/70R22.5	Dual				3970	4110	4275	4410	4455	4610	**4675(G)**	4915	**5070(H)**
	Single				4190	4370	4550	4675	4895	5065	**5205(G)**	5400	**5510(H)**
305/75R22.5	Dual							5840	6025	6235	6610	6640	**6940(J)**
	Single							6395	6620	6850	7160	7300	**7610(J)**
305/85R22.5	Dual				5355	5550	5780	6005	6215	6435	**6780(H)**		
	Single				5840	6100	6350	6610	6830	7070	**7390(H)**		

Diagonal (Bias) Ply

TIRE SIZE	USAGE	65	70	75	80	85	90	95	100	105	110	115
245/75*R22.5	Dual	3465	3615	3765	3915	4055	4195	**4300(G)**				
	Single	3470	3645	3810	3975	4140	4300	4455	4610	**4675(G)**		
265/75*22.5	Dual	3870	4040	4205	4370	4525	4685	**4805(G)**				
	Single	3875	4070	4255	4440	4620	4800	4975	5150	**5205(G)**		
295/75*22.5	Dual	4500	4690	4885	**5070(F)**	5260	5440	**5675(E)**	5795	**6005(H)**		
	Single	4500	4725	4945	5155	5370	**5510(F)**	5780	5980	**6175(G)**	6370	**6610(H)**
285/75*24.5	Dual	4540	4740	4930	**5205(F)**	5310	5495	**5675(G)**	5860	**6175(H)**		
	Single	4545	4770	4990	5210	5420	**5675(F)**	5835	6040	**6175(G)**	6440	**6780(H)**

*Indicates position where R (radial ply) or B (bias ply) designation will appear—i. e., 225/70R19.5.
Letters and **boldfaced** tire-load values indicate tire-load ranges D through J.

Table 13.6 Tire and Rim Association Ratings
Tire-Load Limits (lbs) at Various Minimum Cold-Inflation Pressures (PSI)

		Radial Ply 60	65	70	75	80	85	90	95	100	105	110	115	120
TIRE SIZE	**USAGE**	**Diagonal (Bias) Ply** 55	60	65	70	75	80	85	90	95	100	105	110	115
8*19.5	Dual	2230	2350	2460(D)	2570	2680	2780(E)	2880	2980	3070(F)				
	Single	2270	2410	2540	2680	2800(D)	2930	3060	3170(E)	3280	3400	3500(F)		
8*22.5	Dual	2490	2620	2750(D)	2870	2990	3100(E)	3210	3320	3450(F)				
	Single	2530	2680	2840	2990	3140(D)	3270	3410	3530(E)	3660	3780	3910(F)		
9*22.5	Dual	2960	3120	3270	3410	3550(E)	3690	3820	3950(F)	4070	4200	4320(G)		
	Single	3010	3190	3370	3560	3730	3890	4050(E)	4210	4350	4500(F)	4640	4790	4920(G)
10*22.5	Dual	3510	3690	3870	4040(E)	4200	4360	4520(F)	4670	4820	4970(G)			
	Single	3560	3770	4000	4210	4410	4610(E)	4790	4970	5150(F)	5320	5490	5670(D)	
11*22.5	Dual			4380	4580	4760(F)	4950	5120	5300(G)	5470	5630	5800(H)		
	Single			4530	4770	4990	5220	5430(F)	5640	5840	6040(G)	6240	6430	6610(H)
11*24.5	Dual			4660	4870	5070(F)	5260	5450	5640(G)	5820	6000	6170(H)		
	Single			4820	5070	5310	5550	5780(F)	6000	6210	6430	6630	6840	7030(H)
12*22.5	Dual			4780	4990	5190(F)	5390	5590	5780(G)	5960	6150	6320(H)		
	Single			4940	5200	5450	5690	5920(F)	6140	6370	6590(G)	6790	7010	7200(H)
12*24.5	Dual			5080	5300	5520(F)	5730	5940	6140(G)	6330	6530	6720(H)		
	Single			5240	5520	5790	6040	6290(F)	6530	6770	7000(G)	7220	7440	7660(H)

*Indicates position where R (radial ply) or B (bias ply) designation will appear—i.e., 8R19.5.
Letters and **boldfaced** tire-load values indicate tire-load ranges D through H.

Table 13.7 Tire and Rim Association Ratings, Trailer Tires
Tire-Load Limits (lbs) at Various Minimum Cold-Inflation Presssures (PSI)

TIRE SIZE	15	20	25	30	35	40	45	50	55	60	65
ST155/80*13	540	640	740	815	**880**(B)	970	1040	**1100**(C)			
ST175/80*13	670	795	905	1000	**1100**(B)	1190	1270	**1360**(C)			
ST185/80*13	740	870	990	1100	**1200**(B)	1300	1400	**1480**(C)			
ST205/75*14	860	1030	1170	1300	**1430**(B)	1530	1640	**1760**(C)			
ST215/75*14	935	1110	1270	1410	**1520**(B)	1660	1790	**1870**(C)			
ST205/75*15	905	1070	1220	1360	**1480**(B)	1610	1720	**1820**(C)			
ST225/75*15	1060	1260	1430	1600	**1760**(B)	1880	2020	**2150**(C)	2270	2380	**2540**(D)
ST215/80*16	1090	1300	1480	1640	**1820**(B)	1940	2080	**2200**(C)	2340	2470	****2600**(D)
ST235/80*16	1270	1510	1720	1920	**2090**(B)	2270	2430	**2600**(C)	2730	2870	*****3000**(D)

*Indicates position where R (radial ply) or B (bias ply) designation will appear—i.e., ST155/80R13.

**Load range E/2910 lbs. @ 80 psi.

***Load range E/3420 lbs. @ 80 psi.

Letters and **boldfaced** tire-load values indicate tire-load ranges B through D.

■ CHAPTER 14 ■
HITCHES

itch systems are engineered to connect a tow vehicle and a trailer in a manner that will result in a safe and appropriate marriage between the two. In order for a hitch system to perform well, the correct components must be selected for the job, the equipment must be properly installed, and it must be maintained so it can continue to perform its function successfully.

For conventional trailers, there are two different hitch types: weight distributing and weight carrying. The names are, in and of themselves, accurate descriptions of these types of hitches. Fifth-wheel trailers can utilize two completely different types of hitches.

A weight-distributing hitch includes spring bars that attach between the ball mount and the trailer frame to distribute the hitch weight evenly to the front and rear axles of the tow vehicle, as well as to the trailer axles (Figure 14.1). Used properly, a weight-distributing hitch sustains the tow vehicle and the trailer at level attitudes after the full weight of the A-frame has been imposed on the ball mount. Sway-control devices are commonly used with weight-distributing hitches.

A weight-carrying hitch (Figure 14.2) is designed to support the full A-frame load on the ball mount (or ball if a separate ball mount is not used). Under this condition, the rear of the tow vehicle bears the entire weight of the A-frame at the point of hitch attachment. If the hitch weight is substantial, the rear of the tow vehicle will be forced downward. As the rear of the tow vehicle is loaded, the front of the vehicle will rise, unloading the front axle. This can result in light steering, decreased front-brake effectiveness, and poor handling. This is one reason weight-carrying hitches are rated only for lightweight towing. Sway-control devices are sometimes used in

conjunction with weight-carrying hitches, depending upon the trailer being towed.

A fifth-wheel hitch consists of a platform that is installed in the bed of a truck above the rear axle (Figure 14.3). The uppermost part of the hitch is the saddle, which carries the weight of the pin box (the coupling system that is attached to the trailer). This is, in essence, a weight-carrying unit, because the full hitch weight of the trailer is borne by the rear of the tow vehicle without being distributed fore and aft by hitch components. However, because the hitch point is centered almost directly above or just forward of the rear axle, there is none of the leverage on the rear of the tow vehicle that a conventional trailer imposes. With the hitch point so far forward, a portion of the hitch weight is distributed to the front axle, so the tow vehicle maintains a more level attitude than it would if the same amount of weight were loaded on a conventional hitch. Because of the location of the hitch, fifth-wheel trailers can only be towed by flatbed or pickup trucks with open cargo boxes. Sway-control devices are not necessary and in fact cannot be employed in conjunction with fifth-wheel hitch systems.

■ HITCH CLASSIFICATIONS ■

Conventional hitches are rated by the manufacturer according to the maximum amount of weight they are engineered to handle. The weight rating refers to the total weight of the trailer, with the freshwater tank full, propane tank/cylinder(s) full, all supplies on board, and ready to travel. Class I hitches are rated for towing as much as 2,000 pounds. Class II units are intended for loads up to 3,500 pounds. Class III can be either weight-carrying or weight-distrib-

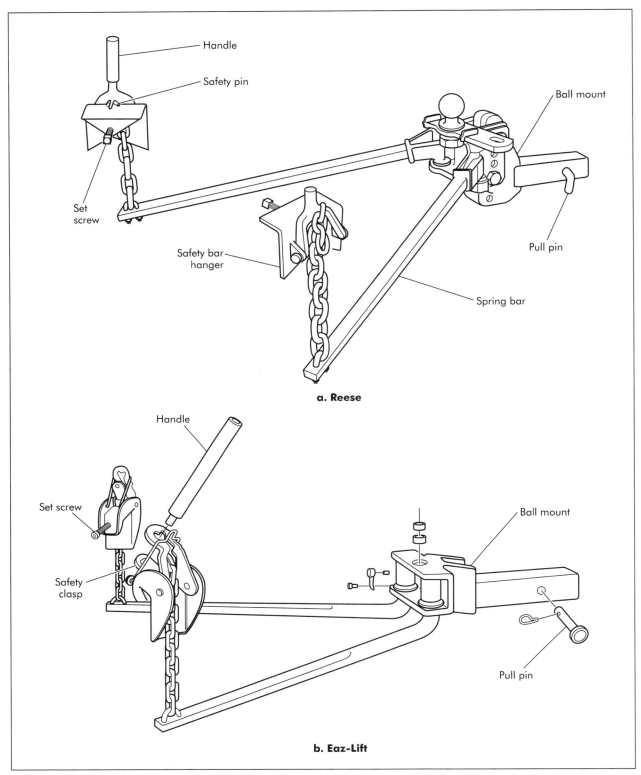

Handle

Safety pin

Ball mount

Set screw

Safety bar hanger

Pull pin

Spring bar

a. Reese

Handle

Set screw

Ball mount

Safety clasp

Pull pin

b. Eaz-Lift

Figure 14.1 Weight-distributing hitches are designed for towing heavier trailers. Reese (a) and Eaz-Lift (b) are major suppliers.

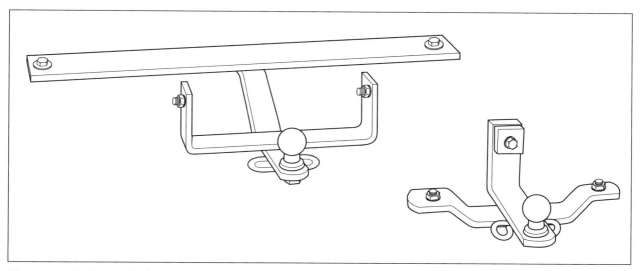

Figure 14.2 Class I (*right*) and Class II (*left*) weight-carrying hitches are available for towing lighter trailers.

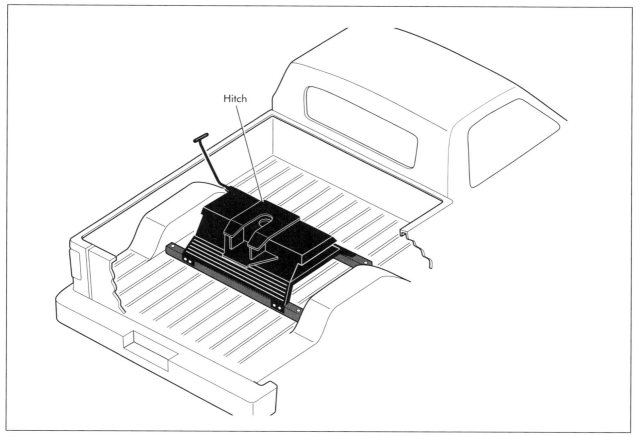

Figure 14.3 A fifth-wheel hitch platform is installed in the bed of the truck, over the rear axle.

Figure 14.4 PullRite hitch

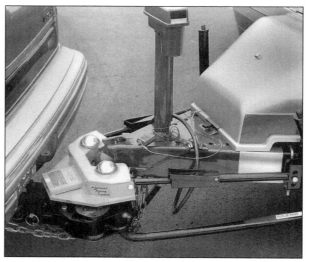

Figure 14.5 Hensley Arrow advanced towing system

uting hitches, rated for trailers up to 5,000 pounds gross weight. Class IV includes both weight distributing and fifth-wheel hitches, rated for trailers between 5,000 and 10,000 pounds.

Beyond Class IV are hitches that are rated for towing loads greater than 10,000 pounds. Reese offers its Titan model Class V conventional receiver hitch that is rated to tow as much as 12,000 pounds in simple weight-carrying mode, or 14,000 pounds in weight-distributing mode. Maximum hitch-weight ratings are 1,200 pounds and 1,700 pounds respectively. One caution should be mentioned here: When using a Class V hitch, the operator must be certain that the tow vehicle is rated for such heavy loads. Simply installing a Class V hitch will not increase the tow rating of the vehicle.

Another hitch system that exceeds the norm is the PullRite, made by Pulliam Enterprises, Inc. PullRite hitches (Figure 14.4) are unusual in that they reposition the pivoting hitch point quite a ways forward under the tow vehicle to a location immediately behind the axle housing. Moving the hitch point forward effectively delivers handling characteristics that fall somewhere between those of a conventional hitch and those of a fifth-wheel hitch. The PullRite Heavy Duty was introduced in 1985 for commercial trailer towing, where heavy cargo and hitch weights exceeded the ratings of standard conventional hitches. This model is rated for towing as much as 20,000 pounds and for han-

dling hitch weights as heavy as 2,000 pounds. Again, the caution for owners is that the tow-vehicle ratings must meet or exceed the loads being towed.

The Hensley Arrow Advanced Towing System (Figure 14.5) is rated at 10,000 pounds gross trailer weight and 1,300 pounds of hitch weight. This is a separate coupler unit designed to be used with a conventional two-inch receiver. No modifications are required to either the trailer or the tow vehicle in order to utilize the Hensley Arrow. The assembly fits between the trailer's coupler and the receiver hitch and consists of an articulated ball mount, a set of weight-distributing spring bars, strut bars, and jack assemblies. All this is designed to eliminate trailer sway, calm the trailer on rough road surfaces, cause the trailer to track more precisely behind the tow vehicle, and reduce the bow wave effect caused by 18-wheelers flying past at high speed.

■ CONVENTIONAL HITCH HARDWARE ■

Receivers

A conventional hitch platform is secured beneath the rear of the tow vehicle. The rearmost part of the platform is the receiver—a section of reinforced square-steel tubing into which the shank of a ball mount is inserted (Figure 14.6).

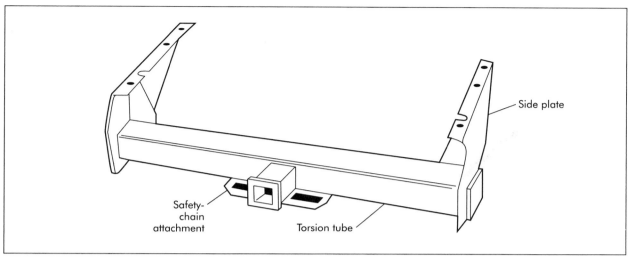

Figure 14.6 Receiver assemblies are secured, preferably using bolts, to the rear of the tow vehicles.

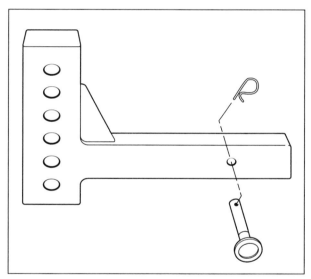

Figure 14.7 Solid steel adjustable ball-mount shanks are available for heavy towing service.

Shanks

For lightweight load-carrying service, there are ball-mount shanks made of square-steel tubing. Heavy towing, on the other hand, requires a solid shank (Figure 14.7). In both cases, the shank has a hole through it that lines up with holes on opposite sides of the receiver. When the hole in the shank is lined up with those in the receiver, a hitch pin is inserted and held in place by a clip or a lock.

Ball Mounts

A ball mount is attached to the end of the shank (Figure 14.8). Some ball mounts are adjustable to accommodate varying coupler heights and permit fine-tuning of the hitch to optimize performance. After the ball mount has been properly adjusted, it need never be readjusted unless it is to be used with a different tow vehicle or trailer. When setting up an adjustable ball mount, level the trailer on a level surface. Measure from the inside of the coupler to the ground to determine the starting ball height. Set the ball so that it is approximately 1 to 1½ inches higher than the measured figure. This is your starting point. Adjustments may be needed after the spring bars are attached. If you plan on using a weld-together ball mount, make sure the welding is done by a certified shop. Adjustable ball mounts that bolt together, however, provide flexibility for unforeseen circumstances.

The Ball

A ball of appropriate size and rating is installed on the ball mount (Figure 14.9). Balls are available in sizes from 1⅞ inches to 2⁵⁄₁₆ inches, with a variety of risers to elevate the ball above the mount. Balls are rated for loads ranging from 2,000 to 10,000 pounds, but raised balls usually have lower ratings. It is critical that the ball rating be equal to or greater than the gross vehicle weight rating (GVWR) of the trailer.

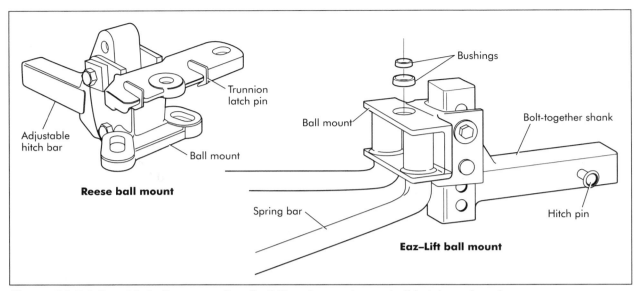

Figure 14.8 Adjustable ball mounts allow flexibility when setting up ball height and angle.

To be safe, three or four threads of the ball shank should be showing past the nut and lock washer when properly tightened. Balls should be greased with a thin layer of ball grease (available at most RV supply stores).

When using a Reese ball mount, if the ball has a 1-inch threaded shank, use bushing no. 55030 to reduce hole size in the ball mount to 1 inch. Place a

lock washer next to the nut. If the ball has a ¼-inch threaded shank and a standard-size (1 inch or more thickness) nut, place a lock washer on top of the ball mount. This reduces interference between the spring-bar trunnion and ball nut during very tight turns. If the ball has a 1¼-inch threaded shank and thin nut (.72 inch thickness), place the lock washer next to the nut. Torque the nut to 200 foot-pounds in all cases.

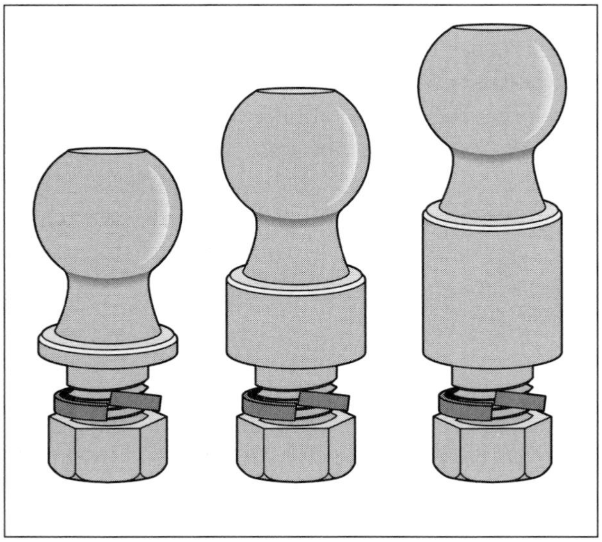

Spring Bars

Spring bars are used with weight-distributing hitches to spread the hitch weight among the axles of both the trailer and tow vehicle (Figure 14.10). Spring bars are rated in various weight capacities, and the correct ones must be employed to allow the load-distributing system to function properly. The rule of thumb is to utilize spring bars that are rated slightly higher (up to 250 pounds more) than the trailer's actual hitch weight. If springs bars of insufficient capacity are used, the rear of the tow vehicle will sag under the weight of the A-frame, or the spring bars will need to be overtensioned to maintain a level tow vehicle. If springs bars of excessive capacity are used, the ride quality could be harsh.

When the spring bars are attached between the ball mount and the trailer frame, tension adjustment

Figure 14.9 Hitch balls are available in 1⅞-inch, 2-inch, and 2⁵⁄₁₆-inch sizes; heavier trailers require a 2⁵⁄₁₆-inch size.

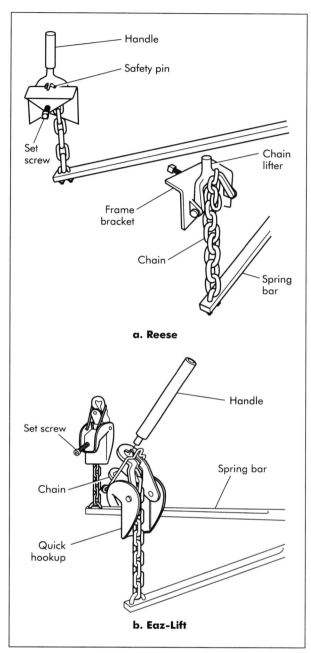

Handle

Safety pin

Set screw

Chain lifter

Frame bracket

Chain

Spring bar

a. Reese

Handle

Set screw

Chain

Spring bar

Quick hookup

b. Eaz-Lift

Figure 14.10 Spring bars are used to spread the hitch weight to the front axle of the tow vehicle and axle(s) of the trailer. Shown here are the Reese (*top*) and the old-style Eaz-Lift (*bottom*).

is made by selecting the appropriate links of the spring-bar chains. This permits fine-tuning of the system for the proper amount of weight transfer. The chains are attached to frame brackets on the trailer

A-frame, and chain lifters (brackets) apply tension to the spring bars as they are locked in position.

Lightly grease the bar ends where they lock into the ball mount to reduce wear on the components.

Safety Chains

It is vital that safety chains and hooks (or other attaching devices) are rated higher than the GVWR of the trailer. The chains should be installed in such a manner that they run from the A-frame to a set of chain loops attached to the hitch receiver. Adjust the safety chains so they are sufficiently loose to allow sharp cornering without binding or other interference, while being tight enough to prevent them from dragging on the ground. Properly hooked up, safety chains should cross beneath the coupler so that if the trailer were to come uncoupled, the A-frame would be supported above the ground in the cradle formed by the crossed chains. Make sure the chains are positioned inside the **V** formed by the spring bars.

■ INSTALLING THE HITCH ■

In every installation, it is vital to insure that the platform is precisely aligned and solidly attached to the tow-vehicle frame. High-grade bolts should be employed, and they should be torqued according to the manufacturer's installation instructions. When using bolts, it's best to use those supplied with the hitch equipment. Cheap, low-quality nuts and bolts seem to be the norm when buying at certain hardware store chains. Look for high-quality grade 5 or grade 8 bolts and nuts, as required by the individual hitch-hardware suppliers. Check with your local industrial supplier for the best nuts and bolts.

Conventional Hitches

Conventional hitch platforms are attached to the rearmost section of the tow-vehicle frame. The platform should be bolted in place with the appropriate hardware. Welded receivers should be considered a thing of the past. Care should be taken by the installer to insure that the attachment points are those required by the receiver manufacturer—usually the strongest points of attachment. Most receiver assemblies are designed for specific vehicles, and the bolt holes are pre-drilled to make installation easy and safe. A major safety point here: Do not try to save money by purchasing a hitch lighter in capacity than you need to safely tow the load. Your safety and the safety of others depends on having the proper weight-carrying capacity for the intended load. All receivers should have their weight ratings clearly labeled.

Fifth-Wheel Hitches

There are several different brands and weight capacities of fifth-wheel hitches on the market, but only two basic types: fixed and tilting-head models. The fixed head is held level with the sides of the bed of the truck and can only pivot in a back and forth direction. The tilting-head model pivots in a back-and-forth direction and in a side-to-side motion, allowing the fifth-wheel to be easily connected on ground that is not level.

Fifth-wheel hitches also come in several weight capacities, from 8,000 pounds to more than 25,000 pounds. Never buy a hitch that's rated lower than the weight that you expect to tow. A good safety margin is to purchase a hitch that is at least 10 percent over the GVWR of your fifth-wheel. If you plan on towing a very heavy fifth-wheel, you should locate the hitch-pin approximately two inches in front of the rear axle line of the truck. This transfers additional weight to the front of the truck. In any case, never locate the hitch pin behind the rear-axle line; doing so can adversely affect handling.

There is a tremendous amount of pressure between the pin and the hitch saddle. To minimize the wear and prevent binding between the pin, the saddle, and the pinbox, you must lubricate the pin with high-pressure grease. A cleaner method of reducing the friction between the pinbox and the saddle is to use a Teflon disk or pad, which eliminates the need for grease. This also makes working around the saddle cleaner without the fifth-wheel hitched.

When installing a fifth-wheel hitch, it is important to bolt the platform directly to the tow-vehicle frame rather than simply attaching it to the sheet-metal floor of the cargo box. Prior to installation of a fifth-wheel hitch, the height of the hitch

point must be determined. Adjustment should be made to allow a minimum of 5½ inches of clearance at the closest points between the top of the truck bed rails and the bottom of the fifth-wheel.

Some applications, such as short-wheelbase trucks, may not allow the hitch to be installed in the ideal location due to clearance problems at the rear corners of the truck cab. Specialized fifth-wheel hitch versions that allow the saddle to be moved rearward when the fifth-wheel must be maneuvered in close quarters are available. You should not tow the fifth-wheel with the saddle in the rearward position. If provisions are not made to allow for greater clearance between the front of the fifth-wheel and the rear of the truck cab, certain collision damages are inevitable.

■ CONVENTIONAL HITCHING PROCESS ■

Successful use of weight-distributing hitch equipment depends upon proper adjustment of all components (Figure 14.11).

1. Begin with the tow vehicle and trailer parked on level ground. Block the trailer wheels. Unhitch the trailer and use the tongue jack to adjust the trailer. Measure the distance between the trailer frame and ground at the front and rear corners, and adjust until the frame is level. Note the following measurements:
   a. Distance from ground to top of the inside of coupler socket.
   b. Distance from ground to lower corner of bumper at all four corners of tow vehicle. You can also use the distance from the bottom of the wheel wells to the ground as reference points.
2. The first adjustment to be made is the ball height. With the adjustable ball mount secured in the receiver, measure from the ground to the top of the ball. Depending upon the hitch weight and the type of tow vehicle, the ball height will need to be adjusted so that it is slightly higher than the distance from the ground to the inside of the top of the coupler. Use the following as a guide:
   a. For trucks with extra-heavy-duty springs, set the ball height equal to the coupler height.

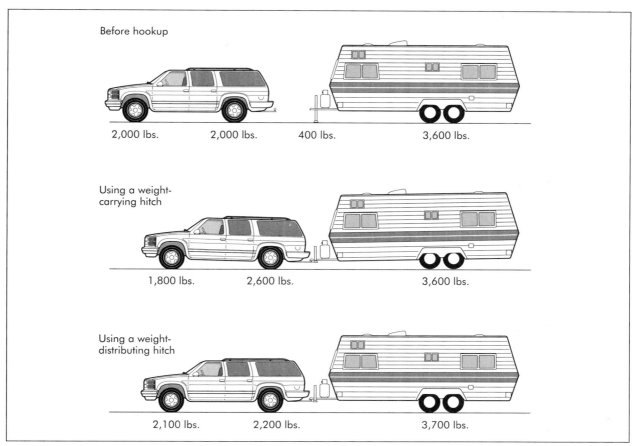

Before hookup

2,000 lbs.   2,000 lbs.   400 lbs.   3,600 lbs.

Using a weight-carrying hitch

1,800 lbs.   2,600 lbs.   3,600 lbs.

Using a weight-distributing hitch

2,100 lbs.   2,200 lbs.   3,700 lbs.

Figure 14.11 Proper adjustment of a weight-distributing hitch will move approximately 50 percent of the hitch weight and spread 25 percent to the front axle of the tow vehicle and 25 percent to the trailer axles(s).

b. For pickups with standard springs, raise the ball height about ¹⁄₃₂ inch for each 100 pounds of hitch weight.

c. For passenger cars, raise the ball height about ¹⁄₁₆ inch for each 100 pounds of hitch weight. After the rest of the hitching process has been accomplished, it may be necessary to fine-tune the system by moving the adjustable ball mount up or down to achieve a near-perfect ball height.

3. Adjustable ball mounts can also be tilted in small increments, raising or lowering the spring-bar tips in relation to the ground, allowing them to be placed in the proper attitude and under the right amount of tension. But this adjustment cannot be made until the spring bars have been hooked up and examined for proper position. To obtain proper ball-mount tilt, insert the spring bars

in the sockets and swing them outward about 25 degrees, which is the same angle as they will have when the trailer and tow vehicle are hitched to one another. Lift up on the spring bar tips to take up slack. Tilt the ball mount to obtain the proper chain adjustment (Figure 14.12); this is your starting point.

4. The next step is to lower the weight of the A-frame on the hitch. Make certain that the coupler-locking mechanism grasps the ball securely. Raise the tongue jack to remove all weight from the hitch and continue upward until the rear of the tow vehicle rises a few inches (this will make lifting the spring bars onto their brackets easier). Insert the spring bars in their mounts and hook up the spring bar chains to the chain-lift brackets on the trailer A-frame. The chains should be as close to vertical as possible, assuming the tow vehicle and trailer are aligned straight ahead. If

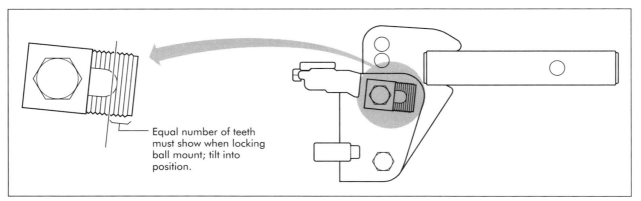

Equal number of teeth must show when locking ball mount; tilt into position.

Figure 14.12 Adjustable ball mounts allow the owner to regulate tilt when attaching spring bars.

necessary, move the brackets forward or backward on the A-frame until the chains are vertical. Insert the safety pin in the brackets before you remove the lifting tool to prevent accidental injury from occurring after the load has been imposed on the spring bars. Make sure chains are not twisted; you may have to make a half-twist to accommodate certain chain positions in relation to the brackets.

A little experimentation is necessary to discover which link of the chain to use. Start with a link that requires moderate force on the chain-lift brackets and then make adjustment up or down by one link until the spring bars distribute the right amount of weight to keep the tow vehicle level. Make sure you have no fewer than four chain links under tension. Using fewer than four links can result in damage to the brackets when turning tight corners. If it is not possible to achieve a level tow vehicle without tightening the chains beyond the four-link limit, then the ball-mount angle must be adjusted or spring bars of a higher-weight capacity must be employed.

5. Lower the tongue jack until all the weight is on the ball mount. Measure again beneath the corners of the tow-vehicle bumpers where you measured the first time to verify that the vehicle has squatted equally front and rear, or if the hitching process has inflicted torque on the frame so that one side is lower than the other. If it isn't correct, readjust the links of the spring-bar chains, or change to spring bars of a different weight rating, until the tow vehicle squats equally front and rear and remains level side to side.

Tightening the chains effectively transfers load along the vehicle frame from the rear to the front of the tow vehicle. Overtightening may result in loss of traction in a rear-wheel-drive vehicle and loss of rear-wheel-braking effectiveness as the weight is removed from the rear axle. Insufficient tension on the chains results in light steering, reduced front-wheel-braking effectiveness, and poor handling of the tow vehicle.

6. After determining which are the correct spring-bar chain links for your trailer and tow-vehicle combination, mark the proper links with paint for future reference.

7. Finish the hitching process by attaching the breakaway cable and plugging in the electrical cord. After removing the blocks from the trailer wheels, test the trailer lights and brakes.

■ FIFTH-WHEEL HITCHING PROCESS ■

Hitching a fifth-wheel trailer is, in some ways, easier than hitching a conventional trailer. This is because the fifth-wheel hitch is usually fully visible to the driver at all times, so there is less difficulty in aligning the hitch and coupler pin. Follow these guidelines:

1. Block the trailer wheels.
2. Lower the truck tailgate.
3. Raise the front trailer jacks until the pin-box plate is slightly higher than the hitch saddle.

4. Remove the handle-locking pin, and rotate the handle to open the pin lock. Some brands of hitches do not require opening the pin lock, but the retaining pin must be removed first. Check with your owner's manual for exact hitching instructions.

5. Slowly back up the truck until the kingpin is firmly seated in the coupler slot. When the kingpin engages the latch plate, the hitch will automatically lock in place.

6. Set the tow-vehicle parking brake to hold slight pressure against the kingpin.

7. Always visually inspect to insure that the kingpin is solidly locked in place. If not, repeat steps 5 and 6.

8. Replace the safety pin to secure the latch.

9. Attach the breakaway cable, plug in the electrical cord, and raise the tailgate.

10. Remove the blocks from the wheels and retract the front landing jacks.

11. Test trailer lights and brakes.

■ SWAY-CONTROL DEVICES ■

Two different types of sway-control devices are in common use in the RV industry. They are the friction-type and the Reese Dual Cam Sway Control. Because of the way friction sway-control units operate, and the forces they impose on the trailer A-frame, they are not recommended for use on trailers with surge brakes or on trailer A-frames with less than .080-inch-wall thickness.

Friction sway-control mechanisms consist of a bracket that attaches to the trailer frame with either brackets or small socket and ball, a friction assembly with a friction plate that is adjusted by turning a screw-in handle, and a slide bar with a small ball socket on the front end. For increased control, two units can be installed, one on each side of the trailer A-frame.

In operation, the slide bar slips through the friction assembly, which is tightened until it acts as a brake on the slide bar, permitting the bar to slide in and out only under the influence of great force. The socket end of the slide bar fits over a small ball located to one side of, and to the rear of, the hitch ball on the ball mount. This sets up a triangle between the trailer frame, the sway control, and the hitch system. The sway-control unit acts as a variable-length side of the triangle. Its length is permitted to change when turning corners, yet the braking action of the friction assembly and slide bar resists unwanted pivoting motion of the trailer and tow vehicle while traveling.

Reese Dual Cam Sway Control is recommended only for trailers with fairly heavy hitch weights (usually larger trailers in the 28- to 32-foot range). They are a bit more complex than friction-type units, with more hardware involved. Once installed, however, no adjustment is needed. For even greater control, the Reese Dual Cam Sway Control system can be used along with one friction-type unit. With the Reese Dual Cam Sway Control system, vertical movement of the tow vehicle and trailer is permitted, but trailer sway is dampened by torsion action of the cam arms because they resist lateral movement.

It should also be pointed out that trailer sway is likely caused by improper hitch weight. If the hitch weight is too light, the trailer naturally becomes tail heavy. A trailer that is tail heavy is always prone to sway or fishtail.

Ideally, a conventional trailer should have a hitch weight that is 12 to 15 percent of the overall trailer weight—limited, of course, by the weight rating of the hitch and the tow vehicle. In reality though, most trailers have closer to 10 percent hitch weight.

First, find out your trailer's hitch weight. With the trailer loaded and ready to go, take it to a certified public scale and, with the spring bars disconnected, the tongue jack on the scale, and the tow vehicle off the scale, weigh the trailer. This will give you the total weight of the trailer. Hitch up the trailer, set the coupler on the ball (no spring bars), and take a second weight; this is the axle(s) weight. Subtract this weight from the total weight and you will have the hitch weight.

Hitch weight can be increased, if necessary, by moving supplies forward.

Installing Sway-Control Devices

Reese Friction-type Sway-Control Device

To install the Reese friction-type device:

1. The Reese friction-type sway-control (Figure 14.13) is installed with the sway-control ball

located 1⅛ inches forward of the hitch ball and 5½ inches outward. Install the ball using a locking washer and nut. Locate the ball in an outwardmost position and torque the nut to 100 foot-pounds.

2. Hitch the trailer for normal towing. The trailer should be aligned directly behind the tow vehicle. If a tow vehicle is not available, position the ball mount in the trailer coupler so the hitch bar is on the centerline. It is important that the hitch bar match the tow vehicle hitch-box angle.

3. Check the position of the nylon pad. The correct position is inside the body between the friction-plate assemblies and with the hole aligned with body holes.

4. Install the handle with the washer into the body. Lubricate the handle threads, the washer, and the handle flange with oil or light grease before installing the handle. Position the slide-bar end 4¼ inches from and parallel to the body. Tighten the handle.

5. Place the slide-bar coupler on the ball. Hold the bracket up to the frame. Position the bracket for optimum handle clearance. All four corner holes must be riveted to secure the frame-clamp bracket to the frame.

6. Drill one ⅜-inch hole through the bracket and frame side. The hole must be straight and round—the drill must not walk. The holes in the bracket are punched undersize so the drill will match bracket and frame holes. Install the drive rivet. Use a washer on the rivet if the frame is less than .120 inch thick. Use a hammer to drive the rivet pin flush with the rivet head.

NOTE: Use drive rivets for frames .080 inch to .188 inch thick. For thicker frames, use SAE grade 5 bolts with nuts and lock washers.

7. Drill three remaining corner holes. Immediately after each hole is drilled, install a rivet or bolt.

8. Check for possible interference between the end of the slide bar and the bracket rear end and between the slide bar and snap-up bracket. Check for interference between bumper, bumper guards, coupler, and sway control. Have an observer check for interfer-

ence while the trailer is slowly turned in both directions. If necessary, loosen and move the sway-control ball inward to obtain greater clearance.

Eaz-Lift Friction-type Sway-Control Device

The Eaz-Lift friction-type sway-control device attaches to a small ball on the ball mount and another small ball on the trailer frame (Figure 14.14). A spring clip is employed to secure both balls in their respective sockets.

To position the ball for installation on the trailer frame, measure 24 inches back from the center line of the coupler ball to locate the center line of the frame-mounted sway-control ball. The sway-control ball can be either welded in place or secured with self-tapping bolts.

Reese Dual Cam Sway Control

Installation is fairly simple for the Reese Dual Cam Sway Control (Figure 14.15). There are two separate units, each the mirror image of the other, one for the right side of the trailer A-frame and one for the left side. Each unit consists of a frame U-bolt pivot bracket, a cam arm, and the cam. The U-bolt bracket attaches to the trailer A-frame, and the pivot end of the cam arm is bolted to the pivot point on the bracket. At the lower end of the cam arm, a clevis is used to connect the spring-bar chains to the cam arm. Using this system, the spring bars are no longer directly chained to the chain-lift bracket. Rather, the lower end of the cam arm fits up into the cam, which is attached beneath the trailing end of the spring bar. As the chain is tightened, the cam arm lifts the spring bar, thereby distributing the load.

Steps for installation are as follows:

1. Assemble the clevis through the chain. Attach the clevis to the cam arm with a ⅜-inch bolt and a ⅜-inch locknut. Assemble the cam arm to the pivot bracket using a ½-inch bolt. Assemble with the bolt head to the outside and tighten the nut securely against lock washer.

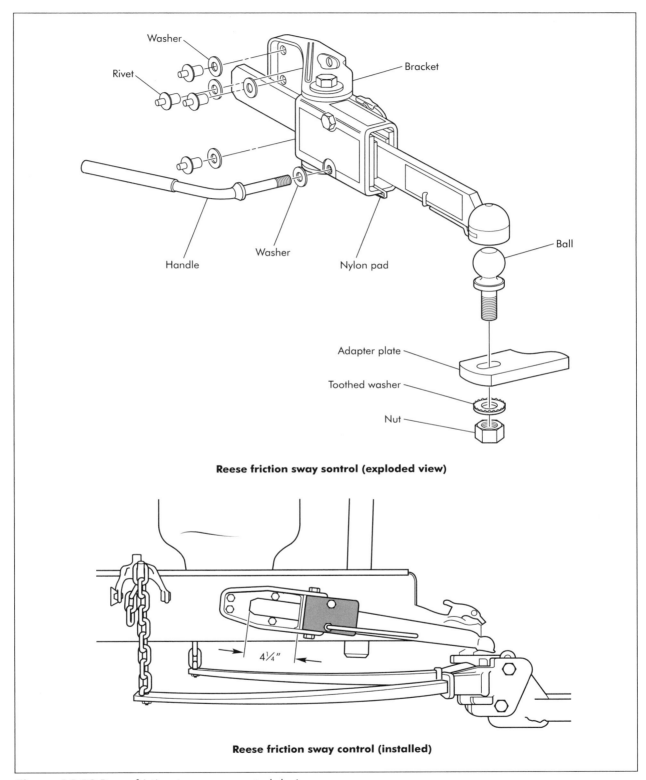

Reese friction sway sontrol (exploded view)

Reese friction sway control (installed)

Figure 14.13 Reese friction-type sway-control device

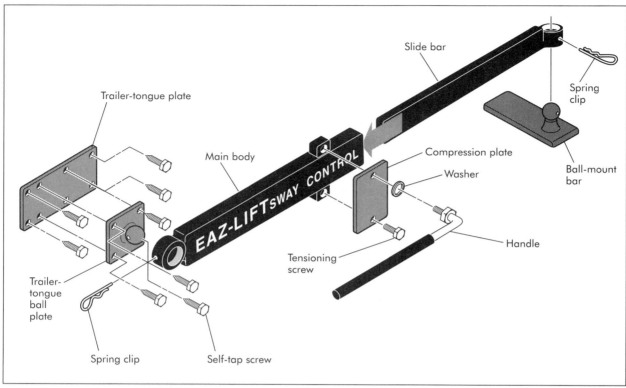

Figure 14.14 Eaz-Lift friction-type sway-control device

2. Attach pivot brackets to each side of trailer A-frame using four U-bolts. Install eight $^7/_{16}$-inch tail nuts—leave nuts one turn loose.

   CAUTION: Be sure U-bolts are at least 2½ inches apart; 5 inches is preferred.

   NOTE: If frame is open on one side (C-channel), install a reinforcing plate in the open side where the pivot brackets are attached.

3. Attach the snap-up bracket to the trailer frame so the chain is vertical, if possible.

4. Attach the cam to the small end of the spring bar using a ½-inch bolt and lock washer, and a ⅜-inch U-bolt with two nuts and lock washers. Torque the ½-inch bolt to 70 foot-pounds. Tighten U-bolt nuts. Rap each corner of U-bolt with a hammer, and torque nuts to 25 foot-pounds.

   NOTE: The cam must be mounted on the bottom side of the spring bar.

5. Measure from the ground to the top plate of the ball mount. Connect the trailer to the tow vehicle. Using the tongue jack, raise the trailer A-frame and the rear of the tow vehicle approximately 5 to 8 inches. Install the spring-bar trunnion in the ball mount. Place the bottom trunnion into the lower socket first. Spring bars may be used on either side. Mate spring bar and cam to cam arms. Pull the chain vertical and place the appropriate link on the hook of the snap-up bracket. Place the snap-up in the up position. Install the safety pin. Then install the second spring bar using the same number of chain links.

6. Lower the tongue jack. Again measure from the ground to the top plate of the ball mount. Measurements should be the same or ½ inch less than before. If not, select the chain link that will bring the tow vehicle to a level position.

   NOTE: Tow vehicle and trailer should be loaded and ready for travel before final leveling.

When hitching with the Reese Dual Cam system, the spring bars are positioned in such a manner that

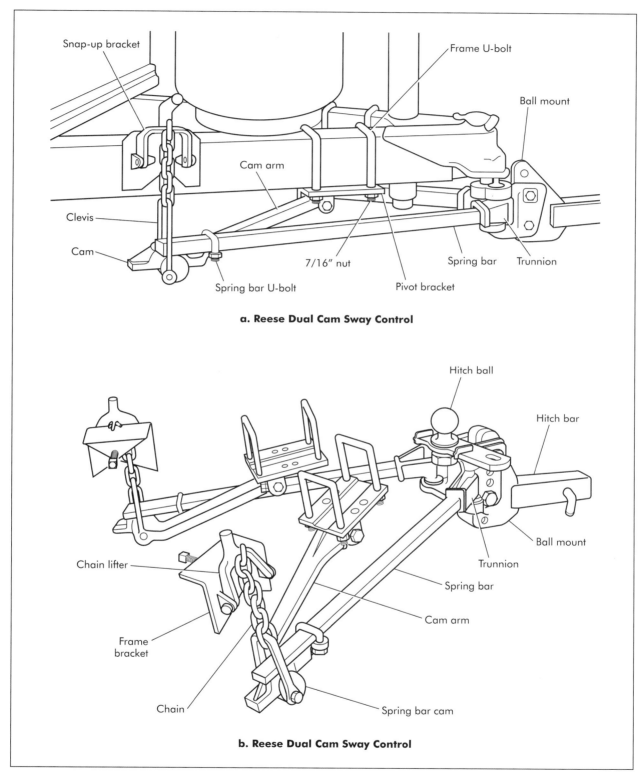

a. Reese Dual Cam Sway Control

b. Reese Dual Cam Sway Control

Figure 14.15 Reese Dual Cam Sway Control (two views)

■ **TROUBLESHOOTING** ■

THE HITCH SYSTEM

Problem	Possible Cause	Correction
Coupler separates from ball	Coupler ball clamp failure	Check ball clamp for breakage or excessive wear
	Failure to properly connect coupler over ball	Double-check ball clamp when hitching up
	Improper ball size	Check ball size and replace if necessary
Spring bar falls out on ground	Broken spring-bar retaining clips	Inspect ball mount for broken or missing spring-bar retaining clips
	Failure to properly insert spring bars	Double-check installation
Spring-bar tension brackets open and release tension	Broken or missing bracket safety pins	Inspect bracket safety pins and replace if necessary
Noise from hitch	Dry ball	Lubricate ball
	Loose receiver bolts	Inspect bolts attaching receiver platform to vehicle frame; tighten if necessary.
	Dry spring-bar ends	Inspect and lubricate trunnion ends of spring bars
Poor tow-vehicle handling	Improper spring-bar tension	Double-check hitching procedure
	Improper ball height	Remeasure and adjust for proper ball height
	Improper ball-mount angle	Adjust ball-mount angle to sustain spring bars level with ground and a minimum of four chain links is under tension
Loss of traction	Excessive spring-bar tension	Reduce spring-bar tension
Light steering	Insufficient spring-bar tension	Increase spring-bar tension
Steering plows through corners	Excessive sway control	Reduce sway control
Trailer sways easily	Insufficient sway control	Increase sway control
	Worn sway control	Inspect sway-control-friction surfaces and replace if necessary
	Insufficient tongue load	Increase tongue load to about 12 percent of total trailer weight

the lower end of the cam arm fits up into the cam beneath the tail end of the bars. The only adjustment made is to insure that the frame brackets are positioned so the system is self-centering. To do this, loosen the U-bolt nuts slightly and drive straight ahead with the trailer in tow for about 100 feet. Check mating of cam with arms and, if the bracket positioning is not correct, rap the pivot brackets with a hammer to jar them into place. Then tighten the U-bolt nuts. Periodic rechecking of alignment is part of standard maintenance.

Adjusting Sway-Control Devices

Adjusting a Reese sway-control friction assembly to work with a particular trailer requires some experimenting. After coupling the trailer to the tow vehicle and hooking up the sway-control device, it is necessary to find the zero-load point of the friction assembly. Do this by tightening the handle while at the same time moving the slide bar up and down in the friction assembly by hand. When the bar won't move any farther, the zero-load point has been reached.

Note the position of the handle, and tighten ½ to 1 turn for small trailers up to about 3,500 pounds. Tighten 1 to 1¾ turns for trailers between 3,000 and 7,000 pounds. (Overtightening can damage the unit.) This will give you a starting point, after which it is necessary to drive the vehicle in order to determine whether more adjustment is necessary. Make additional adjustments ¼ turn at a time until it feels right. An indication that the sway control is too tight is when the vehicle doesn't easily and fully return to a straight-ahead position after turning a corner.

The Eaz-Lift friction-type sway-control device is adjusted differently. Adjustment can be made by tightening or loosening the bolt below the handle, before tightening the handle itself.

Adjustment for the Reese Dual Cam Sway Control system is accomplished by loosening the eight ⁷⁄₁₆-inch nuts. Drive the tow vehicle and trailer in a straight line. This is important. Sight down the center of the hood, and drive approximately 100 feet toward a distant point. Check mating of cam with cam arms. If not mated squarely, rap pivot brackets with a hammer.

Tighten the eight ⁷⁄₁₆-inch tail nuts. Torque each nut to 60 foot-pounds, but be careful not to distort the frame.

NOTE: From time to time, it may be necessary to use a different chain link to properly level the tow vehicle and trailer. This may be due to weight changes in the tow vehicle or trailer or due to trunnion wear. Level the tow vehicle, readjust the dual-cam system, and recheck alignment periodically.

■ HITCH MAINTENANCE ■

Checking Hitch Systems

- Inspect all fasteners for tightness at least every 2,000 miles of operation. This includes the bolts holding the receiver platform to the tow-vehicle frame, the ball-mount bolts, the spring-bar-tension bracket bolts, and the sway-control mounts.
- On fifth-wheel systems, inspect the platform bolts and the kingpin box mounting bolts. Torque all platform mounting bolts to 50 to 55 foot-pounds. Torque kingpin box bolts to 150 foot-pounds.
- On tilt-platform fifth-wheel systems locate and grease all Zerk fittings and pivot points.
- If a Teflon or hard plastic pad is used on a fifth-wheel hitch, you need to inspect it for cracks and large chips. Replace the pad if damaged.
- Inspect the ball clamp and coupler-latching mechanism for freedom of movement before each use. On fifth-wheel systems, inspect the kingpin latch plate and latch bolt for freedom of operation.
- Inspect spring-bar trunnions and mounting sockets for wear before each use. On fifth-wheel systems, inspect the kingpin, the pin-box plate, and the saddle for wear or damage.
- Inspect safety chains for signs of wear or stress before each use. Periodically clean and lubricate the coupler socket-and-ball clamp, the ball, the spring-bar trunnions, and the spring-bar sockets. On fifth-wheel systems, lubricate the latch bolt and pivot point of

---

■ CHECKLIST ■
SWAY-CONTROL DEVICES

- For friction-type sway-control devices, inspect and clean the components. Oil should be applied periodically to the handle and bolt threads, the trunnion bolts, and the ball. No oil should ever be placed on the friction surfaces of the slide bar.
- Reese Dual Cam Sway Control system maintenance consists of lubricating the ball-mount sockets and spring-bar trunnions to prevent rapid wear.
- Trunnions should be lightly lubricated every towing day. Excess oil, dirt, and grit should be wiped out whenever the trailer is uncoupled. It's wise to oil the pivot-bolt joints occasionally at each end of the cam arms, because the system was designed to utilize metal-to-metal friction. If the unit is noisy, it is permissible to lightly coat the cam surface with petroleum jelly.

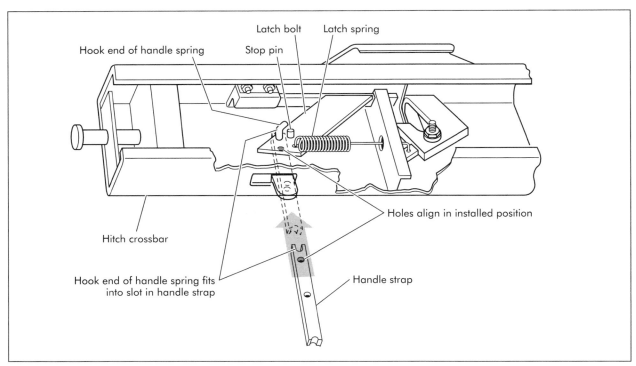

Figure 14.16 Latch bolt and pivot point in fifth-wheel hitches must be lubricated with SAE 30-weight oil every six months.

latch plate with SAE 30 oil at least every six months (Figure 14.16).

■ Grease the load-bearing surfaces of the fifth-wheel hitch with a lithium-base grease every 2,000 miles of operation to reduce wear and provide easier turning, if a Teflon disk is not used. Inspect and clean the fifth-wheel-hitch latch plate before each use. On fifth-wheel hitches, grease the pivot points between the rails and hitch with a lithium-base grease every 2,000 miles of operation.

■ Replace all worn or damaged parts.

■ CHAPTER 15 ■
EXTERIOR CARE
AND REPAIR

Mother Nature has joined with the by-products of our industrial society in what seems like a conspiracy to wreak havoc on our vehicles. Sunshine oxidizes the paint and fades the color. It shrinks and cracks vinyl, dries out and splits rubber, and deteriorates upholstery fabric. Storms can deliver an acid or alkaline bath (essentially the acid-rain fallout of industry) to mar the exterior finish. Rain creates mud to be splashed on the outside of the RV, underneath the RV, and tracked inside. The wind carries dust, dirt, pollen, and myriad airborne contaminants to deposit all over the vehicle. And while all this is going on, the bugs and birds are doing their part.

■ THE SYMPTOMS OF WEAR ■

Gradual deterioration of the exterior is a relentless process. In this chapter, we will define the symptoms of a vehicle in need of attention to exterior maintenance and discuss how to go about providing appropriate care. When using exterior-care products, it is important to follow the directions on the package because similar products may have different directions for use.

Oxidation

When exterior paint takes on a dull, lifeless, chalky appearance, it is suffering from oxidation. This is a gradual process in which oxygen combines with the paint to form new chemical substances. The process is speeded up by the bleaching action of the sun. The end result is gradual deterioration of the surface.

The most effective way to slow down the progress of oxidation is to keep the vehicle covered or garaged, although this may not be practical for large RVs. While oxidation may not be entirely preventable, it is somewhat repairable by using products that remove the oxidized paint layer, thus exposing the fresh paint beneath. Cleaner-waxes and finish restorers will remove light oxidation. Glazes and rubbing compounds remove the heavy stuff. Of course, using these abrasive products eventually results in wearing the paint down to bare metal, at which time it becomes necessary to get a new paint job.

Acid/Alkaline Rain

Emissions from industrial, vehicle, and natural sources introduce sulfur, sulfur dioxide, and nitric oxide into the atmosphere. These chemicals can be carried by wind for thousands of miles. When they combine with water, they form sulfuric and nitric acids, which can then fall as acid rain. Acid rain literally etches the painted surface of a vehicle.

Alkaline rain has a similar genesis and results in the same destruction of vehicle surfaces, accelerating the oxidation process and leaving ugly blemishes. Even waxed and poly-sealed surfaces are vulnerable.

Washing, waxing, and polishing won't help with acid/alkaline blemishes. Special products are formulated for this special problem.

Scratches

Minor scratches may be removed by using a cleaner or cleaner-wax, but deeper scratches will need a polishing compound, rubbing compound, or glaze. These are abrasive products that remove top layers of paint, blending the scratch into the surrounding painted surface so it becomes less visible.

General Grime

Depending upon where you live and where you travel, your vehicle may stay clean for quite a while or it may be covered with dirt every time you turn around. Only you can determine how often your vehicle needs a general cleanup, but certainly bird droppings, insects splattered on the outside, tree sap, road tar, and grime will be good indicators of the need for attention.

Once clean, how long is it going to last? The answer to that question depends upon the environmental conditions where your RV is parked. If you're fortunate enough to have a garage or cover for the rig, you may not need to attend to it very often. But it you're on the road a lot, drive newly resurfaced or salted highways, bake in the Sun Belt, or nest beneath the trees in a sappy forest, you may need to stock up on cosmetic products and keep a supply of clean rags handy.

■ EXTERIOR CARE ■

Washing the Vehicle

Before doing anything else to your vehicle's exterior, it must be thoroughly washed. But washing with household detergents containing alkali or ammonia can harm the surface. Special car-wash products have been developed that will remove the dirt and grime from a vehicle's surface without harming the previous wax job. Some products combine a wash-and-wax job all in one process.

These products are liquid or powder concentrates that are intended to be diluted in a pail of water. A soft cloth, sponge, or wash mitt should be used, and the vehicle should be washed in the shade to prevent spotting. Never throw the washcloth, sponge, or mitt

on the ground when not in use; it can pick up small rocks and other debris that can scratch the vehicle surface when reused. Gently dry with a soft, clean chamois or towel to avoid spots.

Exterior Finishing Products, Waxes, Cleaners, and Polishes

Finish Restorers

In preparation for waxing, the vehicle may need treatment with a finish restorer if the finish has become oxidized and dulled by grime. Milder than a rubbing compound, a finish restorer will remove stubborn grime and oxidation, allowing the true color of the paint to show. Instructions for use vary with different products, so read and follow the directions carefully. Typically, these products are applied gently in a circular motion with a soft cloth. After drying, they are buffed to remove residue. Hard rubbing is not recommended.

Rubbing Compounds

For seriously deteriorated painted surfaces, rubbing compounds should be used. These products will remove layers of oxidized paint, minor scratches, and stains. Extreme care must be employed when working with rubbing compounds, because if they are used too vigorously, they will remove good paint along with the bad. Rubbing compounds can also be used to remove scratches, stains, or rust from chrome finishes.

As always, work on clean, dry, cool surfaces. Apply rubbing compound sparingly and evenly, rubbing in a straight line just enough to remove the oxidized paint, stains, or scratches. Buff lightly with a clean, dry cloth.

CAUTION: Do not use rubbing compounds on flat-black paint, wood panels, vinyl, plastic, or fiberglass.

Waxes

Waxes are applied to the exterior of vehicles to protect the paint from the elements. The theory is to let the wax, rather than the paint, take the beating delivered by sun, wind, blowing dirt, bugs, and all the rest. By keeping a healthy coat of wax between the paint and the elements, the paint will last longer and look better, and it's a simple job to renew the wax periodically.

All wax manufacturers agree that prior to waxing, the vehicle should be washed and cleaned of stubborn grime. If the paint has suffered oxidation, some wax containers specify that finish restorers be used to prepare the surface for the final wax job.

Waxes should be applied to a cool vehicle surface in the shade, using a clean, soft, damp, or dry (according to package directions) terry cloth. Wax should be applied briskly and in a circular motion, laying down a thin, even coat to one section of the vehicle at a time. A separate, soft, clean terry cloth should be used to lightly buff the wax after it has had time to dry to a haze. Turn the buffing cloth frequently and shake out the residue as needed.

You can test the durability of a wax job by watching water bead on the surface. When rain or wash water no longer beads, it's time to freshen up the wax job.

Combination Cleaner-Waxes

Cleaner-waxes are far milder than rubbing compounds, yet they can remove minor stains and oxidation. They offer a one-step process that leaves the painted surface cleaned of dull oxidation and stains, and coats it with a protective wax.

Begin with a clean, cool surface. Apply and finish as you would a regular wax, following specific directions for the product of your choice.

Polishes

Polishes are different from waxes. They are surface preparations that leave a glistening shine, but do not leave a wax layer over the paint. According to manufacturer claims, polishing a vehicle provides superior protection to waxing.

As with wax application, polish should only be applied with a circular motion to clean, dry, cool vehicle surfaces. Oxidized paint will be removed by the polish and retained in the polishing cloth, so it may be necessary to keep several cloths on hand to permit working with a clean cloth at all times. Overlap

areas being worked to insure thorough coverage of all body panels. After the polish dries to a haze, remove residue by buffing with a clean cloth.

Polymer Sealant

Claims of secret formulas and spectacular results circulate in this segment of the automotive-product market. Polymer coatings are claimed to seal the vehicle finish against everything from smog to bird droppings. In theory, the formula actually bonds to the painted surface of any vehicle, whether it be metal, chrome, or fiberglass. It is not, however, intended for use on vinyl, flat paint, plastic, decals, or synthetic or painted wood.

Wash and dry the vehicle, but don't use household detergents or cleaners because they may cause streaking. Apply poly sealant in a circular motion to the entire vehicle surface. Allow to dry thoroughly until a haze appears. Wipe off. Then, with a fresh, dry cloth, buff vigorously.

Metal Polishes

To remove tarnish and minor corrosion, a metal polish is the product of choice. While there are similarities between some of these products, directions for use vary, so it is important to follow the instructions on the product package.

These products are rubbed gently onto the metal surface being treated and then buffed off. Read the instructions carefully, because some products specify that care must be taken to prevent the polish from drying on the surface before being removed.

Tire Dressings

To restore a fresh look to aging tires that may have rubbed against a curb or are just losing their snappy appearance, there are tire protectants available that can be used on both whitewall and blackwall tires.

Whitewalls and white lettering can be restored to a fresh appearance by using products formulated specifically for that job. Follow directions on the container because they vary between products. Basically, the whitewall restorer is sprayed or wiped on and scrubbed or rinsed off, with a short curing duration in between.

Tires subjected to the elements (especially strong sunshine) should be treated every month with a good protectant like 303. A good-quality protectant will have UV blockers and help slow down cracking and crazing and, in general, rubber compound break-down. If the RV is going to be stored outside, cover the tires with plywood or special covers made of vinyl. Tires do not have to be lifted off the ground during the storage period.

NOTE: Never use tire-care products that contain petroleum distillates; they can soften the rubber and cause blistering of the material.

Wheel Cleaners and Polishes

Wheel cleaners come in liquid or paste form. The liquid cleaners are easier to use because all that is required is to spray the product on the wheels, wait about a minute, and then hose off with a strong stream of water. Paste cleaners are applied much like paste wax and require some rubbing and buffing. However, stubborn grime may demand scrubbing, even with the spray-on/hose-off liquid cleaners. And some of the liquid cleaners employ a two-stage system in which two solutions are used—the second neutralizing the action of the first.

CAUTION: Not all types of wheels can be cleaned with all brands of wheel cleaners. Some chrome cleaners will damage aluminum or magnesium wheels, while other products are specifically formulated for these materials. Read the labels carefully before you buy.

Degreasers

Some degreasers on the market are specifically formulated to work on the warm surfaces of an engine to melt the grime away, so working under the hood isn't such a messy job. Others are "all-purpose" degreasers and cleaners that can be used to clean up small areas wherever they are needed.

Labels offer directions for specific use. Often, the products will be used full strength, but sometimes they need to be diluted. Most often, degreasers are sprayed on, then hosed or wiped off.

NOTE: Before washing a dirty motor with solvent, be sure that the runoff is going to a sump designed to contain oils and solvents. Local laws may preclude washing engines where runoff will go into public drains.

Also, use caution not to get any of this material on a painted surface or where graphics are applied.

Glass Cleaners

The numerous glass cleaners on the market are all used in the same manner. Simply spray on and wipe off with a lint-free cloth or paper towel.

But normal glass cleaners should not be used on windows to which a film-type window tint has been applied. For this application, there are special nonabrasive plastic polishes formulated for use on window-tint film, Plexiglas, and convertible-top windows. These products are used by spraying them on a clean, dry surface. They are then spread evenly with a dry cloth, and the surface is buffed to a shine.

To remove bugs and other stubborn dirt from the windshield when normal glass cleaners fail, use white vinegar on a clean cloth. To remove tree sap, try baking soda. It isn't as abrasive as cleanser, but it will cut through the sap.

Tar and Bug Removers

There is no substance as sticky and stubborn as road tar, but bugs come close. Bug and tar remover is designed to clean grease, bugs, and road oil from glass, paint, and polished metal surfaces without damaging the standard automotive paint. It is also effective in cleaning tree sap from the finish.

Dampen a cloth with the bug and tar remover and rub briskly over the grimy surface until it is clean. Wipe with a clean, dry cloth to remove residue. To restore the finish, reapply wax or polish.

An alternate method of removing road tar is to use laundry prewash solution. It cuts the tar like magic. Reapply wax or polish after use.

Rubber-Roof Care

Rubber-roof (EPDM) material needs special care to keep it clean and in good condition. A side benefit of a clean rubber roof is the prevention of unsightly streaks that can run down the RV's sidewalls.

Rubber roofs are glued to a wood decking (substrate), which is usually plywood or lauan that's around ⅜ inch thick. The continuous membrane is attached to the wood using a water-based adhesive. The termination moldings, seams around roof vents, holding-tank vents, roof racks, ladders, and all other accessories screwed into the decking are sealed using a self-leveling lap sealant. Only lap sealant designed for rubber roofs can be used here. Do not use this material on metal or fiberglass roofs.

One of the by-products of weathering is a white, powdery substance (called *chalking*), which is oxidation from prolonged exposure to the sun and other destructive elements in the atmosphere. Chalking poses no threat to the integrity of the material but can cause unsightly streaking on the RV's sidewalls.

The roof should be checked regularly for chalking, deposits from trees or passing birds, and other debris. It should also be inspected for small holes or tears, especially around anything installed on the roof. This includes all air vents, antennas, air conditioner(s), the refrigerator vent, solar panels, and any other extras the owner may have added.

To remove chalking, the rubber roof should be cleaned with borax or other similarly mild abrasive cleaners and a medium bristle brush—and plenty of water. Continue cleaning until no more white residue is revealed.

CAUTION: Do not use any citric-based product or any product containing petroleum distillates.

You may or may not have to treat the rubber roof with a protectant. Rubber roofs are naturally resistant to ultraviolet radiation, sun, and other outside elements. If the chalking returns within a month or two, the cleaning process should be repeated and the surface treated with a good protectant like 303. If your rig's roof has a tendency to chalk, repeat the cleaning/protectant process at least once every six months.

A rubber roof can maintain a good seal for a long period. However, if the RV manufacturer was sloppy and covered protruding or loose screws, pieces of wood, or any other debris with the membrane, normal wear and tear will be accelerated, especially when walking on it. The roof can also be cut or punctured by sharp objects, such as low-hanging branches.

Fortunately, small rips or holes are simple to fix using kits available at RV stores. As long as the hole or rip does not extend into a roof vent, plumbing vent, air conditioner, or termination molding, a patch precoated with adhesive can be used. Kits specifically for this purpose are available at most RV supply stores.

Once the area is cleaned thoroughly and dried, the backing is removed and the patch is positioned over the repair area. The top protective liner is then removed and a ⁵⁄₁₆-inch bead of lap sealant is applied to the entire edge of the patch. Using the feathering tool, the lap sealant is smoothed over, allowing for a secure repair. The patch cannot be used over previous repairs or sealant.

Larger repairs can be made using kits containing a 3-foot-square section of membrane, splice-cleaner, and cement. The process does require more precision since the user must clean the area with soapy water followed by an application of splice-cleaning solution and a base coating of adhesive. Once dry, an additional layer of splicing cement must be applied to the roof surface and membrane patch. The user then affixes the membrane and finishes off the repair with lap sealer.

Smoothing out a large section of membrane can be a little tricky because you really don't get a second chance once the material contacts the roof. Use a 3-inch overlap when sizing the new membrane. In all cases, the repair should be allowed to sit for two hours before moving the vehicle.

The rubber roof should be carefully inspected every time it is cleaned. If the lap sealant around the roof-mounted accessories begins to crack or show holes, you should apply new self-leveling material. Mineral spirits should be used to remove any dirt buildup on the old seals and then allowed to dry for at least fifteen minutes before making the repairs. When applying new lap sealant, make sure the material touches the rubber roof (not already sealed) and the accessory surface. This will insure a tight seal.

Rubber roofs are designed to provide a watertight seal for many years. Under most conditions, they serve their owners well, but only when owners take the responsibility to keep them clean and secure.

Metal- and Fiberglass-Roof Care

One-piece roofs generally do not leak. However, the seams and seals around the vents and accessories can leak if they are not sealed right, using the proper materials. Never coat the entire roof surface with a sealing material; repair only the seams and areas where accessories are installed.

Before making any repairs, scrape off any old material and clean the area with a good solvent. In most cases, the thinner elastomeric sealers will work best since they can find their way into the small cracks and holes. The thicker material, usually formulated with alkyd fibers, should only be used when attempting to fill large holes, creases, or bows in the roof.

When installing new roof vents, holding tank vents, or other accessories, use a good lap sealer over the screw heads and around the seams.

CAUTION: Do not use silicone on the roof.

Aluminum Care and Repair

Aluminum RV exterior skin may be either raw metal or painted. Care of the two surfaces is different in some respects. Harsh abrasives should not be used when cleaning unpainted aluminum because the raw metal surface can become marred by fine scratches. However, a painted aluminum surface can be treated just as a painted steel surface because it is the paint that is being treated and not the aluminum.

To care for and restore the luster of an unpainted aluminum surface, begin by washing thoroughly with a warm solution of automotive wash product. Do not use strong detergents, solvents, or abrasive cleansers. Wash during the cool of the day, in the shade or on an overcast day. Never wash the aluminum skin in direct sunlight.

Before washing, check to see that all windows, vents, compartment doors, and entry doors are closed tightly before washing. Use a large sponge or soft cloth. Begin with the roof. Wash one section at a time, then rinse to prevent the cleaning solution from drying on the surface. Dry with a chamois or soft, clean towel to prevent water spots.

Road tar, sap, and bugs should be cleaned off as soon as possible, before they can harden in place. Use kerosene, turpentine, or naphtha with a soft cloth, taking care not to scratch the surface. Rinse thoroughly with clear water. Wax the affected areas.

The painted aluminum skin should be waxed every three to six months or more often if necessary, as determined by exposure to the elements.

A painted aluminum skin should be washed and cleaned of road tar, sap, and bugs, using the same methods as for unpainted aluminum. When necessary, oxidized paint can be treated by using a polish combination, cleaner-wax, or, in extreme cases, a polishing compound. A good grade of automotive wax should be applied every three to six months, or more often if necessary.

Unpainted aluminum exterior siding used on certain RVs (Airstreams, for example) are treated with a protective coating. You should not wax this surface. In time the protective coating may discolor, fade, or strip away in blotches. Before a new coating can be applied, the old material must be etched off; this requires special chemicals and a safe environment and should be left to the professionals. The use of a polish or rubbing compound to make the surface shiny will make the future application of the protective coating difficult, if not impossible. If you want to make the surface shiny, keep in mind that you'll be a slave to this surface forever.

Aluminum skin that has been physically damaged cannot be repaired and must be replaced. Because aluminum skin is made of large panels of material, considerable work must be done to remove the damaged panels and replace them with new material.

Emergency repairs can be made to prevent moisture or dirt from entering the coach through a damaged exterior wall. Use duct tape to close a puncture or tear. If a panel has come loose, use sheet-metal screws or wood screws (appropriate for the type of coach framework) to secure the panel to the framework until professional repairs can be made.

Replacing Aluminum Siding

The aluminum siding provides protection for the framework of the RV without causing expansion or contraction problems because of the way it is constructed (Figure 15.1). The siding does not rust but does need some protection from the sun to keep the finish from oxidizing, turning dull, and having the decals (striping) or paint from fading. There are dozens of protectants on the market designed to clean and protect the finish, but in most cases, simple soap and water will do the cleaning and normal automotive wax will provide the protection. Keep products with petroleum distillates away from the stick-on striping.

Repairing Damaged Aluminum Siding

Because of the configuration and design of the aluminum siding on most RVs, it almost impossible to repair small sections. RV siding comes in widths of 10 to 18 inches and can be purchased in lengths up to 40 feet. The manufacturer of your RV or your local dealer is the best source for this material. Cost is $3 to $4 per square foot, depending on the style, texture, and paint, plus crating and shipping. Also, if you need a colored section or one with a decal or special striping, the cost will be higher. You will also need to rent, buy, or borrow an industrial stapler/ nailer and special sheet-metal cutters so that the aluminum is not deformed when cut to size for the specific repair. Replacing the siding or, for that matter, making repairs is not inexpensive.

The normal procedure is to gain access to the damaged panel to be replaced by removing the adjacent panels, starting from the bottom or top of the RV, depending on which panel is closer. For example, if the damaged panel is the third one from the bottom, you will have to remove the two lower panels first. You will also have to remove any trim, access doors, vents, door stops, power outlets, water-fill inlets, water-heater access doors, outside refrigerator-service doors, taillights, and any other items that are attached to the sheet metal being removed. (Figure 15.2)

The sheet metal is designed with an interlocking flange at the top of each sheet (Figure 15.3). The metal is stapled at the bottom of each sheet. To remove a single sheet, the metal must be exposed and

Figure 15.2 Exterior door must be removed before disassembling sheet metal siding.

the staples pulled from the bottom of the panel. Then you lift the metal at the bottom and rotate it in an upward or downward direction (Figure 15.4) until the interlocking flange unhooks. In most cases, you'll need a helper for this process. Gently remove the panel from the side of the RV without kinking or bending the metal. Remember that aluminum is soft and will rip and bend very easily. Also be aware that some manufacturers use glue to hold the joints and corners of the sheet metal to the frame. On some RVs, where the outside of the frame is covered with plywood, the manufacturer will simply glue the panel to the wood with a few staples to hold the edges.

NOTE: Always wear gloves when working with sheet metal.

After the skin has been removed from the RV,

Figure 15.1 Aluminum siding is common on trailers, fifth wheels, and campers.

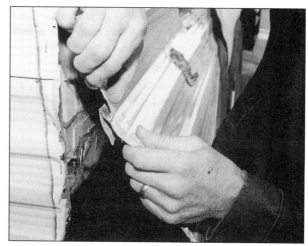

Figure 15.3 Sheet metal has an interlocking flange at the top of each sheet.

Figure 15.4 Once the staples are removed, the sheet metal is rotated upward or downward.

you'll need to perform a careful inspection of the framing to check for damage. Manufacturers use several different materials for framing RVs. If the frame is made of aluminum, then you will be better off going to a service center where there are technicians experienced in welding that material. If the frame is wood, the repair is much simpler. Wood-frame repair will depend on the severity of the damage done to the sidewall. You can, in fact, replace the entire frame if necessary.

To replace the aluminum skin, the procedure is basically the reverse of the removal. The metal is lifted to the side of the RV and rotated until the locking flange (Figure 15.1, page 15.7) connects with the upper panel and then the panel is lowered until flush with the frame. Extreme care must be taken to not bend the panel; flex of only 1 to 2 inches will leave a permanent crease in the sheeting. Follow the manufacturer's original staple placement; glue where the adhesive was originally used. Sealants must be applied to the edges of the panels where they can be clamped by the moldings. Use butyl tape and silicone sealer, attempting to follow the original construction procedure.

The edge and corner moldings must cover the corners of the panels to prevent water from entering the RV. Any doors, windows, service doors, and all other accessories must be replaced into the original locations using fresh butyl tape (gray putty tape can also be used if desired).

Fiberglass Care and Repair

Fiberglass comes in two varieties—painted and gel coat. Gel-coat fiberglass has the pigment applied as the fiberglass panels are manufactured. Routine maintenance of both types of fiberglass is the same: periodic washing (always in the cool of the day or in the shade) with an automotive wash product. Rinse thoroughly to remove soap residue. Dry with a chamois or soft, clean towel to prevent water spots. Apply a coat of good automotive wax every three to six months or more often if necessary to protect the surface.

If damage occurs to a fiberglass surface, repair is fairly easy. A repair kit can be purchased at RV or marine-supply outlets.

Deep scratches can be repaired by applying a coat of fiberglass resin, allowing it to cure, then sanding it until it blends with the surrounding surface. An excellent product for surface repair is Marine Tex, available at boating-supply stores. This product is applied with a putty knife and allowed to cure; then it can be sanded, drilled, sawed, filed, and painted.

If the original fiberglass was painted, a coat of touch-up paint will be necessary to make the repair invisible. If the original surface was gel coat, the color layer may not have been breached, and the clear resin used for the repair may permit the original color to show through, making further touch-up unnecessary. However, if the gel-coat layer is damaged, it may be repaired with a gel-coat repair kit, available at most marine and RV supply outlets

Touching Up Gel Coat

To perform touch-up work on gel coat, follow this routine:

1. Select the proper color gel coat.
2. Brush or spray it on the damaged area.
3. Catalyze it with MEK (methyl ethyl ketone) peroxide, according to the directions on the container.
4. Cover the repair area with a sheet of plastic food wrap to seal off oxygen penetration. This is necessary because gel coat will not cure in the presence of oxygen. Leave the plastic wrap in place for six to eight hours (or

overnight if desired) at a temperature of 70°F.

5. After curing, remove the plastic wrap and wet-sand the area with 320- or 400-grit sandpaper. Follow this by buffing, polishing, and applying paste wax.

To paint over a gel-coat surface, remove any wax, sand the surface, and apply a coat of primer surfacer. Sand the surfacer. Finish by applying paint in a color to match the rest of the coach.

Repairing Severely Damaged Fiberglass

Severe damage, such as cracked or broken fiberglass, is also easy to repair. Follow these steps:

1. Trim away excess broken pieces and restore the remaining fiberglass to its original shape as much as possible.
2. Grind, sand, and clean the surface of the area to remove road grime, oil, and dirt.
3. Mix the fiberglass resin according to instructions on the product container.
4. Cut the fiberglass cloth large enough to cover the area to be repaired and to overlap onto surrounding solid fiberglass by a few inches. If possible, apply a layer of fiberglass to the back side of the damaged area to serve as reinforcement. Then work on the exterior repair.
5. Soak the fiberglass cloth in the resin, and apply the cloth over the surface of the area to be repaired. Smooth it with a roller to help it adhere well to the surface and to eliminate bubbles. The resin will begin to cure immediately, so work swiftly but carefully. Allow the resin to cure the full amount of time specified in the product instructions.
6. After the resin has fully cured, grind and sand the area to make the repair patch blend with the surrounding surface. Apply additional layers of fiberglass as necessary until the repair is built up to the original contour and strength.
7. Grind and sand each layer before applying the next, taking care to maintain the proper body-panel contour. Use a block sander to

prevent ripples. After the final layer of fiberglass has been applied, cured, and sanded, body filler may be used to blend the repair work. To make the repair match the rest of the coach, the area must be painted.

Caulking and Sealing

Age and the elements can dry and crack seam-sealing caulk material, making it unsightly or even resulting in leaks. Periodically inspect all seams and joints to check on the condition of the caulking compound. These areas are found on the roof, around vents, where roof and sidewall panels meet, around the screws used to secure accessories such as roof ladders, along molding strips, and around windows and door frames. If chunks of caulk are missing or badly deteriorated, replacement is advised.

Always clean the area where the old caulking was applied with a good solvent. Use caution not to allow any solvent to run down the sidewalls, soak into the rubber-roof material, or penetrate decorative striping. Although most manufacturers use the thick, gray caulking tape, the black butyl tape is much better. It seals better, is thinner and easier to use, it's more sticky, and it will not ooze as badly. Butyl tape is available in rolls in most RV supply stores.

NOTE: Do not use silicone sealer as a replacement for tape-type caulking.

Moldings and Doors

Exterior trim moldings are often secured to the coach with a double-sided adhesive tape. If the molding begins to pull loose, it can often be repaired by simply replacing the tape and pressing the molding strip back into place.

When cleaning the coach, take a moment to wipe the dirt from the rubber weatherstrip gasket surrounding the door. A shot of silicone lubricant helps keep this gasket fresh.

Periodically inspect the hinges for loose screws. Tighten if necessary. If the hinges squeak, lubricate them with a light oil and wipe away any excess. An occasional drop or two of lock lubricant with graphite will help keep the locks operating freely.

Realigning a Door

Door misalignment can occur as a result of abuse, improper installation at the factory, or normal wear and tear. To realign a door:

1. Determine the cause of misalignment by removing the inside door molding and making a visual inspection to locate where the door frame has shifted in relation to the coach wall.
2. Loosen the screws that hold the aluminum door frame to the RV framework. Work on the hinge side of the door rather than the latch side when making these adjustments.
3. Using ⅛-inch by 1-inch plywood shims, return the frame to square by driving the shims into the appropriate spaces between the door frame and the stud. Continually check the way the door fits in relation to the frame, and make adjustments with the shims until the fit is perfect.
4. Complete the job by tightening the screws to secure the door frame to the coach wall, then replace the molding.

Screens

Replacement of screen material is easy. The screen is held in the frame by a round rubber gasket that is pressed over the edge of the screen and into a groove in the frame. Remove the gasket by carefully prying it out of the groove with a flat-blade screwdriver. Use the old screen intact as a pattern to cut a new piece of matching screen material. Spread the new screen material over the frame and reinstall the gasket. Gently press it into the groove to secure the screen material. Take care to apply just enough tension on the material so it doesn't tear but is tightly stretched across the frame.

Ladders, Roof Racks, and Roof Vents

Periodically check the mounting hardware for tightness and to insure that no cracks or breaks have occurred. Inspect the caulk material used around the mounting hardware, looking for possible breaches in the seal. Repair as necessary.

Roof vents are subject to damage from wind, overhanging branches, and from being stepped on, kicked, or having items dropped on them when loading cargo onto the roof. They also suffer the natural effects of age and the elements.

Periodically inspect the roof vents for cracks, splits, or breakage. Check the caulking compound around the seams and repair as necessary to prevent leaks. Clean out pine needles, leaves, and other debris that naturally collect there.

Replacement of a vent cover is easily accomplished. Simply remove the hardware (depending on the brand and model of roof vent) that holds the vent cover to the hinge; reinstall the vent cover using the appropriate hardware. If you cannot find a replacement cover—if it is no longer in production, for example—replace the entire mechanism.

Trailer A-Frames

There is very little that can go wrong with trailer A-frames. Periodically inspect all the hardware attached to the frame and tighten if necessary. The frame should be washed to prevent the buildup of road grime and dirt. Touch-up paint should be used on all scratches and paint chips to prevent rust. A coat of paste wax will help keep an A-frame clean and protected from the elements.

And What About the Driveway?

We might as well not stop until we've discussed ways to clean up after a vehicle that drips an occasional drop of oil or grease on the driveway.

Cat-box litter, spread out over the oil or grease drip, will help absorb it. Spread it evenly over the oil spot, sweep it back and forth to work it into the spot, and leave it for a few days to do its work. Cat-box litter also helps remove odors from the garage.

Another solution to an oily garage floor is to use dry cement. Scatter it over the spot, sweep it around to work it in, then let it sit for a few days. The cement will absorb the grease and oil, and when you sweep it up, the spot will be gone. If it's not gone entirely, give it another try. It will gradually disappear. There are also commercially available grease, spot, stain, and rust removers specifically formulated to work on concrete and asphalt.

■ CHAPTER 16 ■
INTERIOR CARE

Soil and stains are the worst enemies of any RV interior. Routine, thorough cleaning is the most effective way to prevent damage to interior components. Periodic use of a vacuum cleaner on every dust-catching surface—blinds and drapes (employing a soft-brush attachment on the vacuum nozzle), sofa and chairs, and carpet—will help keep the interior fresh and clean. This is especially important on the carpet, which is vulnerable to dirt tracked in from outside. Particles of dirt can work down into the pile and cut the fibers, gradually wearing out the carpet.

Routine cleaning should also include the countertops, inside cabinets, vinyl flooring, fiberglass tub/shower enclosure, porcelain or stainless-steel sinks, all appliance surfaces (both inside and out), and the wall paneling and woodwork. Allowing spills or water to sit may lead to permanent stains or water spots, so quick action is preferable.

■ CARPET AND UPHOLSTERY STAIN REMOVAL ■

Care must be taken when removing stains from carpet and upholstery fabric. You can't just attack with hot water and strong cleaners or bleaches. The material has been dyed to give it its color, and you don't want to bleed out the dye. Also, most stains are set by hot water, so unless cleaning instructions specifically call for hot water to be used on a particular stain, use cold water.

The general rule is to act quickly, rather than to allow the spot or stain to dry and set. There are exceptions to this—drips of candle wax, for instance, which are more easily removed after the wax has hardened. But in most instances, spots need to be given immediate attention.

The other general rule is to always try out the cleaning product on a small patch of the fabric or carpet before working on the main spots where they are visible. How hard to scrub the spot depends upon the strength of the material being cleaned. The last thing you want to do is remove a patch of fabric along with the spot.

When cleaning a spot, always work from the outside edge of the spot toward the center. This prevents spreading the spot out into a larger area. Keep plenty of clean, absorbent materials (such as paper towels) on hand to soak up the moisture during the cleaning process. With carpeting, you can step on the paper towels to blot up the last of the moisture and residue after the cleaning is done.

Stubborn stains may have to be cleaned more than once in order to eliminate them completely; some stains will never disappear altogether. A lot depends upon the fabric and the chemistry of the stain itself.

There are different remedies for different types of spots and stains. The guide on page 16.2 lists some of the most common types in alphabetical order. When the remedy calls for chlorine bleach, don't use it full strength; dilute it with four parts water to one part bleach. When peroxide is mentioned, use it in the full 3 percent strength, just as it comes from the bottle.

There are also specialty stain-removal products formulated for particular types of stains. Many are in small containers convenient to carry in the RV. Look in the laundry section of grocery or department stores.

■ DRAPES AND BLINDS ■

Periodically vacuum the drapes and blinds, using a soft-bristled brush attachment. Unless there are stains on fabric drapes, thorough vacuuming is the best

---

■ A GUIDE TO STAIN REMOVAL ■

Blood Treat the blood stain with cold water. If it is safe for the fabric in question, follow up with hydrogen peroxide or chlorine bleach. If not, you may want to try an enzyme presoak product or unflavored meat tenderizer on the dampened spot. Finish up with a rinse of cold water, then dry with a clean towel.

Chocolate Several things will work well on chocolate spots: ordinary household detergent, ammonia, an enzyme presoak laundry product, or peroxide. Remember to test a small, hidden piece of the material before trying to clean the main spots.

Cigarette Burns in Carpet One solution is to carefully cut away the scorched fibers from the burned spot. Then locate a segment of the carpet that is never seen (in the corner of the closet floor, for example) and trim out some replacement fibers. Squeeze a little liquid glue into the area to be repaired, and set the fresh fibers in the glue.

Coffee This is one instance when you want to use hot water to remove a spot. Begin by soaking the stain with an enzyme presoak laundry product or, if the fabric can handle it, a color-safe bleach or chlorine bleach. Then finish up by washing the stain out with hot water. Blot up as much of the moisture as possible with paper towels.

Fruit (including catsup) If you can catch it in time (before it dries), remove the fresh stain with cool water. Once the stain is dried into the fabric, soak it in a solution of cool water and a household detergent. Rinse and dry.

Milk, Cream, Ice Cream Soak the spot in a solution of warm water and an enzyme presoak laundry product. Then rinse and blot dry.

Mud Allow the mud to dry out first. Then you can brush it to knock loose as much of the caked-on dirt as possible and vacuum it up. Any mud that remains can be removed by soaking it in cool water. If there is a residual stain, use a household detergent, then rinse and blot dry.

Mustard One proven remedy for mustard stains is to use ammonia, another is peroxide. But always run a test on the material before cleaning to see if damage from the cleaning agents will occur.

Oil/Grease If you're dealing with freshly spilled oil or grease, try to sop up as much of it as possible with paper towels or other absorbent materials to prevent it from spreading. The next step is to pick out an inconspicuous little piece of the material on which to test cleaning agents. You can try using mechanic's hand cleaner on the greasy spot. Liquid detergent and dry-cleaning solvents also work. Carburetor cleaner will work very well for all types of oily stains (this is a highly flammable and high-vapor compound so care must be exercised when using it). Finish up by washing the area with cool water and laundry detergent, then rinse and blot dry.

Tar Road tar can make a real mess of things inside a coach. You can try the remedies suggested for oil and grease, but if they don't work, try turpentine. Surprisingly, mayonnaise will also cut tar. As always, make sure you test a hidden piece of the material before cleaning the main spots.

Urine These wet spots need prompt attention and a good wad of paper towels. Start by soaking up all the moisture possible until the paper towels don't show any dampness when you step on them. Then wash the area with an enzyme presoak laundry product; rinse and blot dry.

Wine Begin with an enzyme presoak laundry product and hot water. If it's safe for the material, try an oxygen bleach and hot water. If the stains remain, and if the material can safely handle it, you can try a chlorine-bleach solution.

---

maintenance. If stains occur, the drapes should be removed and either gently washed or dry cleaned according to the instruction tag on the fabric. If there is no tag containing cleaning instructions, contact the dealer or manufacturer to learn the recommended cleaning method.

Gentle care must be taken when working with aluminum miniblinds to prevent damage to the fragile blades. By lowering the blinds and then adjusting all the way in both directions, the broad surfaces of both sides of the slats can be vacuumed. Special miniblind brushes are available at many department stores; these make cleaning the blades easier. If spills or stains occur on the blinds, a soft, damp cloth and mild detergent can be used. Gently wash the blinds and then dry thoroughly. Adjust the slats so they are separate and allow to air dry.

Wood miniblinds are generally cleaned the same way as aluminum. Instead of washing with a mild detergent, use a cleaner made for wood floors; this will prevent the wood from drying out. Furniture polishes should be used sparingly; some will leave a residue that builds up or attracts dust.

Day/night blinds should be vacuumed frequently because the dust acts as an abrasive, causing the blinds to wear out faster. These shades are difficult to spot clean and cannot be dry cleaned. If spot cleaning is necessary, use a barely damp cloth and wipe gently.

■ FLOOR CARE ■

Vinyl Flooring

Today's vinyl floor coverings are exceptionally easy to care for. All they require is periodic sweeping or vacuuming and mopping. For stubborn dirt, mop with a solution of ammonia and warm water or one of the floor cleaners available in every grocery store. If serious scrubbing is necessary, use a plastic-bristle brush to prevent damage to the vinyl surface. Although most of the vinyl-floor coverings used today have no-wax surfaces, a floor wax can be applied, if desired, to make future cleanup even easier.

Tile Flooring

Tile flooring is very easy to keep clean. Normal washing will suffice under most conditions. A glass cleaner or common household floor cleaner can be used for spot cleaning. Do not use any form of wax on tile floors; wax can create a very slippery surface.

■ WALL AND CEILING PANELING ■

Dust, fingerprints, and grease from cooking can coat the wall paneling and ceiling. Routine cleaning of these surfaces with a soft cloth and mild detergent solution will help prevent a heavy buildup of these elements. Do not scrub or use abrasive cleaners. Wall covering is generally water resistant, but it is not waterproof.

Use caution when treating the paneling; many manufacturers use a photosensitive paper that simulates wood grain. This industrial contact paper allows manufacturers to use a lighter wood and still give the look of natural woods, without the additional weight. Polishes and cleaners designed for real wood should not be used on photosensitive surfaces. In many cases, the cabinet doors and drawer fronts are finished in real wood while the rest is photo paper. Extreme care must be taken when cleaning photopaper; do not use too much water. Never attach a stick-on hanger (for example, one to hold a towel) to photopaper, because it will simply peel off the wood backing.

If the ceiling is covered with a carpet-like material, use a mild detergent solution or carpet cleaner. Some of these ceilings will develop yellowish spots resembling water stains. This is commonly caused by the glue used to adhere the fabric to the ceiling bleeding to the surface. Most times, these stains will not come out.

■ WOODWORK ■

Some of the most beautiful furnishings in an RV are made of wood. They will retain their beauty if treated as fine furniture in the home would be. A high-quality liquid or spray wood treatment can be used. Avoid the use of water-based waxes or polishes.

As beautiful as the woodwork is, it is vulnerable to damaging scratches, chips, and stains. Luckily, wood's characteristic is to have light and dark portions, a texture, and a personality. Unlike paint, wood isn't meant to be monotone. When it comes to repairing wood, these characteristics help make the repair work less obvious.

Low-humidity areas will also require that wooden doors and cabinets be oiled/waxed more often to prevent the wood from drying out.

Repairing Scratched Woodwork

Many different remedies have been suggested for making scratches and dings disappear. They don't mend the scratches, but at least they make them less visible. Read over this short list, then pick out the one that suits your needs.

■ One low-tech remedy is to use old motor oil as a staining medium for furniture. It renders a rich, dark color and oils the wood at the same time. A small amount can be rubbed into the scratches on wood to make them blend into the rest of the wood's grain.

- Instant coffee (one part) and water (two parts) can be rubbed into the scratches with a cotton ball. This solution can be used almost like a furniture polish to remove water spots and leave a soft sheen.
- Water marks can also be removed by the solid application of elbow grease and a soft cloth, if you catch them while they're still wet. Stubborn, dried-on marks may need an oil-based furniture polish to remove them.
- One fellow we heard of swears by Magic Markers as a scratch and ding mender. He just buys the color that most closely matches the woodwork and inks in the bad spot. Buffing over it with a soft cloth immediately afterward helps to "feather in" the edges and make the repair less visible.
- Nut meats have been used to repair scratched woodwork. Just rub the meat over the length of the scratch, then wipe with a soft cloth.
- Paste shoe polish can be rubbed into the scratches to make them vanish. You can buy polish of different tones to match the woodwork. This serves not only to color the scratch, but to wax the surface as well
- Of course, you can keep on hand a small dispenser of stain to match your woodwork. Just dab it on with a cotton ball, rub it in, wipe away the excess, and you're done. A little linseed oil mixed with the stain will help preserve the wood as you mend it.
- Woodworking finishing/repair pencils and crayon sticks can be found in your local hardware store in almost every color. These make wood finish repair very simple.

■ KITCHEN AND BATHROOM CARE ■

Cutting Grease

Grease buildup on kitchen appliances or miniblinds on the kitchen windows may require an application of a grease cutter before washing. Allow the solution to stand for a few minutes. Do not use abrasive cleaners. Make sure you also clean the exhaust-fan screen.

Stove-top burners may be cleaned quickly by lighting the burner and allowing the flame to burn at its lowest level, without going out. Food and other residues will cook off completely. Do not have anything on the burner. Allow the stove top to cool before closing the range cover.

Microwaves will clean with soap and water. If spills or splatters have dried, spray on a little soap or other mild cleaning solution and let sit for a few minutes. This will soften the food and make it easy to wipe off. Consider using a splatter shield to cover foods cooking in the microwave.

Countertops and Sinks

Countertops take a great deal of abuse. Food is chopped up here, dishes drain here, everything spills here. It's an area that needs constant attention.

Some of that attention should be paid in advance. No matter what kind of material your countertop is made of, it can be damaged. Cutting should be done only on a cutting board. This will not only save the countertop, but the knife as well. If spills occur, they should be wiped up as soon as possible. Never use harsh abrasives on countertops since the surface may become damaged or dulled.

Some General Countertop-Cleaning Tips

The following guidelines will help keep countertops in tip-top shape:

- Hard water can leave lime deposits on the counter. One way to remove them without resorting to abrasive cleansers is to use white vinegar and a soft cloth. For stubborn deposits, let the vinegar stand and soak the area for a few minutes.
- Toothpaste and a discarded toothbrush come in handy for cleaning the corners and the grout between tiles.
- Rather than spend time and energy scrubbing off dried-on food, lay a sponge or washcloth, wet with hot, soapy water, over it for ten minutes to soak and loosen it up.
- If scrubbing is necessary, use a plastic scrub pad or brush to prevent damage to the countertop surface.

Corian Countertops

Corian is a high-quality material used for countertops in more expensive RVs. The material somewhat resembles marble and has a beautiful, smooth surface. However, Corian is soft enough to be damaged by a knife, leaving scratches and scars on the finish. Prevention is better than cure, and the use of a cutting board, pot holders, and ashtrays will prevent damage to a Corian countertop. To remove scratches or burn marks, use a very fine-grit sandpaper or a light abrasive rubbing compound. Work gently or you may gouge the surface, a problem that takes extensive training and special materials to fix.

Stainless-Steel Sinks

Just because it's made of stainless steel doesn't mean that it can't get stains (one of the mysteries of life). Keep your stainless-steel sink looking nice and shiny by using a few of the following techniques:

- Most of the time, a stainless-steel sink only needs to be wiped out and dried with a soft cloth after each use in order to keep it looking spotless. This is especially important if you are using hard water.
- Vinegar will remove the buildup of lime deposits and water spots resulting from hard water.
- Rubbing alcohol or baking soda can be used to remove stubborn stains. Follow up with a good washing with hot water and detergent.
- Avoid using abrasive cleansers because they damage the surface of the stainless steel.

Porcelain Sinks

Durable as porcelain enamel is, it can still be damaged by abrasive cleansers. Use a spray-on foamy cleanser or one of the abrasive-free powders. Cleaning may require a bit of elbow grease, but it will save the porcelain finish. An alternate cleanser is dishwasher detergent. Wear rubber gloves when working with these cleansers to save the fine finish on your hands.

There are touch-up paints on the market that can be used to repair a section of the porcelain that's chipped. These are applied like nail polish and come in colors to match most porcelain products. Most hardware stores carry these paints.

Fiberglass Sinks, Tubs, and Showers

Special care must be taken to prevent scratches or cracks in fiberglass. When they do occur, repair can be made by following the specific instructions on a fiberglass-repair kit, available at RV and boating-supply outlets. Although it is possible to repair a scratch or crack in the fiberglass, it is difficult to match the original color. It may be necessary to paint the entire surface.

Everyday care and maintenance of fiberglass is similar to that of porcelain. Use only nonabrasive cleansers that state "fiberglass-safe" on the label. (There are cleansers on the market specifically for fiberglass. Look for these at RV supply outlets, department stores, or supermarkets.) Before the initial use, and again after each thorough cleaning, apply a coat of a good fiberglass wax or protectant. Not only will this preventive maintenance limit the buildup of water deposits, discoloration, and stains, it also helps close the surface "pores," increasing the life of the material.

CAUTION: Do not use a protectant or wax on the tub or shower floor; this will make the surface too slippery and dangerous to walk on.

Vinyl Shower Curtains

After each shower, use the hand-held shower wand to spray clear water over the surface of the curtain to remove soap residue. When it comes time to launder the curtain, either hand wash or machine wash on the gentle cycle, using warm water and a mild soap. Do not use bleach. Remove the curtain from the machine before the final spin cycle and allow to drip dry.

Odor Eaters

Most of us already know about leaving an opened box of baking soda in the refrigerator, freezer, and oven to remove unwanted odors. But there are at least two other methods for removing odors from small enclosures or the entire coach.

1. A pan of charcoal briquettes left sitting out in the open air will eliminate bad smells.
2. Cat-box litter is quite effective as an odor eliminator. Fill a shallow pan and leave it sitting in the RV during storage. It takes care of the musty smells that can build up when the vehicle is not used for some time.

■ GENERAL INTERIOR CARE ■

Carpet runners and/or area rugs can be laid in high-traffic areas to protect the carpet from excessive wear. A washable rug (bath mats for example) positioned just inside the entrance helps enormously. There are service companies that will come to your rig and steam clean the carpets and upholstery. Check the phone book or a local RV dealership.

In low-humidity areas, it helps to spray the vacuum-cleaner head or areas to be vacuumed with an antistatic spray. Otherwise dirt (especially pet hair) clings to the surface being cleaned.

Consider putting a blanket, sheet, or other cover over the sofa and chairs. Doing this will help protect against sun fading, accidental spills, and general wear. This is really helpful if there are pets in the rig. Washing a cover is easier than shampooing the upholstery.

■ CHAPTER 17 ■
ACCESSORIES

Installing accessories on the exterior of an RV not only adds character but also makes traveling and camping more comfortable and convenient. Each accessory offers its own bundle of benefits, but each also calls for periodic maintenance. A prime example is the awning. In the heat of the day, the shade of an awning is an inviting place to spend a little time enjoying the scenery offered by the campsite. If an awning is properly maintained, it is less likely to give the owner fits when operating the mechanism. The same can be said of automatic levelers and tongue jacks, which take much of the work out of leveling and hitching up an RV—they certainly beat using stacks of boards and piles of rocks! But automatic levelers are complex pieces of equipment and require periodic service to assure operational efficiency. These days, many RVs are designed with extension rooms that slide out on mechanisms that require care and maintenance. Television antennas are as common as kitchen sinks and are obviously necessary if the RV is equipped with a television. Simple care of the mechanism is all that is needed.

■ AWNINGS ■

Awnings are the RV counterparts to patio covers, but they are more complex because they have moving parts and are retractable. Awning systems are sized to fit all types of RVs, ranging from the largest motorhomes to the smallest tent trailers. In addition to the main awning that covers the entire side of an RV, smaller awnings are available for use on individual windows and to cover the slide-out area. There's even an awning for the rear of pick-up campers.

The typical RV awning system consists of an awning rail attached to the upper edge of the RV side wall, adjustable rafters and lower support arms to stiffen the awning when extended, brackets for attaching the rafters and support arms to the side of the RV, a roller tube onto which the awning fabric is furled, and a locking mechanism to prevent the awning from unrolling while traveling.

Awning manufacturers have designed their products to operate slightly differently from one another. One of the keys to successful use of an awning system is to study the owner's manual and learn the proper steps to setting up and taking down the awning so there will be no confusion at the campsite.

Awning Maintenance

Fabric Awnings

Some awnings are made of fabrics that are resistant to rot and mildew, while others need special care to prevent this type of damage. Rot and mildew result from moisture being trapped in the fabric. Although instructions published by manufacturers of rot and mildew resistant awning fabrics claim that their awnings can be rolled up wet if necessary, even these awnings should be unfurled and allowed to dry thoroughly as soon as possible. If the fabric is not rot and mildew resistant, even greater care must be taken to dry the material at the earliest opportunity.

It is important to keep the awning material as clean and dry as possible. Even on mildew-resistant fabric, pollen or dust can support mildew growth, which results in stains. In regions of the country prone to salt spray or road salt, the awning fabric and hardware should be washed frequently to prevent deterioration. Air pollution has been found to damage the fabric, and it is recommended that during prolonged exposure to air pollution the awning should be washed a minimum of twice a month.

Cleaning Fabric Awnings To clean the fabric, carefully follow the manufacturer's recommendations. The following are typical recommendations, although the procedures may be different for some brands:

1. Periodically (as the need demands) loosen hardened dirt with a dry, soft brush.
2. Hose off dirt, both top and bottom.
3. Using a mixture of ¼ cup of dish soap and ¼ cup of bleach in 5 gallons of warm water, wash both the top and bottom sides of the fabric.
   CAUTION The bleach must be diluted or it will damage the awning fabric.
4. Roll up the awning for anywhere between five minutes to two hours (depending upon the stubbornness of the dirt) to allow the cleaning solution time to work on both sides of the fabric.
5. Unroll the awning and rinse thoroughly.
6. Allow the fabric to air-dry completely before rolling it back up.
   CAUTION: Never use a strong detergent or stain remover on the awning because it will destroy the fabric's water repellency. Avoid the use of hard-bristle brushes, petroleum-based chemicals, and abrasive or caustic household cleaners on the awning fabric.
7. To remove stubborn mildew, wipe the affected areas with white vinegar, which will kill the mildew. Rinse the fabric with clear water. The fabric may require a second washing and rinsing after this cleaning procedure.

Checking for Leaks in Fabric Awnings Leaks in the fabric may be the result of several causes:

- If the leaking occurs after washing, the cause may be insufficient rinsing. Rinse more thoroughly and allow the fabric to dry, then check for water repellency.
- If water drips through the needle holes in the stitching, use a commercial seam sealer (available at canvas and RV supply stores) or apply a layer of paraffin wax to the top of the seams.

- A pinhole leak can develop if a spot of water-repellent material on the top of the fabric has flaked off. To fix the hole, apply a small dab of VLP (vinyl liquid patch) with the end of a cotton swab. By gently rolling the VLP around the hole, the paint will melt and fill in the pinhole with a perfect color match. Be sure to allow the VLP to dry before rolling up the awning.
- If a leak develops through the fabric where a pool of water has collected, lower one of the support arms to encourage drainage.

Awning-Hardware Maintenance

As with the fabric, different manufacturers recommend various procedures for maintenance of the awning hardware. Carefully read the owner's manual before proceeding. Following are typical recommendations for some awnings:

- Clean all the hardware with a solution of warm, soapy water.
- Rinse and allow to dry.
- Using silicone spray, lubricate the rafter arms and support arms.
- Using silicone spray, lubricate the threaded portion of the adjustment knobs.
- A stubborn pushbutton or lift-handle can be lubricated with silicone spray.
- Lubricate the bottom-bracket release tab for easier disengagement.
- A light oil may be used on the latch section of the base brackets, the threaded portion of the security knobs, and the spring-loaded adjustment knob in the lift-handle. After lubricating, wipe excess oil from all parts.
- Periodically extend all telescoping arms as far as possible and wipe away accumulated dirt.
  NOTE: Do not over lubricate or use WD-40 on any of these parts. This just attracts dust and dirt and will result in more frequent cleaning and wear on the parts.
- Before each travel season, check all fasteners for tightness. Replace any missing parts with factory-authorized replacement parts. If streaks appear or water is seeping behind the awning rail, check for loose screws or damaged sealant at the rail.

■ LEVELERS ■

Hydraulic levelers are used on motorhomes to provide a firm, level foundation when parked in a campsite. When traveling, the levelers ride in the "up" position beneath the chassis. Depending on the type of leveler, when activated, the units either telescope downward or pivot to a vertical position before the hydraulic/electric rams extend downward until they contact the ground. With a leveler located at each corner of the coach (or with one centered in the front and one at each corner of the rear), the chassis can be raised a different amount fore and aft and side to side, until the coach is level.

Some models are automatic, employing a computer-controlled sensing device that operates the system and automatically brings the coach to level. Other systems are manual, requiring that the driver control the leveler for each corner individually.

In this section, we will cover the care and maintenance of both manual and automatic systems. Because of the complexity of installation, we recommend that these systems be installed by experienced personnel.

HWH Leveler Maintenance

Check the following items on the HWH leveler: (See "Troubleshooting the HWH Leveler," pages 17.31–35)

- Inspect the assemblies of each leveler to be sure they are free of road hazards and dirt buildup prior to every trip.
- Make sure the routing of electrical wires and hydraulic lines avoids sharp edges of undercarriage components and heat-producing portions of the coach or AC generator-exhaust system.
- Keep the battery system fully charged. If it is necessary to start the engine prior to operating the levelers, it could indicate a low-battery-charge condition caused by an electrical drain or insufficient charging of the battery.

    NOTE: When inspecting each unit, check if any wires have been pulled loose during the previous trip.

HWH Leveler Lubrication

Periodic lubrication of the various pins and links is important for the proper operation of the HWH leveling jack (Figures 17.1 and 17.2). Begin by cleaning the jack assembly, washing it with a high-pressure hose if possible. Lubricate all moving parts with a light penetrating oil such as WD-40, followed by lubricating these same points with a heavier oil such as 10- to 30-weight engine oil. The grease fitting on the rear of each jack should receive 2 to 3 pumps of grease.

If the main cylinder of the jack is slow to retract, extend the jack, spray the polished rod with WD-40, and manually rotate the foot of the jack as it retracts. Make sure the lower roller is free to roll on the polished rod as it extends.

HWH Leveler Adjustment

Inspect the pin through the lower roller and the two hook bolts; make sure they are not bent. Replace if necessary. The hook bolts regulate the fore and aft position of the jack when it is in the vertical position. It is important that both hook bolts are adjusted to the same length. Make sure the horizontal pin rides equally on the edge of the notched flat bars on each side of the jack when it's vertical.

The stop on the side of the pivot bracket regulates the position of the jack in the stored position. If you want to prevent the jack from swinging all the way up into the stored position, the stop should be moved to a higher hole in the pivot bracket. The stop should be adjusted so the jack can extend in the horizontal position without making contact with any obstructions behind the jack.

HWH 610 Series Leveler Repair

Reduced Lifting Capacity

If the jack extends to the ground but will not lift the coach, two possible problems exist. Follow this procedure to determine the cause of the problem:

1. Disconnect the tube between the shuttle valve and the manifold.

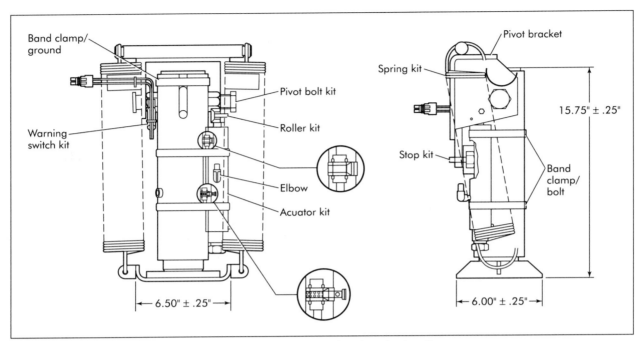

Figure 17.1 HWH kick-down jack for 100, 110, 200, and 310 series leveling systems

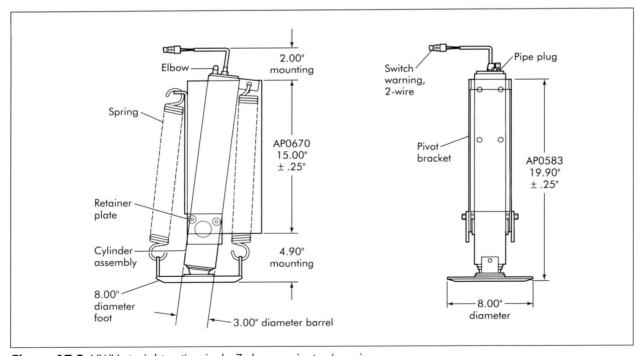

Figure 17.2 HWH straight acting jack, 7-degree pivot, s/s springs

2. Connect a pressure gauge to the fitting in the manifold.
3. Check the pump pressure. It should be approximately 3,500 psi.
4. If the pump pressure is okay, replace the shuttle valve.

Jack Refuses to Retract

If the leveler refuses to retract, follow this procedure:

1. For a 9,000-pound unit, bleed pressure between the jack and the actuator.
2. If the jack still will not retract, replace the jack.
3. If the jack starts to retract, tighten the actuator tube and bleed pressure off between the actuator and the hydraulic-supply line.
4. If the jack fails to retract, replace the actuator.
5. If the jack starts to retract, the problem is probably the outer check valve in the manifold.
6. For 6,000- or 16,000-pound units, bleed pressure between the actuator and the hydraulic-supply line.
7. If the jack fails to retract, replace the jack.
8. If the jack retracts, the problem is probably the outer check valve in the manifold.
9. A stuck shuttle valve could prevent the system from retracting, but if that were the case, none of the jacks would retract.

HWH 510 Series Leveler Repair

Emergency Jack Retraction

Some systems are equipped with drain valves that can be used for emergency retraction of the jacks.

1. On systems with the 3-port drain valve, place a container under the drain valve.
2. Slowly open the drain valve by turning each T-handle counterclockwise 3 turns.
3. Drive the coach forward off the jacks.

A second method of emergency retraction will work if the jacks refuse to retract when the pump comes on after the master solenoid is activated.

1. Disable the pump by disconnecting the cable from terminal number 6 on solenoid B. This will disconnect all power to the pump motor.
2. Run the system through the normal retract procedure.

Jack Fails to Hold Pressure

If a jack retracts slowly after the coach is level and stabilized, the solenoid valve for that jack is leaking and should be replaced.

If one of the jacks drops slightly during the leveling process and then continues, the inner check valve for that jack should be replaced. This problem may also be caused by a sticky shuttle valve.

HWH 610 Series Leveler Straight-Acting Jack Repair

Emergency Retraction

Each solenoid valve is equipped with a T-handle release valve.

1. Turn the handle counterclockwise 3 turns or until the jack begins to retract.
2. The oil will return to the reservoir and the jack should retract.
3. After all the jacks are fully retracted, turn the T-handle clockwise until snug.

Jacks Fail to Lift and Stabilize the Vehicle

If the jack fails to move to stabilize the vehicle:

1. Unplug the pressure switch and try again.
2. If the jack now extends and lifts the vehicle, replace the pressure switch.

Jacks Fail to Reach the Ground

The jacks should lift the vehicle at least ½ inch during stabilizing. If a jack extends but fails to reach the ground or lift the vehicle sufficiently, first adjust the pressure switch. To make this adjustment, follow this procedure:

1. Remove rubber boot from the switch body.
2. Unplug the wire so it can rotate freely.
3. Loosen the locking nut.
4. Turn the pressure adjust body ½ turn clockwise.
5. Try again to stabilize the vehicle.
6. Repeat the adjustment procedure until the jacks are operating properly.
7. If adjusting the pressure switch fails to help, replace the switch.

Jacks Lift Too Much

If one or more of the jacks lifts the vehicle too much, adjustment or replacement of a pressure switch is necessary. If one front jack-pressure switch needs adjustment or is defective, both jacks will lift too much. To adjust the pressure switch and decrease the amount of lift during stabilizing, do the following:

1. Remove the rubber boot from the switch body.
2. Unplug the wire so it can rotate freely.
3. Loosen the locking nut.
4. Turn the pressure-adjust body ½ turn counterclockwise.
5. Try the system again, and repeat the procedure if necessary.
6. If adjusting one front switch doesn't help, try adjusting the switch on the other front jack.

The rear jacks operate independently of one another. If adjusting the switch fails to help, replace the switch. To determine which front switch is malfunctioning:

1. Disconnect either switch.
2. Use a jumper wire to ground the harness pin for that switch.
3. If the jacks continue to lift too much, the switch that remains plugged in is the bad one and should be replaced.
4. If the front jacks now stabilize properly, replace the switch that is unplugged.

HWH 310 Series Kick-Down Jacks

The Jack Fails to Return to Horizontal

If the foot of the jack retracts, but the jack itself fails to return to the horizontal position:

1. Make sure the actuator cables or rollers are okay.
2. If the cables and rollers are okay, replace the actuator.

If all the jacks fail to retract:

1. Check for 12-volt DC power at the solenoid valves.
2. If power is not present, replace the touch panel.
3. If power is present at the solenoid valve plugs, replace the shuttle valve.

The Jack Fails to Retract Using the T-Handle

If none of the jacks will retract when using the T-handles, the shuttle valve is bad. If only one jack fails to retract when using the T-handle, loosen the hydraulic supply line to that jack. If the jack retracts, replace the solenoid valve. If the jack fails to retract, the hose could be kinked or the actuator or jack is bad.

HWH 600 Series 4-Point Air-Leveling System

Air Bags Fail to Inflate

If the air bags fail to inflate, check the following:

1. Check the appropriate fuse for the solenoid in question.
2. If the fuse is blown, the valve or the power wire to the valve may have shorted.
3. If the fuse is not blown, check for power on the corresponding pin in the control box.
4. If power is not present, replace control box.
5. If power is present, there's a problem with the wire to the valve, the ground for the valve, or the valve itself.

6. Replace the valve if power is present and the ground is good.
7. If power is not present, a wire or connection is bad.
8. If a 2-wire plug is used, the white wire is ground. Check for power at the colored wire and make sure there's a good ground.
9. If power is present, check and repair the ground wire (as necessary).
10. If no power is present, check and repair the colored wire (as necessary).

A Front Bag Fails to Deflate

When a front bag fails to deflate, check the following items:

1. Make sure the exhaust ports of the air manifold are not plugged.
2. Check fuse for bag that fails to exhaust air.
3. If the fuse is blown, the valve or the wire to the valve is shorted.
4. If the fuse is not blown, check the pin in the box for the valve.

If power is not present:

1. Unplug the opposite front-pressure switch and retry.
2. If no power is present, replace the control box.

If power is present:

1. The pressure switch that is unplugged is closed.
2. If there is more than 10 psi in the air bag, the pressure switch should be replaced.
3. If power is present, the problem is the wire to the valve, the ground for the valve, or the valve itself.
4. Replace the valve if power is present and the ground is good.
5. If power is not present, a wire or connection is bad.
6. If a 2-wire plug is used, the white wire is ground. Check for power at the colored wire

and make sure there's a good ground.
7. If power is present, check and repair the ground wire (as necessary).
8. If no power is present, check and repair (the colored wire (as necessary).

A Rear Bag Fails to Deflate

The pressure switch will not interfere when deflating the rear air bags. Check the following:

1. Check the fuse for the bag that fails to exhaust air.
2. If the fuse is blown, the valve or the wire to the valve is shorted.
3. If the fuse is not blown, check the pin in the box for the valve.
4. If power is *not* present, replace the control box.

If power is present:

1. Check the wire to the valve, the ground for the valve, or the valve itself.
2. Replace the valve if power is present and the ground is good.
3. If power is not present, a wire or connection is bad.
4. If a 2-wire plug is used, the white wire is ground. Check for power at the colored wire and make sure there's a good ground.
5. If power is present, check and repair the ground wire (as necessary).
6. If no power is present, check and repair the colored wire (as necessary).

Level-Sensing Unit Adjustment

To adjust the level-sensing unit:

1. First, level the coach and verify that it is level by placing a 24-inch level in the center of the coach floor.
2. Adjust the sensing unit until all yellow lights are out.
3. This is done by adjusting the sensing-unit

screws, turning them either clockwise or counterclockwise as the situation demands.

4. If a front light is on, adjust the front screw.
5. If a side light is on, adjust the side screw.
6. If a rear light is on, adjust the rear screw.
7. One or more screws may need to be adjusted in order to turn out all the yellow lights.
8. After adjustment has been made, pull down the sensing unit to make sure the unit is bottomed out on the screw heads.
9. Rock the coach and recheck for yellow lights.
10. Readjust if necessary.

Big Foot Hydraulic Levelers

The Big Foot Hydraulic Levelers by Quadra Manufacturing Inc. use high-pressure hydraulic pumps on each lift-jack cylinder to operate the levelers. These levelers can be used with both normal spring-type suspensions and with air-bag or direct-air suspensions. They can be fitted to Class A and C motorhomes, fifth-wheel trailers, and bus conversions in either a 3- or 4-point configuration. Operation of the system is via a central control panel.

The system has no springs, hinges, or kick-down applications. It is strictly a straight-acting, completely hydraulic system, for both extension and retraction. According to the manufacturer, the straight-acting jacks have a total stroke of 15 inches and should be installed on the RV frame so there is ground clearance of 8 to 10 inches when the jacks are completely retracted. The control panel includes individual Extend/Retract switches for each jack, an All Extend/Retract switch and an Emergency Retract switch.

The Big Foot system is designed to be almost maintenance free. The user should be aware that there's a 100-amp circuit breaker located near the battery (if installed properly) and a 7.5-amp fuse on the back of the control panel. The rest of the electrical system is straightforward, using a point-to-point wiring harness and a simple connector block behind the control panel.

Each jack is a self-contained system (Figure 17.3) with its own pump, pressure regulator, oil tank and limit control; there are no hydraulic hoses or remote connections. The jacks are designed to be repaired or replaced as a unit, requiring very little labor time.

The hydraulic-fluid supply tanks bolt directly to the hydraulic cylinders and are filled with 48 ounces of ether DEXRON I or II automatic-transmission fluid.

Coaches with air suspension need to dump their air before beginning the leveler-operation procedure.

NOTE: Big Foot jacks do not have a "drive-off" safety feature. Make sure you do a visual inspection of the actual position of the jacks before driving the motorhome from its campsite.

Big Foot Troubleshooting Tips

- If you attempt to use the levelers and all you hear is a clicking noise, reset the 120-amp circuit breaker located near the batteries.
- If no lights come on when the control panel is activated, inspect and replace, if necessary, the fuse in the back of the control panel. Make sure the wiring is positioned correctly.
- If the red light stays lit on the control panel, check the limit pins at the foot assembly; make sure they move freely up and down. Also check the spade connections at the limit switches and the switch itself.
- If one or more cylinders will not retract and the green light stays lit on the control panel, check the limit pin(s) on the affected leveler to verify that it moves freely. Also check the tank solenoid by jumping a hot wire across the connections to retract the unit. Check the hydraulic-fluid level in the tank; it should be full. Check for broken hydraulic lines on the jack. Make sure there is no power interruption in the 16-gauge control wire from the main wiring harness. Check the 4-gauge battery cable for proper connections.
- If a cylinder is noisy or drops (collapses) just enough to set off the safety alarm, there may be air in the hydraulic system. Purge the air out of the system by extending the levelers in pairs to their full length. Let the system stand for ten minutes; the air will self-purge the vent caps. After the ten-minute period, momentarily bump the All Retract button and then hold the Retract Levelers button until the jacks are fully retracted.
- If a cylinder appears to be leaking, extend the leg fully for ten minutes and then retract it

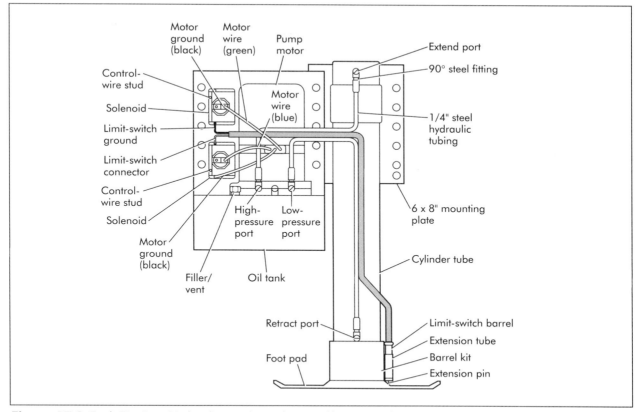

Figure 17.3 Each Big Foot Hydraulic Leveler jack is a self-contained system.

halfway for five minutes. Repeat this cycle two more times. Now extend the jack for another ten minutes and retract it fully. Make sure you bump the All Retract switch before fully retracting the jack. If the cylinder still seems to be leaking, it needs to be replaced.

■ If a jack seems unable to lift the RV, check the needle valve in the pump assembly or replace the cylinder, as necessary.

RVA Leveling Jacks

RVA J-II Leveling System

RVA makes a three-point leveling system with five models, ranging in capacity from 16,000 to 45,000 pounds (Figures 17.4 and 17.5). The systems come as either a manual or an auto-level model.

RVA Maintenance

The system is equipped with a warning device to indicate the position of the jacks and also to indicate low fluid levels. To fill the jacks with oil, you must extend the jack 6 inches from the fully retracted position. The other two jacks should be retracted fully. Unscrew the reservoir cap from the top of the pump. Fill with fluid until the red light and sound signal turn off. Stop filling and replace the cap.

A majority of the fittings in the hydraulic system are pipe threads. The factory covers all male pipe threads with at least three wraps of Teflon tape, except for the first thread of the fitting, to prevent any tape from breaking off and becoming lodged in the valves. A small amount of grease is applied to the tip of the fitting (without the Teflon) and also to the mating female thread. This procedure insures proper sealing without fear of leaks. Make sure that you use the pre-

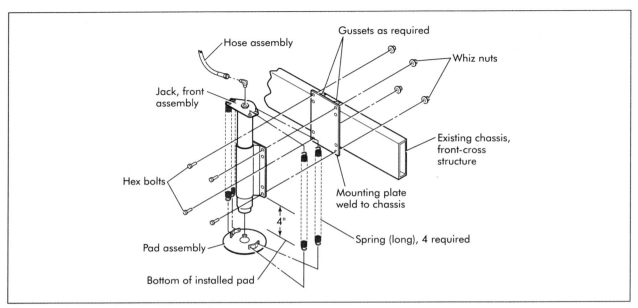

Figure 17.4 RVA front jack installation

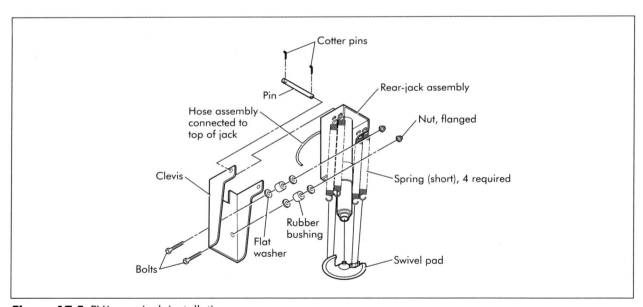

Figure 17.5 RVA rear jack installation

ceding procedure when disconnecting or connecting any of the fittings.

If a component of the hydraulic system such as a jack ram has been removed and replaced, air will probably have been introduced into the hydraulic system. The unit has a self-bleeding system to assist in removing this air. Extend and retract each jack fully at least twice to remove the air. Some additional air can also be trapped in the manual retract valves. To remove this air, you must fully extend the jacks and open the manual retract valves to bleed out the trapped air. This operation will retract all the jacks at the same time. Close the valve handles and check the liquid level in the hydraulic system.

RVA Lubrication

The only lubrication needed on the outside of the jacks is to lightly apply a lightweight oil such as WD-40. Some oil found on the extended jack ram is normal and aids lubrication of the ram.

■ TRAILER TONGUE JACKS ■

To raise and lower the trailer A-frame or the front of a fifth-wheel trailer, tongue jacks or landing jacks are used. These are available in both manual and electric models. While manual jacks are mechanically simpler, their electric counterparts are popular because they require less effort to operate.

Tongue-Jack Maintenance

Basic maintenance of all types of jacks consists of keeping them clean and lubricated. Lubrication should be performed at the beginning of each season or more often as conditions demand.

Lubricating the Atwood Power Jack

Atwood recommends the following procedure for its power jacks:

1. Before each use, inspect the jack tubes and replace if bent or damaged.
2. If wiring is connected to battery terminals, inspect frequently for corrosion. Clean with a solution of baking soda and water, then apply a thin coating of petroleum jelly to the battery terminal.
3. Periodically extend the jack as far as possible and clean the inner ram tube. Coat the tube with a light coating of silicon-spray lubricant.

Emergency Manual Operation for Electric Tongue or Landing Jacks

In case of electrical failure, the electric jacks can be operated manually by following this procedure:

Atwood Power Jack

For the Atwood power jack (Figure 17.6):

1. Remove the hex nuts and the lock washers from the lower side of the motor and cover assembly.
2. Lift both the motor and cover assembly off the jack.
3. Turn the hex drive nut with the wrench or optional manual drive handle.
4. When reinstalling the electric motor on the jack, rotate the hex drive nut so the pin in the hex drive nut is aligned with the slot in the motor drive shaft.
5. Tighten the hex nuts to 25 inch-pounds of torque.

H&H Tongue Jack

Maintenance

On H&H tongue jacks (Figure 17.7), once a year, the power head should be removed by taking out the Allen head set screw (Figures 17.8) and applying a liberal amount of grease directly to the coupling on which the drive pin rests.

The housing cover should also be removed once a year to inspect the gears for wear and proper lubrication. To remove the cover, take out the 4 screws and tap around the edges of the housing to free the cover.

NOTE: Do not use a screwdriver blade to pry off the cover. It will damage the mating surfaces.

Use only high-melting-point lithium-based grease on the jack. Do not pour oil into the top of the jack post.

H&H Outrigger Jacks

The H&H electric outrigger jacks (Figure 17.9) can be used on light travel trailers, fifth-wheels, and Class C motorhomes. Sizes range from 16 to 23 inches of extension with a lifting capability of 1,500 pounds per jack.

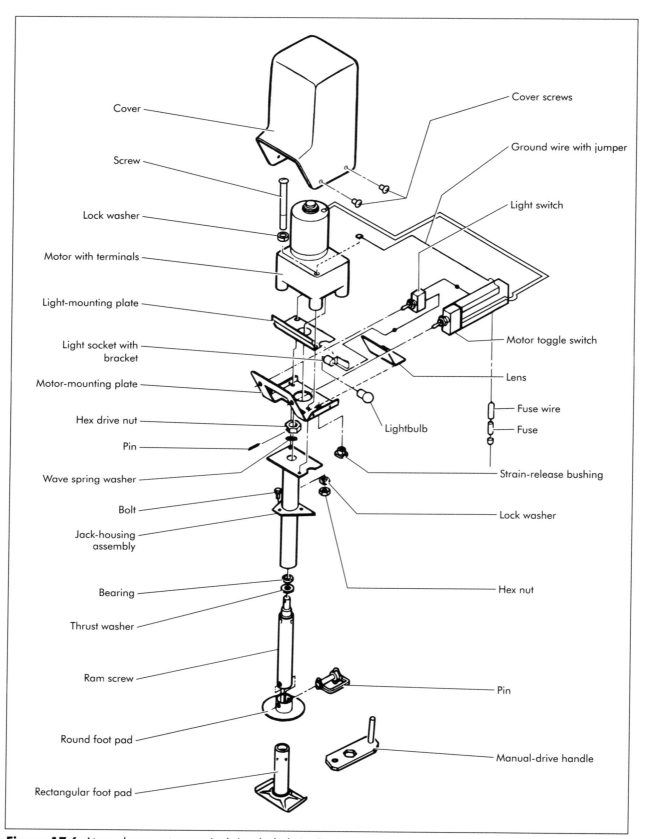

Figure 17.6 Atwood power-tongue jack (exploded view)

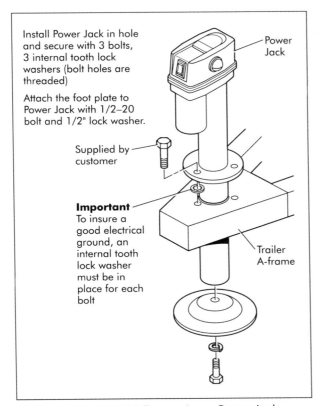

Install Power Jack in hole and secure with 3 bolts, 3 internal tooth lock washers (bolt holes are threaded)

Attach the foot plate to Power Jack with 1/2–20 bolt and 1/2" lock washer.

Supplied by customer

Important
To insure a good electrical ground, an internal tooth lock washer must be in place for each bolt

Power Jack

Trailer A-frame

Figure 17.7 H&H Hi-Torque Acme Power Jack

Maintenance

The inner tube (Figure 17.10) of the jack assembly must be greased annually with Mobil-Lift SHC-460 grease or equivalent. Check and lubricate with a small amount of WD-40 all points of moving contact. No routine lubrication is needed for the gearbox.

■ TELEVISION ANTENNAS ■

In this section, we'll examine the Winegard Television Systems antenna that is widely used on both motorhomes and travel trailers. This antenna is controlled from inside the RV by use of a manual crank that both elevates and rotates the antenna for optimum reception.

Antenna Maintenance

Periodic lubrication of the elevating-gear assembly is the only routine maintenance procedure. To lu-bricate the elevating gear, apply a liberal amount of silicone-spray lubricant to the elevating gear with the lift in the down position. Then run the lift up and down a few times to distribute lubricant over the gears (Figure 17.11).

If rotating the antenna becomes difficult, normal operation can be restored by lubricating the bearing surface between the rotating gear housing and the baseplate (Figure 17.12). Use silicone-spray lubricant for this purpose.

1. Raise the antenna.
2. Remove the set screw from the rotating gear housing.
3. Spray lubricant into the hole and around the edges of the gear housing.
4. Rotate the gear housing until the lubricant coats the bearing surfaces and the antenna rotates freely.

Replacement of Antenna Components

In the event that the elevating shaft and worm gear assembly become worn or broken and require re-placement, follow this procedure (Figure 17.13):

1. Loosen the set screw to release the elevating crank, the spring, and the directional handle.
2. Remove the RGH-2 plug from the top of the gear housing. This will expose the top of the worm-gear assembly.
3. To remove the worm-gear assembly, remove the top pin.
4. Disengage the elevating gear from the worm gear.
5. Remove the elevating shaft and the worm-gear assembly.
6. Cut the replacement elevating shaft to match the length of the original.
7. Install the new assembly by reversing the procedure. The two gears will automatically realign themselves by turning the elevating crank half a turn after all items have been put back together.

To remove the lift assembly from the vehicle without breaking the seal between the baseplate

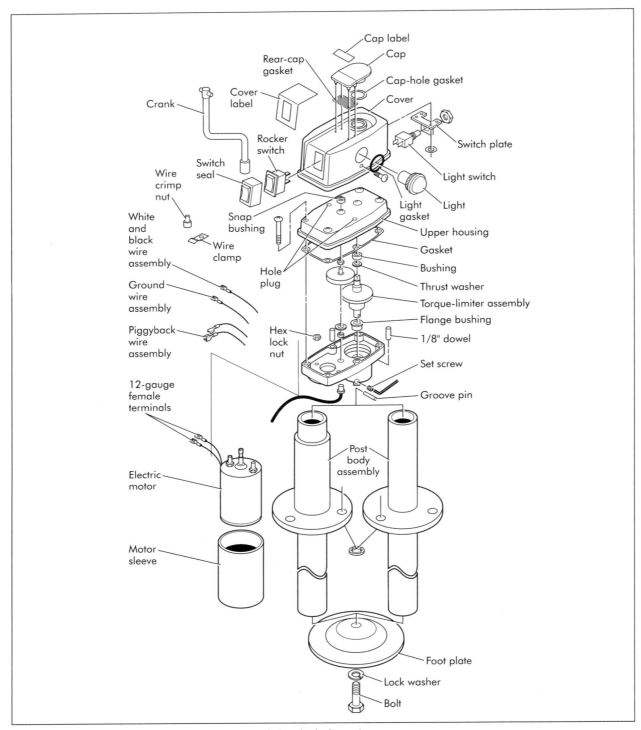

Figure 17.8 H&H Hi-Torque Acme Power Jack (exploded view)

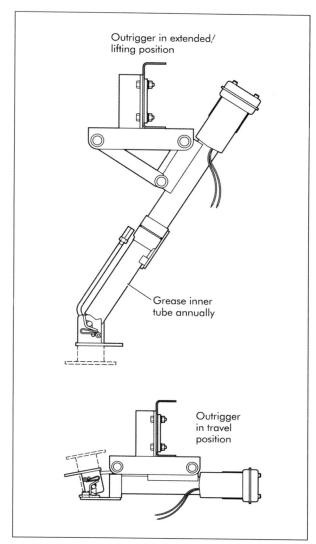

Figure 17.9 H&H electric outrigger jacks

and roof, the rotating-gear housing and base plate must be separated.

1. Loosen the Allen set screw in the elevating crank.
2. Remove the crank directional handle and spring.
3. Using a small flat-blade screwdriver with a blade the same width as the keyway in the rotating gear housing, bend the crimped area of GHN-1 nut out of the keyway.
4. Using a ⁵⁄₃₂-inch drill, clean the threaded portion of the GHN-1 nut out of the keyway.
5. Insert Winegard's Tenna-Tool (Figure 17.14)

or use a spanner wrench over the shaft (depending on mechanism) and rotate until the pins engage the holes in the nut.

   NOTE: A spanner wrench may be constructed from a ⅞-inch- deep socket or 1-inch EMT conduit. Grind the face of the socket down about ⅛ inch, leaving pins to engage the GHN-1 nut (Figure 17.15).
6. Unscrew the nut counterclockwise.
7. The rotating gear housing and all parts connected to it may now be lifted from the base plate on the roof.
8. To reassemble, reverse the procedure. Use a new GHN-1 nut and tighten only enough to remove side play in the lift. Make certain the lift rotates freely. Bend the edges of the GHN-1 nut down into the keyway with a punch when properly adjusted.

   NOTE: The Allen set screw that secures the elevating-crank handle inside the RV is prone to loosening. When this happens, the crank handle can be ejected from the shaft due to the spring that keeps it under tension. Reinstall this set screw using a good-quality thread-lock sealant. Do not use a permanent-type sealant.

Manual Satellite-Antenna Maintenance

There are no user-serviceable parts in the electronics portions of the satellite antenna (Figure 17.16). The mechanical parts are serviced almost exactly like the normal RV television antenna previously described.

Periodic lubrication of the elevating-gear assembly is the only routine maintenance procedure. To lubricate the elevating gear, apply a liberal amount of silicone-spray lubricant to the elevating gear with the lift in the down position. Then run the lift up and down a few times to distribute lubricant over the gears (Figure 17.17).

If rotating the antenna becomes difficult, normal operation can be restored by lubricating the bearing surface between the rotating-gear housing and the base plate. Use silicone-spray lubricant for this purpose.

Replacement of Manual Satellite-Antenna Components

In the event that the elevating shaft and worm-gear assembly become worn or broken and require replacement, follow this procedure (Figure 17.18):

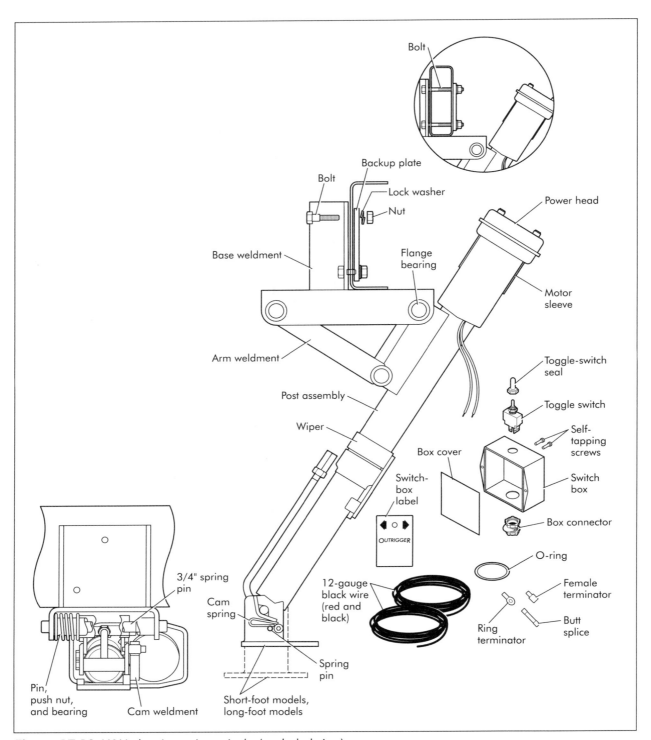

Figure 17.10 H&H electric outrigger jacks (exploded view)

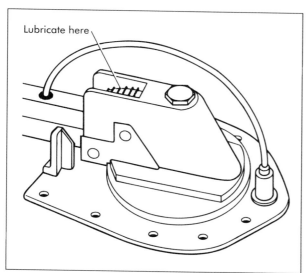

Figure 17.11 Silicone is used to lubricate the elevating gear in the Winegard television antenna.

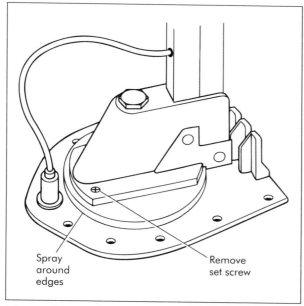

Figure 17.12 If rotating the antenna becomes difficult, the bearing surface must be lubricated with silicone.

1. Lower the antenna to the travel position.
2. Loosen the screw on the elevating crank, remove the crank, the spring, and the directional handle.
3. Remove the hex nuts, cable clip, and washer from the bolt holding the elevating tube in the rotating-gear housing and remove bolt.

4. Remove the plastic plug from the top of the rotating-gear housing, disengage the elevating gear, and remove the elevating-shaft assembly.
5. Lubricate the worm-gear assembly on the new elevating-shaft assembly with silicone-spray lubricant. Make sure the wave washer, the flat washer, and the quad ring are on the lower bearing (Figure 17.19), and then insert the assembly into the housing.
6. Reinstall the bolt, the hex nuts, the cable clip, and the washers that hold the elevating tube in the rotating-gear housing.
7. Replace the directional handle, the spring, and the elevating crank. Make sure the set screw contacts the flat surface on the shaft before tightening.

To remove the lift assembly from the vehicle without breaking the seal between the base plate and the roof, the rotating-gear housing and base plate must be separated. Use the instructions previously described for this procedure on the television antenna mechanism.

Adjusting the RV Antenna/Dish Mount

When installed properly, the base plate is attached to the roof. The gear housing sits on top of the base plate, and a threaded shaft extends through the roof of the RV into the interior. A gear-housing nut is factory installed on this shaft and holds the gear housing onto the base plate from the bottom. If this nut becomes too loose, the dish or antenna could wobble on the top of the RV. This can damage the gear housing causing the TV or satellite picture to weaken or flash on and off.

The tightness of this nut determines how hard or easy the antenna or dish will turn from the inside. In many cases, users of the satellite-dish mechanism have experienced difficulty locking onto the satellite because the gear housing has become damaged. The gear housing nut can be tightened with Winegard's TT-1000 Tenna-Tool (Figure 17.20). If this tool is not used, the adjustment requires removing the base-plate from the roof, which could break the weather seal and increase the chances of a roof leak.

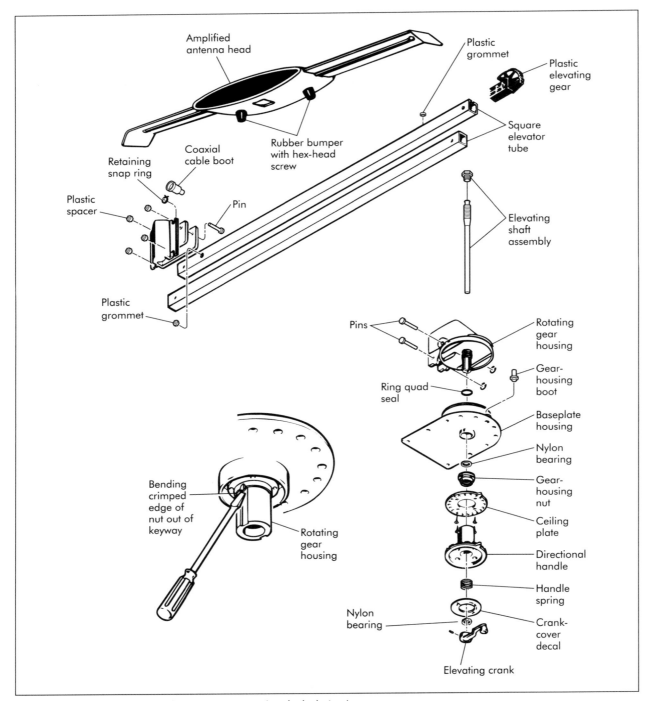

Figure 17.13 Winegard television antenna (exploded view)

Figure 17.14 The Winegard Tenna-Tool

Adjusting the Sensar-type TV Antenna

To adjust a Sensar-type antenna:

1. Loosen the Allen set screw (tool supplied) and remove the elevation crank from its shaft.
2. This allows the crank, the handle spring, the nylon bearing, and the directional handle to be removed.
3. Slide the Tenna-Tool over the elevation shaft, through the ceiling plate and roof, and attach to the gear housing nut.
4. Turn tool to the desired tightness.
5. Remove tool; reinstall parts in reverse order.

Adjusting the Satellite-Antenna System

To adjust the satellite-antenna system:

1. Loosen the Allen set screw (tool supplied) and remove the elevation crank from its shaft.
2. This allows the crank, the handle spring, and the nylon bearing to be removed.
3. Unscrew the clamp-down knob and remove it and the rotate clamp.
4. Remove the directional handle and the rotate plate by gently pulling downward on the mechanism.
5. Remove the 4 Phillips-head screws holding the ceiling-plate group. Keep the plates together as an assembly and set them aside.

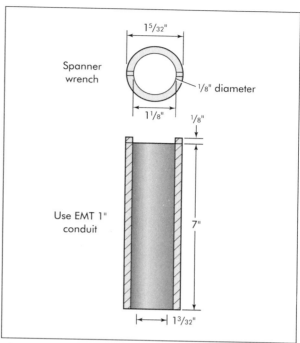

Figure 17.15 A spanner wrench may be constructed from a ⅞-inch deep socket or a 1-inch EMT conduit. Grind the face down about ⅛ inch, leaving the pins to engage the GHN-1 nut. Remove the elevating shaft if necessary.

These pieces must be put back exactly the way they were removed.

6. Slide the Tenna-Tool over the elevation shaft, through the RV ceiling and roof, and connect to the gear-housing nut.
7. Turn tool to desired tightness.
8. Remove tool and reinstall parts in reverse of above.

Adjusting Satellite-Antenna Systems Built after June 1996

To adjust these systems:

1. Using a Phillips screwdriver, remove the elevation crank, the nylon washer, and the spring.
2. Pull down on the directional handle. It and the extension shaft, if used, should come off the elevation shaft.

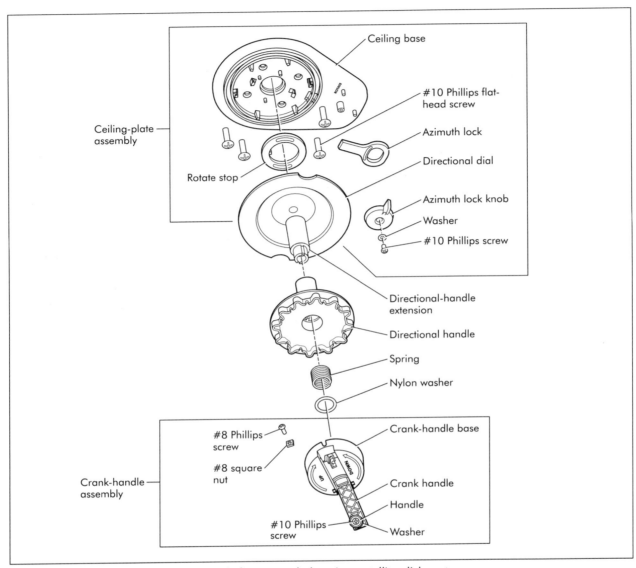

Figure 17.16 Winegard inside controls for manual elevating satellite-dish system

3. Remove the 4 Phillips-head screws in the one-piece ceiling-plate assembly and place assembly aside.
4. Proceed with the adjustment procedure for the other satellite-antenna systems previously described.

Winegard Electronic Self-Seeking Satellite-Antenna System

Self-seeking satellite-antenna systems (Figure 17.21) relieve the user of having to locate and focus on the broadcast satellite. There are no user-serviceable parts either in the electronics or the positioning systems.

Maintenance   Periodic lubrication of the elevating assembly is the only routine maintenance procedure. To lubricate the elevating assembly, apply a liberal amount of silicone-spray lubricant to the hinges and pins with the lift in the down position. Then run the lift up and down a few times to distribute lubricant (Figure 17.22).

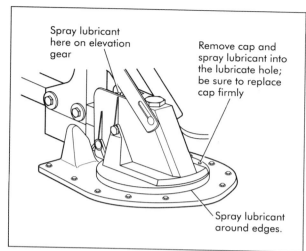

Figure 17.17 Lift mechanism for the Winegard manual satellite system

■ SLIDE-OUT ROOM SYSTEMS ■

There are three general types of slide-out room systems: 12-volt DC electric-motor-driven systems, high-pressure hydraulic systems, and hybrid systems that use either electric, hydraulic, or mechanical power to operate cable-controlled systems. None of these systems is user serviceable or adjustable.

Although all slide-out systems use electric or hydraulic motors, the methods that are used to move the slide are varied. Fortunately, slide-out mechanisms have become very reliable over the last few years and usually require little maintenance.

Electric-powered systems are available in a number of configurations, including those that use a screw mechanism (Figures 17.23 and 17.24), a cable and track (Figure 17.25), a sawtooth rack-and-pinion (Figure 17.26), or a flush-floor rack-and-pinion (Figure 17.27).

Electrically driven hydraulic slide-outs (Figure 17.28) use valving to extend and retract the rams. In some systems, the hydraulic extender ram uses a rack-sensing valve to control the limits of extension and retraction. Flow-divider valves are used to insure that the slide operates equally in an outward and retraction stroke by balancing the pressure between the two (or more) driving rams. Hydraulic extenders that use pulleys and cables operate the same as the electric types, with the only difference being the motive force being used.

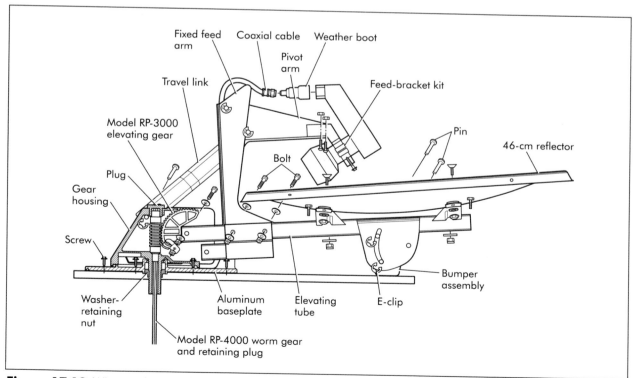

Figure 17.18 Winegard manual-control satellite-antenna system (exploded view)

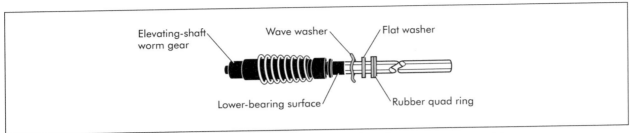

Figure 17.19 Winegard satellite antenna system elevating shaft and worm-gear assembly

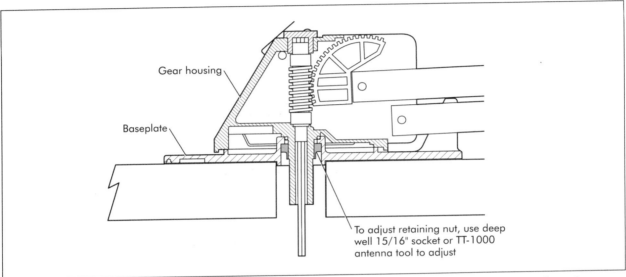

To adjust retaining nut, use deep well 15/16" socket or TT-1000 antenna tool to adjust

Figure 17.20 Gear-housing nut is adjusted with Tenna-Tool, $^{15}\!/_{16}$-inch deep socket, or a homemade tool.

An interesting variant of the hydraulic slide-out room system is the Fleetwood E-Z Glide system (Figure 17.29), which uses only one cylinder per slide and a traversing rod that links the two-room extension/retraction arms together. The system transfers the weight of the room from the side wall of the RV onto the chassis.

HWH Spacemaker Room Extension Systems

Manual Room-Retract Procedure

If one side of the slide-out room fails to move when extending or retracting, release the room-control switch immediately. The rack-sensing valve plunger may be stuck, bent, or not touching the strike plate (Figure 17.30). Also, for further help see "Troubleshooting the HWH Room Extension System" on pages 17.36–38

1. If possible, repair the valve before retracting the room.
2. If repair is not possible, release the pressure on the manual retract winch and remove the check-valve cap from the back of the rack-sensing valve.
3. Remove the check-valve poppet.
4. Replace the check-valve cap.
5. Retract the room using the manual retract winch.
6. If applicable, retract the system leveling jacks prior to manually retracting the room-extension system.
7. Open the hydraulic pump/manifold solenoid valves about 6 turns using the T-handles.
8. Connect the manual retract winch to the room, following the specific instructions provided by the vehicle manufacturer.
9. Slowly retract the room by turning the winch handle clockwise. Winching the

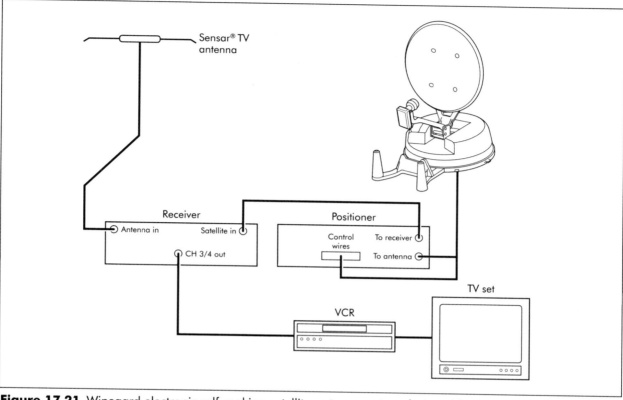

Sensar® TV antenna

Receiver

Antenna in   Satellite in

CH 3/4 out

Positioner

Control wires   To receiver

To antenna

TV set

VCR

Figure 17.21 Winegard electronic self-seeking satellite-antenna system designed for RVs

room quickly will increase hydraulic pressure in the system, making the process more difficult.

10. When the room is fully retracted, engage the room-locking devices and leave the retract winch in place until the system has been repaired.

Cylinder Replacement

To replace the cylinder:

1. Extend the room until the cylinder-mounting bolts are visible.
2. Open the extension solenoid-valve T-handles.
3. Remove the cylinder-adjusting locknut.
4. Measure the distance between the end of the cylinder-adjusting rod and the cylinder-mounting plate. Add ¼ inch to this measurement to allow for easy adjustment of the

room after installing the new cylinder.
5. Remove the two hose-guide mounting bolts.
   NOTE: This step is only necessary if you are removing the left-hand cylinder.
6. Remove the cylinder hoses from the sensing valve and the tee fitting.
7. Plug the hose ends, and attach a wire to the two hoses to help when feeding them back through the extension tubes.
8. Remove the cylinder-mounting plate nuts.
9. Remove the cylinder assembly.
10. In preparation for installing the new cylinder, extend the new cylinder's rod about 1½ feet. Some fluid will exit the fittings as this is done.
11. Install the hoses from the old cylinder on the new one. Take care not to overtighten the fittings.
12. Move the mounting plate to the new rod. Use the measurement from the old rod.
13. Feed the hose and the new cylinder into the room-extension tube.

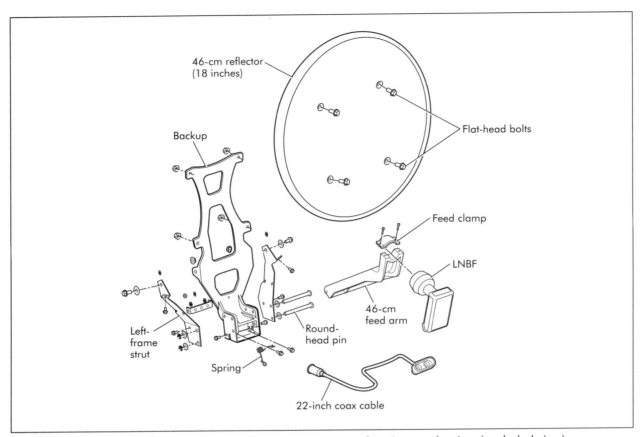

Figure 17.22 Winegard self-seeking satellite-antenna system elevating mechanism (exploded view)

14. Line up the cylinder-mounting holes and replace the bolts.
15. Reattach the hoses and the hose guide.
16. Push the rod in and reattach the cylinder-mounting plate.
17. Close the solenoid valves.
18. Purge the air from the system by doing the following:
    - Retract the room completely.
    - Extend the room 1 foot, and then retract the room once again.
    - Extend the room 2 feet, and then fully retract the room again.
    - Extend the room all the way, and then retract the room completely.
    - Finally, extend the room fully and hold the button toward Extend for five seconds.
    - Check for leaks, and check the oil level in the reservoir.

Cylinder Adjustment

To adjust the cylinder:

1. Extend the room all the way.
2. Turn the cylinder-adjustment rod in or out until the room seals are properly compressed.
3. Replace and tighten the cylinder-adjusting locknut.
4. The In stop is adjusted by loosening the locknut and turning the adjusting nut in or out until the room seals are properly compressed.

Rack-Sensing Valve Replacement

When replacing a rack-sensing valve, the T-handles for both valves on the room extension manifold must be opened 5 to 6 turns to relieve system pressure.

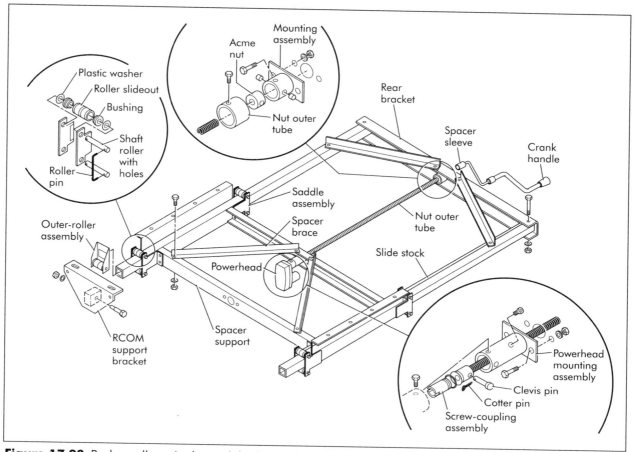

Figure 17.23 Barker rollout single-module slide-out mechanism

The two solenoid valves for the room extension need to be opened.

1. Loosen the rack-sensing valve-mounting bolts.
2. Remove the adjusting bolts and the locknut.
3. Remove the 3 hydraulic lines from the valve.
4. Remove the mounting bolts and the valve-adjusting bar.
5. Replace the valve, but do not tighten the mounting bolts.
6. Replace the hydraulic lines, the adjusting bolt, and the locknut.
7. Adjust the valve so approximately half the plunger is visible.
8. Close the valve-release T-handles.
9. Make final adjustments.

Rack-Sensing Valve Adjustment

To adjust the rack-sensing valve:

1. If the valve side of the room is moving at a *closer* distance to the vehicle, turn the adjusting bolt counterclockwise one turn. If the difference is minor, less than one turn may be sufficient.
2. If the valve side of the room is moving at a *greater* distance to the vehicle, turn the adjusting bolt clockwise one turn. If the difference is minor, less than one turn may be sufficient.
3. Extend the room an additional 12 inches, then retract the room that same 12 inches and check the measurement. The difference

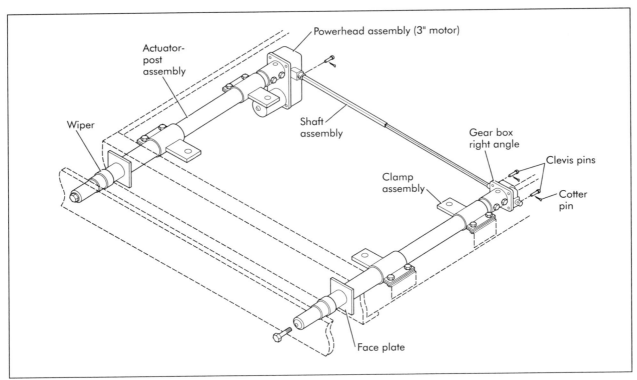

Figure 17.24 Screw-type slide-out room mechanism

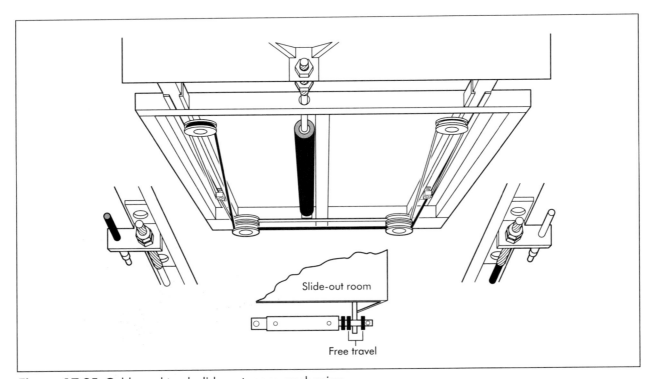

Figure 17.25 Cable and track slide-out room mechanism

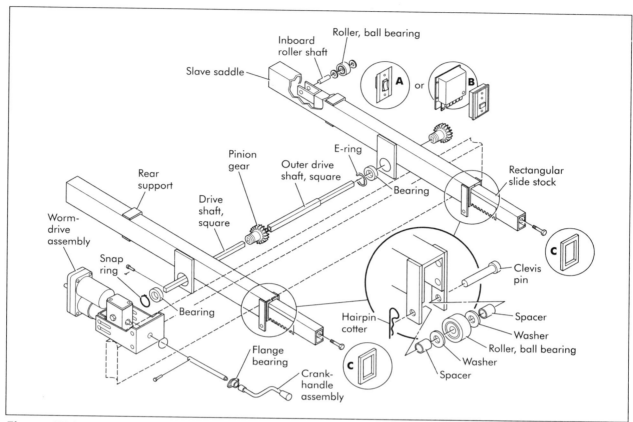

Figure 17.26 Sawtooth rack-and pinion slide-out room mechanism

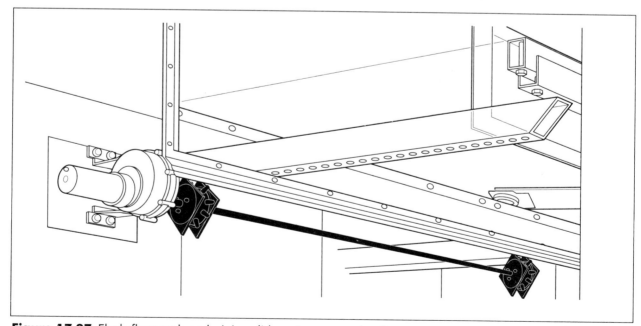

Figure 17.27 Flush-floor rack-and-pinion slide-out room mechanism

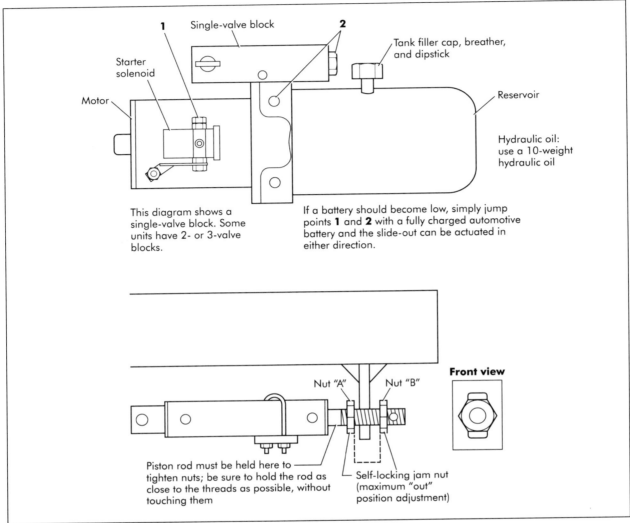

Figure 17.28 Electrically driven hydraulic slide-out room pump and piston rod

in measurement should be less than ½ inch. Repeat this procedure if necessary.

4. Tighten the mounting bolts and adjusting locknut.

Servicing Hydraulic Systems

Maintenance on hydraulic-system slide-out rooms consists almost solely of insuring that the hydraulic pump is kept full of fluid. The proper procedure for filling the fluid reservoir is as follows:

1. Fully retract the room and leveling jacks before checking the oil level.

2. Remove the cap from the top of the reservoir and fill to within 1 inch below the top of the reservoir.

3. Use Dextron II or a high-quality multi-purpose automatic-transmission fluid.

Safety Procedures for Slide-out Rooms

The following procedures must be followed:

1. Keep people and obstructions clear of the room when extending or retracting. This includes chairs, footstools, pet dishes, and so on.

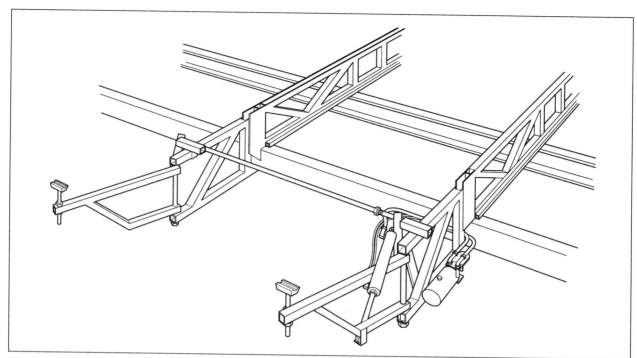

Figure 17.29 Fleetwood E-Z Glide slide-out room mechanism

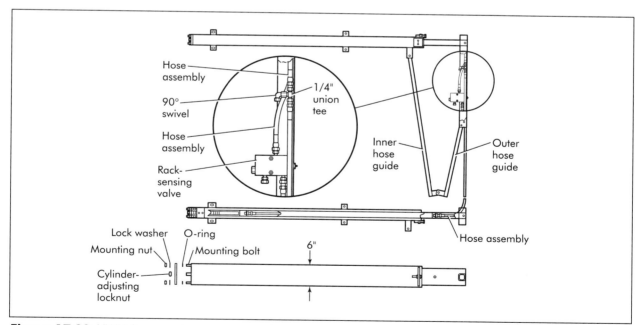

Figure 17.30 HWH Spacemaker room-extension system

2. Always stabilize and level the coach prior to extending the room. This removes much of the stress that can affect the operation of the slide mechanism.

3. Unlock all locking devices.

NOTE: If your extension-room mechanism has a manual winch attached to retract the room, be sure to remove it (disengage) before extending the room.

4. Make sure there is adequate clearance on the outside of the RV to fully extend the room.

■ TROUBLESHOOTING ■
THE HWH LEVELER

Problem	Possible Cause	Correction
Part 1:		
Touch panel lights are on when ignition is off.	Power to control box	Trace the brown or yellow wire in the 3-pin connector to its source. The wire should be connected to accessory or ignition power. Accessory is preferred. Do not use unswitched power for the control box.
Part 2:		
a. With the ignition switch on: Neither the "travel" nor the "jacks down" warning light is on.	With the ignition switch on, the brown or yellow wire in the 3-pin connector should have power.	Trace the wire to its source. Check in-line fuses. Make sure the white wire is properly grounded. If everything is okay, the problem is the control box, the touch panel, or the modular cable.
b. The "jacks down" warning light is on even though the jacks are in the stored position.	Bad warning switch or short problem	Unplug the warning switch. If the light goes out, replace the warning switch. If not, unplug the 9-wire connector for the warning switches at the control box. If the red warning light goes out, the wire to the jack warning switch is shorted. If the warning light stays on, replace the control box.
c.. The touch panel has lights on other than the "travel indicator."	Control box, touch panel, or modular cable	Turn the ignition switch off, then back on. If the lights do not go out, the problem is probably the control box, but it could be the touch panel or the modular cable.
Part 3:		
After pushing the "I" button one time:		
a. The red indicator light above the "I" fails to come on.	Voltage on the brown or yellow wire should be 12.5 volts or more.	Check voltage on brown or yellow wire. Check white wire for proper ground. If good voltage is present, replace the control box, the touch panel, or the ribbon cable. Check that the cable between the touch panel and the control box is properly connected.
b. More than two yellow lights are lit, or the opposite yellow lights are lit.	Control box, sensing unit, wiring	Unplug the sensing unit's connector from the control box. If lights do not go out, replace the control box. If the lights go out, connect a test light to ground. There are 5 pins on the sensing unit— 1 pin for ground and 1 pin for each yellow level-indicator light. Touch each of the 4 pins for the indicator lights. Only one light per pin should come on. If this is so, replace the sensing unit. If not, replace the control box.
c. The "not in park/brake" light is on.	Transmission, park brake, wiring, control box	Check that the transmission is in the "park" position and the park brake is set. Trace the blue wire in the connector to its source. Check for proper position of the diode arrangement. Check the brake switch for proper function. Most coaches complete ground through the brake switch, but some have a 12-volt signal. Make sure the proper box is being used. Use a jumper wire to apply the proper signal to the blue wire. If the light still doesn't go out, replace the control box
d. The pump comes on at this time.	Control box, relay B	Release the park brake. If the pump continues to run, replace relay B. Otherwise, check terminal 5 with a 12-volt test light connected to ground. If 12-volts are present, the problem is with the control box. If no power is present, replace relay B.

■ **TROUBLESHOOTING** ■
THE HWH LEVELER, continued

Problem	Possible Cause	Correction
e. All the indicator lights on the touch panel come on.	Control box	If all the lights come on and stay on, replace the control box. **NOTE**: All lights will flash momentarily when turning the system on.

Part 4:

After pushing the "I" button a second time:

a. The red light above the "I" button does not flash.	Control box	Push the "off" button, then the "I" button twice. If the light does not flash, replace the control box.
b. The low battery indicator comes on, but the pump runs and the jacks go vertical.	Low voltage	The low-battery light will come on if voltage at the control box is below 8.5 to 9.0 volts. The system will continue to function, but the batteries and all connections should be checked. Continuously running the system under low voltage can damage electrical components.
c. The pump does not come on.	Many possible problems. See solutions.	If the low-volts light comes on, push the "off" button, then the "I" button once. Check terminals 1, 2, and 3 of relay A. They should have 12 volts. If terminal does not have 12 volts, the control box is bad. If terminal 2 has no voltage, check the cable, cable ends, and the battery. If terminal 3 has no voltage, connect a test light to terminal 2 and check terminal 8. Terminal 8 supplies the ground for relay A. If the test light comes on, replace relay A. If the test light does not come on, check that all wires are properly connected to ground. The white wire on terminal 8 could be bad. Check the fuse in the in-line fuse holder on the #10 wire connected to terminal 3. The following test must be performed while the red light is flashing above the "I" button. Push the "I" button a second time. With a test light hooked to ground, check terminals 5 and 6 while the light is flashing. If terminal 5 has no voltage, check the pump fuse at the control box. If the fuse is good, replace the control box. If the fuse is blown, the gray wire may be shorted or relay B may be bad. If terminal 5 has voltage but not terminal 6, check terminal 7 with a test light hooked to terminal 2 of relay A. Terminal 7 supplies the ground for relay B. If the test light comes on, replace relay B. If the test light fails to come on, check connections at the grounding stud. The white wire may be bad. If terminals 5 and 6 have voltage, check the connection at terminal 9. Check that the connection at terminal 10 is tight. Check that the pump ground cable is properly attached to the grounding stud. **NOTE:** Some pumps will not have terminal 10 or a ground strap. Check that the pump has a good, solid frame mount. If all connections and mountings are okay, replace the pump.
d. Pump runs under no load and nothing happens.	Pump, shuttle valve	Disconnect the pressure tube between the manifold and the shuttle valve. Check pressure at the manifold. Turn the pump on for five to ten seconds. Pressure should be approximately 3,500 psi. If pressure is low, change the power unit. If pressure is okay, change the shuttle valve.

■ TROUBLESHOOTING ■
THE HWH LEVELERS, continued

Problem	Possible Cause	Correction
e. A jack is vertical and extended, but the red warning light is not lit.	Warning switch, control box	Return the jacks to horizontal. With panel "on," pull each jack vertical by hand while someone watches the panel. Make sure the light for each jack comes on. Unplug jack warning switch for light not working. Use a jumper wire between the 22 pins of the harness connector. If the light comes on, replace the warning switch. If the light does not come on, unplug the orange connector for the warning switches at the control box. Use a test light connected to the ground pin for the warning-switch inputs. Touch each pin in the control box. If the warning lights work properly, the wire from the jack is bad. If the red light fails to come on, replace the control box. **CAUTION:** A jack will abruptly swing to the horizontal position when released.
f. A jack is not vertical, and its red warning light is not on. The jack has not extended in the horizontal position.	Air in the lines, solenoid valve, actuator, control box	On a new installation or after a repair, there could be air in the lines. Turn the system on and off and retry several times. Check that the roller bearing or actuator cable is okay. Check that jack stops are okay. Check that actuator rod moves freely. If there is no change, the problem is either a bad solenoid valve, actuator, or control box. Check the fuse for the malfunctioning jack. If the problem is a front jack, interchange the wires for the front solenoids. If the problem is a rear jack, interchange the wires for the rear solenoids. Retract and try the vertical mode again. If the problem stays with the jack, change the solenoid valve. If the problem follows the change of wires, replace the control box.
g. A jack has extended in the horizontal position.	Roller bearing, actuator cable, actuator	Check that the roller bearing or actuator cable is okay. Check that the stop is okay. If these check out, replace the actuator.
h. After going vertical, a jack returns to horizontal after the pump shuts off.	Control box, solenoid valve, actuator	Push the "off" button. Push the "I" button twice. As the problem jack goes vertical and its red light comes on, push the "off" button. If the jack stays vertical, the control box is the problem. If the jack retracts, the problem is the solenoid valve or the actuator. Check that the emergency-release valve on the solenoid valve is closed tightly. Push the "I" button twice. Push the rails manual button that will operate that jack. Hold the button until the jack kicks vertical and extends and lifts the coach. Release the button. If the jack retracts, replace the solenoid valve. If it does not retract, the problem is probably the actuator on that jack.

Part 5:

When manually operating the jacks: a. A jack extends but will not lift the coach.	Actuator, shuttle valve	If one or more other jacks will extend and lift the coach, and if the jack in question swings to the vertical position okay, the actuator should be replaced. If none of the jacks will lift the coach, disconnect the tube between the shuttle valve and the manifold. Check pressure at the manifold. Pressure should be approximately 3,500 psi. If pump pressure is okay, replace the shuttle valve.

■ TROUBLESHOOTING ■
THE HWH LEVELER, continued

Problem	Possible Cause	Correction
b. A jack fails to retract.	Jack, actuator, solenoid valve	Bleed pressure off between the jack and actuator. If the jack will not retract, replace the jack. If the jack starts to retract, bleed pressure off between the actuator and the hydraulic supply line. If the jack fails to retract, replace the actuator. If the jack starts to retract, the problem is the solenoid valve.

Part 6:

Level indicator does not work properly.	Level sensing unit	The level-sensing unit is a disk normally mounted under the center of the coach, although sometimes it is installed inside the coach. Check that the unit is not mounted, or the wires are not routed near a heat source. Check that the unit is mounted correctly. The unit is adjusted by drawing up or loosening the corresponding screws until the level-indicator lights go out. Using a test light connected to ground, check each pin in the control box for the sensing unit. Check that the proper light on the touch panel comes on when its pin is touched. If there is a malfunction here, replace the control box. If the control box is okay, replace the sensing unit.

Part 7:

One or more jacks are not stabilizing the coach.	One or more jacks do not reach the ground. Or, one or more jacks lift the coach too much.	If the jack does not attempt to move to stabilize the coach, unplug the jack-pressure switch and retry. If the jack now extends and lifts the coach, replace the pressure switch. If a jack extends but fails to reach the ground, adjust the pressure switch. Unplug the wire, loosen the locknut, turn the pressure-adjust body ½ turn clockwise. Reassemble and retry. If adjusting the switch doesn't help, replace the switch. If the jack lifts the coach too much, unplug the wire, loosen the lock-nut, turn the pressure-adjust body ½ turn counterclockwise. Reassemble and retry. If adjusting the switch doesn't help, replace the switch.

Part 8:

After pushing the "I" button once and pushing the "store" button:

a. The pump comes on.	Solenoid B	The pump solenoid is probably stuck. The system cannot retract if the pump is running.
b. A jack will not retract to the horizontal position.	Solenoid valve	Unplug the left front and the left rear solenoid valves. Put the system in the "store" mode. If the right-side jacks retract, replace the left rear solenoid valve. Repeat the procedure for the right side.
c. Red warning lights on the touch panel out, but the jacks have retracted.	Warning switch, wiring, control box	Unplug the warning-switch wire. If the light goes out, replace the warning switch. If the light does not go out, check the wire for a short to ground. If the wire is okay, replace the control box.
d. The master "jacks down" warning light will not go out.	Wiring, control box	Unplug the 6-pin connector and check the ground wire to the master warning light. If it is not shorted to ground, replace the control box. This light should be on whenever a warning light on the touch panel is on.

■ TROUBLESHOOTING ■
THE HWH LEVELER, continued

Problem	Possible Cause	Correction
e. The green travel light will not come on.	Control box	The green travel light will not come on if any red warning lights are on. If no red warning lights are on, replace the control box.
Part 9:		
Jacks fail to retract using the T-handle release on the solenoid valves.	Shuttle valve, solenoid valve, actuator, jack	If none of the jacks will retract using the T-handles, the shuttle valve is bad. If only one jack will not retract using the T-handles, loosen the hydraulic line for that jack. If the jack retracts, replace the solenoid valve. If the jack does not retract, the hose could be kinked or the actuator or jack is bad.

■ TROUBLESHOOTING ■
THE HWH ROOM-EXTENSION SYSTEM

Problem	Possible Cause	Correction
Part 1:		
The pump fails to operate when the extension switch is pushed toward "extend" and/or "retract."	Power, control box	Check power pin on the control box. If power is present, check the "extend" and "retract" pins while pushing the room-control switch. If power is present, replace the control switch. If power is not present, check for 12-volt power on terminal 11 of the room-control switch. If power is not present on terminal 11, check for power to the key switch from the red wire in the room-extension control-switch harness. If power is present, the key switch is bad. Replace the room operator's panel. If power is not present, the red wire from the control box is bad. If power is present on terminal 11, check terminals 12 and 13 of the room-control switch while pushing the switch in both directions. If power is not present on terminals 12 and 13, replace the room-control switch. If power is present, there is a problem with the yellow and black wires in the room-extension control-switch harness.
Part 2:		
The pump runs but the room fails to extend.		
a. The pump runs under no load.	Retract valve	The retract valve is open. Make sure the solenoid valve "T" handle is closed. Check for 12-volt power on the black wire at the manifold. If power is not present, replace the retract valve. If there is power on the black wire, unplug the black wire from terminal 13 of the room-control switch. Check terminal 13 while pushing the switch toward the "extend" position. If there is power, replace the switch. If there is no power, the black wire is shorted to 12 volts in the room-extension control-switch harness.
b. The pump runs under a load.	Extend solenoid valve.	The extend solenoid valve is not opening. While pushing the room-control switch toward "extend," check between the yellow and white wire of the extend-valve plug for 12-volt power. If power is present, replace the extend solenoid valve. If power is not present, check between the yellow wire and ground. If power is present, repair the white wire in the plug. Low power may prevent a solenoid valve from opening. If power is not present on the yellow and white wire, check "extend" fuse at the control box. If the fuse is blown, check the harness for shorts. Then replace the extend solenoid valve if the harness is okay. If the fuse is okay, check the "extend" pin in the connector on the control box while pushing the switch toward "extend." If power is present, the problem is with the harness. If power is not present, replace the control box.

■ **TROUBLESHOOTING** ■
THE HWH ROOM-EXTENSION SYSTEM, continued

Problem	Possible Cause	Correction
Part 3:		
The pump runs, but the room will not retract:		
a. The pump runs under no load.	Extend valve, retract valve, wiring	The extend valve is open. Make sure the solenoid-valve "T" handle is closed. Check for 12-volt power on the yellow wire at the manifold. If power is not present, replace the retract valve. If power is present on the yellow wire, unplug the wire from terminal 12 of the room-control switch. Check terminal 12 while pushing the switch toward the 'retract' position. If there is power, replace the switch. If there is no power, the yellow wire is shorted to 12 volts in the room-extension control switch harness.
b. The pump runs under a load.	Retract solenoid valve, wiring, control box	The retract solenoid valve is not opening. While pushing the room-control switch toward "retract," check between the black and white wire of the retract-valve plug for 12-volt power. If power is present, replace the retract solenoid valve. If power is not present, check between the black wire and ground. If power is present, repair the white wire in the plug. **NOTE:** Low voltage may cause a solenoid valve not to open if power is not present on the black and white wire of the retract valve plug, check the "retract" fuse at the control box. If the fuse is blown, check the harness. Then replace the extend solenoid valve if the harness is okay. If the fuse is okay, check the "retract" pin in the connector on the control box while pushing the switch toward "retract." If power is present, the problem is with the harness. If power is not present, replace the control box.
Part 4:		
The room moves erratically from side to side as it extends or retracts.	Structural problems	Check that the pivot bracket is free to pivot. Check that the inner tubes are free of paint or undercoating. Check that the left cylinder hydraulic lines are not wire-tied to the room closer than 12 inches to the rack sensing valve-support arm. Check that the strike plate is mounted solidly to the room and that the rack-sensing valve plunger is properly positioned on the strike plate. Check that the plunger is not bent. Check that the room itself is not binding on seals or other interferences. Then replace the rack-sensing valve.
Part 5:		
The ends of the room do not move at an equal distance from the vehicle.	Rack-sensing valve	Adjust the rack-sensing valve.

■ **TROUBLESHOOTING** ■

THE HWH ROOM-EXTENSION SYSTEM, continued

Problem	Possible Cause	Correction
Part 6:		
The room creeps out after being retracted.	Extend solenoid valve, extension cylinder, manifold check valve.	If the room creeps out more than 1 inch, the problem is most likely that the manifold check valve is leaking. Retract the room completely. Remove the hydraulic line for the cap end of the cylinder at the manifold. Hold the hose end in an upright position. Press the rocker switch for that room to the "retract" position. If fluid flows from the manifold fitting, the extend solenoid valve needs replacing. If no fluid flows from either the hose end or the manifold fittings, inspect the manifold check valve. There is a spring below the cap. Do not lose the spring. Check for cuts on the poppet O-ring. Check the poppet and cap for burrs. The poppet should easily slide in the cap. If the check valve is okay, or fluid flows from the hose end, the room-extension cylinder should be replaced.
Part 7:		
The room creeps in after being extended.	Oil leaks, retract solenoid valve	Check for visible oil leaks. If there are none, replace the retract solenoid valve for that room extension.
Part 8:		
Room does not seal tightly when fully extended or retracted.	Room stops	Adjust room stops.
Part 9:		
One side of the room will not move while trying to extend and/or retract the room.	Rack-sensing valve	Adjust or replace the rack-sensing valve.

TRAILER LIFE BOOKS
64 Inverness Drive East
Englewood, Colorado 80112

Dear Repair Manual Owner:

Thank you for purchasing this third edition of <u>Trailer Life's RV Repair and Maintenance Manual</u>. In an ongoing effort to improve this book, we are relying heavily upon our readers to share with us their experiences in using it. We are as eager to learn about any negative experiences as we are to hear about positive ones.

We've made it easy for you to be our consultant on this and future versions of the <u>Repair Manual</u>. Your answers to specific items we need to know about will only take a few minutes. However, a questionnaire cannot possibly cover all aspects of critique, so feel free to amplify your comments on any questions asked, or add any comments on topics not covered.

It's important to us that we hear from you. After you've had a chance to look the book over, please send us your completed questionnaire. We want to make a good manual even better, and we need your help to do it.

Sincerely,

Rick Rundall
General Manager
Trailer Life Books

First, please tell us a bit about you and your family:

❏ Male　　❏ Female　　❏ Married　　❏ Single

Your age:　❏ Under 30　　❏ 31–40　　❏ 41–50　　❏ 51–60　　❏ 61–65　　❏ over 65

What kind of RV do you own now?

❏ Class A　　❏ Class C　　❏ Fifth-wheel trailer　　❏ Travel trailer

❏ Tent trailer　❏ Pick-up camper　❏ Van conversion　❏ Other _____

What is your favorite source for RV information (magazines, books, videos, neighbors)?

_____

What is your favorite RV reference book? _____

What is your favorite RV guide book? _____

What is your favorite book? (general)? _____

Have you purchased any other books from (Good Sam Club, *Trailer Life*, *Highways*,

MotorHome)?　　❏ Yes　　❏ No

If yes, what were they? _____

Do you have a computer?　　❏ Yes　　❏ No

If yes, do you access the Internet?　❏ Yes　　❏ No

What other interests do you have (check all that apply)

❏ Woodworking　　❏ Sightseeing　　❏ Boating　　❏ Cooking　　❏ Biking

❏ Golf　❏ Fishing　❏ Museums　❏ History　❏ Crafts (specify) _____

❏ Do-It-Yourself/Home improvement　　❏ Other (specify) _____

What state do you live in? _____　What is your zip code? _____

1. For what purpose do you use the *Repair Manual*?

   ❏ To make your own repairs

   ❏ To use as an aid in diagnosing problems in your RV

   ❏ To use as an aid to communicate with your mechanic

2. How often do you think the *Repair Manual* should be updated?

   ❏ Every 6 months　　❏ Every 12 months　　❏ Every 2 years

   ❏ Every 3 years　　❏ Every 5 years

3. Is the way in which the material presented satisfactory?

❑ Yes   ❑ No

Comment: _____

_____

4. Should we publish loose-leaf, updated supplements to this book periodically?

❑ Yes   ❑ No

Comment: _____

_____

5. If yes, would you be willing to pay:

❑ $5 to $10   ❑ $10 to $13   ❑ $13 to $18   ❑ Over $18

6. Which chapters in the *Repair Manual* do you feel are the most helpful?

Rate from 1 (least helpful) to 5 (most helpful).

___ Electrical Systems   ___ Air-conditioning Systems   ___ Drivetrain Systems

___ LP-gas Systems   ___ Refrigerators   ___ Hitches

___ Water Systems   ___ Ovens and Ranges   ___ Exterior Care/Repair

___ Sanitation Systems   ___ Microwaves and Icemakers   ___ Interior Care

___ AC Generators   ___ Trailer Brakes   ___ Accessories

___ Heating Systems   ___ Dinghy Towing

7. Which additional systems or areas would you like to see covered?

_____

_____

_____

8. Which areas or chapters would you like to see expanded, deleted, or added?

_____

_____

_____

9. Do you feel a companion videocassette would be useful?

   ❑ Yes　　❑ No

10. Would a list of manufacturers' hotline telephone numbers be helpful to you?

    ❑ Yes　　❑ No

11. Of the many new features in the revised *Repair Manual*, which of the following did you find the most helpful? Rate from 1 (not helpful) to 5 (extremely helpful).

    ___ Troubleshooting guides　　　___ Expanded index

    ___ More photos and artwork　　___ More step-by-step instructions for repairing

    ___ Expanded use of checklists　　　or utilizing systems (see page 14.8)

12. Do you use any other repair manuals?

    ❑ Yes　　❑ No

13. If yes, which do you find the most useful?

    ❑ Manuals designed specifically for your vehicle

    ❑ Owner's manual

    ❑ Other RV repair manuals (please list):

    _____

14. Would you be interested in separate, expanded versions of individual chapters or systems described in the manual?

    ❑ Yes　　❑ No

    If yes, which chapter or chapters would you like to see in an expanded version?

    _____

    _____

15. Additional comments (use extra sheets if you need them):

    _____

    _____

    _____

    _____

INDEX

Page numbers in **boldface** refer to figures, tables, and charts in the text.